By I. F. Stone

A NONCONFORMIST HISTORY OF OUR TIMES
The War Years 1939–1945
The Hidden History of the Korean War 1950–1951
The Truman Era 1945–1952
The Haunted Fifties 1953–1963
In a Time of Torment 1961–1967
Polemics and Prophecies 1967–1970

Other Books

The Court Disposes
Business As Usual
Underground to Palestine
This Is Israel
The Killings at Kent State
I. F. Stone's Weekly Reader
The Trial of Socrates

THE
HIDDEN HISTORY
OF THE
KOREAN WAR

1950–1951

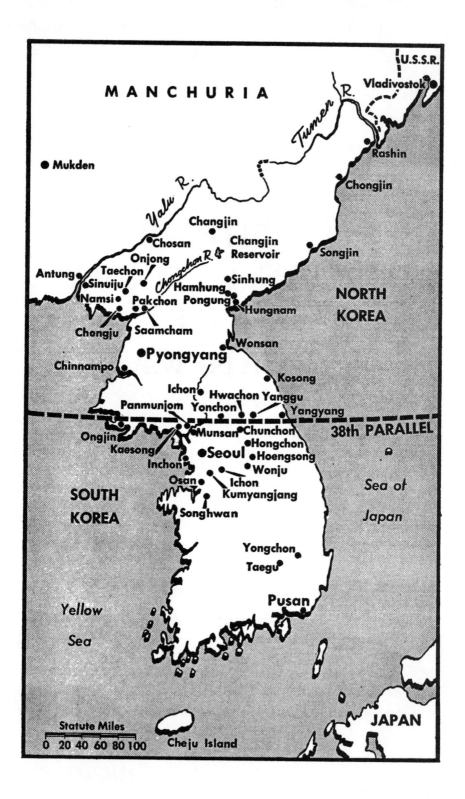

A NONCONFORMIST HISTORY OF OUR TIMES

THE HIDDEN HISTORY OF THE KOREAN WAR

1950–1951

I. F. STONE

With a Preface by Bruce Cumings

LITTLE, BROWN AND COMPANY
BOSTON   TORONTO

Originally published in 1952 by Monthly Review Press

Library of Congress Cataloging-in-Publication Data

Stone, I. F. (Isidor F.), 1907–
    The hidden history of the Korean War.

    (A nonconformist history of our times)
    Reprint. Originally published: Monthly Review
Press, 1952.
    Includes index.
    1. Korean War, 1950–1953 — United States.   2. United
States — Foreign relations — 1945–1953.   I. Title.
II. Series.
DS919.S76   1988   951.9′042   88-12995

ISBN 0-316-81773-2 (HC)
ISBN 0-316-81770-8 (PB)

MV

Published simultaneously in Canada
by Little, Brown & Company (Canada) Limited

PRINTED IN THE UNITED STATES OF AMERICA

To
Leo Huberman and Paul Sweezy
in comradely appreciation

Contents

Map of Korea	Frontispiece
Preface by Bruce Cumings	xi
Author's Preface	xxi

PART I.   *HOW THE WAR BEGAN*

1. Was It a Surprise?	1
2. The Silence of Seoul	7
3. Connally's Warning	14
4. The Role of John Foster Dulles	23
5. Chiang's Pilgrimage	28
6. Time Was Short	35
7. The Stage Was Set	42
8. ". . . Only in Very Rough Outline Form"	53
9. Willoughby Exposes MacArthur	57
10. "The Best Army in Asia"	61

PART II.   *THE U.N. GETS A COMMANDER IT CAN'T COMMAND*

11. Classic Incident	67
12. Stampeding the United Nations	75
13. MacArthur's Blank Check	82
14. MacArthur and Mack Sennett	90
15. Peace Alarums	101

PART III.   *HATING WAR BUT FEARING PEACE*

16. Reversal on the Parallel	108
17. Free Elections?	116
18. First Warnings	124
19. The U.N.'s Dilemma	133
20. A Sudden Change in Plans	139
21. Mystery at Wake Island	145

PART IV.   *CORDIAL INVITATION — TO DISASTER*

22. Twin Dangers	151
23. Mr. Truman Keeps Cool	167

24. The China Lobby Responds ... 175
25. Peking Suspects ... 180
26. Home-By-Christmas ... 185
27. Danger on the Thames ... 192
28. Anti-Peace Offensive ... 199

PART V. *PHANTOM WARFARE*

29. The Enemy Was Horrid ... 208
30. . . . Like a Poorly Made Fire ... 216
31. Phantom Battle ... 223
32. Seoul Abandoned Again ... 232

PART VI. *WAR AS POLITICS*

33. Hiding the Lull ... 248
34. Lost and Found ... 253
35. The Deadly Parallel Again ... 260
36. MacArthur Upsets the Applecart ... 267

PART VII. *STALEMATE AND TRUCE TALKS*

37. Why MacArthur Was Fired ... 274
38. "Every Time Stalin Smiles" ... 280
39. Cease-Fire Switch ... 284
40. Ridgway Stands "Firm" ... 291
41. Postponing Peace Again ... 299
42. "The Dreaded Softening Process" ... 304
43. Talks on Whether to Talk ... 310
44. Ridgway's Own Iron Curtain ... 316
45. Atrocities to the Rescue ... 321
46. Weird Statistics ... 326
47. Six Months of Futile Slaughter ... 335
48. Van Fleet Sums Up ... 345

APPENDIX

New Light on the Korean Mystery: Was the
  War No Surprise to Chiang Kai-shek? ... 349
References ... 353
Index ... 364
About the Author ... 369

Preface

by Bruce Cumings

Americans know the Korean War as a "forgotten war," which is another way of saying that generally they do not know it. A war that killed upwards of four million people, 35,000 of them Americans, is remembered mainly as an odd conflict sandwiched between the good war (World War II) and the bad war (Vietnam). Today most people will find it difficult to connect this war with a modernized South Korea, host to the 1988 Olympics and exporter of family cars and computers.

If people do know the Korean War, they usually know the official story. This presents the war as a simple sequence: in June 1950 the North Koreans, at Stalin's order, suddenly attacked an innocent and defenseless Republic of Korea; the Truman administration responded by invoking the collective security procedures of the United Nations in a "police action" designed to restore the *status quo ante,* the thirty-eighth parallel that divided North and South. General Douglas MacArthur accomplished that task by the end of September, after a brilliant amphibious landing at the port of Inch'on. Thereafter things went awry, as MacArthur sought to unify Korea through a march into the North, soon bringing Chinese "hordes" into the fighting; Truman attempted to limit the war and ultimately was forced to dismiss his recalcitrant field commander in April 1951. Ceasefire talks soon began, but seemingly minor issues, like prisoner-of-war exchanges, kept the war going until July 1953. It ended in a stalemate that left Korea divided into two states, as it had been before the war began.

Almost four decades ago, I. F. Stone challenged the official story with a book that opened and closed on a note of mystery, an inquiry into what Tacitus called *arcana imperii* — empire and its method as a "hidden thing," shrouded above all from the people it ruled.[1] Stone

---

[1] The reference to Tacitus is from Franz Schurmann, *The Logic of World Power: An Inquiry into the Origins, Currents, and Contradictions of World Politics* (New York, Pantheon

described a war in which "an ephemeral elective occupant" at home (Truman) jousted with an "ambitious proconsular Caesar abroad" (MacArthur), "already plotting to turn against the capital the armies with which he had been supplied to hold distant marches against barbarian hordes." Out of print for almost two decades, *The Hidden History of the Korean War* now seems to be a book with nine lives, padding back in again on the cat's feet of its shrewd author, to unsettle the scribes of historical and political orthodoxy.

Stone at first accepted the official story, believing as so many others did that the Korean War was a clear example of unprovoked aggression, which must have had Moscow's sponsorship. But in Paris in the winter of 1950–51, he began to wonder. His new vantage point enabled him to see America as a foreigner would. The late Theodore White once said that "Pekingology" is like watching two great whales do battle beneath the ocean; occasionally they surface and spout a bit, which is your only evidence of what the trouble might be in China. But American politics, too, is often like this: we need to do "Washingtonology" — read newspapers carefully, watch the rise and fall of key figures, look for power struggles. Stone followed this method.

Yet to say these things runs deeply against the grain of American thought, violating our conceptions of politics, of history, of human action and conjuring up conspiracy theory. People with a built-in indifference to history are ill accustomed to retrospective digging, to lifting up rugs, to searching for subterranean forces and tendencies. Exploring the labyrinth of history is alien to the American soul, perhaps because an optimistic people find knowledge of the past too burdensome in the present. This is one reason why Korea has become a "forgotten war."

When Stone went from one publisher to another in 1951, he found warm praise for the quality of his work and off-the-record comments that it was "too hot to handle" — an interesting example of a common, tacit self-censorship that coexists with wide freedom of speech. He put the book aside, until a chance meeting with Leo Huberman and Paul Sweezy in New York's Central Park led to its original publication.

When I first came upon *Hidden History* as a graduate student, during the Vietnam War, a professor warned me against the book, saying it was unreliable and indulged in conspiracy theories. So I read it all the more eagerly, and found that, indeed, Stone's method was in contrast to that of highly recommended scholars: he cared about truth, he was fearless, he didn't equate objectivity with silence on the

Books, 1974). This brilliant book takes a page from I. F. Stone's method, although it is theoretically more sophisticated; like *Hidden History*, it quickly went out of print.

great issues of his day. It seemed that I. F. Stone provided a model of honest inquiry, of which there are all too few examples — particularly in regard to our recent Asian wars. *Hidden History* is above all a truthful book, and it remains one of the best accounts of the American role in the Korean War.

Mary McCarthy once slandered Lillian Hellman by saying everything she said was a lie — down to the last "a, an, and the." We may reverse that with Stone, and say everything he says is the truth (as he sees it) — to the last "a, an, and the." But what is his model, his teaching? It seemed to a graduate student that the task of honest inquiry into the contemporary history and politics of America was a relatively straightforward matter, following Stone, of subjecting the available literature — newspapers, books, official documents — to a careful, critical reading. (Among its many virtues, *Hidden History* is a textbook on how to read.)

Instead one discovers that his method is difficult. Not that close reading is necessarily hard; no, there is something else that is hard: to disabuse oneself of received wisdom is hard, as it bombards you in various forms; to find and ask unasked questions is hard; to confront authority is hard. The hardest thing is to tell the truth, because desire hinders perception and quashes memory.

For example, our desire to love our nation and love justice: Harry Truman was a good and honest man; Stone's sympathetic portrait of him ("as honorable and decent a specimen of that excellent breed, the plain small-town American, as one could find anywhere in the U.S.A.") is right; how could Harry Truman have allowed the provocation of a war by the Republican right (something Stone hints at), or the terror-bombing of a defenseless people, or taken us to the brink of World War III? We have an often unintuited desire to trust our leaders: since they hold high position, ergo they must deserve it (even when their names are Joseph McCarthy or Curtis LeMay).

This is part of what makes critical reading difficult and makes remembering even harder: a faculty of repression, honed by our desire to live at peace with our liberal system and our American brethren, wins out. Indeed, a remarkable aspect of contemporary America is its ineffable capacity to forget those secrets that do happen to penetrate the media, salient facts that surface but quickly drift to the briny deep, owing to an absence of context or the absence of a political sensibility that likes to seek out patterns in the events of the day. Freedom of speech and a fairly extensive disclosure of foreign policy secrets obtain in the United States, but one sometimes wonders if anyone is listening or, if listening, remembering.

Stone's discoveries about the gaps, distortions, and outright lies in the official record should not surprise a person familiar with, say, the American record in Vietnam, beginning with the assassination of Ngo Dinh Diem and the Tonkin Gulf incident in 1964, the latter used to gain Congressional backing for the war. In the 1970s the Watergate episode and a spate of revelations about the CIA were merely prelude to the truly Byzantine covert activities during the Reagan years — ranging from the Contra war in Nicaragua to the Oliver North/William Casey dealings with shady Iranian arms merchants to the unmasking of General Manuel Antonio Noriega of Panama as a major drug-runner, who just happened to have been on the CIA payroll for many years. But somehow such events are not connected to form a pattern, and remain episodic outrages that come and go inexplicably.

Let us take an example from Stone's book, apparently a small one. A soybean conspiracy occurred just before the Korean War began, according to Stone — but also according to Dean Acheson. During the MacArthur hearings in 1951, a Senator asked Acheson if he had heard anything about a corner on the soybean market in June 1950. Acheson replied blandly, "there was, I recall, a very serious situation created by a group of Chinese buying and taking delivery of a certain amount of soybeans, which gave certain controls over prices." However, Acheson did not quite recall who might have been involved, could not really say if perhaps the China Lobby had something to do with it, and so the Senators went on to a new line of questioning. Since we are not supposed to think about conspiracies, no one but Stone followed this story up.[2]

Someone had dumped large amounts of soybeans on the Chicago market to force the price down, while holding bigger amounts in soybean futures. The speculation began in mid-June and was targeted specifically for big selloffs at the end of the week before that fateful Sunday, June 25, 1950. The Commodity Exchange Authority later said that by June 30, fifty-six Chinese held nearly half of all open contracts for July soybean futures — all "on the long side," meaning they were playing for a rise in price (p. 352).

Although it still seems impossible to get the full list of names behind this scam, I. F. Stone at the time correctly named T. L. Soong, brother of fabulously wealthy T. V. Soong, and brother-in-law of Chiang Kai-shek.[3] Furthermore, according to several sources, Senator Joe

---

[2]*MacArthur Hearings*, vol. 3, p. 2187; *New York Times*, June 9, 1951. The *Times* noted that the corner had "aroused official suspicion that they had advance knowledge of a war that caught this country wholly unprepared" (*New York Times*, July 6, 1951).
[3]For declassified information backing up Stone, see Office of Chinese Affairs, box 4223, Anne B. Wheeler to A. G. Hope, July 25, 1950; Hope to Magill, Aug. 1, 1950.

McCarthy profited from the soybean corner. Drew Pearson wrote in his diary, "McCarthy was buying soybeans" at the time when "the Chinese Nationalists did just about corner the market before Korea";[4] Stone said McCarthy had "a successful flier in soybeans" later on in 1950 (p. 349).

Soybean speculation was one of the many errant counterpoints to Washington's official story that Stone homed in on; although it seemed like a minor business, it is a neglected thread in unraveling how this war began.[5] In any case it is a fine example of a key element in Stone's method — to find what he called the "one very queer detail," the "one odd-shaped piece that doesn't fit," and thus demolish the official logic or construct an alternative logic. It is doubtful that anyone has ever been better at this.

Another odd-shaped piece of evidence was the original cable from the American embassy in Seoul announcing the North Korean assault — basing its account on South Korean Army information, which had been *"partly confirmed"* by American sources. Stone asks, "What part of the South Korean version was confirmed? What part was not confirmed?" He then digs up a reference in the London *Times* to brief dispatches from the British Mission in Seoul, merely confirming *"the outbreak of fighting."* This thin reed of partially confirmed information then became the basis for the United Nations decision to involve itself in the Korean conflict.

Stone reads a document the way Sherlock Holmes looks for fingerprints. Readers interested in a lesson in this ferreting out of half-truth and distortion might simply turn to a "ragout of intelligence information" from MacArthur's headquarters about Chinese intervention in the war (pp. 170–173), which Stone surgically dissects until nothing is left. It is one example among many in the book. What is more remarkable, though, is the humor that Stone sustains in the midst of his awful tale.

His description of the phantomlike ephemerality of the Korean People's Army in Tokyo's briefings, for example, is done brilliantly, accurately, and with a satirist's wit. An army that MacArthur claimed to have utterly destroyed after the Inch'on landing two months later was raised "like Lazarus, from the tomb." By Christmas 1950, according to MacArthur's headquarters, "eleven reconstituted North Korean divisions [had] reappeared in the last twelve days"; "Kim Il Sung," Stone wrote, "was made to seem a modern Cadmus." And then

[4] Drew Pearson, *Diaries, 1949–1959*, Tyler Abell, ed. (New York: Holt, Rinehart & Winston, 1974), p. 250.
[5] I cover this possibility at length in *Origins of the Korean War*, vol. 2 (Princeton University Press, 1989).

there was MacArthur's rapid retreat, ostensibly in the face of hordes of Chinese; Stone found this whole business odd, writing that "the Chinese had "failed to 'agress,' " and declassified intelligence now backs him up: at this point the Chinese forces were not terribly large and for long periods there was little contact with the enemy, leading to what British intelligence sources called a "phony war."

In many other episodes as well, declassified documentation backs up Stone's judgment — which he based mostly on careful and wide reading of newspapers. The People's Army was not destroyed in MacArthur's Inch'on landing trap, but instead regrouped, first for guerrilla war in the central, mountainous regions of Korea and then for a combined Sino-Korean assault against MacArthur's march to the Yalu, in which Korean forces were as important as the Chinese.

Stone was right that the State Department had long planned to take a serious outbreak of fighting in Korea to the United Nations and had drafted skeletal memoranda for such an eventuality. John Foster Dulles's own memoranda now show that Stone was exactly on the money in saying that after Dulles joined the Truman administration in April 1950, he "discreetly but unmistakably joined forces with MacArthur on Formosa policy." He was right that China had good defensive strategic reasons for entering the Korean conflict, as a RAND Corporation study subsequently concluded.

He was right about Soviet caution and restraint after the war began, and about Stalin's swallowing one affront after another (such as our planes bombing an airbase near Vladivostok). Khrushchev's memoirs essentially reiterate Stone's point that "the self-restraint of China and Russia" at the Pusan perimeter "made possible an American victory." That is, Stalin (and Mao), fearing the consequences of an American rout, refused to give Kim Il Sung the requisite tanks, planes, and heavy artillery needed to win in the crucial fighting near Taegu and Pusan in August and September 1950. We now know that Acheson had vowed to come back in if American forces were pushed off the peninsula, and the Navy had the massive amphibious power to do it, as demonstrated at Inch'on. Stone was right that MacArthur and his intelligence chief, the odd and duplicitous General Charles Willoughby, contrived both fighting strategy and official reports on the fighting to serve their goal of extending the war to China.[6]

On the larger question of historical responsibility for the disastrous

---

[6]Readers interested in recent literature that, based on excellent declassified sources, backs up many of Stone's observations should consult, among others, Rosemary Foot, *The Wrong War* (Cornell University Press, 1985); Peter Lowe, *The Origins of the Korean War* (White Plains, NY, Longman, 1986); Callum MacDonald, *Korea: The War Before Vietnam* (Glencoe: The Free Press, 1987).

attempt at rolling back communism in North Korea (the operative document, NSC81, called for a "roll-back"), Stone declined to absolve Truman and Acheson and simply blame MacArthur — the easy and comfortable position and something that an entire literature of liberal apologetics has since sought to maintain. "Truman either had to risk the ending of the cold war or its possible transformation into the real thing," Stone wrote; in the event, Truman "gave MacArthur the signal to go ahead."

Stone's portrait of the leading diplomatic light of the period, Dean Acheson (whom James Chace recently called "the greatest Secretary of State since John Quincy Adams"), is unsurpassed in the literature. If Acheson was to our British allies precisely "their picture of what a foreign secretary should be: cultivated, personable, and superbly tailored," he was to many Americans a subversive poseur: "Nothing could be more dangerous to a public figure in America than the mere suspicion of an urbane and compassionate view of history and humanity," Stone wrote, something amply confirmed by Acheson's principled defense of his old friend, Alger Hiss, and the subsequent McCarthyite outrage.

Stone then went on to say, however (p. 204):

> Only in the heat-distorted vision of cold-war America could Acheson be seen other than as he was: an "enlightened conservative" — to use a barbarous and patronizing phrase. . . . Who remembered in these days of McCarthyism that Acheson, on making his Washington debut at the Treasury before the war, had been denounced by New Dealers as a "Morgan man," a Wall Street Trojan Horse, a borer-from-within on behalf of the big bankers?

It is now fashionable to point to Acheson as a wise strategist who, but for McCarthy and MacArthur, would have realized a mutually beneficial relationship with China, a quarter century before Richard Nixon picked the policy out of the dustbin of history. But Stone was far better when he said (pp. 203–204):

> What a public man "really" thinks is difficult to discover and rarely of much relevance when found. It is what the pressure of circumstance upon his own personality leads him to do and say that counts. What Acheson had long said and done committed him to a policy hostile to Communist China. . . . Acheson could not let himself be objective about the Communist revolution in China — and remain Secretary of State.

Stone also accurately dated Acheson's about-face on China from February 1950, with the onset of his "total diplomacy" speeches, designed to prepare the public for the major reorientation of American Cold War policy embodied in National Security Document 68. "The drift to the worst of policies in the absence of the vision and courage necessary for the best," Stone wrote, "was marked by a series of speeches in which Acheson began to set forth a new image of the Chinese revolution, hardly recognizable to a reader of the White Paper" (the State Department's 1949 analysis of the victory of the Chinese revolution).

It is important today to remind Americans of what was done in their name in the 1950s, but in a different era it is also easy to do so. In 1952 it took rare courage for Stone to write, after reading an Air Force briefing of the obliteration with "jellied gasoline bombs" of a North Korean city (p. 179):

> There is an indifference to human suffering to be read between those lines which makes me as an American deeply ashamed of what was done that day. . . . The mass bombing raid on Sinuiju November 8 was the beginning of a race between peace and provocation. A terrible retribution threatened the peoples of the Western world who so feebly permitted such acts to be done in their name. For it was by such means that the pyromaniacs hoped to set the world afire.

Stone was one of the few to write with compassion about the horrible consequences of this war for the Korean people. To think that the American Air Force could have dropped oceans of napalm and other incendiaries on cities and towns in North Korea,[7] leaving a legacy of deep bitterness palpable four decades later, and that this was done in the name of a conflict now called "the forgotten war" — as memory confronts amnesia, we ask, who are the sane of this world?

The book also shows us that I. F. Stone loves a good mystery, that his excavating instincts reveal the soul of a good detective. *Hidden History* is good history, but it is also a tale well told — full of suspense,

[7] In his oral history held at Princeton University, former Air Force Chief of Staff Curtis LeMay relates the following story, from the first days of the Korean War:

> We slipped a note kind of under the door into the Pentagon and said, "Look, let us go up there . . . and burn down five of the biggest towns in North Korea — and they're not very big — and that ought to stop it." Well, the answer to that was four or five screams — "You'll kill a lot of non-combatants" — and "it's too horrible." Yet over a period of three years or so . . . we burned down *every* [sic] town in North Korea and South Korea, too. . . . Now, over a period of three years this is palatable, but to kill a few people to stop this from happening — a lot of people can't stomach it.

surprises, dangling questions, unexpected outcomes. It merges a fictional style with real people and events, and reads with the pace and structure of a good novel. The last chapter concludes the book as it began, on a note mingling tantalizing uncertainty with profound observation. Citing the "astute and sophisticated" lectures that George Kennan gave at the University of Chicago in 1951, he says Kennan's remarks on the Spanish-American War (and its extension to the Philippines by Dewey's attack on the Spanish fleet at Manila) may some day be equally appropriate for the Korean War (p. 345):

> We can only say [Kennan declared], that it looks very much as though, in this case, the action of the United States government had been determined primarily on the basis of a very able and very quiet intrigue by a few strategically placed persons in Washington, an intrigue which received absolution, forgiveness and a sort of public blessing by virtue of war hysteria.

If Stone's theses remain unproved on a possible provocation of the Korean War, or a tacit agreement to let the attack happen, no honest historian today can do anything other than withhold judgment on these dangling questions. There is no doubt that the North Koreans were ready to fight on the morning of June 25, 1950, but there are many remaining questions about South Korean provocations throughout the summer of 1949, now well documented, and Seoul's relations with Chiang Kai-shek's regime on Taiwan, which grew in importance in the spring of 1950.

Stone's virtues are ones that do not come easily. He is a rare person, who can excavate our errors and calamities without developing a corrosive cynicism, who can mix love of country with the courage to confront the high and mighty (indeed, takes it as a duty), who possesses an idealism born of searching examination, not sappy homilies; a man with unflagging curiosity that feeds off an optimism and good humor with inexplicable roots. Behind it all one senses an indefatigable, irrepressible *will* to truth, to independence, to iconoclasm not for its own sake but for our sake. He has found a way to tell the truth and still remain a liberal, still keep his balance and his sense of humor — a remarkable accomplishment. The ideals of the enlightenment are embodied in this man, as he walks in a land that only half-believes them.

His open mind has much to do with his method, a Socratic questioning that is itself open-ended; this is also the secret of the longevity of *Hidden History,* with its many still-unanswered questions. In his seventies Stone embarked on a quest to learn Greek and master the philosophers of antiquity: more questions for a man who must know that closure of questions draws the curtain down on one's creativity, and who also knows that beyond the good historian is the good citizen. As Nietzsche put it in a magnificent essay:

> A historical phenomenon, known clearly and completely and resolved into a phenomenon of knowledge, is, for him who has perceived it, dead: for he has recognized in it the delusion, the injustice, the blind passion, and in general the whole earthly and darkening horizon of this phenomenon, and has thereby also understood its power in history. This power has now lost its hold over him insofar as he is a man of knowledge; but perhaps it has not done so insofar as he is a man involved in life.[8]

---

[8]Friedrich Nietzsche, "On the Uses and Disadvantages of History for Life," in *Untimely Meditations*, trans. R. J. Hollingdale (Cambridge University Press, 1983), p. 67.

Bruce Cumings is professor of East Asian history, University of Chicago, and the author of *The Origins of the Korean War* (two volumes, 1981–1989, Princeton University Press).

Author's Preface

I have tried to write this story as if I were writing a novel, with suspense and with three-dimensionality. In a good novel one does not know all the answers, and I do not know all the answers here. Much about the Korean War is still hidden, and much will long remain hidden. I believe I have succeeded in throwing new light on its origins, on the operations of MacArthur and Dulles, on the weaknesses of Truman and Acheson, on the way the Chinese were provoked to intervene, and on the way the truce talks have been dragged out and the issues muddied by American military men hostile from the first to negotiations. I have tried to bring as much of the hidden story to light as I could in order to put the people of the United States and the United Nations on guard.

Writing in an atmosphere much like that of a full war, I realized from the beginning that I could be persuasive only if I utilized material which could not be challenged by those who accept the official American government point of view. I have relied exclusively, therefore, on United States and United Nations documents, and on respected American and British newspaper sources. I did examine carefully the North Korean Blue Book on the origins of the war, but I must say I found remarkably little in it. Mr. Vishinsky's speeches at the United Nations on the Korean War convinced me only that the Russians themselves must know very little about its origins if this was the best that so able a lawyer as Mr. Vishinsky could do.

I do not think the truth — in this as in all wars — is to be found in the simplistic propaganda of either side. I believe that in Korea the big powers were the victims, among other things, of headstrong satellites itching for a showdown which Washington, Moscow, and Peking had long anticipated but were alike anxious to avoid. There is a certain parallel here with Sarajevo, though the parallel fortunately is still incomplete.

I believe this book serves a threefold purpose. It is a case-study in the cold war. It is also a study in war propaganda, in how to read newspapers and official documents in wartime. Emphasis, omission, and distortion rather than outright lying are the tools of the war propagandists, and this book may help the reader to learn how to examine their output — and sift out the facts — for himself. Finally this book is what it purports to be, not "inside stuff" or keyhole revelations but the hidden history of the Korean War, the facts to be found in the official accounts themselves if texts are carefully examined and reports collated.

In preparing the manuscript with its voluminous references for publication, I have had the devoted help of a small corps of co-workers, including John Rackliffe, Sybil May, Catherine Winston, and Mardean Ryan. I want to thank them for their aid in a task that required much patience and many pains.

New York City   I. F. STONE
March 15, 1952

PART I

HOW THE WAR BEGAN

CHAPTER 1

★

Was It a Surprise?

OFFICIALLY the outbreak of the Korean War was described as a surprise. The White Paper issued by the American State Department spoke of it as a "surprise attack."[1] The United Nations Commission on Korea reported that the South Korean forces "were taken completely by surprise as they had no reason to believe from intelligence sources that invasion was imminent." General Douglas MacArthur's biographer, John Gunther, wrote that "the South Koreans and Americans in Korea, to say nothing of SCAP [MacArthur Headquarters] in Tokyo, were taken utterly by surprise."

If this is true, certain first reactions in Washington to the outbreak of war in Korea remain unexplained. The attack came on a Sunday, and at once recalled that other Sunday, nine years earlier, when the Japanese attacked Pearl Harbor. The parallel was striking, but inquiry revealed a difference. The first indications were that the attack in Korea was not a surprise at all. This difference between Pearl Harbor and Korea was skeptically greeted, grudgingly accepted, and then quickly forgotten—as Freud tells us people conveniently forget inconvenient facts.

When newspapermen that torrid Washington summer day called at the Pentagon, huge headquarters of the United States

[1] All references are placed together following the text, on pages 349-359. Citations are given for the sources of all quotations, with the exception of those which are clearly identified in the text by name and date of publication.

1

Department of Defense, "an aide said privately that the United States expected the attack." This officer pointed to "the fact that ships were ready to evacuate the families of American officers and others in South Korea as evidence that the invasion was not a surprise."

When newspapermen tried to confirm this, they succeeded in reaching America's highest ranking intelligence officer, Rear Admiral Roscoe H. Hillenkoetter, director of the Central Intelligence Agency, which coordinates and distributes information received from all the various American intelligence services. Admiral Hillenkoetter did not insist, as Washington officials so often do, on speaking only "off the record" or "without attribution." He permitted his name to be used, and he made the statement that American intelligence was aware that "conditions existed in Korea that could have meant an invasion this week or next."

The press did not take this statement too seriously. America's most authoritative newspaper, the *New York Times*, treated it as of subordinate importance. The Admiral's response may well have seemed the natural reaction of an official trying to cover up a blunder by pretending he-knew-it-all-the-time. The *New York Times* account next morning stressed the likelihood that the Republicans would make the sudden outbreak of war "a national issue, involving as it does the country's foreign intelligence."

The next day the Admiral was summoned to appear before a private hearing of the Senate Appropriations Committee. He was called on motion of Senator Bridges of New Hampshire, one of the fiercest critics of the Truman Administration's Far Eastern policies. With Senator Bridges on that Committee was Senator Knowland of California, another Republican critic of "appeasement" in the Pacific. Senator Knowland had already issued a statement saying that the invasion had "caught the Administration flatfooted." The Republicans had made a major issue of Pearl Harbor, and were looking forward to a repeat performance.

The Admiral was asked to appear at 3 P.M. but, when a more urgent summons came for the Admiral from the White House, the hearing was postponed until an hour later. For the Admiral, it must have been a trying day. He had to convince the Republicans that American intelligence had not been taken unawares, yet he had to do so without raising too many questions about the Administration's failure to take preventive action on the basis of his reports. Perhaps he also had to explain to the President why he had not called attention more forcibly to those intelligence reports.

The statement the Admiral made on leaving the White House may have reflected the version of events he had just offered the President. The Admiral "said the North Korean forces have had the capability of invading the South for a year, but that it had been impossible to predict the timetable under which they would march, if at all." This was quite different from his statement the day before that indications showed an attack was possible "this week or next." To say that American intelligence had known for a year that the North could invade the South but didn't know when they would invade, if at all, was the same as admitting that American intelligence had been taken by surprise.

This did indeed remain the version at MacArthur's headquarters in Tokyo. John Gunther, in his biography of MacArthur, writes: "On the morning of June 25, the North Koreans launched an attack by no fewer than four divisions, assisted by three constabulary brigades; 70,000 men were committed, and about 70 tanks went into action simultaneously at four different points, . . . Ask any military man what all this means. To assemble such a force, arm and equip it, and have it ready to wheel into precalculated action over a wide front with perfect synchronization, on the appointed date, must have taken at least a month, . . . Yet South Koreans and Americans in Korea, to say nothing of SCAP in Tokyo, were taken utterly by surprise. . . . It was more disgraceful than Pearl Harbor. Our eyes were shut, and even our feet were sound asleep."

Gunther adds, "No doubt this will all be investigated in good time." It was investigated that very first day after the war began when Admiral Hillenkoetter was summoned before the Senate Committee. But when the Senators emerged from

behind the closed doors of the hearing room they were molli-
fied. The Admiral's account at the hearing was quite different
from the vague statement he made on leaving the White
House. He had gone into considerable detail before the Committee, producing a file of intelligence bulletins to prove that
he had not been taken unawares. The latest of these was dated
June 20, only five days before the outbreak of the war. Senators Bridges and Knowland told newspapermen waiting outside the hearing room that they were now satisfied that the
Central Intelligence Agency had been "doing a good job."

It would be strange if, in a country like Korea, American
intelligence were to overlook a military buildup as impressive
as that which went into action on the 38th Parallel that Sunday morning. Korea was one place where American intelligence
was not dependent on meager hints from dubious agents in
country difficult to penetrate. There were 500 American officers
and 700 civilian technicians in South Korea. They were scattered throughout the government and the armed forces. The
government itself was dependent on American aid and eager
to be cooperative. Nowhere was the Iron Curtain less formidable than on the 38th Parallel. The same people lived, the
same language was spoken, on both sides of that artificial
boundary. Much of the frontier ran through rugged country
difficult to patrol and easy to penetrate. It is hard to believe
that an invasion force could be built up on that border without detection.

The bulletins the Admiral showed the Senators that day
were not made public, but America's leading military commentator, Hanson Baldwin of the *New York Times,* a trusted
confidant at the Pentagon, reported that they showed "a
marked buildup by the North Korean People's Army along
the 38th Parallel beginning in the early days of June."

Major elements of four North Korean divisions, Baldwin
wrote, plus two other units described as constabulary brigades,
were in position along that border "where intermittent fighting
and border raids were a part of life." Commencing in early
June, intelligence reported that "light and medium tanks probably of Japanese manufacture, about thirty 122-mm. Soviet-

type field guns and other heavy equipment were assembled at the front, and troop concentrations became noticeable."

If there really were advance warnings, why had nothing been done about them? The question created disbelief. That very first day of the war, when the *New York Times* reported that the Pentagon and the Admiral claimed that they had not been surprised, it quoted other unnamed "observers" as being skeptical of these assertions. These "observers" suggested that if the United States had known that troops were massing on the Korean border for a possible invasion it would have made diplomatic representations "either to the United Nations, to the North Korean government or to Russia." They also pointed out that warning could have been given in a less official way by making some of this intelligence information available to the press. The "observers" were mystified by "the failure of any news reports to tell that such a crisis was brewing along the 38th Parallel."

This also puzzled the Senators at the Hillenkoetter hearing. When questioned by them, the Admiral "could offer no explanation why the receiving agencies had apparently failed to interpret the indications he furnished as evidence of a move to be undertaken soon." One Senator said he would "make it his business to find out." If he ever did, he kept what he learned to himself.

The mystery is why Washington should have been surprised, when there was reason to believe from intelligence reports that an attack might be in preparation. Admiral Hillenkoetter told the Committee that the duties of his agency "did not, in his view, include evaluation of the information it passed on." This bit of information turned up two months later, in August, in the story announcing his replacement as chief of intelligence.

If it was not Admiral Hillenkoetter's job to evaluate this information—to say, "Look, this might mean an attack is coming"—then whose job was it? Primarily, one supposes, the Department of Defense. But the Pentagon is a big place, and its military responsibilities covered a wide area, from occupied Germany in the West to occupied Japan in the East. If war broke out in Korea, at the very threshold of occupied Japan, threatening the peace of the Pacific, the task of coping with the military consequences would rest with MacArthur in Tokyo.

If MacArthur Headquarters in Tokyo evaluated this intelligence as important, that evaluation would have alerted Washington. If MacArthur Headquarters brushed it off as unreliable or unimportant, no subordinate official in Washington would dare insist that it might mean war. And, if Washington disagreed with MacArthur's evaluation, he was not one to keep his light hidden under a bushel. Every publicity device from well-timed unofficial "leaks" to full-dress interviews was constantly being utilized by MacArthur Headquarters to get its point of view across.

Korea was not occupied territory—but neither was Formosa, yet for months the danger of a Red attack on Formosa had been a constant theme at Tokyo Headquarters. Headlines like "REDS MASS FOR WAR ON 38TH PARALLEL" would have been easy to evoke in the American press. It was not necessary to wait for the capture of a North Korean timetable. The mere possibility would have been enough. The absence of inspired press reports out of Tokyo warning of possible Communist aggression in Korea was all the more puzzling because it was so out of keeping with MacArthur's character and usual mode of operation.

CHAPTER 2

★

The Silence of Seoul

WHATEVER the situation in Washington or Tokyo, it cannot be said that Seoul, capital of South Korea, was caught completely unawares. On the contrary, the South Korean government, though also strangely silent in the days immediately preceding the outbreak of the war, had been expecting trouble. Early in May, President Syngman Rhee had made an appeal for combat planes saying, "May and June may be the crucial period in the life of our nation." On May 10, Captain Sihn Sung Mo, Defense Minister of South Korea, had held a press conference at Seoul in which he stated "that North Korean troops were moving in force toward the 38th Parallel and that there was imminent danger of invasion from the North." Robert T. Oliver, an American adviser of Rhee's, had made an appeal for planes for South Korea in the June 9 issue of a publication called *Periscope on Asia*, warning that "unless the decision is 'yes,' and unless the planes are sent promptly, the next Soviet advance in Asia could be down the Korean peninsula."

"Why did the South Koreans do badly at the beginning?" John Gunther asks in his book on MacArthur, a book which embodies the official version of Tokyo Headquarters. "They were taken by surprise, and were miserably short of arms." The surprise is questionable and the inadequacy of their equipment was no secret. The day after the war started, the *New York Herald Tribune* correspondent at Tokyo filed a dispatch on the lack of equipment in the South Korean forces. Its transmission was inexplicably delayed and it was not published until four days later. "Only last month," he reported, "Brigadier General William L. Roberts, then head of the American military mission to South Korea, urged American-supplied airpower for South Korea and spoke of danger if it should not be forthcoming." General Roberts was not subject to MacArthur. No similar warning came out of Tokyo Headquarters.

It is true that on June 27, two days after fighting began, the United Nations Commission cabled the Security Council that the South Koreans "were taken completely by surprise as they had no reason to believe from intelligence sources that invasion was imminent." In the light of information already in the possession of the Commission but not made public until almost three months later, this was untrue.

On September 14, the Commission made public a report which showed that on several occasions officials of the South Korean government had discussed with the Commission signs that the North was preparing for an invasion. The first occasion was in January, 1950, when the Chief of Staff of the South Korean army "informed the committee that he believed the aggressive plans of the North Korean authorities to be mature, and that it was only a matter of time before they would be put into action." He supplied detailed intelligence figures, which are given in the report. The second occasion was a month later when the Chief of Staff "stated that the North Korean forces possessed more powerful and more numerous artillery weapons than did the Army of the Republic of Korea," and gave figures on the increase in the number of tanks, armored cars, and planes on the Northern side. The next occasion was in May when "the attention of the commission" was drawn to a statement made by the South Korean Defense Minister at a press conference on May 10, at which he declared "that North Korean troops were moving in force toward the 38th Parallel and that there was imminent danger of invasion from the North."

The Commission arranged for a meeting with the Foreign

Minister "to ask for information on the seriousness of the danger and the degree of imminence of the invasion, as envisaged by the Defense Minister." A private hearing was held by the Commission at which the Acting South Korean Deputy Chief of Staff and the chief of intelligence of the South Korean army gave "important and detailed information," which indicated an extensive buildup of forces and equipment on the 38th Parallel.

After the hearing, members "informally heard" from two officers on the staff of General William L. Roberts, chief of the United States Military Advisory Group to the South Korean army. These officers "substantially confirmed the information given by the Korean military authorities" but "did not, however, agree on the imminence of any danger and again expressed confidence in the ability of the Army of the Republic to handle the forces of the Northern regime in case of attack." The hearing was on May 12. The war broke out on June 25, less than six weeks later. It is difficult to reconcile this information made public on September 14 with the earlier statement in the UN Commission cable of June 27 that the South Koreans "had no reason to believe from intelligence sources that invasion was imminent."

Another UN Commission document little noticed at the time also makes it hard to understand the Commission's insistence that the attack was a complete surprise. This appears as Document No. 14 in the State Department's White Paper on Korea. It was not transmitted to the United Nations Security Council until June 29 but it was dated June 24, the day before the fighting began. The heading is significant: "Following report dated 24 June from United Nations field observers submitted to Commission on their return from field trip along 38th Parallel commencing 9 June to report developments likely to involve military conflict is forwarded for information."

In view of the warnings by South Korean authorities in May and the intelligence reports later furnished by Admiral Hillenkoetter in Washington, it would seem to have been a good precaution to send out field observers "to report developments likely to involve military conflict." But again it is difficult to reconcile the sending out of observers for this purpose from June 9 to June 24 with the view that there was "no reason to believe from intelligence sources that invasion was imminent."

It would be good to know more about these field observers, how they happened to be sent out, how they were picked out, and how they operated. The field report is signed "Szu-Tu," apparently a Chinese. Next to the United States, Nationalist China was Syngman Rhee's strongest supporter in the United Nations, and Chiang and Rhee worked closely together, notably in their joint campaign for a Pacific Pact to be supported by the United States. The field observers ended their tour and made their report on June 24. If they had waited a few more hours they might have seen how the fighting actually started, for the war broke out early on the morning after their return.

The field report seemed designed to show that the South Koreans could not have had any offensive purposes. "Principal impression left with observers after their field tour," the report says, "is that South Korea Army is organized entirely for defense and is in no condition to carry out attack on large scale against forces of North." The report states: "In general, attitude South Korean commanders is one of vigilant defense. Their instructions do not go beyond retirement in case of attack upon previously prepared positions." It declares there was no evidence of reconnaissance northward "nor of any undue excitement or activity at divisional headquarters or regimental levels to suggest preparation for offensive activity." The lack of South Korean air support, armor, and heavy artillery would make "any action with object of invasion . . . impossible." The timing and the observations, on the very eve of the war's outbreak, provided a remarkably convenient alibi for the South Koreans.

The field report ends with a statement which later helped to create the picture of a surprise attack from the North. It says that no intelligence reports had been received "of any unusual activity on the part of North Korean forces that would indicate any impending change in general situation along Parallel." This would seem to be a debatable conclusion on the basis of the field report itself. It gives several intelligence indications which might reasonably have seemed danger signals. At several points North Koreans had taken possession of "salients on south side parallel, occupation in at least one case being of fairly recent date." In some sectors "civilians had recently been removed from areas adjoining parallel to north to depths ranging from 4 to 8 kilometers." On Thursday night, June 22, the regimental headquarters at Ongjin received intelligence reports "to effect that there was increased military activity . . . about four kilometers north parallel." The reference to increased military activity near Ongjin is striking, for the very first cablegram from the American Ambassador at Seoul reporting the outbreak of fighting said: "Action was initiated about 4 A.M. Ongjin was blasted by North Korean artillery fire."

When we add the information in the United Nations reports to that which emerged from the Hillenkoetter hearing and couple this with the public statements of the South Korean government itself, it is impossible to accept the flat statement by the UN Commission that the South Koreans had "no reason to believe from intelligence sources that invasion was imminent." This statement, with no supporting evidence, was made in the Commission's cable of June 27 to the Security Council, the very day sanctions were voted. But the facts here presented, from which the Commission supposedly drew its deductions, did not come to light until later. They underscore the wisdom of the Yugoslav delegate in urging that the Security Council act less hastily.

What puzzles one in the record of events is why the South Korean government made no effort after its Defense Minister's press conference of May 10 to attract public attention to the danger it feared and the inadequate military equipment of which it had complained.

The silence is all the more striking because the South Korean government was confronted with a political problem more serious than the military problem. This was the question of how far the United States would support the South in war with the North. The question had been brought sharply to public attention by an interview which Senator Connally of Texas, chairman of the Senate Foreign Relations Committee, had given the influential Washington weekly, *U.S. News and World Report*. As the Democratic Party's foremost congressional spokesman on foreign policy, the veteran Senator from Texas spoke with authority. What he had to say attracted more attention in the Far East than at home. The English-language paper in Tokyo, the *Nippon Times*, gave it a front-page spread on May 3: "REDS WILL FORCE U.S. TO QUIT SOUTH KOREA, CONNALLY PREDICTS."

In the interview, Senator Connally was asked whether the suggestion "that we abandon South Korea is going to be seriously considered." The Senator replied that he was afraid that this was going to happen "whether we want it to or not." He thought the Communists were going to overrun Korea when they got ready just as they "probably will overrun Formosa."

When asked, "But isn't Korea an essential part of the defense strategy?" he had replied: "No. Of course any position like that is of some strategic importance. But I don't think it is very greatly important. It has been testified before us that Japan, Okinawa, and the Philippines make the chain of defense which is absolutely necessary."

The next day there was an alarming response in Washington, where Secretary of State Dean Acheson "declined to say whether the United States might have to abandon South Korea to Russia," and a cry of protest from Rhee in Seoul, where he called in the Associated Press for an exclusive interview in which he said, "Senator Connally must have forgotten that the United States has committed herself and cannot pull out of the Korea situation with honor."

Senator Connally's statement that Korea was not part of the essential American defense "perimeter" in the Far East reflected a strategic decision made months before and well known in Washington. It was this strategic decision not to defend South Korea which led Syngman Rhee's former American adviser, Robert T. Oliver, to write later in his book, *Why War Came in Korea*, that one of the reasons for the Communist attack was that "American authoritative statements indicated that we would not defend Korea."

If Rhee feared attack, it was important for him to try to change that decision. A campaign was indeed begun in the press to publicize Korea's danger. A dispatch from Seoul in the *Nippon Times*, May 7, said: "The brave South Koreans would go north at a drop of a hat—Uncle Sam—but this appears unlikely. The question unanswered is, when will Russian-backed North Koreans come South?" The story went on to say that "this situation has brought Korea to the world's attention. The UN has struggled with the problem. Statesmen have proclaimed Korea must not be deserted in the face of the Communist deluge of Asia and others have replied such a fate is a matter of time, so why prolong it at the expense of the American taxpayers"—presumably a reference to Senator Connally and the unfeeling Democrats. On May 10, the South Korean Defense Minister held the press conference at which he said North Korean troops were moving in force toward the 38th Parallel and there was imminent danger of invasion from the North. This was the last public appeal made by the South Korean Republic. Why the silence after that date?

There were no statements from Seoul. There were no inspired press dispatches from Tokyo. There were no speeches in Congress. Could it be that Rhee received advice that it would be wiser to invite or provoke attack, and then trust to the impact on American public opinion to change American policy? Rhee was apparently content to let that basic American strategic decision go unchallenged, to draw up his troops into defensive positions, to give them orders to withdraw in event of attack, and to arrange for United Nations observers to see how defensive all his military dispositions were. The observers brought in their reports on the 24th. That night, in their absence, the war began. Rhee announced that it began with an unprovoked invasion from the North. The North Korean government, on the contrary, reported that South Korean forces crossed the Parallel in three different places, were hurled back, and the North Korean forces then went over to the offensive.

CHAPTER 3

★

Connally's Warning

MAC ARTHUR relished the role of big brother to little Syngman Rhee. True, MacArthur took the Japanese side in disputes between South Korea and Japan over reparations and the rankling compulsory registration imposed on all Koreans living in Japan. But MacArthur had shown himself protective in all that concerned South Korea's relations with its Communist neighbors. At the Seoul ceremonies which established the Rhee regime in August, 1948, MacArthur had proclaimed: "In this hour, as the fortunes of righteousness advance, the triumph is dulled by one of the great tragedies of contemporary history—an artificial barrier has divided your land. This barrier must and will be torn down." It is difficult to believe that Rhee did not turn to Mac-Arthur for aid and advice when he began to fear that this barrier might be torn down from the wrong side.

In 1949, when Rhee went to Tokyo for a brief visit, Mac-Arthur saw him off—as the cables reported—with a pat on the back and a declaration: "You can depend upon it that I will defend South Korea as I would defend the shores of my own native land." Could it be that Rhee did not let MacArthur know of the threatening preparations on the 38th Parallel? John Gunther explains that the General had no "political or military responsibility" for Korea after the occupation ended on August 15, 1948. "It is only fair to state this with emphasis," Gunther writes, "inasmuch as several of his critics have sought

14

to lay to his door some responsibility for our negligent intelligence. The General was not to blame. Korea was not part of his domain." On the other hand, Gunther adds, as commander in chief of the Far East Command, MacArthur "might well have given developments in Korea a more penetrating scrutiny than he did."

Gunther's account reflects an almost exuberant eagerness on the part of Tokyo Headquarters to admit what seems an extraordinary bit of stupidity. "The South Koreans and Americans in Korea, to say nothing of SCAP in Tokyo," he relates, "were as blankly astonished as if the sun had suddenly gone out. The North Koreans achieved complete tactical and even strategic surprise." This was certainly not true of the South Koreans. Could it have been true of Tokyo Headquarters? Could MacArthur have overlooked the warlike preparations noted in the Central Intelligence bulletins in Washington? More extraordinary than the oversight itself is MacArthur's readiness to admit it. This is what seems so out of character, in a commander who would normally tend to cover up the slightest retreat or the most excusable defeat in high-sounding circumlocutions.

What adds to the difficulty of believing that MacArthur was quite *that* unaware is the visit paid to Korea at the time by John Foster Dulles, Republican adviser to the United States Secretary of State. Dulles spent three days in Korea and then several days in Tokyo with MacArthur the week before the war began. On his way home, three days after the fighting started, Dulles stopped at Honolulu, where he said he had known the situation was "critical" when he was in Korea but that the attack from the North "came sooner than expected." No one asked him when he expected the attack, or whether he had mentioned the possibility to MacArthur.

When Dulles left Washington on June 14, he said he was going to Korea "on the invitation of the President of the Korean Republic." Surely Syngman Rhee must have spoken to Dulles about the invasion he feared and about the inadequacy of the South Korean military equipment? Dulles was in a sense the godfather of the South Korean Republic. "In

1947, and again in 1948," as he said in that same statement on leaving Washington, "I had the responsibility in the United Nations General Assembly of representing the United States in the sponsorship of the resolution which led to the reestablishment of Korea's independence under a representative government administering the free part of Korea." He might have added that the South Korean Republic was also the first fruit of another institution he had successfully sponsored at the UN—the Interim Committee or "Little Assembly," a device for circumventing the Soviet veto power on the Security Council. It was the Interim Committee which, despite the serious misgivings of Canada and Australia, voted to authorize the separate elections in South Korea that led to the establishment of the Republic. For Dulles, Korea was a symbol. As acting chief United States delegate to the General Assembly during the debate on Korea he had "made it clear that the United Nations action on Korea was to be taken as an endorsement of the wider opposition of American foreign policy to Communism."

It is this record which makes it so hard to understand why Dulles did not seek by some public statement to focus American and world attention on the danger which menaced the South Korean Republic. Dulles left Washington June 14. We know from Hanson Baldwin's account in the *New York Times* that the marked buildup of armed force on the 38th Parallel in what might well be preparation for an attack "was described in a [intelligence] report of June 9 and substantiated on June 13." These intelligence bulletins, as Admiral Hillenkoetter had explained to the inquiring Senators, were distributed to those persons in the government authorized to see them. Were they made available to Dulles in preparation for his trip? He was chief Republican adviser to the Secretary of State. He had played the leading American role in the creation of South Korea. He was going to the Far East at the request of the President and the Secretary of State to study the question of a Japanese peace treaty. The outbreak of war in Korea would at once affect the political and military calculations determining America's Japanese policy.

Dulles stayed three days with his Korean hosts and protégés, and spent one of these days inspecting their defenses on the 38th Parallel. Could it be that they did not discuss their fears, military needs, and intelligence with him? If so, what made him think while he was there that the situation was "critical," but that the attack (as he said in Honolulu) had come sooner than he thought it would?

Dulles addressed the Korean National Assembly on June 19. The speech, while fervid, was confined to cold-war generalities, but it implied aid in resisting Communist aggression. He told the Assembly that the Korean people were "today . . . in the front line of freedom, under conditions that are both dangerous and exciting . . . you encounter a new menace, that of Soviet Communism . . . [which] has seized in its cruel embrace the Korean people to the north of the 38th Parallel and . . . seeks by terrorism, fraudulent propaganda, infiltration and incitement to civil unrest, to enfeeble and discredit your new Republic." He assured them, "You are not alone . . . so long as you continue to play worthily your part in the great design of human freedom."

The South Korean officials must have been eager to learn in private talks with Dulles whether these were mere words, or whether they could count on concrete aid if war broke out. That aid would have to come first of all from Japan. It is asking a great deal to believe that Rhee, fearing an impending attack, did not ask Dulles to take the matter up with General MacArthur in Tokyo.

We do not know what Dulles discussed with Rhee in Seoul or afterward in Tokyo with MacArthur, but Rhee's urgent problem was part of a larger problem in which MacArthur had shown an intense interest for months: the problem of whether the Truman Administration could be brought to commit itself to military support of the remaining anti-Communist regimes in the Far East.

For Rhee the problem had two aspects, one internal, the other external, and it is in the light of both that the generalities in Dulles' speech at Seoul must be examined. This was the internal problem: the Korean National Assembly that

Dulles addressed on June 19, six days before war began, was the first meeting of a new assembly, the fruit of elections Rhee had tried hard to avoid. By decree, on March 31, he had ordered these elections postponed until November on the excuse that more time was needed to complete the budget. Eight days later he rescinded the decree, after receiving a sharp warning from Secretary of State Acheson on April 7 that South Korea would lose United States aid unless the elections were held as originally scheduled on May 30, and inflationary practices curbed. The elections, the first free elections in Korean history, brought out ninety percent of the voters and proved disastrous for Rhee. The opposition centered its campaign on the brutal police practices of the Rhee regime and only 27 members of the old assembly that Rhee had dominated were reelected. At least 128 of the 210 seats were won by independents, and Rhee supporters were sure of only 45 seats.

The North had begun a campaign for unification, and urged the South to throw Rhee and his cabinet out as traitors. Rhee had one major weapon to utilize against peaceful unification. The Korean Aid Bill passed by Congress in February of 1950 carried the proviso that aid would be terminated "in the event of the formation in the Republic of Korea of a coalition government which includes one or more members of the Communist Party or of the party now in control of the government of North Korea." It is in the light of this provision that one must read Rhee's statement to the Assembly on June 19: "We refuse to compromise with or make any concessions to the Communists. That would be the road leading toward disaster." It would also be the road leading to loss of American aid. But what if, with peaceful unification blocked by Congressional policy, there should be an internal revolt in the South, or an attack by the North, or both? Would there be aid from the United States? And how much?

The Korean situation was becoming a smaller version of the Chinese situation, and it displayed official American policy in the same baffling inconsistencies. Dean Acheson, by insisting on free elections, had created a crisis for the Rhee regime. But Congress, by its proviso on aid, was preventing that crisis from being resolved peacefully, in conformity with majority aspirations for peaceful unification—on both sides of the Parallel. Would Rhee be driven out of South Korea as Chiang had been driven off the mainland of China? This was hardly a question to which MacArthur could remain indifferent. And now Senator Connally, in saying that the Reds would overrun Korea when they got ready just as they "will probably overrun Formosa," touched a sore point at MacArthur Headquarters which was itself enough to draw MacArthur's attention forcibly to Korea. The Formosan question had been for months the center of a running battle between the Truman Administration and its headstrong military occupation chief in Tokyo.

The question of Formosa indeed was not without bearing on how Dulles happened to become chief Republican adviser to the Secretary of State in the spring of 1950. He had created some ill-feeling at the White House during his unsuccessful campaign for the Senate in 1949 by attacking Truman's Fair Deal as "a clear . . . danger to human liberty." Dulles' attempt to link his Democratic rival, former Governor Herbert H. Lehman, with Communists and Communism also left a bitter aftertaste with Truman. And yet Dulles owed to Truman his appointment year after year as a member of the various American delegations to the meetings of the United Nations General Assembly and the Council of Four Power Foreign Ministers.

It was Formosa, in a sense, which returned Dulles to favor again. In December, 1949, Chiang Kai-shek, facing the threat of a Communist invasion of his last stronghold, Formosa, was imploring Washington for military aid. In Washington Chiang's representatives utilized their powerful connections with the Republican party. On January 2, former President Herbert Hoover and Senator Robert A. Taft of Ohio demanded that the United States Navy be used to prevent a "Communist invasion" of Formosa. The next day, like a well-planned bombshell, the United Press revealed the contents of a private circular the State Department had sent out to American diplomats abroad on December 23 saying that Formosa's fall to the Chinese Communists was to be expected and that the United States would not interfere. The next day Secretary of State Dean Acheson was summoned to explain by the Senate Foreign Relations Committee at a hearing set for January 10. Truman's hand was thus forced, and on January 5 he told his press conference in a written statement that the United States would not give "military aid or advice" to Chiang on Formosa and would not "pursue a course which would lead to involvement in the civil conflicts in China." This statement of nonintervention in Chinese internal affairs remained the official American policy for not quite seven months. It was reversed by the outbreak of war in Korea.

Where did the United Press obtain the document which put Truman on the spot? In Tokyo. General MacArthur ordered an investigation on the 6th, the day after Truman's statement, but nobody in Tokyo seems to have done anything about finding out how the United Press got that scoop from its correspondent at MacArthur Headquarters in Tokyo. An investigation did soon begin to make headlines, but not the investigation of that curious "leak" in Tokyo. It was the investigation precipitated in Washington by Republican Senator Joseph McCarthy of Wisconsin, who delighted Chiang's friends at the capital by attacking the State Department as "Red," with special emphasis on those who had helped to establish America's skeptical attitude toward Chiang Kai-shek. When the heat became intense, the Department sought to bring Dulles back as Republican adviser, hoping that he might win it some Republican support and give it some protective coloration. The White House reluctantly named Dulles on April 6. His first assignment was preparation of the Japanese peace treaty.

If Truman had misgivings about the Dulles appointment, they soon proved well founded. In the Far East, Dulles turned up in MacArthur's "corner." He made a speech in Tokyo saying, "Our material might was exemplified by the atomic bomb; our moral might is exemplified by General MacArthur." The flattery might have been forgiven, if put to the Administration's purposes. But the day after laying it on—and with a shovel, as Disraeli advised with royalty—Dulles discreetly but unmistakably joined forces with MacArthur on Formosa policy. Fresh from a ninety-minute talk with MacArthur, Dulles told a press conference that his own presence in the Far East "indicated that the principle of bipartisan foreign policy now might be extended for the first time to Asia." When "questioned specifically regarding Formosa" at that Tokyo press conference, he said America's foreign policies "are constantly under review, taking account of changing situations. This generality applies to Formosa also." The "changing situations" which did reverse the Formosa policy that very next week were those created by the outbreak of war in Korea.

It is against this background that the silence of both Dulles and MacArthur on Korea is so tantalizing. Here were two men who had demonstrated consummate skill in politics and in the creation of public opinion, both anxious to commit the United States more strongly against Communism in the Far East. At a time when there was reason to believe North Korea might be preparing an aggression against South Korea, neither uttered a word of warning. Is it possible that the outbreak of war in Korea was preceded and followed by a chain of errors, falsehoods, forgeries, and negligences so extraordinary as to leave MacArthur unaware of what was going on? It would be easier to believe, in the light of what happened afterward—when the Korean War reversed American policy not only on Korea but also on Formosa—that MacArthur preferred to "play dumb," that Korea was a pawn to be sacrificed in a bigger game, a gambit offered as in chess, and that he did not want to do or say anything which might put his opponents on guard.

This is only surmise. Much that is otherwise inexplicable would fall into orderly place in the chain of events if it were true. Whether the outbreak of the war in Korea, like the assassination at Sarajevo which unleashed World War I, had its own unsavory secret history no outsider yet knows. But there was at least one well-informed American at the time who did not think impossible the kind of tactics this would imply. This man was Senator Connally.

There was a warning against the "preventive war" mentality in the *U.S. News and World Report* interview with Senator

Connally. The interview dealt with the prospects of peace and focused, as might be expected in the existing American atmosphere, on the intentions of Russia. The chairman of the Senate Foreign Relations Committee didn't think Russia wanted war. He didn't think Russia needed war: "They got along after World War I," he said, "without a war." He didn't consider war between the United States and the USSR inevitable. "They might change their policy," the Senator said, "we might change our policy so that there wouldn't be any cause for a war."

The interviewer asked whether the widespread view in America that war was inevitable wasn't based "largely on the fear that some incident might . . . inflame the parties into war." The Senator didn't look at it quite that way; he seemed to think some people were actually looking for an incident. "Well," was his reply, given verbatim in this full-dress question-and-answer interview, "a lot of them believe like this: They believe that events will transpire which will maneuver around and present an incident which will make us fight. That's what a lot of them are saying: 'We've got to battle some time, why not now?' " Was some such "maneuvering around"—to *create* an incident—the key to events in Korea?

CHAPTER 4

★

The Role of John Foster Dulles

WHEN John Foster Dulles left Washington for Korea on June 14 he spoke of himself as going out to "wage peace." He had been waging peace for a long time, though in different ways. In the spring of 1939 he joined Senator Burton K. Wheeler in attacking the Roosevelt Administration for "worsening the prospects of world peace" by supporting England and France against the Axis. A month after the war began in Europe he declared the United States could only "fulfill its destiny of showing the way to a permanent, constructive world peace" by staying out of the conflict. The moral revulsion he was later to exhibit in relation to the USSR did not appear in his attitude toward the Axis. According to the *New York Times* next day, he "traced aggression by the German, Italian and Japanese nations . . . to 'resentment, bitterness, and desperation' arising from in-equalities." This was not so different from the official apolo-getics at Berlin, Rome, and Tokyo.

In the year 1943, the year of Stalingrad and the North African invasion, Dulles launched a campaign for a "Chris-tian" peace, that is, a peace of forgiveness. As head of a Com-mission to Study the Bases of a Just and Durable Peace, he published a famous "Six Pillars of Peace" in March of that year. The Commission was established by the Federal Council of Churches of Christ in America.

The year 1943 was also the year Dulles began to take a prominent part in politics, appearing as foreign policy adviser to the Republican Governor of New York, Thomas E. Dewey, who was to run against Roosevelt the following year. At the famous meeting of the Republican Postwar Advisory Council in September, 1943, Governor Dewey put forward the idea of basing world security after the war on "a continuing military alliance" with Great Britain—almost three years before Churchill's similar speech at Fulton, Missouri. This created a good deal of dismay at Washington, for it promised to provoke Russian suspicion and undermine Allied unity at a time when German propaganda's last hope was to split East and West. "What would England and the United States do," Goebbels had asked in a radio broadcast on February 18, 1943, after the Stalingrad disaster, "if the worst happened and the European continent fell into the hands of the Bolsheviks?"

It was the position taken by Dewey on postwar security plans in the 1944 campaign against Roosevelt which brought Dulles his first invitation to Washington and "bipartisanship." The Roosevelt Administration was basing its plans on the conviction that any new world organization could succeed only if the victorious powers maintained their unity after the war, thus preventing Germany from again playing East and West against each other. It was on this idea that the Republican candidate focused his fire, attacking "Russian plans" for postwar "domination" by the Big Four as "imperialism," "cynical power politics," and an "immoral . . . military alliance." Why domination of the world by the Big Four was more "immoral" than Dewey's idea of domination by an Anglo-American Big Two was not explained. This speech in August, 1944, led Secretary of State Cordell Hull to invite Governor Dewey to a conference on postwar security plans, in an effort to head off Republican opposition to a United Nations organization. Dewey sent Dulles as his representative, and it was as a result of this conference that Dulles appeared the following spring as Republican adviser to the American delegation at San Francisco.

The isolationist had now become a full-fledged "internationalist." He was appointed thereafter to every United States delegation to the sessions of the United Nations General Assembly, and appeared as adviser at the various sessions of the Council of Foreign Ministers which had been established at the Potsdam Conference. He also expanded his activity as a Presbyterian layman in the Federal Council of Churches of Christ in America, and helped to organize the World Council of Churches of Christ.

From 1947 on, Dulles became the object of bitter attack from Moscow and was labeled a warmonger by Vishinsky. No figure in American public life was more deeply concerned with the "menace" of Sovietism; none more pessimistic about the possibility of cooperation with Moscow. As early as June, 1946, he was dubious about the possibility of peaceful coexistence, implying in a public speech that the USSR must seek to crush freedom everywhere. "The Soviet Union," he said, "cannot be kept purged of freedoms if elsewhere those freedoms are rife." After the Moscow conference of 1947 he urged the Western powers to go ahead with the solution of the problems of peace without Russia—presumably by separate treaties with the defeated powers. He helped draft a manifesto by the Federal Council of Churches that year calling for a world-wide "moral offensive" by the United States to spread the doctrine of freedom as opposed to the Soviet doctrine of the police state; and at the first constituent assembly of the World Council of Churches at Amsterdam in August, 1947, he attacked the Soviet regime as "atheistic and materialistic" and accused its leaders of rejecting "the concept of moral law." The man who in 1943 had been pleading for a "Christian peace" with the Axis now seemed to be advocating a "Christian war" against the USSR.

These multifarious political and religious activities, all centering on the menace of Communism, contrasted sharply with the quiet life Dulles had been content to lead in the years before the war. He then figured very little in the news, either as a political or religious leader. A successful lawyer, long a partner in Sullivan & Cromwell, America's leading corporation law firm, he was little known outside financial and legal circles. His only quasi-public assignment during those years came after Hitler took power in Germany, when a group of New York banking houses chose him to represent their German dollar bond interests in negotiation with Hjalmar Schacht. If the Nazi regime offended his religious sensibilities, he gave no evidence of it.

At first there was protest from Americans who remembered this prewar record and distrusted the active role Dulles was playing in decisions affecting the future of Germany. In post-war Congressional cartel investigations, his name often turned up as a former counsel for German financial interests. When Secretary of State Marshall announced that he was taking Dulles along as adviser to the meeting of the Council of Foreign Ministers in Moscow in the spring of 1947, a "National Conference on the Problem of Germany," convoked in New York on March 6 by a group that included Mrs. Franklin D. Roosevelt and Edgar Ansel Mowrer, urged that attorneys like Dulles having interests in Germany be barred as advisers to the American delegation. As recently as November 3, 1949, former Secretary of the Interior Harold Ickes in a public speech opposing the Dulles campaign for the Senate recalled this pre-war past and quoted Dulles as having said in 1939 that "only hysteria believes that Germany, Japan or Italy contemplates war against us." But protest soon died down, especially after Vishinsky listed Dulles among the "warmongers" in his UN General Assembly speech of September 18, 1947. For after that, to attack the Dulles record was to appear to be following the Soviet line, a hazardous occupation in the hysteria which the cold war was developing in America.

Peace with Russia seemed to be what Dulles feared. Early in March, 1950, when dispatches quickly cleared by censorship in Moscow again suggested that Stalin would like to meet with Truman, and peaceful speeches were made by Molotov and Malenkov, Dulles addressed a public meeting in New York, together with former Postmaster General James A. Farley, denouncing the Russian "peace offensive" as "deceptive cold-war strategy." Not long before Dulles left for Korea, he seemed to feel that something more than cold war was needed. In a broadcast from Washington on May 14, he declared, "as things are going now . . . we must develop better techniques. . . . They [the Russians] can win everything by the cold war they could win by a hot war."

Dulles seemed less discouraged after his three days in Korea. When he arrived in Tokyo from Korea on June 21, he was in an exuberant mood and told reporters he expected "positive" results from his scheduled talks with MacArthur. Next day, after his long talk with the Supreme Commander, Dulles "predicted," according to the Associated Press, " 'positive action' by the United States to preserve peace in the Far East."

What kind of "positive action" did Dulles have in mind? There were several ways in which "positive action" might have been taken to preserve peace. He could have warned that the South Koreans feared an attack, and put Peking and Moscow on notice that such an attack would be regarded as their responsibility. With Dulles and MacArthur in Tokyo at the time were the American Secretary of Defense, Louis Johnson, and General Omar Bradley, head of the United States Joint Chiefs of Staff. So influential a quartet of American public figures had it in their power, if they so chose, to focus world attention on the danger of war in Korea and to put the Soviet bloc on notice that any attack would bring grave consequences. Dulles told the Associated Press that by "positive action" he meant that the United States intended to "preserve international peace, security, and justice in the world—and that includes this part of the world as well as the so-called Western world." Pressed for some further explanation of "positive action," Dulles explained that he thought his conclusions pooled with those of Bradley and Johnson would lead to "some positive action, but I cannot forecast what."

What made Dulles so sure of "positive action"? The "positive action" could not have referred to the question of a Japanese peace treaty, because that same day he told the Allied and Japanese press that no decision had even been reached on "whether to proceed with a peace treaty with Japan."

This was on June 22. The only "positive action" which followed was the outbreak of war in Korea on June 25 and the commitment of the American government to large-scale intervention against Communism in the Pacific area on June 27. Was this what Dulles had in mind when he predicted "positive action . . . to preserve international peace, security, and justice in the world"?

CHAPTER 5

★

Chiang's Pilgrimage

WHEN Dulles said he expected "positive action" by the United States to show that it intended to uphold international peace, security, and justice in "this part of the world as well as in the so-called Western world," he was conjuring up a policy the State Department and the White House had rejected. The Korean War led them to accept it. For more than a year, Chiang Kai-shek had been trying unsuccessfully to get the United States to commit itself in Asia as it had already committed itself in Europe. On May 11, 1949, Chiang's ambassador in Washington, V. K. Wellington Koo, had suggested to Acheson the conclusion of a Pacific Pact similar to the Atlantic Pact. There was an echoing statement next day from Australian Prime Minister Chifley and two days later from Syngman Rhee, also calling for a Pacific Pact.

Acheson was forced to take a public position, and at a press conference on May 18 he said that "despite serious dangers to world peace existing there" he did not think the time ripe for such an alliance. It would have committed the United States to military support of Chiang against the Chinese Reds, and the Secretary of State pointedly said he endorsed Prime Minister Nehru's view that internal conflicts in the Asian countries must be resolved first. As a matter of fact Nehru's own position, which was soon to prove an obstacle to Chiang's plans, went beyond this. He had told the Indian Parliament on

March 8 that India would try to keep clear of both cold-war blocs and avoid "binding covenants" with other Far Eastern nations, though he envisaged the possibility of an Asian regional organization "largely confined to consultation and cooperation." This was not at all what Chiang wanted.

Chiang did not allow himself to be discouraged by that first rebuff from Acheson. In July, he visited the Philippines and obtained the support of President Quirino for an anti-Communist union of Pacific nations. Quirino explained that the proposed Pacific bloc would not depend on support from the United States but would "do our bit in the American-led crusade against Communism." In August, Chiang visited South Korea and he and Rhee issued a joint statement proposing that a conference be held in the Philippines to organize the proposed Pacific Pact union.

Quirino in the meantime had gone to Washington, but the best he could get from a visit with President Truman was the assurance on August 11 that the United States would "watch sympathetically" as non-Communist countries in the Far East worked together for collective security. In addressing Congress, Quirino had to say that while he understood why the United States might not "welcome the obligations" of becoming a member of a Pacific Union, "active American participation" was not necessary to its formation.

The only result of these laborious hints was a still more serious rebuff in September when the North Atlantic Council of Foreign Ministers, meeting in Washington, turned thumbs down on a Pacific Pact. British Foreign Secretary Bevin and French Foreign Minister Schuman indorsed the American view that it was useless to try to "save" non-Communist China. In October, on his own visit to America, Nehru called talk of a Pacific Pact "premature." When Quirino persisted in calling a Pacific conference the following spring, he had to accept two conditions. He announced on April 17 that he had dropped plans for a military alliance and sought only a political, economic, and cultural union of non-Communist states in the area. And, when the conference finally met at Baguio on May 26 to May 30, 1950, with representatives of India,

Indonesia, the Philippines, Australia, Ceylon, Pakistan, and Thailand present, it was plain that Quirino had been unable to win assent for an invitation to Chiang and Rhee. This significant exclusion of the prime mover of a Pacific Pact and his faithful friend in South Korea was attributed to the refusal of India and Indonesia to do anything which would imply a departure from strict neutrality in the East-West cold war.

The Baguio conference produced no formal regional organization nor any declaration of regional opposition to Communism. Moreover, it was marked by the first faint signs of regional opposition to Big Power interference in Asia. The conference went on record as demanding that the Big Powers take no action in the Far East without consulting the Asian nations. This, which might have been the beginnings of an Asian Monroe Doctrine, was also a potential stumbling block to Chiang's plans, for his last hope was somehow to precipitate American intervention.

May 30, 1950, the day the Baguio conference ended, was thus a black day for Chiang, as it was for Rhee, for it was also on the 30th that he was forced to hold the elections in which he lost control of the South Korean National Assembly. Chiang awaited an invasion from the mainland, Rhee was faced with the prospect either of peaceful unification or of invasion from the North, with little likelihood that he could survive either. Both were badly in need of some "positive action" which would bring American intervention in their behalf.

For Chiang, the situation was complicated by the fact that even if the Reds did not launch that invasion of Formosa against which MacArthur had been warning, it looked as if it were going to become increasingly difficult to keep Communist China out of the United Nations. The Indian press in June reflected renewed efforts to bring Peking in. "U.N. HEADING FOR CRISIS OVER RED CHINA ADMISSION," said a headline in the *Hindustani Times* of New Delhi on June 22, over a Press Trust of India dispatch from New York saying that Trygve Lie was "trying to get France and Egypt" to vote for the admission of Peking. Since Acheson had said that America would not veto

Peking's admission, and Washington had been dropping hints for weeks that it wished the other nations on the Security Council would "force" it to accept Red China in the United Nations, those two votes would lose Chiang his place at the Security Council.

Were Peking to be admitted to the United Nations, the Chiang regime on Formosa could hardly maintain itself much longer. What, then, would happen to the island? Chiang's friends in Washington had made Formosa into an American national issue. On the surface the dispute was a strategic question—was distant Formosa really necessary to the defense of the United States? In reality this was a political question. To commit the United States to hold Formosa was to commit it to a hostile policy against the new China. This suited three different but allied points of view in the debate over American policy. One wished to extend "containment" to the Pacific. The second looked, as Chiang did, for an eventual American war of "liberation" against the mainland. The third believed that a new war between the United States and the Soviet bloc was inevitable, and the longer it was delayed the stronger the USSR would become.

What made the debate over Formosa obscure was the need to keep the essential question submerged. Under cover of argument about the need for Formosa in the American perimeter of "defense," Chiang and his friends were merely rearguing the case for a Pacific Pact in a subtler and more effective way. If Formosa was necessary to American defense, then America must prevent the new China from taking possession; if America and the new China were to be enemies, then America must support those other Asian anti-Communist forces on China's flanks. The real issue was never stated. If there was to be war, then it was folly to give up any advance base. On the other hand, if there was to be peace, Formosa was not necessary to American "defense."

What Chiang and those obsessed with the need for an anti-Communist crusade feared was the further corollary. If Formosa was not necessary to American "defense," then there was no obstacle to the stabilization of good relations and trade with the new China. This meant peace. And peace is what they feared—for from their point of view peace would merely permit the new regime to consolidate itself, to give satisfaction to mass needs, and to take root, perhaps too strongly for destruction later.

On the eve of the Korean War, those who saw Formosa as the fulcrum of the future conflict with the mainland were looking around for alternative means of accomplishing their ends. The Pacific Pact was too enormous in its implications; Congress balked at the sheer ultimate cost, Western Europe at the diversion of armament. The campaign to "sell" Formosa as necessary to American defense was petering out. A third idea was being broached, which was to play a part in shaping Truman's decisions after the war began.

The day before the fighting started, O. H. Brandon, the well-informed Washington correspondent of the London *Sunday Times*, cabled his paper that General Bradley and Secretary Johnson would urge use of a new device to take over Formosa. "It will be stressed," Brandon cabled, "that, with the Japanese peace treaty still pending, America could take the island temporarily in trust. Mr. Johnson is said to favor ultimately a United Nations trusteeship over Formosa." This was a device worthy of two such able corporation lawyers as Johnson and Dulles, for under the trusteeship provisions of the United Nations Charter the power in possession can fix the terms on which it will hand the territory over to "trusteeship" and can retain effective control behind the new façade. Such legalistic devices could clearly not dispose of so explosive a question as Formosa, but "trusteeship" was enough to keep Washington and Peking embroiled, and prevent the stabilization of relations with the new China.

The same unspoken considerations which lay beneath the dispute over Formosa were also to be found under the surface of the related dispute over the question of a Japanese peace treaty. From the standpoint of those who wanted war with the Soviet Union, or thought it inevitable, Japan was the most valuable American base in the Far East, and a vast reservoir of first-rate military manpower. To end the occupation and give up this base was, from this point of view, folly. From the stand-point of those who hoped for peace, the continued occupation of Japan, its utilization as a base, and its prospective rearma-ment were calculated to feed Russian suspicion, maintain ten-sion, and make war all the more "inevitable." Here, again, as in the case of Formosa, the question was really whether one feared war or peace.

How serious were the implications of the Japanese treaty issue for those who feared peace may be seen in three columns on the question which Walter Lippmann wrote in June of 1950. Lippmann spoke for those who favored an early treaty ending the occupation. He argued from the difficult trans-Atlantic supply problem in the last war that a commitment to feed and defend a nation twice as populous as the United Kingdom and twice as far away, with no merchant marine of its own, would be a defense liability. This was true. But if one felt, as many of the American military did, that war could not be avoided, then Japan became an invaluable taking-off point for bombers even if it had to be sacrificed later.

In the final Lippmann article, one can see what most alarmed the "preventive war" crowd. For Lippmann argued that the real way to protect Japan from Soviet expansion was to "neu-tralize" the country and then give it an American guarantee against aggression. This would ease tension by assuring the Russians and Chinese that Japan would not be utilized as a base for American aggression while putting them on notice that any attack on Japan would mean war with the United States. Japan itself would be allowed limited rearmament for self-defense "and for internal security."

Lippmann then suggested that "developments of this sort in Japan" would have "great repercussions in Germany and in Europe." The application of such a policy to Japan would "raise the question of when the occupation of Germany, which causes the military partition of Europe, is to end. This is the supreme European question. It is the crux of the problem of 'peace.' If the occupation of Japan can end, then men will be sure to ask why the occupation of Europe should not end also." These quiet words were dynamite.

The perspective opened by Lippmann's final observation on the significance of an early Japanese peace treaty, made the week before the Korean War began, was possible only to those with attitudes fast disappearing in America. To look at the world in this way required (1) good-will toward other men, whatever their system of society, and (2), more fundamentally, a faith in one's own society and in freedom so deep and unshakable as to be impervious to the panic urge of fear and hate. These were indeed the characteristics of Franklin D. Roosevelt and of the Roosevelt era. By 1950 they had been made to seem naive, outmoded, and dangerous—if not downright subversive.

The new perspective coming to power, not yet but almost fully dominant in Washington, had a brilliant but paranoid logic. To end the occupation of Japan and Germany with their "neutralization" would be to leave them free to resume their normal trade ties, the former with China, the latter with Eastern Europe. But to permit this trade to be resumed with a Communist China and a Communist East Europe would be to free Germany and Japan from the economic needs which bound them to the dollar and made it possible to use them for that war which obsessed this particular mentality. Worse, this trade would mean allowing Germany and Japan to contribute to the reconstruction and the industrialization of these backward areas, ending their exploitation as reservoirs of cheap materials and cheap labor, and demonstrating the creative possibility of socialism for such areas, however repellent the regimes from the standpoint of personal liberty and intellectual freedom. Capitalist America's evident fear of peaceful competition testified to an ignominious lack of faith. Somewhat similar anxieties explained the iron curtain erected round the Soviet bloc lest nascent socialism look too frightfully austere beside the lush pastures of American capitalism. It was this mutual fear, itself the reflection of a subconscious unwilling admiration, which bound Washington and Moscow to each other in a cold war which brought out the worst in both, like a dreadful marriage of hate.

CHAPTER 6

★

Time Was Short

IF JAPAN were to be held, there had to be "positive action" quickly. Elections there on June 4, as in Korea on May 30, injected a new element of instability into the situation. In Washington, Truman had finally sided with Acheson in favor of an early peace. In Japan, public opinion was growing unhappy over continued occupation. The elections for the upper house of the Japanese legislature showed that the Liberals, the right-wing pro-American government party, which favored a separate treaty with the United States, could command no clear majority. Its percentage of the vote polled fell from 45 to 36 percent. The Ryokufukai, a group of independent conservatives who had usually supported the government, now "tended to support . . . the Opposition parties' demand for a general peace treaty and thereafter the removal of American bases from Japan." The big surprise of the elections, according to Frank Hawley, the Tokyo correspondent of the London *Times*, whom MacArthur found unpalatably independent-minded, was the emergence of the Socialists as the second largest party in the upper house, with 61 votes to the Liberal Party's 76. The Socialists were the leaders of the opposition to a treaty which would exclude the Chinese and the Russians and allow the Americans to keep their bases in Japan.

"Both General MacArthur's Headquarters and Mr. Yoshida (the Liberal Prime Minister)," Hawley cabled, just a few days before he was declared *persona non grata* at MacArthur Headquarters, "were today engaged in propaganda to convince the world of the pro-American feelings of the present Japanese government, so that a separate peace treaty can quickly be pushed through. The election results are for that reason interpreted officially in a manner that dumfounded Japanese observers. The significant results are the great increase in the strength of the moderate Socialist Party, and the defeat of the Communists."

Though the elections showed that the Communists had won not more than four and perhaps as few as two of the 132 seats involved in the election, MacArthur continued to press vigorously for their outlawry, despite the "free" constitution he had himself imposed on Japan. Perhaps the secret of this concern with an internal Communist danger of pygmy proportions may be read between the lines of an editorial in the Tokyo *Asahi* which warned that "such action [outlawing the Communists] might prove incompatible with Japan's desire not to be involved in any international conflict." Perhaps it was the desire to commit the Yoshida government firmly to the Western camp which explains the pressure on it to declare the Communist Party illegal, and the Yoshida government's stubborn reluctance to make any such move. Two days after the elections, MacArthur himself ordered the twenty-four members of the Central Committee of the Communist Party purged from public life, an order which brought a protest from the Russian representative on the Allied Council in Tokyo.

Perhaps MacArthur also had in mind the need to strengthen those elements which in Japan, as in Germany, could alone be trusted to engage wholeheartedly in remobilization for war. "Leading financial circles," the London *Times* correspondent reported after the MacArthur purge order, "declared today that, while Communism is incompatible with the reconstruction of this country, efforts must be taken to prevent the present government from reestablishing 'special secret police.' Everywhere today there is the fear that now, with the backing of the allied authorities, nothing will be allowed to stand in the way of the revival of the old totalitarianism. . . . Many Japanese express the hope that the Supreme Commander will come to realize that, as the old Japanese proverb puts it, 'It is dangerous to hunt tigers with wolves.' "

When Secretary Johnson and General Bradley arrived in Japan on June 18 for their conferences with MacArthur, Johnson revealed unsuspected gifts as a humorist by saying, "Freedom-loving people everywhere are encouraged by what is happening in Japan." In the wake of attacks on GIs in Tokyo on Memorial Day, the first such outbreak since the occupation began, a ban had been imposed on all rallies and demonstrations "of an extreme nature"—a ban so rigidly enforced that (according to the London *Times*) even a lecture on hygiene and a violin concert had to be abandoned. The day before Johnson arrived, the ban had been lifted under pressure from Allied Headquarters where a spokesman said, "We are not going to allow re-creation of a police state in Japan"—one of the few times that Allied Headquarters made itself felt in MacArthur's realm.

The arrival of Johnson, Bradley, and Dulles for conferences with MacArthur came, according to the London *Times* correspondent, at a time "when there is a feeling of greater tenseness than there has been for at least two or three years." The newspaper *Asahi* was quoted as saying sadly that "it could have wished that Mr. Dulles could hear also the voice of the people, which has no voice."

While the Japanese people were hoping for peace, the American and British military seem to have been planning for war. There is no stranger coincidence in this story of strange coincidences than the fact that the British, Australian, and American military authorities should have held top-level conferences in the Pacific area just before the Korean fighting broke out. If there had indeed been a decision to risk a civil war in Korea, such conferences were a necessary measure of foresight. Korea had been a strategic crossroads for centuries, trampled by contending Chinese, Russian, Japanese, and more recently American, armies. The Japanese saw it as a pistol aimed at them from the mainland; the Chinese, as the historic bridgehead for Japanese penetration into their country; the Russians, as a threat to Vladivostok; the Americans, as a key point in the noose of "containment" with which they hoped to choke off any further expansion of Communism. Were war to break out between the Russian satellite north of the 38th Parallel and the American satellite south of the Parallel, there was obvious danger of a clash between their respective sponsoring powers, since first one and then the other might be led to intervene. War in Korea might easily become—it may still prove to be—the beginning of World War III.

Was this possibility considered at the top-level military conferences which preceded the beginning of the war? Was this possibility, perhaps, the real occasion for these conferences? We do not know. Little is known of the conferences held with MacArthur in Tokyo by General Omar Bradley, head of the United States Joint Chiefs of Staff, and Secretary of Defense Louis Johnson. Less is known of those held in Australia.

The Sunday before the war began, the authoritative London *Observer* published a dispatch from its correspondent in Sydney saying that "unparalleled peacetime security precautions are being taken concerning the conferences now proceeding in Melbourne of the Chief of the Imperial General Staff, Field Marshal Sir William Slim, and the Australian defense chiefs." All that could be learned was that the conference dealt with the coordination of Commonwealth defenses "with particular emphasis on the Pacific in view of the growing Communist menace south from China." United States representatives did not take part, but "American liaison officers in Melbourne are being informed of decisions." Did these liaison officers exchange intelligence information? Was the Imperial General Staff apprised of the preparations which might portend war on the 38th Parallel? Did it consider what might happen if the war spread to China and China struck back, perhaps at Malaya, source of the tin and rubber so vital to the American and West European war machines?

More attention was paid to the flight of Bradley and Johnson to Tokyo, though not much more is known about their purpose and talks. Two explanations were given at the time for their visit to MacArthur. One was that the head of the United States Joint Chiefs of Staff and the Secretary of Defense, the top military and civilian officials respectively of the American military machine, had gone off on "a tour of inspection." The other was that they were to discuss with MacArthur the security aspects of a Japanese peace treaty. Some light was shed on both explanations by a dispatch which the *New York Times* published from its veteran Tokyo correspondent, Lindesay Parrott, on June 20, five days before the war began.

The Japanese were hoping that a peace treaty would be the result of these conferences. Parrott cabled that these hopes had been "reduced" by a blunt statement from MacArthur Headquarters which said: "The purpose of Secretary Johnson's visit is to inspect the installations, operations and organization of the Far East command and does not involve the political situation in the Far East." Parrott did not seem to think too highly of this explanation either, for he went on to say that "the confidential atmosphere in which the conferences are being held indicates that they are of rather greater importance than a discussion of the condition of barracks, the progress of training and other routine matters that would scarcely bring top defense officials all the way from Washington to Tokyo."

Bradley and Johnson themselves, when interviewed on arrival in Tokyo June 17, would only say cryptically that "they had come to learn facts 'affecting the security of the United States and the peace of the world.' " The information reported by American intelligence on the imminent possibility of an attack in Korea would seem to qualify for inclusion in facts "affecting the security of the United States and the peace of the world." General Bradley and Secretary Johnson spent three days being briefed on the military situation in the Far East by General MacArthur and his staff. Was nothing said about the information from Korea?

If the Korean situation was discussed, did no one suggest the possibility of heading off an attack by alerting American and world public opinion—as it has more recently been alerted on the possible danger to Yugoslavia? Or was it decided to keep silent about the danger, though it might finally bring about that long-expected conflict with the USSR? The evidence, meager as it is, does suggest that MacArthur, Bradley, and Johnson did pay considerable attention to the possibility of war with Russia.

The fullest account of the content of the Tokyo discussions seems to have been supplied by Richard Hughes, one of the best-informed British correspondents in Tokyo. In a cable to his paper, the London *Sunday Times,* on the eve of the conferences, Hughes supplied the content of an advance briefing on what MacArthur intended to discuss with Bradley and Johnson. This seemed to indicate that MacArthur's primary concern was war with Russia.

While the Japanese were waiting eagerly for a peace treaty which would finally free them from occupation, MacArthur's concern seemed to be how to satisfy this desire for a peace treaty without giving up the occupation. His thesis, as reported by Hughes, was to be that "American armed forces must be retained in Japan for the duration of the cold war at no less than their present occupation strength . . . whatever the decision on a theoretical 'separate peace treaty.'" The reason was that Japan would be needed if the cold war turned hot.

Hughes went on to explain that existing occupation bases in Japan were "held to be essential for American interception of Soviet bombers flying over the roof of the world to attack American cities, and for effective counterattack on Soviet air bases in the Vladivostok area." MacArthur and his aides would insist that "sober military necessity must override political arguments for the withdrawal of American forces." They would point out that while Okinawa was 1000 miles from Vladivostok, the B-29 airfield on North Honshu was only 500 miles from the Soviet window on the Pacific.

The detailed military calculations reported by Hughes showed how intense was the preoccupation of Tokyo Headquarters with a possible Russian war. Hughes was even given a kind of preview. He was told that the existing occupation forces should be able to resist invasion, though Russian submarines "could isolate Japan at the outbreak of war," and it would be necessary to organize "an airlift of hundreds of planes . . . for supplies." Hughes quoted "a high American officer" as saying, "Japan will not be a second Bataan." The Russians, according to this officer, could "bomb Tokyo and other cities and all our airfields. But our counterattack could destroy Vladivostok and its supply dumps, cut the Trans-Siberian Railway to pieces and throw open all Siberian centers to round-the-clock attack."

No American correspondent seems to have cabled any such detailed account of what was on the mind of Tokyo Headquarters. The news reports on the conference were very meager but Lindesay Parrott did report to the *New York Times* that the three-day briefing given Johnson and Bradley "was said to have included the most accurate information available here on the Soviet Union's military position on the mainland and its potentialities for aggression in the Pacific in case of war." If this was just the usual sort of thing general staffs engage in, why did Johnson and Bradley have to fly the Pacific for routine theoretical war planning? Why just at the time intelligence reports showed war in Korea was an imminent possibility?

CHAPTER 7

★

The Stage Was Set

IT IS as if the scene had been set with masterly care. On the eve of the war, there was no indication that Mac-Arthur and the MacArthurites disagreed with the American government's decision that Korea was outside the American defense perimeter. From all appearance, an attack by the North on the South seemed to be accepted as inevitable and deplorable but of no vital American concern. The visit of John Foster Dulles to Korea, and the ensuing conferences in Tokyo among MacArthur, Dulles, Louis Johnson, and Bradley, produced no word of warning to the Communist world against an attack on South Korea, nor any statement to alert public opinion back home to the intelligence reports which for several weeks had indicated a steady buildup of forces north of the Parallel. After May 11, as if by agreement, the South Korean government also kept silent on the danger and the known inadequacy of its military equipment. The South Korean army was drawn up in defensive formations. The United Nations Commission in Korea sent out field observers who could later attest this lack of offensive design. The instructions given the South Korean commanders, according to the report turned in by these observers the day before the fighting began, did not "go beyond retirement in case of attack upon previously prepared positions." South Korea may have looked from the North, especially after Rhee's defeat in the May 30 elections, like a plum ripe for the picking.

Whether on June 25 the North attacked without provocation or went over to the offensive after an attack from the South, the attempt to pick that tempting plum solved many political problems on the anti-Communist side. Within two days it gave Chiang Kai-shek American protection against an invasion from the mainland. It shelved the question of a general peace treaty for Japan and put off the withdrawal of occupation troops and the abandonment of American bases there. It gave Syngman Rhee, long sourly regarded by the State Department, a sudden respectability and the support of the United States and the United Nations at the very moment when his hold on South Korea seemed to have been ended by the convocation of the new legislature on June 19.

Conversely, the attack created new problems on the Communist side. The Chinese Reds could not proceed with the occupation of Formosa, to which they were committed, without coming into frontal conflict with the United States. Those Japanese bomber bases so near Vladivostok were to be retained by the United States indefinitely. The hope that the South Korean regime would collapse under the impact of the first free elections, the Northern demands for unification, the possibility of an easy "liberation" march southward from the 38th Parallel—all these vanished.

The repercussions were equally disadvantageous to Moscow on the broader panorama of world affairs. Trygve Lie's lonely pilgrimage for peace, between a hostile Washington trying to blanket peace with "total diplomacy" and a suspicious Moscow unwilling to appear too anxious, was brought to a sudden end; his appeal for direct peace talks between Washington and Moscow was made public and buried in the same day's newspapers which brought the tragic news of the Korean War. What Moscow most feared, the campaign to rearm the Germans as well as the Japanese, was given a sudden impetus in Washington. Finally, the mobilization of America's vast industrial power was set in motion for war, and "containment" in a more severe form than before was extended from the Atlantic to the Pacific—as had long been demanded by Chiang and MacArthur.

Could it be that for so minor a prize as South Korea the Russians were prepared to pay so high a price? Was the war Stalin's blunder? Or was it MacArthur's plan? Did the attack begin from the North? Or could it be that, with the scene set and the ensuing political strategy planned, the Northern attack was deliberately provoked by minor forays from the South—as the North Koreans claimed? Has the real truth been hidden in the murk of dispute between pro-Communists and anti-Communists, the former unwilling to admit that the North may well have prepared and planned an invasion, the latter unwilling to look at facts which cast any shadow on South Korea's role as the poor little Serbia or Belgium of what might become World War III? The hypothesis that invasion was encouraged politically by silence, invited militarily by defensive formations, and finally set off by some minor lunges across the border when all was ready would explain a great deal. It would even help to explain the way those first reports were presented to the United Nations.

There is, for example, one very queer detail in the story told by John Gunther, one odd-shaped piece that doesn't fit the picture. Gunther was in Japan when the fighting began. He and his wife were to set off that morning in MacArthur's private railroad car with MacArthur's chief political adviser, General Courtney Whitney, and Mrs. Whitney, on an expedition to Nikko, ninety miles to the north. At the last moment, about 8:20 A.M., the General said he would be unable to go along. He had just received word that MacArthur "needed him in the office that Sunday."

The Korean War had begun four hours before. According to a cable sent the State Department by John J. Muccio, the American Ambassador in Seoul, "Action was initiated about 4 [A.M.] . . . About 6 [A.M.] North Korean infantry commenced crossing the Parallel." Syngman Rhee seems to have turned at once to MacArthur for assistance. "When word of the Northern attack came," Lindesay Parrott cabled the *New York Times* from Tokyo, "Korean President Syngman Rhee appealed to General MacArthur for United States assistance." Dulles, then weekending at Kyoto, "hurried back to Tokyo

by plane" and "immediately met" at Headquarters with Mac-
Arthur.

Parrott did not mention exactly what time this conference
was held. The State Department White Paper shows that the
cable from Ambassador Muccio was received in Washington
at 9:26 P.M. Eastern Daylight Time, Saturday night, June 24.
That was 10:26 A.M. the next day, Tokyo standard time, six
hours after the fighting had begun. This cable is referred to
in the White Paper as the "first official report" on the fighting.
Whether there were earlier unofficial reports is not explained.
Tokyo must have heard at least as soon as Washington did.

And now back to the Gunther account. He says that "two
important members of the occupation" went along on the ex-
cursion to Nikko and that "just before lunch" one of them
"was called unexpectedly to the telephone." He came back
"and whispered, 'A big story has just broken. The South
Koreans have attacked North Korea.'" Gunther here adds
blithely that "it will always be a matter of mild interest to me
that this news, so wildly inaccurate as to who the aggressor
was, but which signalized the opening of the Asia War of
1950, came just after I had spent an hour in stocking feet
inspecting stone monsters carved in 1636. . . ." What John
Gunther examined that morning in his stocking feet remains
of milder interest to the historian than the fact that an "important member" of the occupation should have been informed
eight hours after the fighting began that it had been precipitated by a South Korean attack.

Gunther himself feels that "the fact that the first information reaching Tokyo, as relayed to our party, was of an attack
by South Korea on North, instead of vice versa, is not particularly important." He says "the message may have been
garbled in transmission"—whether by this he meant the telephone message to Nikko or the message from Korea to Tokyo,
is not clear. "Nobody knew anything much at headquarters
the first few hours, and probably people were taken in by the
blatant, corrosive lies of the North Korean radio." The conjecture that MacArthur might have been misled by the North
Korean radio is fantastic.

There was doubt in Seoul as well as in Tokyo, but this doubt was kept from the United Nations. The official account later published by the United Nations says: "At 3 A.M. on Sunday, June 25, the deputy United States representative to the United Nations, Ernest A. Gross, urgently telephoned Secretary-General Trygve Lie. Mr. Gross read a message from the American Ambassador to the Republic of Korea to the United States Department of State reporting that North Korean forces had invaded the territory of the Republic at several points in the early morning hours." An attack under these circumstances, Gross said, "constitutes a breach of the peace and an act of aggression" and he asked for an immediate meeting of the Security Council.

But an examination of the documents published in the White Paper shows that Gross did *not* read to Trygve Lie the actual cable from Ambassador Muccio. Gross read instead a statement of four short paragraphs, the first of which paraphrased the much longer cable from Ambassador Muccio. It was this statement, prepared in the State Department, which appears in the White Paper as the "enclosure" which Gross first read to Trygve Lie and then sent him with the request "to bring the message to the immediate attention of the President of the United Nations Security Council."

The message from Washington differed from the message from Seoul. The message from Washington said flatly, "The American Ambassador to the Republic of Korea has informed the Department of State that North Korean forces invaded the territory of the Republic of Korea at several points in the early morning hours of June 25."

This is not, however, what the message from Seoul said. There was, in fact, an ambiguity about the message which would have been at once apparent, if it had been made available at the time to the Security Council and the press. The American Ambassador did indeed end his cable by saying, "It would appear from the nature of the attack and the manner in which it was launched that it constitutes an all-out offensive against the Republic of Korea." But he began by making clear that he was not yet prepared to state on his own authority just how the fighting had begun. The cable began: "According to Korean [i.e. South Korean] Army reports which are partly confirmed by Korean Military Advisory Group field adviser reports, North Korean forces invaded Republic of Korea territory at several points this morning." The "Korean Military Advisory Group" was the official name of the American military mission attached to the South Korean forces.

The difference between the 171-word cable from Seoul and the 38-word State Department sentence paraphrasing it was considerable. What did the United States Ambassador in Seoul mean when he said that the South Korean reports on how the war began were "partly confirmed" by Americans serving with the South Korean forces? What part of the South Korean version was confirmed? What part was not confirmed? That invading forces were crossing the 38th Parallel was obvious, and must certainly have been confirmed. But did the Americans serving with the South Korean forces also confirm the South Korean allegation that the North had struck first?

"I am conferring," the American Ambassador said, "with Korean Military Advisory Group advisers and Korean officials this morning concerning the situation." What was the outcome of that conference? Did it throw any further light on the question of who had attacked first? We do not know. The text of the cable from Seoul did not become public until almost a month later, when the State Department finally published its White Paper on the Korean crisis. No other cable from the Ambassador is given. This cable is referred to in the White Paper as "the first official report" of the invasion. What reports did the Department receive earlier? Which side was called the aggressor in those reports? What reports were received from the Ambassador later that same day and the next? What light did they throw on the origins of the war? Why is the White Paper documentation on the outbreak of the war in Korea, as seen by American sources on the spot, limited to this one ambiguous document, and why was this document itself withheld from the Security Council? Because of the questions it might have provoked?

The Yugoslav delegate, though speaking for a country itself

under bitter economic and propagandistic attack from the Soviet bloc and dependent on American good will in the event this little Balkan cold war turned hot, had the courage and common sense to insist that "there seemed to be lack of precise information that could enable the Council to pin responsibility." He urged a cease-fire but opposed the naming of North Korea as the aggressor without further investigation.

Had the Security Council been in possession of the American cable from Seoul, other members might have felt the same hesitation. For the ambiguities in the Ambassador's cable paralleled the cautious wording of the only other report before the Council, the cable from the United Nations Commission on Korea, which was in Seoul at the time. The State Department's White Paper says this report "confirmed the attack on the territory of the Republic." That the Commission's cable confirmed the invasion is correct. It is not correct if read, as the unwary will read it, as confirming the South Korean allegation that the attack first came from the North. On the contrary the cable from the United Nation Commission in Seoul confirms the impression that observers on the spot were still unable to decide which was the aggressor. The Commission merely reports that the South Koreans alleged that they had been attacked and that they also denied the North Korean radio account—that the South attacked first, that the North repelled the invaders and then went over to the offensive. The Commission expressed no opinion other than to say that the outbreak "is assuming character of full-scale war and may endanger the maintenance of international peace and security." The text of its broadcast from Seoul that day appealing for peace also expressed no opinion on who started the war and called for peaceful unification—the very outcome which the North had been claiming as its own goal, and which Rhee most feared. It may also be significant that the Commission report that day to the Council adds that the American Ambassador had appeared before it but declares only that he "stated his expectation Republican Army would give good account of itself." Had he expressed no opinion on who started the war?

Considering how little information was available to the Security Council and the gravity of the measures asked by the United States, it was unfair and tricky to withhold the text of the Ambassador's cable at that time. For the United States not only asked the Security Council to brand North Korea the aggressor, without hearing or investigation, the United States resolution as introduced "asked for a cease-fire directed solely at North Korea." The Department is full of able lawyers, trained in the analysis of evidence, any one of whom would have spotted instantly the crucial difference between the cable and the paraphrase. And probably any one of them, knowing that the substitution was made, would deduce that the substitution was deliberate. It had its effect. The effect was to help stampede both Trygve Lie and the Security Council.

The cable arrived in the Department, as we have seen, at 9:26 P.M. Saturday night. Trygve Lie was awakened at 3 A.M. the next morning to have the State Department paraphrase read to him. In the five and a half hours which intervened was the question of whether to forward the cable itself discussed? And the idea rejected? Why did they wait until 3 A.M.? If the matter could hold until 3 A.M., why not until some more reasonable hour like 8 A.M.? Were the facts still too vague to be calmly considered? In London, the Foreign Office on Sunday would not comment "because of the lack of official information reaching London." It was still waiting for information from Captain Vyvyan Holt, British Minister to Seoul. "For the time being," the Foreign Office said, "we are following the American lead." On Tuesday morning the diplomatic correspondent of the London *Times* reported, "Only brief dispatches, *confirming the outbreak of fighting,* have been received from Captain Vyvyan Holt." (Italics added.) At the Security Council the British representative had already voted on Sunday to brand North Korea the aggressor. But Britain's own representative in Seoul seemed to be able to do no more than confirm "the outbreak of the fighting."

At the Security Council, the American representative, Ernest Gross, declared that the "unprovoked assault" was an attack on "the vital interest which all the members of the United

Nations have in the organization." Perhaps it was. But there was also a vital interest in the maintenance of fair procedure within the United Nations. It was neither honorable nor wise for the United Nations, under pressure from an interested great power, to condemn a country for aggression without investigation and without hearing its side of the case. This was especially true when the ambassador of that power on the scene itself, and the United Nations' own Commission, were not yet prepared to declare which side was guilty of aggression.

The doubt as to just how the fighting was precipitated never was cleared up. The White Paper says that when the Security Council met on Tuesday to vote military sanctions it had before it "a number of cablegrams" from the UN Commission on Korea. The text of two is given in the White Paper. The first was a summary report on the background events preceding the outbreak of hostilities. The second was a short cable which seemed to embody the finding reflected in the final sentence of the summary, "All the evidence continues to point to a calculated coordinated attack prepared and launched with secrecy." What was the nature of that evidence?

The White Paper quotes the first cable as saying, "Commission's present view . . . is, first, that judging from actual progress of operations Northern regime is carrying out well-planned, concerted, and full-scale invasion of South Korea, second, that South Korean forces were deployed on wholly defensive basis in all sectors of the Parallel, and, third, that they were taken completely by surprise as they had no reason to believe from intelligence sources that invasion was imminent."

This looks impressive until one turns to the texts as published in the back of the White Paper to see what words the Department omitted and replaced by those three innocent neutral little dots. The Department quoted the document this way: "Commission's present view . . . is, first," etc. Perhaps the cable was too long? No. The omission was exactly four words. These words were: "on basis this evidence." Why would the State Department want to omit a reference to evidence in a situation where evidence from non-South-Korean sources was so conspicuously lacking? Perhaps because this evidence was evidence on events which preceded the outbreak of the war, and evidence on the current hostilities, but still not evidence on how it actually started.

The four omitted words, "on basis this evidence," referred to the first sentence of the cable, which was *also* omitted from the quotation as given in the White Paper itself. (It is given in the appendix.) The first sentence said, "Commission met this morning 1000 hours and considered latest reports on hostilities and results direct observation along parallel by UNCOK [United Nations Commission on Korea] Military Observers *over period ending 48 hours before hostilities began.*" The italics are mine, and the difference between the way the document is presented in the body of the White Paper and the full text in the appendix is simply this: until the reader sees the full text, he does not realize that the only "direct observation" by the UN's own observers along the Parallel all ended forty-eight hours before hostilities began!

These direct observations, later made public June 29, are those to which we have already referred in showing that the UN Commission was guilty of misstatement when it said the South Koreans "had no reason to believe from intelligence sources that invasion was imminent." That these observers reported the wholly defensive deployment of the South Korean forces has already been noted. The only other observation in the Commission cable of June 26 is that "judging from actual progress of operations Northern regime is carrying out well-planned, concerted, and full-scale invasion of South Korea." This was correct, but it still does not say how the fighting began and which side started it. If the South Korean commanders had orders, as these same field observers noted, calling for "retirement in case of attack upon previously prepared positions," the invaders would quickly be able to make considerable progress. The "actual progress of operations" is not so impressive in the light of these orders to fall back if attacked. The invasion neither proved nor disproved the South Korean allegation that the North struck first nor the North Korean allegation that they counterattacked after repulsing invasion at three points. The North Koreans may have been lying. On the other hand the South Koreans may, as alleged, have deliberately provoked the war by three feints across the border. The feints would not excuse the invasion, which was certainly well planned and coordinated, but neither would it leave the South Koreans so blameless as to merit immediate military sanctions in a situation which might easily develop into world war.

Perhaps it was this very doubt, together with considerations of ordinary prudence and orderly procedure, which led the UN Commission in a third cablegram the same day, June 26, to suggest mediation rather than sanctions. Its cable proposed that "Council give consideration either invitation both parties agree on neutral mediator either to negotiate peace or requesting member governments undertake immediate mediation." This was the procedure followed in the Palestine and Kashmir disputes where both sides were also already fighting when the United Nations intervened. The Kashmiri, both Hindu and Moslem, and the Palestinians, both Jew and Arab, may count themselves lucky that—unlike the Koreans—they were the objects of mediation rather than of "liberation."

CHAPTER 8

★

". . . Only in Very Rough Outline Form"

THE State Department was not as surprised as it pretended to be. It had already drafted a resolution to be used at the United Nations in the event of an attack. But this did not become public knowledge until almost a year later, on June 5, 1951, during a routine hearing by the Senate Appropriations Committee on the State Department budget. The witness was John D. Hickerson, Assistant Secretary of State for United Nations Affairs. He was talking of the estimates submitted for the Department's Office of Political and Security Affairs, and mentioned the role it played in the outbreak of the Korean War.

Hickerson began by picturing the outbreak of the war as a complete surprise:

> MR. HICKERSON: On the night of June 24, 1950, at 10:45 my telephone rang and I was summoned to the State Department and we had our first news of the Korean difficulty. The first person I telephoned when I got to the State Department was the head of this Office of Political and Security Affairs.
>
> SENATOR MCCARRAN: Did he not know about the Korean situation before that?
>
> MR. HICKERSON: The attack, so far as I was concerned, came without warning, sir, and it was news to me.

So the record might have stood. But this was the same Senate Appropriations Committee which had heard Admiral Hillenkoetter in executive session the day after the war began. Senator McCarran pressed the witness. "Did you not know," the Senator asked him, "that the Central Intelligence Agency had reported to both the State Department and the executive department and that the reports were on file?" The reply, despite its argumentative tone, was actually an admission. "They reported that an attack might come," the witness said, "but they had reported the same thing about other places." This answer did not satisfy Senator McCarran.

> SENATOR McCARRAN: Was it not reported that they had cleared a corridor of 20 miles north of the 38th parallel and had tanks and guns and munitions being unloaded from Russian ships in North Korea?

The Assistant Secretary of State did not give a direct answer. He neither confirmed nor denied the receipt of such a report. "We knew," he replied, "they had the capability and that certain preparations had been made, but we did not know when the attack was coming."

In the discussion which followed, Senator McCarran insisted: "We had ample warning. If you were formulating policy as to what you would do under certain contingencies, the warning was in your hands as to what was coming. That has been before this committee. The warning was in your hands. You had ample warning." There was no comment from the witness. A little later in the hearings, however, Hickerson sought smoothly but without success to repair some of the damage. The only result was a new admission.

> MR. HICKERSON: Mr. Chairman, we, frankly, had to improvise when the Korean thing came. We did not have the detailed plans, perhaps we should have. We could not have detailed plans for every spot in the world where there was likely to be trouble. We had gone as far as we could, sir.
>
> SENATOR McCARRAN: I come back to the same proposition, this Appropriations Committee last year brought before it the head of the Central Intelligence Agency. He testified as to what he had reported and gave us the report,

which is today in the safe in the office of the clerk of this committee. That report was filed with the White House, with the State Department, and was filed with the Department of Defense, according to his testimony. So you were advised ahead of time. It is hard to say you did not know what was coming.

MR. HICKERSON: That is correct.

Senator Ferguson elicited another series of admissions hardly compatible with the statement that the attack came "without warning." Hickerson had acknowledged to Senator McCarran that there had been some warning. Senator Ferguson wanted to know what the State Department had done about those warnings.

SENATOR FERGUSON: Did you have a plan laid out as to what you were going to do when you got notice of the attack?

MR. HICKERSON: We had done some thinking about that, sir, yes.

SENATOR FERGUSON: Well, thinking is rather indefinite. What had you done on paper? What had you planned to do?

MR. HICKERSON: We had planned to take it to the United Nations for immediate action.

SENATOR FERGUSON: Did you have a proposed resolution drawn up?

Again the first answer was a denial, followed under pressure by an admission. The first answer was, "We did not have a proposed resolution drawn up on Korea, because we did not know when an attack might come." Senator Ferguson persisted.

SENATOR FERGUSON: Then you did not have a plan.

MR. HICKERSON: We knew we were going to take it to the United Nations. We knew in general what we were going to say.

So, though caught "without warning," they "knew in general what we were going to say" to the United Nations. Senator Ferguson made a scornful remark which drew a fresh admission.

SENATOR FERGUSON: That did not take much thinking because that was your department.

MR. HICKERSON: Yes. We had a skeleton of a resolution here first.

So the State Department did have a "skeleton of a resolution." "What was the resolution," Senator Ferguson asked, "you had in the office anticipating if this came that you would use?"

MR. HICKERSON: It is based on earlier aggression. The first thing you do is to tell them to stop it and go back where they came from. Surely, we had that blocked out, but only in very rough outline form.

The Assistant Secretary of State had begun his testimony by asserting, without qualification, that the attack came "without warning." In the end, he confessed that warnings had been received, preparations discussed, and "a skeleton of a resolution" drawn up for submission to the United Nations. This reluctance to disclose preparations which one would normally expect the Department to cite as evidence of foresight leads one to suspect there is more to the story than has yet been told. Why was the Department unwilling to have the public know that its officials did have some advance warning of trouble in Korea and did do some advance planning for the outbreak of war?

CHAPTER 9

★

Willoughby Exposes MacArthur

THE Korean War posed another puzzling question: why didn't the Republicans press for a Pearl-Harbor-style investigation to provide more information on the events leading up to the war? The answer to that came in December, 1951. MacArthur's intelligence chief, Major General Charles A. Willoughby, in an attack on American press coverage of the Korean War, inadvertently disclosed that MacArthur had misled both the United Nations and the Senate Committee which investigated his dismissal. There were skeletons in MacArthur's closet as well as in the State Department's. Another "Pearl Harbor" inquiry would have embarrassed not only the Republican John Foster Dulles but MacArthur himself. Dulles, who was never even called by the Senate inquiry into MacArthur's dismissal, might have been questioned about the advance discussions in the State Department before his visit to Korea, his conversations with Rhee, and whether Rhee asked definite assurances of American aid. MacArthur might have been forced to make damaging admissions about the quality of his intelligence staff and the honesty of his official reporting.

If General Willoughby's revelations are correct, then MacArthur gave the Senate Committee a false impression. He told them in May of 1951 that he had no responsibility for Korea and had paid little attention to what was going on there before the war. "I had no jurisdiction whatsoever over Korea," Mac-

Arthur told the Committee. "I had nothing whatsoever to do with the policies, the administration, or the command responsibilities in Korea until the war broke out." When Senator Morse questioned MacArthur specifically about responsibility for intelligence in Korea, this was the colloquy:

> SENATOR MORSE: General, regarding this matter of our intelligence information, as to what was going on north of the Thirty-eighth Parallel, whose responsibility was it in the military organization to supply whatever intelligence could be made available?
>
> GENERAL MACARTHUR: I fancy that it was the South Korean Government. . . .
>
> SENATOR MORSE: And if they did and they found any information that would be of importance to the military defense of this country, were they under obligation to make that available to your command?
>
> GENERAL MACARTHUR: I would assume they would. It was not in my area, but it was adjacent to my area, and I would have been vitally interested.

MacArthur did not tell the Senators that his G-2 followed Korean events closely and had "a reportorial unit" in Korea. This admission was not made until six months later, when Major General Charles A. Willoughby, MacArthur's chief of intelligence, wrote his article, "The Truth About Korea," for the December, 1951, issue of *Cosmopolitan* magazine. General Willoughby wrote that while MacArthur was "not responsible for intelligence collection or surveillance" in Korea, "Tokyo Headquarters could not remain indifferent to the general situation" and "quietly maintained a reportorial unit in Korea." Willoughby stated that information collected by this unit "was relayed to Washington, and as early as March, three months before South Korea was invaded, it unmistakably traced the North Korean buildup for war."

General Willoughby did not add, however, that MacArthur's intelligence unit for Korea also unmistakably informed Washington—every bit as unmistakably—that these reports of a North Korean buildup for war were not to be taken seriously.

This fact appears from two documents introduced in the record of the MacArthur inquiry by Secretary of State Dean Acheson a month after the MacArthur testimony. These documents showed that one reason some quarters in Washington may have been surprised by the outbreak of war in Korea is that MacArthur's intelligence service had brushed aside advance warnings, and had informed Washington, "It is believed that there will be no civil war in Korea this spring or summer."

Acheson made the two documents public when the Senators began to question him about the quality of American intelligence service in Korea. "I do not believe," Acheson said, "there was a failure of intelligence." He went on to say: "There has been considerable mention of two reports which are examples of intelligence information concerning the intentions of the North Korean Forces, which were available prior to June 25." One of these was the joint weekly intelligence cable from Commander in Chief, Far East, which noted on March 10, 1950: *"Report received that People's Army will invade South Korea in June, 1950."* The Commander in Chief, Far East, was of course MacArthur.

But to this report MacArthur's joint weekly intelligence cable had appended a comment casting doubt upon its credibility, and followed this up fifteen days later with a second cable dismissing the warning altogether. The cable of March 10 began its comment by saying, "The People's Army will be prepared to invade South Korea by fall and possibly by spring of this year indicated in the current report of armed-force expansion and major troop movements at critical thirty-eighth parallel areas." But it added, "Even if future reports bear out the present indication, it is believed civil war will not necessarily be precipitated; so that intentions in Korea are believed closely related to Communist program in southeast Asia." The cable continued:

> Seems likely that Communist overt military measures in Korea will be held in abeyance, at least until further observations made by Soviets of results of their program in such places as Indochina, Burma, and Thailand. If the Soviets are satisfied they are winning the struggle for these

places they probably will be content to wait a while longer and let South Korea ripen for future harvest. If checked or defeated in their operations in these countries in Asia they may divert large share of their effort to South Korea, which could result in a People's Army invasion of South Korea.

Two pro-MacArthur Senators, both Republicans, Hickenlooper and Bridges, perked up at this, but did not quite seem to grasp its significance:

> SENATOR HICKENLOOPER: What report was that?
> SECRETARY ACHESON: This is from Commander in Chief, Far East.
> SENATOR BRIDGES: Well, that was a pretty definite statement that they had word that the attack was coming in June.
> SECRETARY ACHESON: Pretty definite statement? They said a report was received they would attack in June. Then, the comment said, "We don't believe this statement."

To make his point clear, Secretary Acheson put into the record the second cable, dated March 25, from "G-2 of the Far East Command." Willoughby was in charge of the Far East Command's G-2. This cable, exactly three months before the outbreak of the Korean War, said flatly, "It is believed that there will be no civil war in Korea this spring or summer."

These cables indicate the embarrassment to which MacArthur would have been subjected if there had been a Pearl-Harbor-style inquiry into the outbreak of the Korean War. His own intelligence chief, in that *Cosmopolitan* article, disclosed that MacArthur was not telling the truth in his very first report to the United Nations. "The character and disposition of the Republic of Korea Army," MacArthur had blandly maintained in his report to the United Nations of July 25, 1950, "indicated that it did not expect this sudden attack." But General Willoughby eighteen months later spoke about the "alleged 'surprise' of the North Korean invasion," and said, "The entire South Korean army had been alerted for weeks and was in position along the 38th Parallel."

CHAPTER 10

US intelligence

★

"The Best Army in Asia"

IN THE months before the outbreak of the war, American intelligence seemed to agree on two points. One was that neither the Chinese nor the Russians would support the North Koreans in any dangerous adventures, and the other that the South Korean army was fully capable of taking care of itself if there were an attack by the North Koreans. The earliest evidence of these opinions may be found in a report by Senator H. Alexander Smith of New Jersey, a Republican supporter of the bipartisan foreign policy, on November 29, 1949. This report was made privately to the Senate Foreign Relations Committee, of which Smith was a member, on his return from a visit to the Far East in September and October of that year. It did not become public until July of 1951 when Senator Smith made it available to Senator Russell, chairman of the Senate committee investigating the MacArthur dismissal. The report was thereupon printed—and buried—in the voluminous appendix to the MacArthur hearings.

Senator Smith was a guest of MacArthur in Tokyo and, on MacArthur's "special advice," paid a visit to Korea. The Senator conferred there with the American Ambassador, with President Syngman Rhee, and with the men in charge of ECA operations. Senator Smith reported on the basis of these conferences that the South had an army of 100,000 men which was believed "thoroughly capable of taking care of Southern Korea

61

in any possible conflict with the North." This also seems to have been the opinion at MacArthur Headquarters right up to the very beginning of the war. Gunther reports that the week before the war began "a high American intelligence officer" expressed the opinion that "if an outbreak did occur, the South Korean forces ('the best army in Asia') could wipe out the North Koreans with no difficulty."

The most interesting part of Senator Smith's report dealt with the intelligence information available to the American government about Russian and Chinese intentions in regard to Korea. "I was advised," Senator Smith reported, "that the Northern Koreans had endeavored to enlist the aid of the Chinese Communists in order to take over and conquer the Southern Koreans, but the Chinese Communists turned them down on the ground that they had too many responsibilities in other parts of China." This also agrees with the information given Gunther in Tokyo. "At this period," he writes, "not many people thought the Chinese would enter the Korean war. One story was, in fact, to the effect that they deplored it— strange as this may seem now. For the North Korean aggression had, for the moment at least, cost Mao Tse-tung a prize he coveted above all—Formosa."

Senator Smith reported that he was "also advised that the Northern Koreans tried to get the Russians to intervene directly in taking over Southern Korea but the Russian reply was that they did not wish to initiate World War III by creating an incident in a minor area like Korea." According to the testimony of a former Red Army officer, who stated that he had been a member of the Soviet military mission to North Korea at the end of 1948, the Russians were afraid that the North Koreans might cause trouble, and refused for this reason to give them an air force.

The Russian officer was a Colonel Cyril Dimitrievitch Kalinov, who fled from the Soviet zone of Germany in the summer of 1949. He was an artillery specialist who claimed at one time to have been attached to the Soviet general staff. A book he wrote appeared in France in 1950 under the title, *Les Maréchaux soviétiques vous parlent* ("The Soviet Marshals

Speak to You"). Five installments dealing with his experiences in North Korea were published in August, 1950, in *France-Soir*, a sensational right-wing evening paper in Paris, under the title, "I Saw the North Korean Army Organized."

Judging from these articles, the Russian military were as dubious of the North Koreans as many American military men were of the South Koreans. The second installment, in *France-Soir* for August 4, 1950, carried the headline: "THE POLITBUREAU REFUSED TO GIVE PLANES TO THE NORTH KOREANS. GENERAL ZAKHAROV EXPLAINED TO ME, 'WE DO NOT WANT THEM TO BE ABLE SOME DAY TO ATTACK JAPAN AND DRAG US INTO A WAR WITH THE UNITED STATES.'" According to Colonel Kalinov, the members of the Soviet military mission wondered why in preparing a modern army for North Korea nothing was done to organize an air force. On one occasion another colonel declared that an air force was indispensable but was told that for political reasons they were not to organize one. They were told that the Central Committee of the Korean Communist Party had appealed to the Politbureau for an air force and been refused.

General Zakharov explained to the members of the military mission that it would have been easy to organize an air force of 1000 planes since there was no lack of pilots. There were nearly 500 Koreans who had served with the Red Army and as many other Korean pilots who had flown with the Chinese Army. But, General Zakharov explained, "It is necessary to be careful with these Koreans. . . . We are going to form a modern army, . . . but we are not going to act like the sorcerer's apprentice, creating a force which could make mischief in the Far East." The General said that the North Koreans, if given an air force, might sweep down to Pusan, bomb war vessels in the straits which separate Korea from Japan, and strike at Japan itself. "This would bring war with the United States," the Soviet General said, "and we are not interested in provoking such a war."

If the Russians were afraid the North Koreans might embroil them with the United States, there were Americans no less concerned lest the South Koreans set the Far East aflame.

In October, 1949, about the time of Senator Smith's visit, Syngman Rhee boasted in a public speech that the South could take Pyongyang, the Northern capital, in three days, and complained that he was stopped from doing so only by the United States which feared that such action might precipitate World War III. Rhee's Defense Minister, making a "purely social call" on MacArthur on October 31 and "not asking for more aid," told a press conference his troops were ready to drive into North Korea. "If we had our own way," he said, "we would . . . have started up already. . . . We are strong enough to march up and take Pyongyang within a few days."

The bellicose attitude of Syngman Rhee was well known. This may have led United States military and political observers to discount warnings of North Korean invasions which originated from South Korean intelligence sources. Acheson gave a brief account of these past warnings to the Senate Committee after making public the two cables from MacArthur intelligence:

> Now, it is interesting to note in this connection that on October 12, 1949, the intelligence summary from Commander in Chief, Far East, G-2, passed on a report that an attack was to be started on the 15th of October, 1949, but stated that it was probably fabricated.
>
> November 5, 1949, the intelligence summary had expressed the view that previous rumors of an invasion during August, September, and October of 1949 had been started by the North Koreans for the purpose of causing unrest in South Korea. Also, in his report of December 30, 1949, he advocated that a report that an invasion was to occur in March or April 1950 was not necessarily correct.
>
> The report of January 1, 1950, and February 19, 1950, also contain reports of invasions in March and April 1950, and were discounted.
>
> Therefore, you would have had reports that this attack was going to occur almost every month, and the intelligence of the Far East believed that this was not the case.

Why were these reports discounted? "The view was generally held," Acheson said, "that since the Communists had far from exhausted the potentialities for obtaining their objectives through guerrilla and psychological warfare, political pressure and intimidation, such means would probably continue to be used rather than overt military aggression." This was also the opinion expressed by MacArthur's G-2 in the cable of March 25. "The most probable course of North Korean action," it said, after declaring "civil war" improbable that spring or summer, "is furtherance of its attempt to overthrow the South Korean Government by the creation of chaotic conditions in the Republic through guerrilla activities and psychological warfare."

The moment chosen did seem an unusually poor one from the standpoint of the North. The preceding Monday the new legislature had just convened in Seoul with an overwhelming anti-Rhee majority. Why attack a government which might soon be transformed from within into a new regime willing to negotiate unification? There was a second reason for not attacking at that time. The Russians had been absent from the Security Council since their boycott of the United Nations, begun the previous January in protest against the refusal to seat Red China. The other "East European" seat on the Security Council was occupied by dissident Yugoslavia. If an attempt were made to mobilize the United Nations against North Korea, there would be no friend present on the Security Council to veto action.

The Hickerson testimony showed that the State Department was worried about this very point. He revealed that the State Department had thirty people at work the Sunday morning the war began. Senator Ferguson wanted to know, "How could you use thirty people on a thing like that?" "Senator, I assure you," Hickerson replied, "you have no idea of the complexities of a thing of this sort." The chief "complexity," it soon appeared, was what to do if the Soviets ended their boycott and turned up at the Security Council table:

> MR. HICKERSON: We did not know whether Malik would turn up and veto this resolution.

SENATOR FERGUSON: What were you going to do if he did turn up? You knew he would veto it.

MR. HICKERSON: He did not turn up, though.

SENATOR FERGUSON: I say, if he had.

MR. HICKERSON: We were going to ask the Secretary-General to call a special session of the General Assembly. We had one small group of people working on the plans for that and drafting a sort of statement that we would make if he did that.

The State Department had planned for that contingency, too. But Malik did not show up. It is not impossible that Moscow was more surprised than Washington by the outbreak of the war. If the Russians were planning or had approved the North Korean attack, why should they have done so at a time when they were absent from the Security Council and therefore could not veto action against their protégé? When Senator Bridges raised this question with General Marshall during the MacArthur hearings, Marshall said, "It was rather fortunate they were not present on the Security Council at that time."

The failure of Malik to show up at the Security Council suggests that the Russians were taken unawares. There is also reason to believe that the North Koreans were taken by surprise. During the course of a briefing at MacArthur's Headquarters on July 30, 1950, a month after the war began, an intelligence staff officer told the correspondents that "the North Korean army had not carried out its mobilization plan at the time the war began June 25 . . . only six full divisions had been ready for combat when the invasion started, although the North Korean war plans called for thirteen to fifteen." It is hard to believe the North would launch an attack before it was fully mobilized, and moreover at the very moment when it looked as though a hostile legislature might overthrow Syngman Rhee from within.

PART II

THE U.N. GETS A COMMANDER IT CAN'T COMMAND

CHAPTER 11

★

Classic Incident

THERE were the strongest reasons against military sanctions, especially when the bulk of the military force would come from the United States. These reasons were stated with force and clarity by the *Manchester Guardian*, the day after war began.

"The invasion," the *Guardian* said, "is a classic example of the type of incident which endangers world peace when the world is divided into two camps. The procedure for dealing with it is also familiar from past experience. The objectives are the cessation of hostilities, withdrawal of troops, *and, above all, the exclusion of the Great Powers from the conflict.* These must be the aims of the Security Council." Certainly Palestine and Kashmir would have been turned into a shambles, their peoples rendered homeless, and a new world war risked if in those armed struggles, as in Korea, there had been military intervention from either the Western or the Soviet bloc.

"Fortunately," the *Manchester Guardian* editorial continued that first morning, "neither the United States nor the Soviet Union has any direct military commitment to take part in the defense of either North or South Korea. The officers of the American military mission in South Korea have kept aloof from the fighting, and there is no evidence of direct Russian intervention on the side of the North."

The *Guardian* warned against the very gamble the United

States was to take in the next twenty-four hours. "It would be extremely dangerous," it said, "for any of the Great Powers to gamble on the unwillingness of the others to precipitate war. For centuries Korea has been recognized as a vital strategic area in Asia." Little Korea was as capable of detonating a new world war as little Serbia or little Belgium.

Perhaps it was the absence of any direct American military commitment which explains President Truman's first reactions to the outbreak of hostilities. Truman arrived in Missouri Saturday afternoon June 24 for a quiet weekend in his home town of Independence, after an optimistic speech in Baltimore that morning about the prospects of peace. He received his first word of the Korean outbreak Saturday night in a telephone call from Acheson. After the call he received what was described by the *New York Herald Tribune* as "a copy of the official cable from Korea notifying the State Department." He nevertheless went ahead with his weekend as planned—rose at 8 A.M., motored over to visit his brother at Grandview, and after his return informed waiting reporters through a secretary that he had no comment to make. "He's naturally interested and concerned," the secretary told the press, "and wants to be kept informed of everything that happens. He's not alarmed or anything of the sort." It was only after a telephone call from Acheson at midday Sunday that Truman decided to fly back to Washington. Even then his word to reporters before taking off was: "Don't make it alarmist. It could be a dangerous situation but I hope it isn't."

Truman met that evening in Washington with the Secretaries of State and Defense, their senior advisers, and the Joint Chiefs of Staff. The outcome of that meeting was a formal statement by the President issued the following morning which showed that he was still unprepared to permit direct American intervention in Korea. The statement spoke of "unprovoked aggression." It expressed pleasure "with the speed and determination" shown by the Security Council in ordering a withdrawal of the invading force to the 38th Parallel. It said the United States would "vigorously support" the effort of the Council "to terminate this serious breach of the peace," and would demonstrate its "sympathy and support" for the people of Korea "by the cooperative action of American personnel in Korea, as well as by steps taken to expedite and augment assistance of the type being furnished under the Mutual Defense Assistance Program."

Military intervention by the United States, directly or under United Nations auspices, was not mentioned. The atmosphere of Washington that first Monday of the war was one of gloom. I was then working as a Washington correspondent, and I remember vividly the general feeling of depression and uncertainty. The assumption in the State Department and the Defense Department was that the United States would do nothing effective to prevent the North from overrunning South Korea. "The pattern for action," the *New York Times* reported Tuesday morning, "appeared to be to keep South Korea supplied with all the arms that General Douglas MacArthur could rush to the beleaguered country . . . but to avoid any semblance of direct military intervention by this country."

In the Senate, the Democratic spokesman on foreign policy, Senator Connally, "shook an admonitory finger at critics of the Administration" and said the President "does not want to take a course which will involve the people of the United States in armed aggression or in war." The Senator said that the President "is not going to tremble like a psychopath before the Russian power." Oddly enough, the Republicans, though critical of Administration Far Eastern policy that first day in the Senate, were also opposed to armed intervention.

The Senate Republican Policy Committee held a meeting that Monday before the Senate convened. After the meeting Senator Eugene D. Millikin, acting as spokesman, announced that his Republican colleagues were "unanimous that the incident should not be used as a provocation for war." At Lake Success, too, all the indications were that the United States, in accordance with strategic decisions taken long before, would not intervene militarily. Thomas J. Hamilton, the chief correspondent of the *New York Times* at the United Nations, reported that while the United States had been "studying the possibility of asking the Security Council to authorize the use of United States troops . . . a usually well-informed source said tonight [Monday, June 26] that he did not believe it would go this far because of the increasing deterioration of the situation in Southern Korea." In other words it appeared that the imminent collapse of the South Korean armies was a further argument not for intervention but against it.

We now come to the second big mystery of the Korean War. The first was, why had there been no single word of warning out of Tokyo from MacArthur or Dulles or from Bradley and Johnson on intelligence reports indicating that an invasion from the North was an imminent possibility? The second is, what happened Monday night June 26 to change American policy? The Washington correspondents had hardly finished reading the dispatches we have quoted and similar ones in every newspaper in the country (only the *Daily Worker* predicted American intervention), when they were summoned to the White House to receive for noon release the historic statement of June 27, which committed the United States to the policy Chiang and MacArthur had been urging for months.

The statement of June 27 was in all but one respect the Pacific Pact which Chiang, Rhee, and Quirino, with help from MacArthur, had been advocating. It pledged the United States to military intervention against any further expansion of Communist rule in the Pacific area. It promised more military aid to Indo-China and the Philippines. It "ordered United States air and sea forces to give the Korean Government troops cover and support." And it ordered the Seventh Fleet to "prevent any attack on Formosa," declaring that the determination of the island's future status "must await the restoration of security in the Pacific, a peace settlement with Japan, or consideration by the United Nations." The only difference was in the President's declaration that "as a corollary of this action I am calling upon the Chinese Government on Formosa to cease all air and sea operations against the mainland," adding, "The Seventh Fleet will see that this is done." The President was not yet prepared to go beyond a protectorate over Formosa. He was still unwilling to commit American power to support of Chiang's ambition to "liberate" the mainland.

In one other respect, also, the President was not yet prepared for the "all-out" action some people wanted. The June 27 statement said, "The attack upon Korea makes it plain beyond all doubt that communism has passed beyond the use of subversion to conquer independent nations and will now use armed invasion and war." Yet at 4 P.M. that day newspapermen were summoned to a special press conference at the State Department and read an announcement saying that in Moscow the American Ambassador had been instructed to request the Soviet Foreign Office to use its good offices to help bring the Korean fighting to an end. The Truman announcement at noon rested on the implied conclusion that the events in Korea proved that "Moscow" would now use military force to spread Communism. The announcement at 4 P.M. implied that the Korean conflict was a purely civil war which Russia might help to end.

How did this inconsistency arise? The noon statement was what MacArthur had been seeking for months. The 4 P.M. statement reflected the same cautious attitude which Truman had demonstrated before and was to show afterwards—an attitude which strove to prevent the conflict from spreading. The chief Washington correspondent of the *New York Times*, Arthur Krock, with access to the best of sources at both the White House and the Pentagon, said in his dispatch published Wednesday morning, June 28, that "the President's communiqué, issued today [Tuesday] *to about half the length of the original draft,* was to make no charge that Moscow had supplied the North Korean Communists with the added material required for the invasion." (Italics added.)

Krock added that the decision to omit this and any other direct reference to the USSR from the June 27 communiqué "left the Kremlin free to disavow all responsibility or active interest" in Korea, and "free also to accept the invitation of this government, through Ambassador Kirk, to assist with its good offices in Korea—an invitation, it was decided, the Ambassador should be instructed to extend." It appears from this account that the original draft, twice as long as the one finally issued by the President, contained references to Russia and Russian supplies which would have made it more difficult to obtain Russian cooperation in bringing the conflict to an end.

The June 27 communiqué seemed so striking a reversal of Truman's previous position on Formosa that it made many people wonder how he came to change his mind. Arthur Krock's story was calculated to create the impression that the reversal had been a case of "the President's leadership," but he adds that "another" cause for the harmonious way in which the new decisions were made "was the fortunate timing of the very recent visit of Secretary Louis A. Johnson and General Omar N. Bradley to Japan."

"The conferees," Krock continued, "were thus equipped with on-the-spot reports, in addition to those forwarded by military intelligence units under General Douglas MacArthur, and by John Foster Dulles, who had just left Korea. These were agreed by all to sustain the soundness of the President's position and to support the details by which he proposed to enforce it."

It is hard to see what the "on-the-spot" reports of Johnson and Bradley could contribute, if they were as unaware of the dangerous potentialities in Korea as their silence the week before the war would lead one to believe. That these would "sustain the soundness of the President's position" was not surprising, since the President's position as taken in the statement which issued from the conference was almost identical with that of MacArthur and Dulles. But, as recently as the preceding Friday, Acheson at the State Department, when asked about hints from Dulles in Tokyo that American policy on Formosa might soon be changed, had flatly declared the President's "hands off" policy of January 5 was still the policy of the United States. Thus Acheson, it may be added, could hardly have known what was brewing in the Far East or he would not have unnecessarily invited Republican wrath by reiterating on Friday a policy which events were to change by Tuesday.

What part did MacArthur and Dulles play in bringing about the President's reversal of policy? It is difficult to believe that they were content with a passive role. We have seen that as soon as fighting began Syngman Rhee "appealed to General MacArthur for United States assistance" and that Dulles, then in Kyoto, "hurried back to Tokyo by plane when news of the North Korean declaration of war was received." When the first supplies were rushed to Korea, the announcement in Tokyo Monday "made it plain that evacuation and the provision of supplies were being undertaken under orders received from Washington after conferences here between General MacArthur and John Foster Dulles, State Department Republican adviser, who came to the Far East to gather information regarding the United States position here and remained to find himself the ranking civilian policymaker on the field in the outbreak of Korea's ideological civil war." That "the ranking civilian policymaker" present when war began should have been a Republican who agreed with MacArthur must be added to the long list of happy coincidences in the Korean War.

What did MacArthur and Dulles advise? It is to be hoped that the files will some day be thrown open to the historian. How was their advice communicated? We do not know. For a man notoriously vain, with a staff notoriously eager to build up their adored chief, MacArthur seemed unexpectedly modest about taking any credit for the change in policy. John Gunther gave two versions in his book. At one point, as an example of how MacArthur's entourage helped build up the General's prestige, he writes, "After the Communist attack on Korea, the word was quietly passed around that it was solely MacArthur's vigorous intervention in Washington which led Mr. Truman to announce that the United States would give military assistance to the South Korean government." He adds that when the military news turned sour, the line changed and "credit" for the intervention was given to Secretary Johnson.

In a later section of the book, which discusses the Korean War, Gunther gave the other version. He wrote that when the text of the June 27 statement was published in Tokyo "it pierced the atmosphere like an electric-shock treatment. At first it was thought that MacArthur himself was the chief influence in moving the President to his decision." Gunther explained, however, that "MacArthur got his instructions from the Joint Chiefs, just as any other general in the field should, in a long 'conversation' held on the teletype just before the Truman announcement was released. He was, in the words of a witness, 'completely surprised at the decision, but gratified because it reflected positive policy and action.' His responsibilities would be grave, but he was delighted by the order to go ahead."

Gunther, as we have seen, was riding around in Mac-Arthur's private railway car with high officers of the occupation. He had the friendliest relations with MacArthur himself and at MacArthur Headquarters. Why were they so anxious in this case to understate MacArthur's role in the change of policy?

In the circumstances, it was not only natural but essential for Washington to consult MacArthur and Dulles, the leading military and civilian officials respectively in the area. And it would be natural for them to claim their fair share of credit in reversing policies they had long considered wrong. Could it be that in this case they preferred to say as little as possible about their role because it might, if fully known, have raised embarrassing questions and provoked criticism—might have made the whole Korean affair look too much like a well staged job?

When MacArthur saw Dulles off for home at the airport in Tokyo that Tuesday morning, did they feel they had at last achieved that "positive action" Dulles expected?

CHAPTER 12

★

Stampeding the United Nations

THE stampede was on. The Truman Administration had been stampeded, and it in turn stampeded the United Nations. The effect of the statement issued by Truman at noon was to place a *fait accompli* before the Security Council when it met that same Tuesday at 3:15 P.M. When Truman "ordered United States air and sea forces to give the Korean Government troops cover and support" he was in effect imposing military sanctions before they had been authorized by the Security Council. The Council had to vote sanctions or put itself in the position of opposing the action taken by the United States. For governments dependent on American bounty and themselves fearful of Soviet expansion, that was too much to expect, though again Yugoslavia had the courage to vote "No," an act of principle for which it got no credit from the Soviet bloc while antagonizing the United States to which it owed its Council seat.

The relationship of the United Nations to the Korean question had been from the beginning marked by the strategy of the *fait accompli* on the American side, and a quick and quiet acquiescence on the part of the United Nations. Were the other powers less dependent on American aid, they might well have rejected Secretary Marshall's proposal in September, 1947, to hand over the Korean problem to the United Nations. The United Nations was not intended to handle questions arising in connection with the conclusion of peace with the Axis powers. Korea was as little a United Nations problem as Germany, Italy, Japan, or Austria. It was a Four Power problem. The organization was founded on the idea that peace and its own survival depended on Big Power unity. To take a hand in disputes between the United States and the USSR was itself unwise, especially when it might seem that one of these powers was mobilizing the United Nations against the other.

There were many who had long hoped to drive the Soviets out of the United Nations and convert the organization itself into an instrument of "containment." The submission of the Korean question to the General Assembly by Secretary Marshall on September 17, 1947, was accompanied by proposals to restrict the veto on the Security Council and to establish that "Little Assembly" which the Russians feared could be used to bypass the Security Council altogether. The combination of the three proposals was in accord with the "get tough" policy enunciated by Truman, but hardly calculated to make it easier for the United Nations to avoid becoming involved in direct conflict between the two great powers.

Of all the often petulant Soviet boycotts, its boycott of United Nations action in the Korean affair was perhaps the soundest from a legal and constitutional point of view. If the United States could "hand over" the Korean question to the General Assembly, where it was sure of an overwhelming majority in any direct issue with the Soviet bloc, what was to prevent its "handing over" the German question or the Japanese question in the same way?

In accordance with this boycott, the Soviets had refused to allow the UN Temporary Commission on Korea to hold elections in the North as well as the South. The United States —through Dulles—overrode Canadian, Australian, and Indian objections to holding separate elections in the South, a move which only Nationalist China strongly supported within the United Nations and only those Rightists led by Rhee had been advocating in Korea. The elections—held on May 10, 1948—were to be followed by consultation between the elected representatives and the UN Temporary Commission on Korea with the aim of transferring power from the military occupation authorities. The Commission itself was to report to the General Assembly, but this report was not made until October 8 and also had to be written in the light of a *fait accompli.*

"Under Rhee's leadership," the late George McCune wrote in *Korea Today*, "the National Assembly acted with the co-operation of the American command to assume full responsibility for the organization of government in South Korea. On August 12, China extended formal diplomatic recognition to the Republic of Korea, and on the same day the U. S. Department of State released a statement which amounted to giving *de facto* recognition to the new government. On August 19, the President of the Philippines extended to the Republic of Korea 'sincerest wishes . . . for the success of the new State of Korea.' Thus the establishment of a government based upon the elections of May 10 was an accomplished fact well before the General Assembly was scheduled to meet in Paris." This was the government which claimed to be and was given recognition as the lawful government of North as well as South, whence its official designation "Republic of Korea."

In much the same way the Security Council was led on June 27, 1950, to authorize by resolution what the President of the United States had done the night before and announced earlier the same day. The door was shut on the mediation advocated by the United Nations Commission. American military intervention on behalf of the South Korean regime was given *post facto* legality, as UN military sanctions, by a resolution recommending that "members of the United Nations furnish such assistance to the Republic of Korea as may be necessary to repel the armed attack and to restore international peace and security in the area." Three days later, Truman authorized the bombing of "specific military targets in Northern Korea," a naval blockade of the entire Korean coast, and the use of American ground troops by MacArthur. The American intervention that MacArthur wanted was complete at last.

The finishing touch was to make the "United Nations" forces subject to MacArthur without making MacArthur subject to the United Nations. This came on July 7 in a resolution introduced jointly by Britain and France. This is commonly supposed to have established a United Nations Command. Actually it did nothing of the sort. It set up a "unified command" which was authorized to use the United Nations flag but was not subject in any way to United Nations orders. This may be seen from the text of the resolution. It recommended "that all Members providing military forces and other assistance" in accordance with the Security Council resolutions on Korea should "make such forces and other assistance available to a unified command under the United States." It requested the United States "to designate the commander of such forces." It authorized them to use the United Nations flag. The only provision which suggested any maintenance of some United Nations surveillance over forces supplied on its own motion, operating under its authority and using its flag, came in the final clause, which said vaguely that the United Nations requested "the United States to provide the Security Council with reports as appropriate on the course of action taken under the unified command."

The "unified command" was not obliged to consult the United Nations, nor to report to it, regularly or otherwise. The resolution even "omitted any reference to the establishment of a Security Council committee to receive and transmit offers of assistance to General MacArthur." Sir Gladwyn Jebb explained that he believed there was "no real need for such machinery, at any rate at the present time." The United Nations had given MacArthur his blank check.

Events were soon to prove how hazardous this was in a situation where "United Nations" military action might, by accident or design, precipitate war between the "United Nations" and China or Russia or both. How did Britain and France come to decide on a move both were soon to regret? Within a few weeks they were to deplore and protest the consequences of their own resolution. What led them to frame so sweeping a grant of power?

When the resolution was introduced at Lake Success, the American representative, Warren Austin, remained exquisitely silent during the discussion. Afterward he told the Council he could not speak because of "the big and special responsibilities" it imposed upon the United States, adding that the United States was prepared to make "the sacrifice that is involved in carrying out these principles of the United Nations." One was almost tempted to ask, with Mark Antony, "Was this ambition?"

Austin was as disingenuous as Caesar in agreeing, as if unwillingly, to the "sacrifice" thus thrust upon the United States. There was evidence that the proposal was no surprise. "Although the President appeared to be doing nothing that the United Nations had not authorized him to do," the *New York Times* said next day in its story on the appointment of MacArthur as "United Nations" military commander, "it is known that United States officials had been pressing for some time for just such a decision as the Security Council made." There had been "numerous conferences" on the subject, and the device of the single commander and the UN flag had been accepted "as a workable compromise with the demand of many for an outright United Nations police force." Had there been an "outright United Nations police force," it would have been more difficult to keep it firmly under United States control and direction.

The British and French should have known quite well what they were getting into, for SCAP at Tokyo was exactly the same kind of operation—in theory a unified allied command, in reality a MacArthur kingdom. In theory, as Supreme Commander for the Allied Powers, MacArthur was responsible to thirteen allied nations, including Russia, which took part in the war against Japan. John Gunther thus described the setup: "The occupation is 'allied,' but Americans constitute the only personnel. (For a time a few Englishmen and one notable Canadian held positions in SCAP, but no longer.) The thirteen nations whom MacArthur 'represents' meet in Washington on the Far Eastern Commission, . . . But in Tokyo the whole performance is American. . . . the United States, alone among the member nations, has the right to give SCAP what are called 'interim directives.' So far as I know the FEC has never dared to overrule MacArthur on anything."

Aside from the FEC, there was also an Allied Council in Tokyo with four members, one each for the United States, the Soviet Union, and China, and one representing jointly the United Kingdom, Australia, New Zealand, and India. Its function, according to Gunther, "was to consult and advise with SCAP on the spot, in reference to decisions made by the FEC; MacArthur was supposed to call it into consultation on any important matter. Of course he has never done so." Gunther described a visit he paid to one meeting "of this shadow Council" which opened at 10:03 A.M. and closed at 10:04 A.M. "Some of the British," Gunther adds, with a certain bewilderment, "do not like these methods, even though their net effect, by strangling the Council, is to strangle the Russians too."

MacArthur had been given a Japanese empire to rule, and his methods and temperament had become known. Now he was being given a "little" war and a "United Nations" army. The danger was as obvious in Washington as it should have been in London. "Diplomacy and a vast concern for the opinions and sensitivities of others are the political qualities essential to his new assignment," wrote James Reston, the diplomatic correspondent of the *New York Times*, "and these are precisely the qualities General MacArthur has been accused of lacking in the past."

MacArthur had already, as Reston explained, "demonstrated his old habit of doing things in his own way, without too much concern about waiting for orders from Washington." And the question of the 38th Parallel had already begun to cast its shadow over events. "His instructions in the first few days of the Korean operation were to restrict his [air] attacks to the area in Korea south of the 38th Parallel, but despite official denials responsible officials here [Washington] still insist that his planes attacked the North Korean capital before President Truman [on June 30] authorized any such action."

Washington's fear of MacArthur made all the more culpable its behind-the-scenes negotiation to persuade the United Nations to give him a blank check. Reston reported that, since the bombing affair, "he has been instructed . . . to stay out of the area of the Soviet Union's main Far Eastern port of

Vladivostok, and to keep his planes and ships away from the territory and territorial waters of the Soviet Union and Communist China." The United States, Reston emphasized in summarizing Washington official opinion, "is trying to localize the Korean War, not attempting to extend it." Why then arrange for the United Nations to give carte blanche to a commander one suspected either of irresponsibility or of trying to extend the war, when the United States itself was not sure that it could control him?

CHAPTER 13

★

MacArthur's Blank Check

THE day the United Nations Security Council—minus China and Russia—handed over its forces to the "unified command," the President authorized the United States Army, Navy, and Air Force to discard peacetime limits and use wartime Selective Service machinery for compulsory enlistment of whatever manpower proved to be needed. Should some border incident or bombing, accidental or otherwise, suddenly extend the war from Korea to China or China's ally, Russia, MacArthur had a blank check from the United Nations and an unlimited draft on manpower from the United States. The date, July 7, was hardly two weeks after the Korean fighting had begun. Henceforth the Korean War becomes not only a military struggle between North and South Korea but a political struggle between MacArthur and Truman, the latter fighting a rearguard action to keep the struggle localized, the former engaging in provocative maneuver whenever peace seemed possible, constantly risking extension of the conflict and more and more openly advocating a course which could hardly end otherwise than in World War III.

MacArthur's first major political move was to inform the United Nations that the North Koreans were drawing men and supplies from beyond their borders. "From the continuing appearance on the battlefield of large numbers of enemy personnel and equipment," MacArthur said in a formal report to the Security Council on July 25, "it is now apparent that the North Korean aggressors have available to them resources far in excess of their internal capabilities." If North Korea was drawing not only equipment but "personnel" from beyond its borders, then either Russia or China or both were covertly waging war against the United Nations. If the Russians or the Chinese or both were waging war in this way against MacArthur's "unified command," should it not be free to retaliate? This, the next question, was to be amplified by MacArthur more and more strongly in later reports.

But was it true that the North Koreans were then drawing men and supplies from beyond their borders? The day the *New York Times* published the text of this MacArthur report, it also published an article on the Korean War by its military commentator, Hanson Baldwin. He put forward precisely the opposite opinion. He noted "encouraging signs that the Soviet Union was strictly limiting its commitment," stating that "so far, no reinforcements of the North Koreans by forces drawn from Manchuria or elsewhere in Asia have been detected." He cited also as fact that there had been no interference by Russian submarines nor any "conclusive evidence of the participation of Soviet-type jet planes in the Korean fighting."

How could Baldwin assert that no reinforcements from Manchuria or elsewhere "have been detected," when the Supreme Commander himself reported to the United Nations that the North Koreans were drawing "personnel and equipment" from outside their territory? A tentative answer was soon supplied out of Tokyo. It began to appear that MacArthur was in a minority of one at Tokyo Headquarters. Either the Supreme Commander had failed to pass his information on to his own intelligence, or his intelligence had failed to keep him fully informed.

Judging from the information supplied by Tokyo Headquarters the day after MacArthur's report was made public, the United Nations was being misinformed on a very vital point, with the most serious kind of political implication. On July 26 MacArthur's own intelligence staff held its first formal briefing of the Korean War at Tokyo Headquarters. At this briefing, Headquarters estimated that the North Koreans had been pushing their main attack "with about 80,000 men but, despite the heaviest casualties, they have been able to keep their ranks filled partly by impressing South Korean civilians for labor and even in combat service." If the North Koreans had to impress South Koreans "for labor and even in combat service," relying on unwilling, possibly hostile and untrained, manpower, that did not sound as if they had available "resources far in excess of their internal capabilities"—unless MacArthur was being witty and referring to personnel and equipment from South Korea. The spokesman at that briefing session also explained that "there was no indication that the North Korean tank losses were being replaced by further supplies from the Soviet Union, which furnished the original armor and lent instructors who taught the North Koreans how to use it."

In another report to the *New York Times* from Tokyo Headquarters the same day, it was stated that "the weapons captured from the North Koreans have been a wide assortment, even including some World War I rifles," that "the latest estimates . . . are that neither the North Korean army nor the air force has any postwar Soviet weapons," that the latest date "known to have been observed on the nameplates of captured equipment is 1945, except possibly for trucks," and that a recent report "that Communist-flown jet planes have been sighted over South Korea now is evaluated as an error in identification."

Two days later a military spokesman at Tokyo Headquarters said the North Koreans were so short of men that "some prisoners now being captured had had only four days training," and that there had been " 'heavy conscriptions' both north and south of the 38th Parallel to help fill the gaps in Red ranks." He spoke of the North Korean air force as "depleted," noted that while North Korean columns of twenty-five or thirty tanks had formerly been reported "now sightings were of groups of only four or five," estimated that most of the North Korean tanks had been destroyed or damaged already, and said "there were no signs that these vital tank losses were being replaced."

These official intelligence estimates from Tokyo Headquarters hardly supported the picture so ominously implied by the MacArthur report to the UN: "From the continuing appearance on the battlefield of large numbers of enemy personnel and equipment, it is now apparent that the North Korean aggressors have available to them resources far in excess of their internal capabilities." On the contrary the intelligence made available by his own Headquarters indicated that the North Koreans, after only one month of fighting, were already desperately short of men and supplies. This suggested not the large-scale aid from Russia or China or both implied by MacArthur, but a reluctance on both the Chinese and the Russian side to commit men or supplies on any considerable scale to the Korean struggle.

With the forces of the "unified command" withdrawing to the Pusan pocket and the possibility of an Asian Dunkirk in view, it was clear that, as Hanson Baldwin stated, "Generalissimo Stalin can kick us into the sea in Korea if he really wants to," though he "might well regret it later." It was becoming equally clear that Stalin did not want to make it possible for the North Koreans to "kick us into the sea," for fear that he "might well regret it later." The implication of military events toward the end of July was that the Russians and the Chinese were in no mood to intervene in the Korean conflict on any large scale, much less go to war for Korea. The prospects for localizing the conflict were good. Perhaps the best estimate of the real situation was given in a little-noticed speech at Charleston, South Carolina, by a former United States military governor in South Korea who thought the North Koreans had started the war on their own, because "if the Russians had started the advance, they would have taken the entire section in two weeks" and would have started it in the winter "when the roads are hard and the monsoon season is not prevalent." His opinion was: "The Russians in Korea are like men who have a lion by the tail and can't let go."

On the diplomatic as on the military plane, the Russians

showed they were not unwilling to localize the conflict and end it by mediation. The Nehru explorations in July and the quiet encouragement given them by Truman provide the background for MacArthur's next major political move, his dramatic visit to Formosa at the end of July.

To understand this phase of the war one must go back to Truman's request on June 27 for Moscow's "good offices" to help end the Korean struggle. When this move was dramatically announced at a special press conference in the State Department at 4 P.M. the day the Security Council voted sanctions, it seemed at first a tactful way to let Moscow save face and even acquire credit for peace. This was implied by the wording of the announcement about the request for Moscow's "good offices."

The text of the note actually delivered in Moscow was not made available. Had this been done, it would have been seen that Truman's olive branch had been made as thorny as possible by those who drafted the note. The tone was not a friendly request for mutual cooperation in ending the conflict, nor did it even use the phrase "good offices." It had a rasping and peremptory tone. The request for "good offices" was phrased to sound like an ultimatum: "The refusal of the Soviet Representative to attend the United Nations Security Council meeting on June 25, despite the clear threat to peace and the obligations of a Security Council member under the Charter," required the American government to bring the North Korea invasion "directly to the attention" of the Soviet government. It concluded, "In view of the . . . close relations between the Union of Soviet Socialist Republics and the North Korean regime, the United States Government asks assurance that the Union of Soviet Socialist Republics disavows responsibility for this unprovoked and unwarranted attack, and that it will use its influence with the North Korean authorities to withdraw their invading forces immediately."

The announcement in Washington that the President had asked for Moscow's "good offices" led us all to imagine a communication couched in friendly terms, not this humiliating and hectoring demand. Whether Truman was aware of how the American note was phrased is not known. The reply, under the circumstances, was astonishingly mild, though Moscow would have been wiser if it had by some concrete proposal opened the way for peace talks. The reply made three points. The first was that "in accordance with facts verified by the Soviet Government," the events taking place in Korea "were provoked by an attack by forces of the South Korean authorities on border regions of North Korea. Therefore the responsibility for these events rests upon the South Korean authorities and upon those who stand behind their back." The second was that the Soviet government had withdrawn its troops from Korea earlier than the American government had, "and thereby confirmed its traditional principle of noninterference in the internal affairs of other states. And now as well the Soviet Government adheres to the principle of the impermissibility of interference by foreign powers in the internal affairs of Korea." The third point was that the Soviet government had not "refused" to take part in meetings of the Security Council but had "not been able to take part . . . inasmuch as, because of the position of the United States, China, a permanent member of the Security Council, has not been admitted to the Council, which has made it impossible for the Security Council to take decisions having legal force."

The nature of the reply left a door open to neutral mediation, and on July 13 Prime Minister Nehru of India sent notes to Prime Minister Stalin and Secretary of State Acheson urging the two big powers to restore peace and keep the war from spreading. Two days later Stalin "welcomed" Nehru's efforts and said the first step should be to "reactivate" the Security Council—meaning, presumably, to admit Red China. Acheson replied that any such move would subject the United Nations "to coercion and duress."

It was politically impossible for the American government to agree to the seating of Red China under these circumstances without overwhelming attack from the Republican opposition and the press, but Truman in his message to Congress on July 19 said of Formosa, "I wish to state that the United States has no territorial ambitions whatever concerning that island," and that its "present military neutralization . . . is without prejudice to political questions affecting that island." James Reston, commenting in the *New York Times* on the diplomatic problems created in India and elsewhere by the Korean War, said Truman hoped by this statement "to reassure Asiatic opinion that the United States had no territorial designs in Asia, and at the same time to reassure the Chinese Communists that Washington was not intending to remain in Formosa after the crisis had subsided in that part of the world."

That the President was still in a mood to reassure the Chinese Communists about Formosa must have been alarming to Chiang Kai-shek and his friends. It meant that if the Korean War ended, Chiang would be left in the same precarious position as before—perhaps worse off, since a general settlement under United Nations auspices was likely to include recognition of Peking's claim to Formosa. Equally alarming to Chiang was the action taken by the Soviet Union. If it was politically impossible for Truman to acquiesce in the seating of Red China at the moment, it was politically painful for Moscow to end its boycott of the Security Council and "reactivate" that body while Nationalist China was still represented on it. The Soviet representative had walked out of the Council on January 13 and since then the Russians and their satellites had walked out of thirty-three separate United Nations organizations rather than sit down with the representatives of Chiang Kai-shek. Jacob A. Malik, the Russian representative, had stated that the USSR would not return until Chiang's representative had been expelled and Red China given his place on the Security Council. To call off the boycott, to accept at least temporary defeat, to sit down with the Nationalist representative, was a humiliation which perhaps only a dictatorship, with no domestic opposition, could afford to take. On July 27, Malik announced that on August 1 the Soviet Union would return to the Security Council. Under other circumstances, in a different atmosphere, the American press might well have claimed that Stalin was eating humble pie for the sake of peace.

It was at this moment, when mediation still seemed possible, that MacArthur made his dramatic flight to Formosa. The day, July 29, was two days after the Malik announcement. In Formosa MacArthur issued a special communiqué declaring that arrangements had been made "for effective coordination between the American forces under my command and those of the Chinese Government the better to meet any attack," hailing Chiang's "indomitable determination to resist Communist domination," and asserting that this "parallels the common interest and purpose of Americans that all peoples in the Pacific area shall be free—not slaves." This clearly implied an alliance with Chiang against the mainland. The tone was not that of the "neutralization" pledged by President Truman but of an alliance with Chiang, in a common crusade of "liberation" against the new regime on the mainland. The effect was to make the Chinese Communists feel that Truman's assurances could not be trusted. The visit must also have served to force a more intransigent tone on Malik when he returned to the Security Council, lest Russia appear to be selling out its Chinese ally by backing down on the boycott just when MacArthur and Chiang seemed to be planning war. The task of mediation was made more difficult. MacArthur, from Formosa, drowned out the quiet voices that still were urging mediation and peace.

CHAPTER 14

★

MacArthur and Mack Sennett

THERE were moments when the running battle between Truman and MacArthur began to look like one of those giddy interminable circular pursuits in a Mack Sennett movie comedy, where you finally lose track of who is the pursued and who the pursuer. After MacArthur's flight to Formosa, Truman sent W. Averell Harriman to Tokyo as his "special emissary," and Harriman on his return declared that American policy on Formosa had not changed. MacArthur himself was forced to issue a statement on August 10 assailing as "malicious gossip" the notion that he was giving political support to Chiang Kai-shek.

But MacArthur's real views may be seen in a United Press dispatch from Tokyo on August 6 giving a résumé of what MacArthur expected to tell Harriman on his arrival: "The United States ought to take a vigorous position against Communism everywhere in Asia, and Korea ought not to be an isolated case." Two days after the "malicious gossip" statement, as if to make sure that Korea would not remain an "isolated case," the border bombings began. On August 17, a flight of B-29s made a 500-ton bombing raid on Rashin, a North Korean seaport only seventeen miles from the Siberian border and 110 miles from Vladivostok.

This was followed by a series of raids and strafings along the border between Korea and Manchuria. Peking on August 28 protested to the United Nations that American and British planes had strafed airfields and railways on the Chinese side of the Yalu near Antung. In reply the United States Air Force declared that its fliers were "meticulously briefed to scrupulously avoid such incidents." There followed a second border raid and a second protest. This time, on September 1, the USAF acknowledged that one of its F-51s might have strafed Antung on August 27. A month later, on October 3, the Antung attack was officially admitted—as a "mistake."

The border raids seemed to be MacArthur's way of thumbing his nose at Truman, every time the President interfered to curb the General's political maneuverings. The raids on the Chinese border followed immediately after the affair of the MacArthur letter to the Veterans of Foreign Wars, as the raid near the Siberian border had followed on the political disavowal forced on MacArthur by the Harriman visit.

Like the sudden flight to Formosa, the MacArthur letter to the Veterans of Foreign Wars came just when the prospects for mediation at Lake Success seemed to be improving. On August 25, after a telephone conversation with Truman, the United States delegate, Warren Austin, sent Trygve Lie a seven-point letter welcoming United Nations consideration of the Formosan question and declaring that the temporary "protectorate" thrown over the island by the announcement of June 27 was "an action designed to keep the peace," not to intervene in the Chinese civil war or to take over Formosa for the United States. Washington was signaling Lake Success to take the Formosan hot potato off its hands.

The next day Truman learned that MacArthur, without clearance in Washington, had sent a message to the convention of the Veterans of Foreign Wars attacking Truman's policies on Formosa in all but name. MacArthur assailed "the threadbare argument by those who advocate appeasement and defeatism in the Pacific that if we defend Formosa we alienate continental Asia." He argued that by holding Formosa the United States could "dominate with air power every Asiatic port from Vladivostok to Singapore"—a boast that must have read almost as alarmingly in London as in Moscow, since the British were not yet ready to acquiesce in a "protectorate" over Malaya. Truman ordered this MacArthur message "with-drawn"—it was already in print and could not be suppressed. That same day American bombers first hit Chinese territory on the Manchurian border.

It cannot be said that MacArthur hid his views. His view was that the time had come for the United States by military force to oppose Communism everywhere in Asia. Nor can it be said that the effect of his military and political interventions was difficult to decipher. Their effect was so constantly to risk, as to seem eagerly to invite, extension of the conflict. The law says that a man is assumed to will the necessary consequences of his acts: if he is caught time and again setting matches to inflammable tinder in a neighbor's house, he cannot evade conviction for arson by pleading innocent intent. In a court of law, it would be held that MacArthur was trying to drag the United States and the United Nations into war with China and Russia. He was trying to start World War III. Neither Washington nor London nor Paris could claim that they had not been forewarned.

The gigantic "preventive" war to be inferred from Mac-Arthur's words and actions was already being openly advo-cated in America. Clearly the fruity rhetoric and itching trigger finger of the Supreme Commander would have to be curbed—and curbed before the emotional momentum making for war became irresistible. On August 25 Secretary of the Navy Francis P. Matthews—prominent as a Catholic layman —made a speech in Boston advocating preventive war and declaring this would "cast us in a character new to a true democracy—an initiator of a war of aggression . . . the first aggressors for peace." On August 26 George N. Craig, national commander of the American Legion, urged the United States to warn Moscow that any "further aggression" by its "satel-lites" would be "the signal for our bombers to wing their way toward Moscow." The *Pilot*, organ of the Roman Catholic Archdiocese of Boston, declared in its issue of September 1 that offensive wars were moral under certain conditions and that a preventive war against Russia might be necessary. Hanson Baldwin, discussing the question of a preventive war in the *New York Times* that same day, said that the speech by Secretary Matthews was "a trial balloon" launched by his superior, Secretary of Defense Louis Johnson, "who has been selling the same doctrine of the preventive war in private conversations around Washington."

The Truman Administration did indeed take steps to squelch this talk of "preventive war." The day after the Matthews speech, the White House and the State Department both disavowed it. But, while Matthews was forced to declare, "I was speaking for myself," he was allowed to stay on in his top post at the Navy Department. The Administration continued to be a house divided against itself. Ambassador-at-Large Philip Jessup, answering Matthews for the White House and State Department on the radio on August 27, said, "The destruction of war is so catastrophic that no stone must be left unturned in the effort to maintain our security and our highest values by peaceful means." On September 1, Major General Orvil A. Anderson was suspended as commandant of the Air War College, for having taught a course of lectures in "preventive war" strategy and for an interview in which he advocated an attack on Russia, saying, "Give me the order to do it and I can break up Russia's five A-bomb nests in a week." The General apparently even looked forward to debating the question on his own terms with the Prince of Peace, adding, "And when I went up to Christ—I think I could explain to Him that I had saved civilization." Such were the apocalyptic views to be found among men entrusted with the sober responsibilities of the American defense establishment.

Truman replaced Louis Johnson with General Marshall at the Department of Defense in the hope of curbing such pyromaniac tendencies. Furthermore, alarmed by the repercussions abroad, he himself took to the radio in a "fireside chat" on September 1, declaring, "We do not believe in aggressive or preventive war." But events were to show that, so long as MacArthur remained Supreme Commander in Tokyo, the power to precipitate "preventive war" remained in hands which might be disposed to it. The lesser men in Washington might talk dangerously, but they could do little more than talk. MacArthur was in a position to act. Why did Truman leave him in command?

To this there were many answers. MacArthur was a political power. An election was coming on in November. He could not be removed while the troops of the "unified command" were being pushed into the Pusan pocket—this would look as if Truman were not backing a subordinate in defeat. It became harder than ever to remove him after the "Battle of the Beachhead" ended and the Inchon landing brought Mac-Arthur's forces victoriously back to Seoul by the end of September. How remove a commander in his moment of victory? How resist the temptation to share in the glory during the crucial electioneering weeks before November?

The Battle of the Beachhead was the climax of the war, a psychological as well as military turning point. Had Russia wanted war, that was the time to begin it. Soviet air power and sea power by intervening could have pushed the Pusan defenders into the sea. The North Koreans might have done it alone, if they had not been starved for supplies. For the North Koreans were desperately short of planes and tanks and even of heavy arms. When the tide turned so dramatically, a dispatch to the *New York Times* from the Inchon front on September 17 reported, "Both headquarters and field officers said there was no indication of enemy artillery." The Communists had only "mortars, machine guns" and "small arms" with their dwindling number of tanks. It was easy to believe the reply of field officers to a question from MacArthur that day about enemy morale: "Morale is very low."

Though it looked as though the North Korean forces at that time had been abandoned in defeat, the report Mac-Arthur sent to the United Nations next day gave a contrary impression and evoked interventionist headlines, "RUSSIANS AND CHINESE REDS HELP FOE, MACARTHUR SAYS." Conclusion No. 5 of this lengthy report said, "Positive proof has been obtained that during 1949 and 1950 the Soviets have supplied the North

Korean forces with munitions and the Chinese Communists have supplied trained manpower." A section headed "Foreign Support for North Korean Forces" began by saying that it was "appropriate to review existing evidence of material and technical assistance rendered to North Korea, specifically evidence of munitions which the Soviet Union has provided and is now providing to the North Korean forces, as well as evidence of trained military personnel which the Chinese Communist forces have furnished."

The hasty reader, and the hasty newspaperman "boiling down" this verbiage for the hastier newspaper reader, were apt to overlook the opening phrase. It *was* an appropriate time to review the existing evidence of Russian and Chinese aid to the North Koreans. But those few who read the text of the report carefully must have been struck by the fact that, even as reviewed by General MacArthur, the existing evidence was extraordinarily meager.

The examination of the "existing proof" began with what hardly required proof, since it had never been denied. MacArthur stated that the North Korean army "has from its inception been trained, supervised and logistically supported by the Soviet Union." The South Korean army had been "trained, supervised and logistically supported" by the United States. The Soviet representative at the United Nations had announced a few days earlier that no Soviet arms had been supplied the North Korean forces after the withdrawal of the Russian occupation troops in 1948. This appeared next in MacArthur's order of proof. The supply of arms before 1948, he said, was now "openly acknowledged by the Soviets." The wording gave the impression of a confession wrung from unwilling lips.

The report went on to say that, despite the Soviet claim that no arms had been supplied after 1948, "a wide variety of definitely identified Soviet equipment captured from the North Koreans in battle bears the manufacturing date of 1949 or 1950." This was dramatically acted out by the American representative at Lake Success when the report was read.

Warren Austin pulled from under the Security Council table a submachine gun with 1950 Soviet markings and was photographed with the corpus delicti in his arms.

This was, as we say, "hot stuff." If anybody bothered to read the text of the report, after such stirring visual evidence, he would have found, however, that the reference to a "wide variety" of such arms captured from the North Koreans was rendered less impressive by what followed. The report went on to say that "physical proof" (one wondered for a moment whether "spiritual" proof could be used to identify armament) of this "wide variety" of armament "now includes ten specific items." If "ten specific items" of Soviet equipment marked 1949 or 1950 were all that could be acquired after weeks of fighting, there could hardly have been very much post-1948 equipment available. These ten items "fully reported, including photographs, as well as the physical items" had been "forwarded to appropriate United States Army services." Why not to the United Nations, as proof of Soviet intervention? Why was only the submachine gun sent on to Lake Success?

Judging from the report itself, the answer seems to be that the submachine gun was the only impressive item. The report went on to say that "among forwarded definitely identified items were a 7.62 mm. PPSH-41 submachine gun; an aircraft radio receiver type RSI-61-1; two types of hand grenades, and ammunition of varying types and calibers." The submachine gun, the radio receiver, and the "two types of hand grenades" make four items; if anything more striking had been found it would certainly have been mentioned; it looks as if the other six items of "physical proof" consisted of "ammunition of varying types and calibers." It is significant that even the photographs were not submitted to the United Nations.

The final anticlimax of the Russian aid section came in the reference to "other pieces of equipment," that is, equipment which did not bear dates after 1948. The report said that "in addition to these [the ten items] some forty-one other pieces of equipment, including small arms, armored vehicles, artillery and ammunition, have been captured from the North Koreans and are definitely established to be of Soviet manufacture."

Again, it would seem that the North Koreans could not have had much Russian equipment even from before 1948 if only forty-one such items had been captured.

The next section dealt with what the opening paragraph had called "evidence of trained military personnel which the Chinese Communist forces have furnished." Few stopped to consider that there seemed to be no evidence at all of intervention by Russian personnel. Few went on to consider the actual evidence presented of intervention by Chinese personnel. The marshaling of this "evidence" began with an extraordinary admission: "To date, there has been no confirmation of direct or overt Chinese Communist participation in the Korea conflict." The report continued: "However, they have furnished substantial if not decisive military assistance to North Korea by releasing a vast pool of combat-seasoned troops of Korean ethnic origin, which provided the means for expansion of the North Korean Army."

This conjured up for the unwary the flood across the Chinese border of some "vast" horde of seasoned troops vaguely described as of "Korean ethnic origin," perhaps to imply without so stating that they were actually Chinese citizens. This assistance, according to MacArthur, was "substantial if not decisive." Obviously it had not been "decisive" since MacArthur's forces had just succeeded in breaking out of the Pusan beachhead and driving these troops back across the Parallel. But the wording sounded portentous.

If Red China had released a flood of trained soldiers—of Korean or any other "ethnic origin"—across the border after the fighting began, that would be intervention. What proof did MacArthur have? Let us watch his words closely. "This fact," his report went on, "originally established by miscellaneous information emanating from the Manchuria-Korea area *during the past four years* [italics added], is now *fully* confirmed by numerous prisoner-of-war interrogations since the outbreak of hostilities in Korea." If the return to North Korea of Korean veterans of the Chinese Red forces was "established" by intelligence emanating from the border regions "during the past four years," that hardly proved intervention by Red China after the fighting began in June of 1950. If these reports were "fully" confirmed by "prisoner-of-war interrogations since the outbreak of hostilities," that would seem to indicate that the information obtained during those four years had not been absolutely verified beforehand. But again, it does not prove release of such manpower during the fighting. Now we come to the most significant statement of all. General MacArthur gave a summary of intelligence reports on these Chinese-trained veterans. He spoke of an "acceleration" of this movement back into North Korea "during the early part of 1950, and by the middle of February, 1950." But he made no specific allegation later than February and he did not go beyond the general accusation that "the Chinese Communist Army returned many of these North Korean troops to North Korea during the past year." The significant point to notice is that, when MacArthur got down to details, he did not charge that Red China sent even its Korean veterans to join the North Korean forces after the war began.

The presentation of the "evidence" was slickly and disingenuously phrased, as if by a clever lawyer trying hard to make much of little. Had an impartial United Nations body dealt with this same evidence, it would have reported that there was (1) no evidence of Russian or Chinese military intervention, (2) little evidence of Russian supplies coming in after the war began, and (3) that while many North Korean veterans of the Chinese Red Army had been going home during the past four years and had become an important part of the North Korean forces, there was no evidence of such movements across the border after February. This is, indeed, what MacArthur actually said. The difference was in how he said it. The way he said it showed how hard he was still working to make the conflict appear a wider conflict, to bring the United Nations into collision with Russia and China.

The effect on public opinion in America was to inflame the anti-Communists and worry the waverers, for few got beyond the headlines into the report itself. MacArthur, for all his almost clownish exhibitionism, showed himself a master of the American art of "public relations." The report was received and the submachine gun produced the very first day of the United Nations Assembly. They had their effect, though the diplomats gathered in New York for the Atlantic Pact Foreign Ministers Conference and the General Assembly realized that the impression they created was the obverse of the truth.

On the eve of the opening of the Assembly on September 18, Thomas J. Hamilton, chief correspondent of the *New York Times* to the United Nations, reported that the consensus of opinion among "the diplomats gathered here" is that Moscow did not expect the United States to defend South Korea and that "many believe, in fact, that the Soviet Union now realizes that it made a mistake in giving the go-ahead signal to the North Korea regime." The result had been that the United States "has girded itself for military preparations on a scale that would not have been dreamed of only three months ago, and is also trying to arouse its European allies to the urgency of the need for greater military forces." Hamilton reported that "the Soviet Union's relatively decorous behavior since the Korean war started has confirmed the belief of many delegates that the Kremlin does not want a shooting war now, at least not one in which the Soviet Army would be engaged."

The evolution of events in the military sphere seemed to indicate that the Russians did not wish to put Truman's back to the wall. Had the United States forces been pushed off the Pusan beachhead, as could easily have been done by reinforcements of men and supplies, the bitterness of defeat would have made it politically impossible for Truman to negotiate peace in Korea. The self-restraint of China and Russia at this point made possible an American victory. With face saved and a military triumph at his disposal just in time for the elections, the stage was set for Truman to add the olive branches of an honorable peace to the laurels of a brilliant military victory. The American troops were back in Seoul. The Northern invaders had withdrawn hurriedly beyond the Parallel. The Russians at Lake Success attracted attention by their unusual moderation, notably in their mild reaction to the shooting down of a Soviet bomber off the Korean coast early in the month. "SOVIET MODERATION IN U.N. INSPIRES HOPES, SUSPICIONS," said a *New York Times* headline on September 21. The day after MacArthur's triumphal parade in Seoul on September 28, a *New York Times* headline said wonderingly, "VISHINSKY SEEMS UNRUFFLED, AS IF KOREAN REDS HAD WON." The circumstances seemed ideal for the peaceful liquidation of the Korean affair.

But just as it looked as if the fires of war might be localized and extinguished, the sudden chilling fear of peace made itself felt in Washington.

CHAPTER 15

★

Peace Alarums

ANXIETY increased in Washington with the possibility of peace. On September 21, Thomas K. Finletter, Secretary of the Air Force, warned at a luncheon of the Aviation Writers Association that "if there is an improvement in the international scene, and, in particular, if the Korean War ends soon and successfully" this would afford no reason for slackening the national rearmament effort. Finletter was chairman of the Presidential Air Policy Commission whose famous report, *Survival in the Air Age*, made public in January, 1948, had recommended expansion of the air force to seventy groups by January, 1950. Little headway had been made on this program because of its huge cost, until the outbreak of the Korean War. Finletter told the aviation writers at the luncheon that the $11,500,000,000 additional for defense which Truman had just asked of Congress would increase the basic size of the Air Force from forty-eight to fifty-eight groups "and start it on the road to a projected strength of sixty-nine." Finletter thought it important that whatever happened in Korea the United States should go ahead "on the basis of a cold and long-term calculation of our needs, and not on the basis of the more immediate happening in the world scene."

Concerted steps seemed to be under way to alert those who helped to create public opinion. Several days after Secretary Finletter spoke to the aviation writers, General Omar N. Bradley, chairman of the United States Joint Chiefs of Staff, addressed the National Press Club in Washington. There he "declared . . . that the greatest danger facing the West lay in the possibility that the United States might 'let down its guard' after victory had been won in Korea." General Bradley seemed to fear the effect of peace on American public opinion, and on Congress. "Having agreed to certain forces for Western Europe," he told the Washington correspondents, "we cannot vacillate and fall back on these agreements." If American forces in Europe were to be expanded, a new approach to military problems was necessary. This had already been broached by General Marshall, shortly after he had been sworn in as Secretary of Defense on September 21. He had made his first official speech a plea for universal military training, something no American Congress had ever been willing to vote during peacetime. The idea of universal military training had always been intensely unpopular in the United States; the peaceful settlement of the Korean War was unlikely to make it more palatable. In America, the soldier's duty had always been regarded as a regrettable occasional necessity, not as an important profession, or a glorious career. Events were to show how much greater the alarms had to become before Americans would begin to accept the idea of interrupting every young man's life for a term of military service.

There was a similar anxiety at the State Department. Two important steps had been taken in September. In advance of consultations with the other Pacific powers, the United States had announced that it was planning to go ahead with a separate treaty with Japan, containing no restrictions on rearmament. Similarly, on the eve of the meeting of the Atlantic Pact Big Three Foreign Ministers, the State Department had announced that the United States wanted to arm the West Germans and thought they could raise about ten divisions for a joint North Atlantic command. "This," according to the diplomatic correspondent of the *New York Times*, "upset both the French and the British, who were opposed to arming the Germans" and as a result the Big Three conference, "despite the absence of Vishinsky and the mutual objectives and respect among the other three," had proved "a disappointment." The rearmament of Japan and Germany, thus initiated by the United States without consulting even its Western allies, could be put over only by a stepped-up campaign about "the Russian menace." "What attitude the neighbors of Japan will take toward the United States proposals," the chief correspondent of the *New York Times* at the United Nations noted on September 23, "seems to depend upon whether they are now more afraid of the Soviet Union than of a revived Japan." A settlement in Korea at that moment would lessen fear of Moscow, for it would mean the acquiescence of Russia in the defeat of a satellite, the acceptance of a serious blow to Soviet prestige for the sake of peace. "However," the same correspondent went on, "it would seem that unless the Kremlin now is ready to do something to reduce the tension, both the French in Europe and the island nations of the Pacific will have to give way fairly soon to the American proposals."

The Soviets seemed willing enough. On September 25, a delegation from a "Maryland Committee for Peace" put four questions to Soviet Deputy Foreign Minister Jacob A. Malik in New York. One question was, "Do you favor (or will you agree to) a meeting between the top leaders of the United States and the Soviet Union to negotiate their differences to help achieve full peace?" The answer was "Yes." A spokesman for the State Department quickly brushed this aside as smacking of "the Stockholm peace petition." The marks of prearrangement were indeed obvious, but it should also have been obvious that when a diplomat arranges to have himself asked whether his government wants peace talks, so that he can say "Yes," he must be anxious for peace talks. Perhaps the State Department did actually fear that the Kremlin was "ready to do something to reduce the tension." And, if tension were reduced, how persuade the French (and the British) to give way on German rearmament, and the "island nations of the Pacific" to give way on Japanese rearmament?

These were the fears of the American moderates. Generals Marshall and Bradley, Secretaries Acheson and Finletter, were not fire-eaters; they were not associated with the "preventive war" crowd. It was already clear enough that of course peace would be a calamity for those who eagerly wanted a "show-down," for the German and Japanese military who wanted to rearm, and for Chiang Kai-shek whose only hope was a new world war. It began to appear that in this respect there was a fatal if unspoken and unintended coalition forming between these desperadoes and the "moderates," despite their mutual fear, hatred, and contempt. They had a common stake in avoiding peace as long as possible—the desperadoes in the hope that something might yet turn up to provoke a general war, the "moderates" in the hope that they could stave off negotiation and relaxation of tension a while longer. Thus President Truman, who only a few weeks before had been trying to curb MacArthur and to mobilize public opinion against the idea of a "preventive war," now suddenly turned anxious in the hour of victory and began to combat the idea of peace.

Almost since the beginning of his Administration, under one slogan after another—"the get tough policy," "contain-ment," and "total diplomacy"—Truman had predicated his whole attitude toward the Soviet bloc on the belief that the United States could somehow refuse to make peace without being led to make war. The Soviet bloc was to be treated with hostility, subjected to political boycott and economic block-ade, and forced to divert its energies from reconstruction into an ever greater arms race, in the hope that the pressure would cause the Soviet regime to collapse from within, to withdraw into its prewar boundaries, or to sue for peace on any terms. This policy required the maintenance of tension at home and abroad, in order to make politically possible the imposition of a heavier burden of armament and taxes, the rearmament of western Germany and Japan, and the imposition of ever greater restrictions on trade with the Soviet bloc. The settle-ment of the Korean question by peaceful means would in-evitably create a burst of good feeling Washington wished desperately to avoid. It is only in this perspective that one can understand the alarmed tone of Truman's press conference the day of MacArthur's triumphal return to Seoul.

"President Truman," said the *New York Times*, "predicted that as a result of the apparent total victory impending in Korea, a sincere effort would be made to block the whole mobilization and rearmament program, which has been conceived for long-term preparedness against the threat of Russia's military might and aggressive policy. He said he hoped that this effort would not be successful."

Truman always said he wanted peace. Why was he becoming alarmed over its approach? Was he insincere in his peaceful protestations? I do not think so. In the ten years from 1940 to 1950 I worked as a Washington correspondent. To me, with a slight personal acquaintance and a long professional observation to judge by, Truman always seemed a good human being—however exasperatingly inadequate to the terrible responsibilities thrust upon him by the death of Roosevelt—and as honorable and decent a specimen of that excellent breed, the plain small-town American, as one could find anywhere in the U.S.A.: not a man who would deliberately do any harm, but the victim of circumstances and forces stronger than himself. He did not want war. But unfortunately and at the same time he did not want peace, and in a sense could not afford peace.

Behind the truths, half-truths, and fictions which supported the notion that Communism could not be dealt with but must be "contained," there were simpler political realities less unfamiliar to the experienced Missouri politician. Instinctively left-of-center, like Roosevelt, Truman had also constantly to struggle with the same kind of abuse. The Fair Deal, like the New Deal, was denounced as "communistic." How better disprove this charge than by active hostility to Moscow? On the other hand, how fight off the Red-scare bogey at home, if one was also open to attack for making an agreement with Moscow? The difficulty of dealing with the Russians was clear enough, but even clearer was the political danger at home. How negotiate without give-and-take? But how give anything at all without being charged with "appeasement"? To "get tough," to avoid negotiation, to carry on a sniping campaign just short of actual warfare—this was the line of least political resistance.

Roosevelt was fortunate in that during his first two terms in office the urgent problems were domestic, and these—instantly translatable into bread-and-butter terms—were not issues on which the Red-scare tactic could be effective—as election returns demonstrated over and over again. And when foreign policy did become crucial, the German attack on Russia and the Japanese attack on the United States temporarily deprived anti-Sovietism of respectability, especially since many of its devotees were too obviously fellow-traveling a line parallel to that of the Axis.

But President Truman's years in office have been overshadowed abroad by the immense problems of achieving a new world balance of power between the two great victors, and colored at home by the fact that government expenditures, as necessary in Truman's day as in Roosevelt's to maintain full employment, depended more and more on the alarms and fears engendered by Soviet-American rivalry. The Red scare, which had made its debut as an instrument of attack on the domestic reformers, became in Truman's hands an instrument of government, an easy way to obtain from Congress those expenditures he needed to "prime the pump" of prosperity, first by relief and reconstruction abroad, then by rearmament. Those who would not be moved by pity or moral obligation to alleviate suffering abroad could be frightened into appropriations by fear of Communism. Powerful domestic interests ready to combat enlarged expenditure for social purposes could be led to acquiesce readily in "Keynesianism" if it took the profitable form of an armament boom. For Truman, to "contain" the Russians seemed the only way to contain the Republicans.

Truman wanted something which was neither war nor peace. MacArthur wanted war. Indecision made Truman at best an irresolute superior, at worst a passive collaborator in MacArthurism. Absolute firmness was required if there was to be any chance at all of "containing" a dynamic military commander, colossal in his self-assurance, contemptuous of half-measures, and determined to force a showdown. To leave MacArthur in command was bad. To be unsure of whether one really wanted the war to end was worse.

If the war was Stalin's blunder, the blunder was now obvious to Moscow. If the war was MacArthur's plan, the plan itself was plainly visible. The events which followed, the crossing of the 38th Parallel, the demand for "unconditional surrender," and the provocative advance to the Chinese and Russian borders must be read in the light of Truman's fear of peace. This is the third, the decisive, element in Korea's tragic story.

PART III

HATING WAR BUT FEARING PEACE

CHAPTER 16

★

Reversal on the Parallel

SOMETHING worse than indecision made itself felt in
the President's attitude the day of MacArthur's triumphal entry into Seoul. It appeared in connection
with the disputed question of whether the United Nations
forces should cross the 38th Parallel. Exactly a week earlier
Truman had said that this was for the United Nations to
decide. Now he suddenly grew, as one headline put it, "reti-
cent" on the subject.

At his press conference on September 21, Truman had been
asked if he had made any decision about what the American
troops should do once they reached the 38th Parallel. "He
replied," said the United Press next day, that "he had reached
no decision and that after all it is up to the United Nations
to decide, as American troops are only part of the over-all
UN Army opposing the North Koreans. He promised to abide
by any decision reached by the United Nations."

A week later what had been clear now became cryptic. When
the question came up again at the press conference of Septem-
ber 28, the President "said he could not say publicly whether
General Douglas MacArthur's forces would cross the 38th
Parallel." The question was still being debated in the United
Nations at Lake Success, but the word "publicly" in the Presi-
dent's reply implied that he already knew privately what Mac-
Arthur's forces would do.

A change in policy was naturally suspected by the press

corps. In fact, a State Department spokesman, explaining the American position at Lake Success, had maintained that the original Security Council resolution of June 27 already gave authority for "pursuit of the Communist forces across the line." A reporter called Truman's attention to this interpretation. Truman "remarked that the resolution was very broad."

Next a reporter asked whether this meant that MacArthur as Supreme Commander had implied authority to cross the line. "Mr. Truman remarked . . . that General MacArthur was under direct orders of the President and the Chiefs of Staff and that he would follow those orders." What, then, were those orders? Did they give MacArthur authority to cross the line? "Mr. Truman said he could not answer the question."

At this point, Truman "was reminded that recently he had said that the question of crossing the line was one for the United Nations to decide and he was asked how this squared with his statement that the commander was under his orders." The Chief Executive "replied that the UN would have to act first and that certainly it would relay any new instructions through him."

"This reply," said the *New York Times* next day, "suggesting further action at Lake Success, appeared to be in conflict with the position stated by the State Department spokesman and left the world with an enigma."

Some light was cast on this enigma by a brief three-paragraph dispatch sent out of Washington the day before by the Associated Press. This quoted "responsible informants" as saying that General MacArthur had been authorized "to send United Nations troops into North Korea if necessary as a military measure to destroy the power of the fleeing North Korean Army" but that "the longer-range political question of establishing order in North Korea and occupying that area of the peninsula must be decided by the United Nations."

"The decision on crossing the boundary," said the Associated Press, "presumably was approved by President Truman and reviewed by Secretary of State Acheson with the foreign policy chiefs of friendly governments at United Nations headquarters in New York."

If this report was correct, then Truman's sudden "reticence" on the subject was something less than candid. Actually, Truman already knew that MacArthur had been authorized to take an even more important step, namely, to fix the terms of surrender. He had already cleared with Washington a proclamation calling for the unconditional surrender of the North Koreans. This presupposed the right to cross the line and use military measures if they did not lay down their arms. For it would look ludicrous if the Supreme Commander were to call for "unconditional surrender" and the United Nations were then to order his troops to halt at the Parallel while it negotiated peace with the North Koreans.

The question of crossing the line was a political, not a military, question so long as the North Koreans had retreated across it. Then and since, the question was deliberately rendered obscure by irrelevant argument. The 38th Parallel was an imaginary line, but so were many other frontiers. With a war going on, a commander could not be held to an imaginary line—true. But, if a pause came, he might very well be ordered to halt, especially at a frontier, while political decisions were made. Whether a peace was to be negotiated or the opposing army totally destroyed was a political decision, and one which arose naturally at that moment. To cross the line *before* the political decision was reached was, in fact, to *make* the political decision by military means: to end the pause, to force the enemy to fight or retreat to the point where he would have to fight or surrender, and thus to commit the United Nations to the total destruction of the North Korean army. Whether such a decision would be wise or unwise was not the point at issue. The only point was whether the United Nations was to be allowed to make this decision for its Commander, or whether the Commander was to be permitted to make this decision for the United Nations.

Linked with this was another question which Washington permitted MacArthur to decide: the question of the surrender terms. The United Nations could have offered to negotiate with the North Korean regime. It could have asked surrender, but on specified terms. It could have promised country-wide elections with Russian and Chinese observers invited. It could have offered a temporary United Nations trusteeship for the whole country with a guarantee of safety for the defeated Communists in the North. The possibilities were many, and called for serious consideration and orderly decision. All this was foreclosed by MacArthur's proclamation calling for unconditional surrender.

The way in which the proclamation was made public provided a perfect image of the lineup of forces. MacArthur wrote the proclamation. MacArthur had it broadcast to the North Korean commander and his forces. Warren Austin provided Trygve Lie with a copy. This was how the United Nations learned of "its" proclamation. The proclamation itself began of course with MacArthur's favorite pronoun: "I, as the United Nations Commander in Chief, call upon you [the North Korean commander] and the forces under your command, in whatever part of Korea situated, forthwith to lay down your arms and cease hostilities under such military supervisions as I may direct." The Syngman Rhee regime was claiming jurisdiction over the whole country. What if its officers were to supervise the surrender? Would the Communist soldiers be treated as an honorably defeated foe, or as persons guilty of an attempt to overthrow the lawful government of Korea?

True, MacArthur went on to say in his proclamation that "North Korean forces . . . will continue to be given the care dictated by civilized custom and practice and permitted to return to their homes as soon as practicable." The Supreme Commander's lofty assurances may not have seemed enough. The kind of treatment the Northern forces may reasonably have feared had been indicated by a Reuters' dispatch earlier in the war. Dateline *"Advance Headquarters in South Korea,"* it reported: "Twelve hundred Communists and suspected Communists have been executed by South Korean police since the outbreak of hostilities, Kim Tai Sun, chief of the National South Korean police, said today. Those executed were considered 'bad security risks,' he said." The North Koreans might have considered unconditional surrender in such circumstances a bad security risk, too. Actually, the demand for unconditional surrender left the North Korean Communist forces with little, if anything, to lose by fighting to the bitter end. The unconditional surrender demand insured the continuation of the war. And, by insuring the continuation of the war, it kept alive the risk that MacArthur's forces penetrating toward the Chinese and Russian borders would come into conflict with either or both those neighboring powers.

The demand by the United Nations Commander for unconditional surrender may have taken the United Nations by surprise. It was no surprise to Truman. Although the surrender broadcast was not made until October 1, he knew of it on September 28. This helps to explain the confusing reply he gave that day on the question of the 38th Parallel and shows too how far from frank were his answers.

A reporter asked Truman to comment on reports from New York earlier that day that the United States was preparing a six-point peace program for Korea. And then the President made a revealing slip which the press was honor-bound not to publish at the time. Truman did not understand the question, and asked whether the reporter "meant the broadcast asking the North Koreans for surrender." He then went on to explain that MacArthur was making such a broadcast but that reporters must consider this information "off the record" until the broadcast had been made. Truman said he understood the broadcast would be made that day, Thursday, September 28.

The Associated Press, in sending out this story after the broadcast two days later—when little attention was paid to it —said that apparently Truman had the impression that the broadcast already had been given. "The surprised reaction of the reporters," the Associated Press recounted, "showed this was not the case, however." It added that the President said "the statement [the MacArthur broadcast] had been taken up with him."

Truman's action in making this information "off the record" for the time being was natural. But he is open to criticism in failing to admit plainly that the United States was not waiting for United Nations action in Korea, even on so crucial a question as surrender terms, much less on the crossing of the Parallel.

Once again, the United Nations was confronted with a *fait accompli*. When events are thus reconstructed, it becomes easier to understand what was happening at Lake Success. On September 28 the United Nations representatives of Britain, Australia, Canada, Norway, and the Philippines were reported to have been moved by "a sense of urgency" to tentative agreement on the text of a resolution giving MacArthur "what sponsors call tacit consent" to cross the 38th Parallel. The consent had already been given by Washington, and there was not time to wait for passage of the resolution. Next day United Nations diplomats were quoted as saying that "in the absence of specific instructions to the contrary . . . General MacArthur has the power to decide on military terms for surrender—and the power to decide whether to order a crossing of . . . the 38th Parallel." The unconditional surrender proclamation had already been cleared by Washington.

As the *New York Times* said on September 30, "military advances" were "fast outstripping the diplomatic pace." MacArthur restored Rhee to Seoul on September 28. Perhaps if the military advances had been slower, the diplomats at Lake Success might have had time to work out some kind of political program with which to persuade the North to lay down its arms. It may be that this is exactly what MacArthur—and Truman—wanted to avoid.

There is evidence which suggests that the military pace was speeded up at great cost in life and also in damage to the city of Seoul in order to be able to "outstrip the diplomatic pace" and stampede the United Nations into accepting "unconditional surrender."

I want to recall first the bitterness expressed by the "Army and Marine commanders who liberated Seoul." They contended it could have been taken "without the heavy loss in lives" and "destruction" by both the Communist defenders and the UN attackers, attributed "to demands that Seoul be taken 'as soon as possible.' "

"The coolness of the welcome received by the liberators," said a United Press dispatch from Seoul just after its liberation, "is understandable in the light of the millions of dollars worth of damage. . . . Despite communiqués that Seoul was spared, there is evidence everywhere of the pummeling it took from United States planes and artillery."

This cable, published in the *New York Times* on October 1, reported that "one Army commander said the UN attack accomplished absolutely nothing of military value." Marine commanders, "whose troops suffered the heaviest casualties," contended that the city could have been surrounded "and left to die on the vine."

"An Army officer who led the eastern flanking attack," the United Press said, "attributed the city's destruction to 'international politics. . . . We had promised the Korean people that their capital would be spared. It could have been.' . . . A lieutenant colonel said, 'A triumphal entry into the city was needed as soon as possible, and we gave it to them, but it cost us and the Koreans plenty.' "

The high cost to the soldiers was indicated in a dispatch the same day by a *New York Times* correspondent, Michael James. He reported that one battalion of the First Regiment of the United States First Marine Division suffered 297 casualties from the time it hit the Inchon beach to the end of the fighting in Seoul.

"The total casualties for the division cannot be divulged until the figures are released by Washington," this dispatch went on, "but some indication of the total manpower damage can be drawn from the fact that more than 6000 casualties were evacuated from the beachhead in the first eleven days of the northern campaign"—the campaign for Seoul.

What was the hurry? It would seem from Truman's slip at his press conference on the 28th, the day MacArthur triumphantly restored Rhee to his gutted capital, that the President thought the surrender broadcast had been made the same day. Truman had already seen it, so it must have been prepared well in advance. It would have been very dramatic to broadcast the surrender the same day, and MacArthur is nothing if not dramatic; General Eisenhower, when once asked what he learned as chief of staff to MacArthur in Manila before the war, grinned and said, "Dramatics."

But there was more involved than play acting. There was also, as that army officer said, "international politics." The longer the fall of the capital and the drive to the Parallel were delayed, the more time the diplomats had at Lake Success to work out a peace program, the less chance there was of forcing "unconditional surrender" on the United Nations. This was important to Syngman Rhee, and it was also important to Harry Truman.

CHAPTER 17

★

Free Elections?

A KIND of Gresham's Law was in operation, driving the better coinage out of politics in favor of the worse. Just as Truman opposed war but wasn't quite sure that he wanted peace, so while crusading for "democracy" in Korea he wasn't quite sure he wanted to take the risk of permitting free elections if peace came. Just as his indecision on war or peace made him first the victim and then the accomplice of MacArthur, so his basic indecision about free elections brought him in the end to support the program of a man he ought to have despised, Syngman Rhee. It is here that one must look for the answer to the question, why the American government was in such a hurry to take Seoul and call for "unconditional surrender" before the United Nations could think out the problem on its own.

In July, when Pandit Nehru began his efforts at mediation, the State Department asserted that "a cease-fire and a return to the Thirty-eighth Parallel" were the "minimum and irreducible conditions" for peace. This did not seem at all unattainable. It was noted in United Nations circles that while the Soviet government had attacked the validity of the June 27 resolution of the United Nations Security Council authorizing military sanctions and the July 7 resolution providing for MacArthur's "unified command," it had not questioned the validity of the June 25 resolution which called for a cease-fire and the withdrawal of the North Koreans to the 38th Parallel.

116

On these two points, the cease-fire and the withdrawal of the invading force, "there appeared to be complete agreement."

There seemed to be basis for agreement on another point also. If the original United Nations General Assembly directives on Korea were now at last to be carried out, there would be country-wide elections and the establishment of a unified government. This had been blocked before by the Soviet boycott of the United Nations on Korea and by the little iron curtain dropped at the 38th Parallel to shut out two successive United Nations Commissions. The Russians now seemed to have changed their minds. After the Nehru message to Stalin in July, "foreign diplomats" in Moscow were quoted as saying that the Soviet Union wanted to see a peaceful settlement and also general elections "in both North and South Korea to elect a single government for the whole peninsula." The speed with which this was cleared by the Soviet censorship gave it added significance.

Now it was the other side which began to hold back. The dispatch from Moscow appeared the same day with a dispatch from Lake Success, where the chief United Nations correspondent of the *New York Times*, in discussing prospects for mediation, reported: "Some saw a possibility that the Kremlin may also suggest that elections be held afterwards in both North and South Korea to set up a government for the entire country—in the expectation, of course, that this would produce a Communist majority, *thus bringing about the same result as if the United Nations had not intervened.*" (Italics added.)

The fear that the Communists would win such elections was reflected in a speech made by Warren Austin at Lake Success on August 17, which "revealed that the United States wants them [the elections] to be held on the basis that the Republic of Korea's jurisdiction would be extended over North Korea automatically." The "Republic of Korea" was the official name for the Southern regime. If its jurisdiction were automatically extended over the North, it would supervise the elections. Already two United Nations Commissions had reflected unfavorably on the way the Syngman Rhee regime handled elections and manhandled political opponents; threats to confiscate rice ration cards were noted as one of the milder forms of coercion by the United Nations Temporary Commission which observed the elections establishing the Rhee regime.

"The difficulty," the *New York Times* correspondent at Lake Success explained, "is that there is a strong probability of an over-all Communist majority if the elections were held before the communization of North Korea had been undone, and before a UN reconstruction program had assuaged the bitterness of North and South Korea against the destruction of their homes during their liberation by UN forces. In that case communism would win by an election what it failed to obtain by an invasion."

There were others at the United Nations who felt differently. The need for political planning was being discussed at Lake Success in August. The question of whether MacArthur was to be allowed to cross the 38th Parallel was being debated, and some were asking "What can be done to eliminate some of the unsavory elements of the Republic of Korea?" It was said that the job which needed to be done in Korea was much like that which General Marshall had attempted in 1946 in China, when he tried to induce Chiang Kai-shek to make reforms—"and it is hoped here that the United Nations will have better success."

United Nations circles were disturbed at the time by a speech which Dr. John M. Chang, Syngman Rhee's Ambassador to Washington, had just made on August 20 at Lenox, Massachusetts. The speech was an attack on suggestions for a temporary United Nations trusteeship over Korea or at least North Korea while elections were held for a unified regime. "We do not accept the validity of the 38th Parallel as a military, political, or economic division," Dr. Chang said. He declared his government would insist on the "unconditional surrender" of the Northern forces, and that it would have nothing to do with any proposals for "trusteeship" or for a "coalition" government representing both North and South. He also declared that the Rhee regime would expect United Nations forces to turn over all civil functions to it at the earliest possible moment. At the United Nations it was said this speech showed the need for "determined measures to bring about a more realistic attitude in the Republic of Korea."

Unfortunately the determination proved to be on the other side. Rhee was taking no chances. The swift recapture of Seoul and the unconditional surrender proclamation served to nip off threats developing from two quarters. On September 27 there were persistent reports at Lake Success originating "from a couple of Western delegations" that the Chinese Communists had suggested that India sound out the possibility of a peace based on a cease-fire, withdrawal of Communist forces to the 38th Parallel, withdrawal of the United Nations forces to the Pusan beachhead, and the holding of country-wide elections. "Republic of Korea officials said emphatically," it was reported, "that the only terms acceptable were unconditional northern surrender."

There was danger from another direction. The resolution tentatively agreed upon at Lake Success on September 28 by Britain, Australia, Canada, Norway, and the Philippines, while tacitly allowing MacArthur to cross the Parallel, did provide for country-wide elections. At least one of the delegates who helped to draft this resolution not only expected elections to produce a Communist majority but was prepared to acquiesce in such an outcome.

"This delegate said," the *New York Times* reported, "that it was probable that under this plan a unified Korea would go Communist within four or five years. Chances of a democratic victory will be increased, it is believed, if the elections are delayed until a United Nations relief program begins to replace the destruction of the war and an attempt to counteract Communist influence in North Korea can be made. In any event, the feeling of the delegates sponsoring the resolution was that the United Nations could not prevent the establishment of Communist governments if this took place by peaceful means."

The American government was in no mood to accept any such prospect. A few days earlier the diplomatic correspondent of the *New York Times*, James Reston, had reported that while United States officials "expect the General Assembly of the United Nations to define the policy to be followed in North Korea," they were also "clarifying what their policy in Korea has no intention of doing." Apparently the United Nations was to define the policy but the United States would accept that policy only if it suited United States purposes.

While the United States, it was explained, "does not intend to impose Dr. Syngman Rhee and his government upon the North Koreans," it also does not intend "to permit the present Communist leaders of North Korea to obtain their ends by subverting any coalition government that may be established." How could they be prevented from "subverting" the government? Presumably only by outlawing these leaders and making it impossible for their followers to exercise their freedom of choice. But how have free elections if part of the Koreans, apparently a considerable part—perhaps a majority, as the United States delegation seemed to fear—were to be deprived of their full political rights?

Rhee himself was more direct because less hampered by hypocrisy. The day the foregoing dispatch appeared in print, the South Korean delegation to the General Assembly held a press conference to present their own nine-point program. This called for the extension of their jurisdiction over all Korea. Elections were to be held only in the North. They were to be limited to filling the hundred seats originally left symbolically vacant in the Southern legislature for Northern representatives when and if elections could be held there. Obviously a program of this kind required unconditional surrender, and Dr. Chang at the same press conference declared the crossing of the Parallel necessary "to obtain peace for the world. It is absolutely necessary and we expect General MacArthur to do this." The Rhee regime preferred to let the war go on rather than accept anything less.

When Austin addressed the Political and Security Committee of the General Assembly at Lake Success on September 30, the day before MacArthur broadcast his unconditional surrender proclamation, the American government seemed finally to have accepted Rhee's point of view. Austin was smooth but the meaning was unmistakable. In discussing the pending six-power resolution, he said that while the United States agreed with the principle of establishing a unified and independent Korea, "at this moment, we cannot foresee the precise circumstances in which unification is to be accomplished."

Austin maintained that "detailed blueprints for such a complex operation" would be "ill-advised," though he did not explain what would be so complex about country-wide elections. Complexity arose only if elections were to be limited to the North and confined to filling vacant seats in the South Korean legislature. Austin endorsed the idea of a strong United Nations Commission "empowered to devise practical and effective measures for achieving United Nations objectives." Apparently country-wide elections were not "practical" enough. This Commission, Austin said, would of course consult "with the Unified Command and with the democratically selected representatives of the Korean people"—doubtless MacArthur and Rhee. Then "at an appropriate time, elections by secret ballot, free from fraud and intimidation . . . would have to be arranged."

Would these elections be held throughout the country or only, as Rhee proposed, in the North? Austin did not answer this question directly but he went on to point out that "free, democratic elections already have been held south of the 38th Parallel. The General Assembly has formally declared the government of the Republic of Korea formed as a result of these elections to be the lawfully constituted government in that part of Korea in which the United Nations Commission was able to observe elections."

Austin dwelt lyrically on the sufferings and sacrifices of the war as if these were Rhee's credentials: "It is the territory and people of this government that have been ravaged by war; it is the soldiers of this government whose valor and patriotism have been strengthened by the United Nations forces." Austin was indeed willing to concede at least in principle what Rhee was unwilling to recognize in practice. "The manner and procedures required to unify the country," Austin said, "are functions for the United Nations to perform, but the government of the Republic of Korea has unquestionably earned the right to be consulted in all matters relating to the future of Korea."

It was easy to imagine the storm in Congress if the war had ended then and there, with plans for unified elections, and if those elections had brought to power a government containing Communists. Truman only had to imagine this to see the point of Syngman Rhee's program. What happened at Lake Success or elsewhere to hold up the unconditional surrender proclamation for two days remains a mystery; perhaps there were last-minute behind-the-scenes efforts to negotiate a peace; perhaps there was even a short-lived revolt on the part of other powers in the United Nations against a humiliating *fait accompli*. In any case the proclamation finally was broadcast on October 1, cutting short all negotiation, and paving the way for the crossing of the Parallel.

The war was to go on. The "liberating" bombardments were to continue, the cost in suffering to rise beyond conception. The last bitter mouthful for the Korean people to swallow must have been the news that the course on which Rhee, MacArthur, and Truman had launched them was wholeheartedly approved in Japan. "Conservative Japanese" had been "quietly informing foreign friends that the United Nations must pour troops in force across the 38th Parallel and put a definite end to the Communist state in the North if they expect to reap the fruits of their hard fight against the North Korean invasion."

Otherwise the Northern forces might some day try again to make Korea a Russian dagger pointed at Japan. It might then, they warned, "become a matter of extreme difficulty to hold Japanese hotheads back from joining what they would then consider the winning force in Asia." One wonders whether this was the line of the slick Japanese at MacArthur Headquarters.

"The Japanese, of course," it was admitted at the same time, "have a secondary reason for hoping for a quick United Nations counterinvasion of North Korea. . . . This is the prospect of greatly enhanced Japanese export trade should the United Nations succeed in unifying Korea and—with American capital—undertake the enormous task of reconstruction . . . actually the heaviest industrial damage has been wrought in North Korea by Allied bombers. If the United Nations should succeed in unifying both sections there would be a double market for the goods Japan hopes to sell in rebuilding Korea and sufficient stability to insure that orders placed and fulfilled would be paid for without possible interference by a new outbreak of civil war or revolt."

The greater the damage the bigger the market for Japanese goods. But until the Reds were wiped out, payment for these goods could not be assured. The war to make Korea safe for democracy seemed to be a war to make Korea safe again for Japanese exploitation. Five years after its liberation from Japan, Korea was being "liberated" back again.

CHAPTER 18

★

First Warnings

BOTH Lake Success and Washington understood that it was risking trouble to let MacArthur cross the Parallel and then take a chance on keeping him away from the Chinese and Russian borders. Hanson Baldwin, writing in the *New York Times*, noted as early as September 1, "The Chinese Communists are making troop dispositions that will enable them to intervene militarily in Korea if they wish." From Hong Kong on September 8 came the news that overshadowing earlier preparations for a Formosan invasion, which now seemed definitely postponed, was "the transfer of Chinese Communist troops from South and even West China northward to Manchuria"; it was estimated that at least 300,000 troops were on the move northward.

On September 21 Marshal Tito told a visiting delegation of American Congressmen that he thought it would be best for the United Nations troops to halt on the Parallel. Yugoslav sources explained that this was advocated "to prevent a further deterioration in the relations between Communist China and the United States" and to give the North Korean Communists "an opportunity to experience complete disillusionment with Moscow's aggressive policy, as opposed to a magnanimous policy pursued by the West." On September 24 the diplomatic correspondent of the *New York Times* reported: "So far as one can discover, the United States does not wish to place a large and hostile army near the Soviet or Manchurian frontiers. It does not want to provoke the Russians or the Chinese Communists into occupying the North of Korea." The same day, from Hong Kong came a dispatch saying that "reports from coastal cities on the China mainland indicate the Korean War is now being discussed . . . in terms of whether the United Nations forces will go beyond the line that formerly divided North from South Korea." Peking had acknowledged the day before that Korean veterans of the Chinese Red armies were fighting in Korea; and the Hong Kong correspondent of the *New York Times* cabled that the "disposition of Chinese Communist troops on the Yalu River boundary" and the acknowledgment that Koreans had been allowed to leave Manchuria to enter the war "may be designed to point up the threat that Chinese troops could enter Korea too if the United Nations forces got too close to the Manchurian border."

The decision was not an easy one. Hanson Baldwin pointed out in the *New York Times* on September 27 that if the Parallel was crossed "the Chinese Communists might well be provoked to action." On the other hand, if it was not crossed, "the North Korean army may live to fight again." Baldwin hinted that American military leaders were opposed to the risk of sending American troops all the way to the border. He said that while some limited operations above the Parallel might be necessary before a United Nations directive were issued, "we shall certainly not undertake the unlimited task of pushing right up to the Manchurian frontier and of pacifying the entire country, if our military leaders are listened to." Obviously the military leaders he meant were those in Washington, not Tokyo. "Any such job, if done," Baldwin added, "must be done by South Koreans and/or other United Nations forces." Whether such a compromise was ever seriously discussed is not known. One cannot exclude the possibility that the acquiescence of Britain and France in the crossing was won by offering them the alternative of supplying their own troops in sufficient force to do the job, or letting MacArthur do it.

There were warning hints from Moscow and a direct warning from Peking. On September 29, the Associated Press reported from the Soviet capital that "the Soviet Union, which, like Communist China, borders on North Korea, would unquestionably take a grave view of any effort by United States or Allied forces to push up beyond the 38th Parallel." This was given added weight by the fact that it had cleared Moscow's stringent censorship. On October 1, with MacArthur's troops already rolling across the 38th Parallel, Premier Chou En-lai, in an address on the first anniversary of the Chinese Communist State, warned that his country would not "supinely tolerate" an invasion of North Korea. This was given prominence in the Soviet press, and Tass reported from Peking, "Tactics of a prolonged war of resistance will undoubtedly give the Korean people the possibility of overcoming many difficulties and winning final victory." Diplomatic officials in Washington were quoted as minimizing Chinese warnings in connection with the crossing of the Parallel. "Why should they suddenly consider crossing the 38th Parallel an invasion if they labeled the whole South Korean defense an invasion all along?" these officials were quoted as saying. One of them added, "I don't think that China wants to be chopped up," hardly a model of diplomatic tact under the circumstances.

The comfortable notion that Communist China could be counted on not to intervene, because if it had intended intervention it would have done so before the North Koreans had been defeated in the Battle of the Beachhead, was to make its reappearance at a later stage of the war as well. It followed logically from the unspoken assumption that China's primary interest was in the victory of the North Koreans. But if the premise were incorrect, if China had interests of its own to protect irrespective of the North Korean defeat, then it might well intervene to protect those interests.

That China had interests of its own in North Korea which might lead it to intervene even if the North Korean cause looked hopeless was indicated by a *New York Times* dispatch from Hong Kong on October 3 which called attention to "important economic as well as political and military stakes of the Peiping regime in North Korea." The correspondent pointed out that the Yalu River generating plant on the Man-

churian border just inside Korean territory "has been supplying electrical power for the Manchurian industrialization
program" which the Chinese regarded as their "pilot zone" for
a China-wide industrial development program.

By that time it was already too late to stop the crossing of
the 38th Parallel. Some defenders of MacArthur have attempted to deny this. The *Economist* of London, for example,
ran a long editorial, "The Record of Korea," in its issue of
March 10, 1951, in which it argued that "however embarrassing
may have been the Supreme Commander's verbal excesses" he
did not force "the hand of the United Nations." It said: "The
United Nations forces, as distinct from South Korean troops,
did not cross the 38th Parallel until they were authorized to do
so by this resolution (of October 7). They had reached it
already on October 1, but General MacArthur halted them for
eight days until the Assembly had taken its decision. The only
crossing in pursuit of the defeated North Korean forces was
made by the South Korean troops, and this reflected the independent attitude of the South Korean government which,
although willing to subordinate its forces strategically to the
supreme United Nations command, denied that it was politically subject to such authority in Korean territory."

What are the facts? First, as to the South Koreans. On July
19 President Rhee appointed MacArthur Supreme Commander
of "all land, sea, and air forces" of the Republic of Korea. The
two commands were merged in one. As a matter of fact it
would seem that the Korean and United Nations forces were
closely integrated, for Secretary Marshall explained in one
public speech early in October that it was "the integration of
30,000 South Korean troops into United States forces" which
"saved the situation in Korea."

The crossing of the Parallel by the South Korean troops
before the United Nations had acted on the October 7
resolution was indeed, as the *Economist* suggested, an act of
political defiance. The consequences were foreshadowed at
Lake Success on October 3 when Percy C. Spender, the
Australian Minister for External Affairs, challenged the "flat
and unequivocal" claim made the day before by Rhee's repre-

sentative to jurisdiction over the whole peninsula. Mr. Spender declared that an entirely new government should be set up by the United Nations.

This was one of the principal questions left vague by the resolution of October 7. It was referred for decision to a new United Nations Commission which was to be set up under the terms of the resolution. In practice, however, military events might decide the question. "Some delegates declared," it was reported, "that if the trend in the United Nations was against its claim, the South Korean regime might seek to achieve a *fait accompli*. This would make it difficult for the United Nations Commission to challenge its status."

The *fait accompli* was already in the making. The day of this debate, October 3, advancing South Korean forces took Kosong, fifty miles north of the 38th Parallel. Did they do this without MacArthur's orders or consent, as the *Economist* implied?

The evidence is all to the contrary. Let us begin by noting that on Saturday, September 30, Colonel Lee Sun Keun, information officer for the South Korean Army, announced that units of the South Korean Third Division were at the Parallel but were "under orders not to cross" and "will not cross the 38th Parallel unless ordered to do so by the United Nations." This news came in a United Press cable from Taegu, Korea, which was printed in the *New York Times* of the same day.

At 11:45 A.M. Sunday morning, October 1, this South Korean Third Division began to cross the border. It did so, according to a dispatch to the *New York Times* from Tokyo, "under orders of the United States Eighth Army." The order, according to a dispatch to the same paper from its correspondent at Eighth Army Headquarters in Korea, "was dropped from a small observation plane by a United States major . . . late Saturday afternoon." The *New York Times* correspondent was permitted to speak by radio to Lieutenant Colonel Dick Emmerich, the United States Army officer acting as liaison officer with the South Korean Third Division. Colonel Emmerich was "at the forward Korean Third Divisional command post" and confirmed the fact that the troops which had crossed the border were not retiring. "We are not coming back," he said.

MacArthur pretended not to notice. "Although the border crossing by South Koreans is now known to the world and is even accompanied by United States officers," the *New York Times* correspondent at Tokyo reported next day, "it is still shrouded in complete official silence both at General Mac-Arthur's Headquarters and at the field command in Korea."

The "official silence" contrasted with the continued flow of *unofficial* information. "Headquarters allowed it understood," the same dispatch said, "that United States warships as well as the Air Force were supporting the South Korean advance north of the Parallel along the east coastal road, where cruisers and destroyers were lying offshore." In fact Press Release 520 by Far East Naval Headquarters that day said, "United States Navy support forces on the east coast provided direct naval gunfire support for the rapidly advancing R.O.K. [Republic of Korea] Third Army Division." Mac-Arthur was Supreme Commander of the naval and air forces as well as of the ground forces in the area. Major General Edward M. Almond, formerly MacArthur's chief of staff, then commanding the Tenth Corps, denied "formal knowledge" of any crossing, but, when pressed by correspondents, said, "Well, it's their country, isn't it?"

It would have been easy to deny that the advance had been made under Eighth Army orders, to refuse air and naval cover for the advance, and to disavow responsibility for the crossing. Neither denial nor disavowal was ever made. The evidence indicates that the South Koreans moved on United States Army orders and that their advance was coordinated with American air and naval action. MacArthur Headquarters, by refusing for several days to admit "official" knowledge of what was occurring, confessed its own complicity.

On October 3, with the South Koreans fifty miles above the Parallel, MacArthur Headquarters for the first time admitted the crossing. The reasons for the reticence were made clear at a Headquarters briefing. "Because the 'police action' in Korea had been undertaken at United Nations orders, which left somewhat indefinite the extent to which the 'policemen' should advance and because of the potential reaction to the border crossing by North Korea's Communist neighbors in China and the Soviet Union, the situation, it was explained, was quite an explosive one."

The conduct of American air and naval operations was not making it less explosive. The same dispatch, reporting the military information given out that day at Tokyo Headquarters, described how "United States planes . . . came down low to bomb and strafe truck convoys moving south toward Wonsan and down from near the Manchurian border on the Yalu River. . . . Although no United States troops yet had crossed the Parallel, the Air Force was giving maximum support to the South Korean advance. . . . Their right was covered by United States warships giving fire support to the South Korean advance."

In other words, on October 3, four days before the United Nations had passed its resolution, MacArthur was supporting South Korean forces moving more than fifty miles north of the Parallel, and MacArthur's bombers were in action just below the Yalu. This is not quite the "correct" hands-off attitude implied by the reasonings of such defenders of MacArthur as the *Economist*.

The South Koreans were invading not only on the east coast but at many points along the Parallel. The South Korean Third Division crossed, as we have seen, on October 1, and moved up the east coast. On October 2 the South Korean Capital Division, "moving from the west, swung in behind it at Yangyang" and was already reported fifteen miles north of the Parallel while a third South Korean division—the Sixth— "moved forward in the center to the border above Chunchon." By October 3 South Korean movement across the border had become so extensive that the military spokesman at the Tokyo Headquarters briefing that day explained the "bomb line" for B-29 Superforts had been moved "up about thirty-five miles north of the Parallel in eastern Korea lest explosives dropped below that limit hit South Korean allies."

Troops locked in battle cannot stop at a fixed line, but

there was no such military excuse for the South Korean advance. A *New York Times* correspondent with the forces advancing up the east coast reported on October 5 that "up to today, it was almost a sightseeing tour for the tired South Korean soldiers . . . who have not met any major opposition for more than ten days." They were then fifty-four air miles and seventy road miles north of the Parallel and had just had their first real brush with the enemy, a road ambush which caused "several casualties."

The rapid Korean advance may not have served any urgent military purpose but it certainly served the political purpose of putting South Korean troops in control of as much Northern territory as possible before the United Nations could decide against automatic extension of Rhee's authority to the North. The *fait accompli* was in the making. It is worth noting that the South Korean Third Division, which got its orders late Saturday afternoon, September 30, moved across the 38th Parallel at 11:45 A.M. Sunday, October 1, exactly fifteen minutes *before* MacArthur broadcast his surrender proclamation.

It was this proclamation, combined with the South Korean invasion, which forced the United Nations' hand. It could not decide on negotiating without disowning its own "commander's" unconditional surrender demand. To attempt to disown it would have been to come into frontal conflict with Washington where, as we have seen, the "unconditional surrender" statement had already been cleared with the President. Apparently neither MacArthur nor Washington were taking any chance on having the United Nations meddle with that proclamation, for though it said, "I, as the United Nations Commander in Chief," the United Nations had no foreknowledge of what its Commander in Chief was about to do in its name.

"The exact terms of the message," it was reported from Lake Success after the MacArthur broadcast, "had been a well-kept secret here, although rumors were prevalent for some time that General MacArthur was preparing an important message to the North Korean troops and military leaders. An expert with the United States delegation said that none of the other diplomatic missions at the United Nations had any specific information and probably had been less informed than the newspapermen."

No one knows for sure that peace could have been negotiated on a satisfactory basis with the North Koreans. But the United Nations should at least have been free to try negotiations if it so chose. The decision was, in effect, taken out of its hands by the broadcast. South Koreans started across the Parallel on United States orders fifteen minutes before the surrender proclamation, as if to underscore the fact that even surrender would not save the North Koreans. The stage was set for continuation of the war.

The same day, several hours before the news of the MacArthur broadcast, Ambassador Austin, the chief United States delegate at the United Nations, made a speech which was regarded as a "warning" and "clear notice that the United States felt that General MacArthur had the right to order a crossing of the Parallel and that, with or without a surrender, UN forces would march across the line." As a matter of fact, the first American forces to cross the Parallel officially did so at 3:14 A.M. Eastern Standard time Saturday, October 7. The United Nations resolution which by implication authorized the crossing of the Parallel, though it did not do so directly, was not passed by the General Assembly until late that same afternoon, more than twelve hours later. MacArthur could not wait.

We have seen that MacArthur had been authorized by Washington as early as September 27 to cross the Parallel without waiting for United Nations instructions, and to issue the unconditional surrender proclamation without waiting for the United Nations to make its own decisions on the terms of peace. MacArthur in turn, by allowing Rhee's troops to cross the Parallel without waiting for the United Nations, was giving Rhee a chance to create the *fait accompli* the United Nations feared. On October 7, as on June 27, the United Nations could do little but act as rubber-stamp for Washington's wishes and MacArthur's.

CHAPTER 19

★

The U.N.'s Dilemma

THE United Nations resolution of October 7 did not specifically authorize the crossing of the 38th Parallel. The American delegation insisted that authority to cross the Parallel was already implied by the Security Council resolution of June 27 which called on members of the United Nations to "furnish such assistance to the Republic of Korea as may be necessary to repel the armed attack and to restore international peace and security in the area." The Indian delegation was strongly opposed to a crossing, "certainly not without the specific authorization of the Security Council or the General Assembly," overlooking the fact that under the Charter the Assembly could only "recommend" and had no power to authorize military measures. "Several other delegates also believe," it was reported during the debate at Lake Success, "despite the arguments of the United States delegation, that such authorization is legally necessary, and that in any event its absence would make a bad impression in Asiatic countries." As passed, the resolution said that the General Assembly "recommends," among other things, "that all appropriate steps be taken to ensure conditions of stability through the whole of Korea" and that "United Nations forces should not remain in any part of Korea" longer than necessary. These two clauses were held by Washington to imply authority to cross the Parallel, since such a crossing might be an "appropriate step" to ensure conditions of stability, and United Nations forces could hardly be asked not to stay longer than necessary "in any part" of Korea without assuming that they had authority to be there.

Why was this authorization left to implication? The delegates who favored a crossing or at least favored acquiescence in American insistence on a crossing were confronted by twin difficulties. They feared that if there was no authorization by the United Nations the Soviets could point to this as further proof of United States "aggression." On the other hand they feared that if the Assembly authorized the crossing "it might provoke the retaliation of Communist China and so produce a world war." This deserves closer examination. If MacArthur crossed the border and China intervened openly, wouldn't that mean world war anyway? Apparently some people thought that war between China and the "unified command" under MacArthur might be limited to war between China and the United States if other powers, though supporting the Korean "police action," were not committed in advance to a wider conflict.

To vote against the crossing would be to antagonize Washington, which was determined on a crossing, with or without new authority. To permit the crossing to be made without a debate on the question at the United Nations would be to make its subordination to American wishes too unpalatable for countries like India still striving for an independent role, and too naked for West European public opinion. To authorize the crossing would be to commit oneself in advance to its consequences, which might be war with China or Russia or both. Perhaps the draft as passed seemed a clever compromise, for it appeased American wishes, and satisfied the Indian demand for a vote, but left the grant of authority so vague that it could later be disowned without too much loss of face if it threatened to provoke war with the Chinese or Russians.

The notion that safety could be found in such legalistic devices was too clever. A resolution adding momentum to a dynamic situation was not a mortgage or a sales agreement, in which an ingenious disclaimer could serve as protection against obvious risk. Once the war was widened by the crossing of the Parallel, events depended on whether the commander in the field acted with circumspection and obedience. If he took advantage of his authority to provoke China or Russia, it would be their reaction, not the nice wording of a clause at Lake Success, which would determine whether or not there was to be a further widening of the war. And if the United States found itself at war with China or Russia through the instrumentality of the "unified command," there was little chance that Britain or France could keep out by clinging to so frail a reed as was provided by the calculated obscurity of the resolution they voted on October 7.

They had hardly finished voting the resolution when Mac-Arthur dramatically demonstrated its dangerous potentialities. On October 8 two American fighter planes attacked a Soviet airport sixty miles north of the Korean frontier and forty miles south of Vladivostok. The Soviet government addressed a note of protest to the American Minister-Counselor in Moscow on October 9, formally charging that the attack was made by two United States Air Force planes of the Shooting Star F-80 type, that they approached the Soviet airdrome in "a hedge-hopping flight" and then "fired at the aerodrome from machine guns." The Soviet government asked "strict punishment" of those responsible and assurance that the American government "will take the necessary measures to prevent such provocative actions in the future."

The American Minister-Counselor in Moscow refused to accept the note, on the ground that this was a United Nations matter—presumably because any planes operating in the area would be part of the "unified command" set up in the United Nations. The next day the State Department took what seems to have been a step without precedent. It "formally . . . refused to acknowledge" the Soviet charge. The State Department's press officer, Michael J. McDermott, "told reporters that the Soviet protest was not officially before the United States government because of United States insistence that the alleged attack was a question for the United Nations to consider."

McDermott announced that the Defense Department and General MacArthur were notified, but that this was "more or less automatic," and he indicated that there would be no investigation. He explained that the Defense Department "would have been asked to investigate the charge if the United States had accepted the Soviet note." In Tokyo, the English-language and Japanese papers carried full stories on the Soviet protest, a sensational development which might easily portend war with Russia. The only reaction out of MacArthur Headquarters was a statement by the official spokesman for the Far East Air Forces saying that he "knew nothing of the Russian charges."

The incident was revealing. If the charge was untrue, the United States had everything to gain by indicting the USSR before the United Nations for falsehood. If the attack was accidental, a reply pointing this out would have allayed the fears felt at the United Nations that just such an incident might occur to widen the conflict. If MacArthur Headquarters was concerned about United Nations reactions, it might have felt a little diplomatic lying advisable. If it wanted to keep the war localized, Tokyo Headquarters would certainly have not acted with what may be termed effrontery. The message to the USSR was unmistakable: "Yeah, and whaddye gonna do about it?"

The USSR obviously was determined not to be provoked into war. The attack, according to its protest, occurred at 16 hours 17 minutes local time, or a little after 4 P.M.—in full daylight. Two American planes hedge-hopping sixty miles north of the Korean border could hardly have missed noticing the Soviet markings on the airdrome, and if they swung low enough to use their machine guns the Russians certainly saw the markings on their planes. It is impossible to believe that a military airdrome so close to a dangerous border and a key port like Vladivostok would be without anti-aircraft defenses. A plane strafing an airdrome with machine guns is close enough to be hit in return by machine-gun or even rifle fire from the ground. The note did not say there was fire in return or that the planes were shot down. The attacking American planes had been allowed to make off unharmed.

The refusal to accept the protest or investigate the complaint was arrogant. If Russia were not a dictatorship, if Stalin like Truman had a vocal domestic opposition to contend with, there might have been a war. Stalin seemed to swallow the affront. No note was sent the United Nations; to make a protest to the United Nations could have implied an acknowledgement of what the Russians had all along denied—the lawful international character of the "police action" in Korea. It would also have served to bring the USSR into direct frontal conflict with the United Nations in Korea. The Russians seemed for the moment to have chalked the incident off to profit and loss; the extraordinary denouement of this extraordinary incident was a speech by Vishinsky at Lake Success on October 13 asking the United States to give up the "get tough" policy and to return to wartime cooperation, pledging the Soviets to meet the United States "halfway."

But suppose the USSR had acted differently? Suppose fighting had broken out over the airdrome and spread? The United Nations would have found itself drawn toward war with the USSR through the medium of a "unified command" which operated in its name but was not under its control.

The Joint Chiefs of Staff in Washington did not always seem either well informed or wholly happy about their nominal subordinate in Tokyo. At Lake Success, United Nations officials knew as little about the orders MacArthur gave his air force as they did about the orders Stalin gave his. The way MacArthur and the State Department treated the charge of a provocative attack across a national frontier was as much an affront to the United Nations as to the Russians. The United Nations was suddenly given responsibility in a situation where it had no authority: the *fait accompli* in new guise.

A month earlier there had been a similar incident. The Soviet Union charged that a double-engined Soviet bomber "with neither bombing nor torpedo equipment" was attacked and destroyed by eleven fighters of the United States Air Force while on a training flight. The attack was alleged to have taken place while the bomber "was entering the limits of the naval base of Port Arthur, 140 kilometers from the Korean coast." Port Arthur is at the tip of Manchuria, north of the 38th Parallel and on the other side of what is called "Korea

Bay." At that time, too, the American representative in Moscow refused to accept a protest note on the ground that "the forces that shot down the bomber were operating under United Nations orders, and that therefore the United States could not accept the Soviet protest." At that time the American delegate at least reported to the United Nations Security Council, alleging that the bomber was shot down after it fired upon an air patrol "operating as part of United Nations forces in Korea."

On that occasion "chief interest" at Lake Success "was centered on the apparent fact that . . . the Soviet Union seemed to have no desire now to make a first-class international affair out of the shooting down of the bomber." Perhaps MacArthur Headquarters was emboldened by the mildness of the Soviet reaction. Austin said at the time of the first incident that it pointed up the urgency of taking steps to prevent the spread of the war in Korea. One of the places where such steps seemed to be needed was at MacArthur Headquarters in Tokyo. The incidents pointed up the danger of giving the Supreme Commander a blank check north of the 38th Parallel, even if the signature were left a little blurred as in the Assembly resolution of October 7. The bombing itself, however, was to have an unexpected sequel.

CHAPTER 20

★

A Sudden Change in Plans

RESIDENT TRUMAN, always a devoted family man, had planned to take time off the week of October 8 for a festive occasion. His sister, Miss Mary Jane Truman, was about to be "installed" as Worthy Grand Matron of the Grand Chapter of Missouri, Order of the Eastern Star, the highest honor the Missouri chapter could bestow. The White House announced on October 10 that Truman would fly to St. Louis to attend in person the ceremonies conferring the Worthy Grand Matronship on Miss Truman.

These pleasant plans, redolent of happier normal times in small-town Midwestern America, were suddenly interrupted by grave cares. On October 11, the President's press secretary, Charles Ross, himself an old-time Missouri newspaperman who had made a distinguished reputation on the crusading liberal *St. Louis Post-Dispatch*, called in the White House correspondents to announce that the President had decided to fly on from St. Louis after the ceremonies to meet MacArthur somewhere in the Pacific.

This decision remains something of a mystery. Why the sudden change in plans? The announcement said the President wished to discuss with the Supreme Commander "the final phase" of the United Nations action in Korea. The final phase would bring the forces of the "unified command" up to the Chinese and Russian borders, increasing the risk of wider intervention and an enlarged conflict. Perhaps the bombing of the

Soviet airdrome sixty miles north of the Korean border served to remind the White House how grave the risks were. The bombing was on the 8th, the Soviet note calling it to Washington's attention was on the 9th, Truman's decision to see MacArthur personally on "the final phase" of the war was announced on the 10th. The sequence may be significant.

The meeting with MacArthur took place on Sunday, October 15. On Thursday, October 19, Warren Austin, chief United States delegate to the United Nations, presented to the Security Council a note from General MacArthur admitting the attack on the Soviet airdrome, attributing it to "navigation error and poor judgment" in that the attack "was made without positive identification of the target," and saying that the commander of the Air Force group concerned had been relieved and disciplinary action initiated against the two pilots.

Why the commander of the group should have been relieved if the pilots were acting, not under orders, but in consequence of their own "navigation error and poor judgment," was not explained. The note went on to say that "in connection with the above report of the Commander in Chief of the United Nations Command, the United States Government desires to express publicly its regret that American forces under the United Nations Command should have been involved in this violation of the Soviet frontier." The note said that "as evidence of its good faith the United States Government is prepared to supply funds for payment of any damages determined by a United Nations Commission or other appropriate procedure to have been inflicted upon Soviet property." In Washington the Air Force made public the names of the aviation commander and of the two pilots.

This was not only an apology but a startling reversal of the position taken by the State Department, which had insisted that the matter must be taken up with the United Nations. No note had been sent to the United Nations by the Soviet government, and no request for an investigation made by the Security Council. The American note went so far as to say that it was prepared to pay damages determined by "a United Nations Commission or other appropriate procedure," which meant that if Moscow still refused to handle the matter through the United Nations the United States was prepared to accept determination of damages by some other "appropriate" agency. It looks as if the White House stepped in energetically to force a reversal of position by the State Department and to insist on an investigation and punitive action by Tokyo Headquarters. It would be interesting to know whether privately the Soviet government threatened countermeasures, or whether perhaps the British government—alarmed by the incident—made a strong private protest to the President, or whether Truman himself "hit the ceiling" over this incident. Certainly to have let it pass, as MacArthur Headquarters and the State Department seemed determined to do, would be to encourage MacArthur to let his bombers range again far across the border.

It may well be that the border bombing precipitated the meeting with MacArthur. Possibly such a meeting may have been discussed beforehand and the bombing provided dramatic evidence of the need for an "understanding" with MacArthur after the 38th Parallel had been crossed. It is interesting in this connection that the President's press secretary, Charles Ross, should have stressed the fact that "while the decision to hold the meeting" was "on the initiative of Mr. Truman" and "had been made rather suddenly" it was "not the result of any emergency." Why did Ross himself bring up the question of an "emergency"? Certainly the only concrete and visible event immediately after the conference which might possibly have resulted from it was this apology for the bombing of Soviet territory.

After dismissing the possibility of an emergency, Ross remarked that the President had never met MacArthur personally. This did not seem enough to explain the sudden flight 6000 miles to the center of the Pacific. The overwhelming impulse to personal acquaintance seemed a little sudden if there was no emergency involved, and "even certain high defense and other officials were taken by surprise when it [the trip] was announced." The reference to "certain high defense" officials made one suspect the Pentagon had not been consulted, and the cryptic reference to "other officials" made one wonder whether it was not also a complete surprise in parts of the State Department. Truman sometimes acted like one of those sultans in the *Thousand and One Nights* who are constantly trying to evade overbearing grand viziers and over-solicitous palace guards.

The President's own announcement was quite different in tone from the provocative manner in which MacArthur Headquarters and the State Department had handled the protest about the bombing. Truman insisted that the United States had no other aim in Korea than to carry out the "great purposes" of the United Nations. He said, as if repeating for emphasis, that "we have absolutely no interest in obtaining any special position for the United States in Korea, nor do we wish to retain bases or other military installations in that country." The United States would like to get its armed forces "out and back to their other duties" at the earliest possible moment. These statements were meant to be reassuring, though the Chinese may well have wondered in some bewilderment what elaborate game the President and the General were playing.

What was really in the President's mind may be indicated in the statement issued by Senator Millard F. Tydings of Maryland, one of the conservative Democrats in the peace wing of the party, applauding the decision for the meeting. Senator Tydings—campaigning for reelection—said, "We have lost too many lives in Korea keeping the peace to lose it only through some misstep."

There was almost a pleading note visible in the dispatches reporting the President's views and purposes on his way to see MacArthur. An important aim of the approaching meeting, said the *New York Times* correspondent accompanying the Presidential party, "is understood to be to try to convince General MacArthur that the Administration's policy relating to the Far East is the correct one and that he ought to support it, now that the Korean situation is about to pass from a military to a diplomatic phase." This is the very way an ephemeral elective occupant of the consular office in the last days of the

Roman Republic might have approached some ambitious proconsular Caesar abroad, already plotting to turn against the capital the armies with which he had been supplied to hold distant marches against barbarian hordes.

Truman was going out, not to command but to persuade. "The basic principle of policy that the Administration would like General MacArthur to support," the same dispatch en route explained, "is that Communism, especially in China, cannot be overcome by armed force." The wording is almost pathetic. This was what the Administration "would like General MacArthur to support." And if he did not choose to do so?

There was also reflected a certain bad conscience about the destruction wreaked in Korea, notably by bombings. "The Administration recognizes," it was said, "the effect that the war ravages have had on the Oriental peoples, and the exploitation of it by Communist propaganda." This seemed oddly out of accord with the picture of the war as painted for American public opinion. If the war was a "police action" against "aggression," a crusade to liberate Korea from Communist slavery, then one would expect the people of Korea to blame the damage on the Communist aggressors and accept its cost as necessary to their liberation. Perhaps some preferred the slavery to the liberation. Perhaps even some who hated Communism also felt that there had been much unnecessary destruction by American airpower, that the bombing squads had been a little too lighthearted in their "saturation" operations. Truman's original order of June 30 to permit MacArthur to bomb above the 38th Parallel was limited, according to the White House announcement that day, to "specific military targets in Northern Korea wherever militarily necessary." The evidence, as we shall see, suggests that this was quite generally and even gaily ignored, not only north of the Parallel but below it. Perhaps Truman, instinctively kindhearted and not without imagination, would urge MacArthur to be more careful.

Truman approached the Supreme Commander with high-flown flattering phrases. In announcing the visit, the President said MacArthur had been "carrying out his mission with the imagination, courage, and effectiveness which have marked his entire service as one of our greatest military leaders." From Tokyo came no answering response, neither expression of pleasure at an opportunity to make personal acquaintance with the President nor even some formal word of acknowledgment. "General MacArthur's headquarters," was the news from Tokyo, "maintained an official silence regarding the forthcoming weekend meeting between the United Nations Commander and President Truman." There was a cold stare between the lines.

If Truman was preparing to expound policy to General MacArthur, the General was apparently no less ready to "put the President straight." Officially Tokyo Headquarters was silent on the visit. Unofficially it indicated that the General would urge "a stronger, more unified policy in the Far East both by the United States and the United Nations to block Communist penetration of other parts of the Orient." The General was not a man to relinquish his views easily.

While Truman had already said that the United States wanted to get its troops out of Korea as soon as possible and sought no bases on the peninsula, a contrary view could be read in the advance briefings out of Tokyo Headquarters. While recognizing that the United Nations had "pledged that the country would not be militarily occupied" except as necessary for elections and unification, Tokyo Headquarters felt that "at least for some time North Korea presumably must be garrisoned" possibly with "token forces" from other nations "as well as by Americans." Tokyo Headquarters thought that "in some fashion protection of the new unified state against further aggression must be guaranteed." This seemed to imply military occupation for some time after unification, and perhaps permanent bases to protect the peninsula "against further aggression." And MacArthur's Headquarters added, "Just how this can be done is a subject on which General MacArthur's views almost certainly will be sought." One suspected that, sought or unsought, the views would be presented.

CHAPTER 21

★

Mystery at Wake Island

WHAT happened at Wake Island? None but a handful know. Little was told the reporters present at the time. Little was told the Senators investigating the MacArthur removal a year later.

"I see nothing in the Wake Island conference," Senator Hickenlooper told General Bradley when he appeared before the MacArthur inquiry, "that could not have been readily and speedily canvassed by simple routine reports. Therefore, my question is, What was the purpose of the Wake Island Conference? Why did the President travel 18,000 miles in order to have that conference?"

General Bradley's answer was threefold. He said the President "thought that a personal meeting with General MacArthur might be helpful in arriving at an understanding between the two of them." He said, "Also you will notice in the report from which you have read that there have been certain things omitted for security reasons." But this part of the answer did not impress the Senator.

> SENATOR HICKENLOOPER: I have read the deletions.
> GENERAL BRADLEY: I don't remember what they are.
> SENATOR HICKENLOOPER: So far as the deletions are concerned, they would add nothing to the serious import of this conference. There are certain statements there that, perhaps, for general purposes, could well be deleted, but there are only a few lines. . . . I just wanted to make this observation and ask why the Wake Island conference was

145

held, because the report gives me no aid in answering that question.

(Deleted)

What was hidden in that "deleted" remained unknown, but there was still the third part of General Bradley's answer to provide a clue. "There is nothing in this report," General Bradley said, "concerning that hour's conference between the two of them," that is, Truman and MacArthur. The secret of the Wake Island conference lies in what President Truman said to General MacArthur in the private conference they held on the island with no one else present.

There was extraordinarily little time spent on Wake Island. The President arrived at 6:30 A.M. and took off on his return trip at 11:35 A.M. The elapsed time was five hours and five minutes. Let us see how this time was split up.

General MacArthur had arrived the night before and was on hand to greet the President when he arrived. They then conferred privately without their advisers. The newspaper accounts at the time said this took about an hour, but Senator Hickenlooper, who had access to the classified material disclosed to the MacArthur inquiry, spoke of it as "their 45-minute conversation." The general conference covered by General Bradley's notes opened at 7:36 A.M. and ended at 9:12 A.M. "Informal discussions," the Bradley report ends, "continued for 1½ hours between various members of the two groups."

The hour-and-a-half general conference covered a great variety of subjects: Korean rehabilitation, the question of a new election in Korea, the possibility of Chinese and Soviet intervention, the problem of war crimes, and the question of a "Truman Doctrine" for the Pacific as suggested by Mac-Arthur. The only subject on which a real difference of opinion may be suspected was the one on which it was denied. Truman said there was no need to discuss Formosa. "General Mac-Arthur and I have talked fully about Formosa. There is no need to cover that subject again. The General and I are in complete agreement." Conversation was desultory, and the

Bradley report supports Senator Hickenlooper's observation. It may be noted that General Bradley did not take issue with the Senator. The General did not, as he might have, point to anything in the report to challenge Hickenlooper's view of the conference. He merely cited the deletions—and again did not challenge Hickenlooper when the latter said he saw nothing of any momentous importance in the deletions, either —and pointed to the fact that the report contained nothing on the private conference between Truman and MacArthur. It would seem that the real reason for the trip lay in that private conference.

There were, in fact, not two but three separate conferences that day on Wake Island, but no one on the MacArthur inquiry seems to have noticed the second one. The first conference took place between the President and the General alone, and according to Senator Hickenlooper lasted about forty-five minutes. If so, it ended about 7:15 A.M. The general conference with which Bradley's notes deal did not begin until 7:36 A.M. In the intervening twenty-one minutes another short conference was held.

What is the authority for saying that there was a short conference in between the private one and the general conference? The authority lies in the President's own formal statement as issued to the press: "After I had talked with General MacArthur privately," it says, "we met together with our advisers. These joint talks were then followed by technical consultations in which the following participated . . ." The list of those who participated in these "technical consultations" does not mention any of those "advisers" whom MacArthur brought with him from Tokyo except John J. Muccio, the United States Ambassador to Korea.

When MacArthur left Tokyo for Wake Island it was announced that he was accompanied by his "immediate personal staff, including Brigadier General Courtney Whitney," his chief political adviser. The announcement from Tokyo Headquarters said "also in the party" was Ambassador Muccio, adding pointedly that he accompanied MacArthur "at the request of Washington."

It would seem from this that neither General Whitney nor any other member of MacArthur's staff was invited to participate in the second part of the conference, though this was referred to in the President's statement as devoted to "technical consultations." Ordinarily it is for the "technical consultations" that an official's staff is required.

Those who participated in the "technical consultations" with Truman and MacArthur were John Muccio; the President's Special Assistant Averell Harriman; Secretary of the Army Frank Pace; General of the Army Omar Bradley, chairman of the United States Joint Chiefs of Staff; Admiral Arthur W. Radford, Commander in Chief of the Pacific Fleet; Assistant Secretary of State Dean Rusk; and Ambassador-at-Large Philip C. Jessup.

If these were merely "technical consultations," it seems odd that they would require the attention of the chairman of the Joint Chiefs of Staff, the Secretary of the Army, and the Commander in Chief of the Pacific Fleet, but did not merit the time of General Whitney or any other of MacArthur's staff. What if technicalities arose at these "technical consultations" which MacArthur, like any other top executive, was unable to answer? Could it be that the term "technical consultations" was here used for purposes of tact to cover the exclusion of General MacArthur's staff from the conference?

Could it be that General MacArthur naturally brought along his staff for the conference, that the President met with them cordially and then suggested that for the "technical consultations" he had in mind their presence would be unnecessary?

Certainly to take the term "technical consultations" here in its ordinary sense would lead to an absurdity. One would then have "joint talks" with "our advisers" on broad questions of policy, in which General Whitney and other members of MacArthur's staff participated, followed by "technical consultations" from which they were excluded. The Truman Administration, though notorious for its topsy-turvy moments, could hardly be that whimsical.

A discussion of less than two hours with so many key officials present is not one in which fundamental differences can be resolved, especially between two men each as stubborn in his own way as Truman and MacArthur. The private talk, the brevity of the general conference, the imposing character of the President's entourage, and the exclusion of MacArthur's staff from the "technical consultations," suggest a different explanation for the Wake Island meeting. It suggests that this was a conference at which the President informed MacArthur of certain decisions already reached in Washington, offered the General an opportunity to state and argue any objections, and sought thereby to pin MacArthur down.

The circumstances suggest that Truman, after several unhappy experiences in trying to get MacArthur to obey orders, chose by a face-to-face encounter of this kind to assure himself that MacArthur fully understood certain decisions and would abide by them. Truman's purpose in bringing so authoritative a group of officials with him would be to lend weight to his orders, in dealing with a willful and wily commander, and to support the President if MacArthur took advantage of the opportunity to engage in lengthy argument. At the same time, the preliminary private talk would make it easier for the Supreme Commander to acquiesce in certain decisions without too much loss of face.

It was noted at the time that "the conference was rushed to a conclusion several hours ahead of what had been the schedule." It would appear from this that MacArthur accepted the decisions without as much argument as was expected. When they were questioned by the press afterward, it was the President who seemed elated, the General who seemed sour. "Mr. President," Truman was asked, "how did things shape up?" The reply was, "Perfectly. I've never had a more satisfactory conference since I've been President." MacArthur declined all comments when asked about the conference. "All the comments," he said, "will have to come from the publicity man of the President." The President is not a vaudeville performer; he does not have a "publicity man." The reference was ill-mannered, and the tone surly.

"President Truman," the *New York Times* correspondent

accompanying him cabled from Pearl Harbor on the way back, "left Wake Island highly pleased with the results, like an insurance salesman who has at last signed up an important prospect while the latter appeared dubious over the extent of the coverage."

The coverage was to prove dubious enough, but the evidence suggests that it dealt not with broad questions of Pacific policy but with some immediate and pressing issue in connection with the Korean War.

The more I consider the Wake Island conference the more I am inclined to believe that the private talk between Truman and MacArthur was held primarily to discuss the bombing of Soviet territory. The bombing occurred on the 8th. The Soviet note calling it to Washington's attention was on the 9th. Truman's decision to see MacArthur personally was announced on the 10th. The Wake Island meeting took place on the 15th. Four days later Warren Austin presented the United Nations with a note from MacArthur admitting the attack on the Soviet airdrome and promising disciplinary action against those responsible. I believe that when the full facts are known the secret of the Wake Island conference will be found in this sequence of events. And I suspect there must have been something from the Russians tantamount to an ultimatum, to make Truman dash halfway across the Pacific to deal with this affair and to elicit an apology from MacArthur. Soviet territory was not bombed again. The Air Force confined its "mistakes" thenceforward to the Manchurian border.

PART IV

CORDIAL INVITATION—TO DISASTER

CHAPTER 22

★

Twin Dangers

THERE were two dangers in the approach of Mac-Arthur's troops to the Manchurian frontiers. One was military, the other political. The military danger was the possibility of a clash on the frontier between troops of the great powers. The political danger—for some people—was that no such clash would occur. The liquidation of the Korean War, which had been unsettling the Far East, would end military operations and clear the way for political decisions. In an atmosphere of peace, it would be difficult to keep Communist China out of the United Nations and prevent its recovery of Formosa. And MacArthur after Wake Island held "unalterably" to the view that Formosa must not be allowed to "fall into the hands of a potential enemy."

Here Chiang Kai-shek and MacArthur had a common outlook, while Rhee for the first time threatened to diverge from them. The intervention of Communist China in Korea could be utilized in the United States to raise Chiang from an inconvenient dependent to a full ally, while the need to hold Formosa as an American base would be made undeniable by the logic of war. For Rhee, on the contrary, intervention would mean the loss of Korea again. And when the Chinese—as we shall see—did intervene, "some South Korean officials were suggesting," the *New York Times* noted cryptically on November 5 in its weekly news summary, "a deal with Peiping

—withdrawal of Chinese troops in return for a guarantee of continued power" from the Yalu dams.

Only those with some knowledge of American advertising and publicity methods can fully appreciate the Korean War. It was a war fought with one eye on the headlines. Tokyo Headquarters had something to "sell." What it was trying to "sell" was the idea that the Korean War was not and could not be "localized." In accord with this strategy, every bit of evidence which might show, or be made to show, Chinese or Russian intervention was highlighted and exaggerated *except* during one short period. In that period, the three weeks after the Wake Island meeting, when Chinese military intervention actually began, every effort was made by Tokyo Headquarters to discount and disparage reports of this intervention, *as if to avoid new directives from Washington to prevent a large-scale clash.*

The sequence of events is most revealing. On October 20 MacArthur's troops captured the North Korean capital of Pyongyang. MacArthur, personally directing a sensational paratroop jump to cut off the escape route of its fleeing defenders, declared the Korean War was "definitely" coming to an end. At the same time, on the other side of the peninsula, the First Marine Division had moved into the port of Wonsan and MacArthur had "ordered the South Korean divisions under his command to push for the Manchurian border as fast as they could go."

It did indeed look as if the Korean War was over. On October 21 Hanson Baldwin reported from Wonsan: "There are increasing evidences that the Russians have cut their losses in Korea and are pulling out altogether. The flow of traffic down the east coast highway from Vladivostok apparently has been halted altogether and the Russian advisers and technicians, who were present in fairly large numbers here at Wonsan and elsewhere, apparently have fled over the border after attempts to destroy or conceal the supplies and material they could not evacuate."

The Chinese Reds also appeared to be ready to accept the North Korean defeat in Korea and to concentrate on their main interest, Formosa. On October 24 a Peking radio broadcast said Chinese Premier Chou En-lai had asked Trygve Lie to make arrangements for a Peking delegation to attend Security Council talks on Formosa. "This," the United Press reported from Tokyo, "was a complete about-face for General Chou." A week earlier the Peking radio said the Premier had rejected an invitation to take part in that discussion. It looked as if peace might be about to break out.

That there were increased concentrations of Chinese troops in Manchuria near the Korean frontier was well known. Movements toward that frontier had been reported, as we have seen, from Hong Kong and elsewhere. Hanson Baldwin's dispatch from Wonsan on the 21st, from which we have just quoted, said there were believed to be 250,000 Chinese Communist troops massed near the frontier, with another 200,000 elsewhere in Manchuria, and that while the number of planes at their disposal was unknown it might, including Russian planes at Port Arthur and Dairen, amount to more than 3000.

"The increased concentration of some of these planes and troops near Korea," Baldwin cabled, "although it is being carefully watched, is not viewed too seriously. . . . With South Korean troops moving steadily northward up the east coast and with Pyongyang, the North Korean capital, in United Nations hands, it is considered natural for the Chinese Communists to strengthen the frontier."

"However," Baldwin added, "it is possible that the Communists' concept of defense might include an advance south of the Korean frontier for a limited distance to set up a buffer zone between Manchuria and Korea. . . . The Chinese Communists and perhaps the Russians too may be sensitive about the Yalu River power complex, which supplies not only North Korea but parts of Manchuria, including Port Arthur and Dairen, with power. The grids and distribution system are believed to be on the North Korean side of the frontier."

The 38th Parallel had been crossed on the 7th of October by non-Korean forces without provoking Chinese intervention. It appeared that Peking had abandoned North Korea and decided to reverse itself and take part in United Nations discussions on Formosa but had massed troops to protect its frontier. Its vital interests in the power facilities of the Yalu border were well understood, and the American government seemed to be doing all in its power, too, to avoid a clash. On October 24 a spokesman for the United States First Corps in Korea announced that "foreign troops," that is, non-South-Korean troops in the peninsula, "would halt forty miles south of the Manchurian border in their pursuit of the shattered North Korean Communist army."

United States and British troops were then still about sixty miles from the border, while South Koreans were already within thirty miles of it. The "directive," said a cable from the *New York Times* correspondent in Tokyo, would not cover the South Koreans but meant that "United States, British, and other non-Korean forces will refrain from invading the strip of 'buffer territory' between the international boundary and the lands wrested from Communist control." The same dispatch also announced the establishment of a new "bomb line" to protect advancing South Koreans. But this did not mean that there would be bombing "directly along the Yalu River where a series of power plants provide electric current both for Manchuria and North Korea, and might be considered vital to the interest of the Chinese Communist government, the Air Force spokesman emphasized."

Something else had happened in North Korea, which was not made known until later—when its significance was distorted. When the forty-mile buffer zone was announced by the United States First Corps in Korea, troops had already been sent southward across the border by the Chinese Reds to protect the dams. These are the facts: On October 16 "the 370th Regiment of the 124th Division of the Chinese Communist Forty-Second Army, consisting of approximately 2500 troops," crossed the Yalu River, the frontier between China and Korea, "and proceeded to the area of Chosan (Changjin) and Fusan (Pujon) dams in North Korea."

On October 20 "a Chinese Communist task force known as the 'Fifty-sixth' unit consisting of approximately 5000 troops" crossed the Yalu frontier "and deployed to positions in Korea south of the Suiho dam." These troop dispositions showed the intention of the Chinese Reds to protect the dams. They also showed the danger of a clash if UN troops, especially American or British troops, were sent into the area.

The buffer zone order was announced by the spokesman for the United States First Corps in Korea on October 24. Two days later President Truman told his press conference in Washington that "it was his understanding that only South Korean troops would occupy the north frontier of Korea in the final drive of the war there." In reply to questions he announced that this "would apply to the entire northern border."

That same day, October 26, the South Koreans finally reached the Yalu frontier. And, that same day, the *New York Times* man cabled from Tokyo: "General Douglas MacArthur's headquarters for the first time formally denied repeated reports that United Nations forces would halt south of the Chinese Communist line and establish 'buffer territory' along the Yalu River in an attempt to avoid possible international incidents. A spokesman told correspondents, 'The mission of the United Nations is to clear Korea.' This, a spokesman asserted, he had been 'authorized to state'—presumably by General MacArthur."

I believe that this was a clear act of insubordination on MacArthur's part. Perhaps MacArthur gambled on the hope that with the Congressional elections less than two weeks away on November 7 the President would hesitate to make an issue of it. If so, the gamble proved correct. MacArthur got away with it. If MacArthur was also gambling that penetration of the buffer zone by non-Korean troops would be sure to provoke Chinese intervention, he won that gamble, too.

The day after MacArthur Headquarters made clear its intention to defy the President, the news from the battlefield was that "enemy resistance for the first time in several days included large organized bodies of troops, artillery, and mortar fire." "The most dangerous situation came around Onjong, where the South Koreans had been thrusting in that area toward the Yalu River's great Supung dam that provides electric power not only for North Korea but for Mukden and Dairen—a matter of considerable importance to both Manchurian and Soviet industry."

Were these the Chinese Communist troops deployed to protect the dams? A radio message from the Second Regiment of the South Korean Sixth Division on October 26 said it had been surrounded by three Chinese Communist battalions near Onjong, but a spokesman for the United States Eighth Army "ridiculed" these reports in a briefing on October 28.

"The Eighth Army spokesman," said a cable datelined *"With U.S. Forces, Korea"* in the *New York Times* that day, "said investigation showed the report was based on the stories of two prisoners of war 'each of whom told six different stories, adding up to twelve stories, which added up to nothing.' "

Were these prisoners Koreans or Chinese? The dispatch did not say, but it did go on to report that the Eighth Army spokesman "pointed out that individual Chinese were in the North Korean Army and occasional ones had been taken prisoner as far south as the Pusan front two months ago." A few weeks earlier MacArthur Headquarters would not have allowed the possibility of "individual" Chinese in the North Korean forces to be dismissed so lightly.

Were there only "individual" Chinese fighting in North Korea at that time? Then the dispatch quietly made an amazing statement: "The Army concedes the possibility that a token force of Chinese Communists, perhaps a regiment, may be somewhere in North Korea but discounts the possibility that any large force from across the Manchurian border is now in action." Why was the possibility of "a token force . . . perhaps a regiment" conceded?

This raises two further questions, which we shall consider seriatim. The first is, was this fact "conceded" because Army intelligence already knew of those crossings? The second is, if military intelligence already knew of those crossings, why did it say nothing about them, choosing instead to ridicule reports of Chinese intervention?

The authority for the statement on the border crossings of October 16 and October 20 is General MacArthur himself. The source is the special report he sent the Security Council on November 6, 1950, the text of which was published in the *New York Times* of November 7, 1950.

The report does not say when this information became known to American military intelligence—much less why it was held back until November 6. But the wording of the paragraph on the first crossing, that of October 16, would seem to indicate that it became known immediately. This is how it reads: "The 370th Regiment of the 124th Division of the Chinese Communist Forty-second Army, consisting of approximately 2500 troops . . . proceeded to the area of Chosen (Changjin) and Fusan (Pujon) dams in North Korea . . . [and] came in contact with United Nations forces approximately forty miles north of Hamhung." It does not say they clashed. It merely says they "came in contact." If United Nations forces came in contact with Chinese Communist troops in the area of these dams, they must have notified Headquarters at once. Apparently they were not ordered to advance and fight, to repel the invaders or capture the dam area. Why not? Was there a kind of truce at the point in pursuance of earlier directives?

In any case that first crossing was on the 16th. Ten days later MacArthur made it clear that, despite the President's views and earlier announcement of a "buffer zone," he intended to send not only South Korean but other troops all the way to the Yalu frontier. Was he still ignorant of the fact that his troops were already "in contact" with Chinese Communist troops who had crossed the Yalu ten days earlier and proceeded to the area of the Changjin and Pujon dams? Was he still ignorant of the fact that four days later another Chinese Communist task force had crossed the Yalu and been "deployed" (the word is his) south of the Suiho dam?

The MacArthur report of November 6 to the Security Council is also significantly silent as to when he learned about the border crossing of the 20th. Beyond what we have already quoted, all it said about this task force was that "a captured Chinese Communist soldier of this task force states that his group was organized out of the regular Chinese Communist Fortieth Army stationed at Antung, Manchuria." When was he captured? How was he captured? The report does not say there was any clash between this task force and MacArthur's forces, yet they must have been pretty close to take a prisoner from the Chinese Communists. Was he a scout? Was there an unofficial truce at that point, too?

We do not know. What we do know from the MacArthur report is that there was almost immediate "contact" with the first force and that a soldier had been taken prisoner from the second. We also know MacArthur did not lack aerial reconnaissance in the area; unlike the bombing flights, reconnaissance flights were officially permitted all the way to the border. It is almost impossible to believe that by October 26 MacArthur Headquarters did not know of the second border crossing six days before. That MacArthur's intelligence knew would explain why the Eighth Army spokesman on October 28 gratuitously "conceded" the possibility of "a token force . . . perhaps a regiment" of Chinese Communists below the border.

If military intelligence already knew of these crossings, why would it keep silent and allow a military spokesman instead to "ridicule" reports of intervention? The answer may be that if the crossing of the border by Chinese Communist troops to defend the dam areas had been publicized, public opinion would have been alerted to the danger of permitting the buffer zone to be invaded even by South Korean troops—a danger still greater if the troops were American and British.

The day the Eighth Army spokesman ridiculed reports that Chinese Communist troops were in Korea, the day's war roundup from Tokyo said that United States Marines on the east coast, after landing behind South Korean lines, were preparing to move forward. "Their first destination," the dispatch said, "was understood to be the Hamhung-Hungnam area, from where they could strike up the coast toward the Soviet border or through the mountains to the headwaters of the Yalu River." The Marines, in other words, were headed straight for trouble, either on the Soviet or the Chinese border.

At the same time there was evidence of some squirming at MacArthur Headquarters, perhaps under the impact of alarmed protests from Washington on the buffer zone question.

The confusion and equivocation were apparent when Parrott cabled the *New York Times* that day from Tokyo that "Meanwhile, a somewhat complex situation has arisen over President Truman's declaration that the Yalu frontier would be occupied by South Koreans, not Americans, coupled with statements by responsible officers here that the mission of the United Nations is to clear North Korea, and United States divisions are free to advance wherever the tactical situation demands."

This reference to "tactical" considerations, as an excuse for strategic decisions with basic political implications, was typical of MacArthur Headquarters whenever the 38th Parallel or any other line on which to halt short of the frontiers was suggested. The possible "tactical" need to repulse an enemy foray became an excuse for large-scale advances in contravention of political decisions.

The kind of rearguard excuses which were passing over the "telecon" from Tokyo Headquarters to the Pentagon may also have been reflected in what Parrott added. "Speculation is," he cabled, "that the plan was to permit the South Koreans and other United Nations troops to advance to the border by themselves, supported only by United States planes, guns, and armor, *if they proved able to do so.*" (Italics added.) That sounded as if Tokyo Headquarters was hedging by admitting that the South Koreans were supposed to advance while the American troops held back but insisting that a loophole had been left for aid by American ground forces "if necessary." Unlike the camel and the needle's eye, whole American divisions seemed to thread with ease through loopholes of this kind under MacArthur's expert hand.

"In any case," Parrott concluded, "it was indicated the border zone would be 'occupied' by South Koreans after hostilities end." Was this Tokyo Headquarters' concession to the Pentagon? It slyly dodged the one main point, which was not who would occupy the border zone but how to avoid clashes between the troops of the great powers in the closing days of the war.

While the argument went on, the advance of American,

British, and Australian forces into the border area continued. MacArthur Headquarters on October 29 "continued to minimize reports from the South Korean Army that 40,000 Chinese Communist troops had crossed the border to join in the defense of the perimeter along the Yalu River, with its important hydroelectric plants serving both North Korea and the Sino-Soviet Mukden-Dairen industrial complex."

That day, however, MacArthur Headquarters started to change its tune a bit. "A spokesman for the intelligence section of General Douglas MacArthur's headquarters asserted," the same dispatch went on, "that the United Nations Command's G-2 was not in a position either to confirm or deny the presence on the front of some Chinese soldiers." Were the facts in the front lines becoming too obvious?

Headquarters was still anxious to soft-pedal talk of Chinese intervention. "It was the headquarters belief," the cable continued, "that these will prove to be more Manchurian-bred Koreans, like the men of the two Korean divisions of the Chinese Communist Army, which were transferred to the North Korean Red regime after the Chinese Civil War. The situation, the spokesman said, was 'not alarming.' "

The reader will note how flexibly these two Korean divisions of the Chinese Communist Army were "deployed" by MacArthur Headquarters. Not many weeks earlier, as we have seen, they were marched out as evidence of Chinese Communist intervention. Now they are used in a quick flanking action against reports of such intervention. This may not be in accord with Clausewitz, but it was smart by Batten, Barton, Durstine & Osborn standards. It was slick "public relations."

When front-line dispatches reported that "Chinese and North Korean elements" were trying to block the advance of the Eighth Army's First Division to the border, Lieutenant General Walton Walker, the Army's commander, "declined comment but he appeared inclined to doubt that the capture of a few Chinese soldiers in the border area had great significance."

Never were Army officers so anxious to deny what only a few weeks earlier they had been striving to prove. "Officers of

the United States Eighth Army in Korea," a cable from Tokyo
reported, "said that as far as verified information was concerned, the United Nations forces were still in contact only
with the North Korean army. A few allegedly Chinese prisoners, who were taken near Unsan last week, the spokesman said,
told several conflicting stories regarding their presence in
Korea, and there certainly has been 'no great influx' of
Chinese soldiers across the Yalu River."

The term *Chinese* was even put in quotation marks in reports emanating from these briefings, as if to indicate its
dubious worth. "The tendency," the cable went on, "was
to regard the 'Chinese' captured on the front as Koreans from
the border zone where—on both sides of the river—the Korean-
Chinese population is strongly intermixed and often bi-
lingual."

While the Peking radio on October 29 termed the Mac-
Arthur advance to the frontiers a threat to Manchuria and
called on the Chinese people to support the Korean people
against "American imperialism," Headquarters still insisted
on the 30th that "hardening resistance" and the appearance
of "Soviet-made armor, in somewhat larger numbers than a
week ago" merely indicated that the North Koreans had
pulled together their remaining weapons for "a last stand,"
not that "any large-scale reinforcements had been received
from Communist China." By that time the contrast between
what the front lines knew and what Headquarters admitted
must have been so wide that if MacArthur had been a New
Dealer instead of a right-wing darling, he would have been
suspected of covering up for the Reds.

On October 31, MacArthur Headquarters began at last to
concede that Chinese Communists were fighting in Korea. A
spokesman for the Tenth Army Corps in Tokyo that day identified as soldiers of the Chinese Red Army a force which had
cut the communications of South Korean Capital Division advance guards "pushing in from the east coast toward Pujon
reservoir." He said unofficial reports indicated that the Chinese
Communists "were at least in regimental strength and possibly
numbered as much as one division."

This first tentative admission followed "repeated assertions by South Korean Army leaders that their men for several days had been facing elements of the Chinese Fortieth Corps, which supposedly had been concentrated along the Yalu River."

Correspondents in Tokyo began to notice offstage rumblings which sounded remarkably like preparations to exploit this intervention. From Tokyo that day the *New York Times* correspondent reported, "Some sources here believed that this stiffening resistance and the reports of a Chinese counteroffensive indicated a breakdown in the plan to permit South Koreans and possibly other non-American United Nations troops to drive to the Manchurian border while United States forces remained outside some 'buffer area' south of the Yalu."

In Washington, the State Department's press spokesman, Michael McDermott, said with premature clairvoyance that if the reports of Chinese units in Korea should be proved "the matter would be one for the United Nations," and "probably would result in a report from General Douglas MacArthur to the world organization." McDermott was a little ahead of schedule.

General MacArthur still seemed reluctant to acknowledge the fact of Chinese intervention. *The longer the fighting continued, the harder it would be to order him to disengage his troops and withdraw.* A United States or United Nations order to disengage and withdraw would have set the stage for peace negotiations. On the other hand, a gallant military order by MacArthur himself for his troops to withdraw before this new onslaught would set the stage for a demand that China be labeled the aggressor.

On November 1 the battle report from Tokyo based on that day's military briefing said: "The Communists were fighting with the assistance of Russian-made weapons and Chinese troops to force the United Nations to wage a costly, difficult campaign in the unmapped snow-covered hills." But the Headquarters spokesman insisted it "always" had been known that North Koreans "throughout the war" had received from Manchuria "men trained in the Chinese Communist forces" and "General MacArthur's intelligence section frankly [*sic*] does not know whether or not actual Chinese

Army units—as such [*sic*]—have been committed to the Korean War, the spokesman continued."

The spokesman insisted that the evidence was still "insufficient to confirm that Chinese Communist forces in Chinese Army organizations under the direction either of Chinese or North Korean general headquarters were taking part in the conflict." Ten Chinese soldiers had been captured in combat two days before, and some had already been flown back to Seoul for questioning. "An intelligence officer insisted there was no deliberate attempt to withhold information on this touchy political subject but he said he did not know," the same dispatch reported, "in what language the prisoners were being interrogated." Why was the presence of Chinese soldiers in Korea suddenly a "touchy" subject at Tokyo Headquarters?

The evaluation of the extent of Chinese intervention, Tokyo Headquarters insisted on November 1, must come from the commander in the field. But while MacArthur Headquarters was being so coy on the subject, a delayed dispatch dated two days earlier but published the same day in New York from the *New York Times* man at Tenth Corps Headquarters reported "the first official confirmation that a large force of Chinese as such was fighting against the UN forces in Korea." Confirmation, it said, came from Major General Edward M. Almond's Headquarters after a day filled with reports of heavy Red Chinese movements into Korea, and concluded, "Cheerful hopes that the war was virtually over were squelched here this evening." It would be interesting to know why this dispatch was delayed two days in transmission, and whether MacArthur Headquarters on November 1 was still as ignorant as it claimed to be of a fact which Tenth Corps Headquarters had officially confirmed two days earlier.

On November 1, as heavy fighting spread in the border regions, jet-propelled fighter planes made their first appearance in the air on the Communist side, as did a new type of heavy rocket fired from launchers on the ground. There were grave indications of a readiness on the Chinese and Soviet side for a showdown as MacArthur's forces approached the frontiers. But on November 2, while a corps spokesman during the daily Tokyo briefing officially admitted that "Chinese troops" were in action, he added, "We don't know whether they represent the Chinese government."

Such delicacy was unusual. Perhaps one reason for it was alarm in Washington. There were indications that a halt might be ordered. The only United Nations gains on the ground November 1 were made by the Twenty-Fourth Division. But it halted, and "reports from the front said orders to suspend the advance had come from Headquarters of the United States Eighth Army, a statement that was not confirmed there, however." On November 2 there were "unconfirmed reports" again in Tokyo "that the United Nations forces would not thrust to the Chinese border, but would leave a 'buffer' territory between them and the sensitive international frontier."

Whatever might have been brewing over the "telecon" between Washington and Tokyo on November 2, an attack on a particularly sensitive spot was launched next day. A Tenth Corps spokesman said United States Marines started a general attack November 3 "toward the Changjin reservoir." It was the Tenth Corps Headquarters which had first officially confirmed the entrance of Chinese forces into the Korean War. The day before the attack opened "toward the Changjin reservoir," Major General Edward M. Almond, the Corps commander, denied to correspondents that any limit had been put on the United Nations forces, and said they would "fight their way all the way to the frontier."

It was this same front-line dispatch dated November 2 which first disclosed the October 16 crossing. The dispatch cited General Almond himself as authority for saying that a regiment had crossed the Yalu at that time, but said his Headquarters "still does not choose to name the unit or either confirm or deny that there are more Chinese in the area." "Korean officers and United States advisers who are considered to be in a position to know," the dispatch continued, "say that the Chinese are of the 370th Regiment of the 124th Division of the 42nd Corps of the Chinese Communist Eighth Route Army. The South Koreans feel certain that the whole corps has been assigned to duty in Northern Korea."

Under the circumstances, the launching of a general attack

by American forces on Changjin reservoir on November 3 can only be regarded as a deliberate invitation to a fight with the Chinese Communists. The meagerness of the information squeezed out of Headquarters would seem to indicate that the General did not want the brazenness of his challenge understood by public opinion at home. If the Chinese had sent troops in to guard the reservoirs, that was a good reason for staying away from those areas; control of them was not necessary to complete the victory in Korea.

The effort to hide the dangerous potentialities in the situation reached its climax in the attitude of an Air Force spokesman who was questioned on November 3 about the jet fighters which had suddenly made their appearance. The spokesman insisted there were still air strips left on the Korean side which could handle fighter aircraft "possibly even jets." Although the existence of neighboring air strips on the Manchurian side was well known, "Headquarters stuck to the thesis that 'the war exists in Korea' and an Air Force spokesman declined to discuss the Manchurian air strips."

Fighting increased in intensity, but MacArthur Headquarters was still reluctant to admit Chinese intervention. Of all the weird statistics emanating from MacArthur Headquarters none was stranger than its estimate of November 4 as to the size of the North Korean forces. Six days earlier, on October 30, "a spokesman for General MacArthur" said in Tokyo that the North Korean Army had suffered 460,000 casualties in dead, wounded, and captured, and had only 37,000 men left, including guerrillas. On November 4, a spokesman at MacArthur Headquarters said the North Koreans "now had at least elements of twelve divisions and five independent brigades in the northern area." The *New York Times* correspondent noted that at the peak of North Korea's war effort it had only thirteen divisions in the field, and added that the enemy "apparently had an almost equal number of organizations again available for action, although some of the present 'divisions' probably numbered only a few thousand men."

MacArthur Headquarters was still speaking only of "North Koreans." It acknowledged that a major battle was under way in the western area and that the UN position was "uncomfortable" but denied that the situation was "critical." The official spokesman "insisted that the United States and South Korean forces still were on the strategical offensive with the enemy making tactical counterattacks."

MacArthur might be "recruiting" his North Koreans rather rapidly—to avoid a direct admission of Chinese intervention—but his friend Chiang on Formosa was not deceived. "Whatever Chinese Communist involvement in Korea may mean to the rest of the world," said a cable from Formosa on November 4, "to Nationalist China it is held to mean new hope and restored confidence. . . . Prices disastrously high during the summer because of doubts over Formosa's status, have swung downward sharply in the last four days. Currency is moving upward against gold. . . . Many persons feel there is hardly any doubt that Nationalist China now will be admitted as a full partner with the democracies opposing Communism."

At Lake Success on November 4 it became known that the United States was considering the possibility of "accusing Communist China of participation in the Korean War." In London the Foreign Office was reported alarmed over the extent of the intervention. On November 5 the Associated Press from Seoul was estimating the number of Chinese troops in Korea at 75,000, and the *New York Times* from Tokyo was talking of estimates of 50,000.

Behind a kind of smoke screen of denials, evasions, and underestimates from Tokyo, full-scale fighting was under way. On November 5 the American government was "reported tonight to be considering telling Communist China that power plants on the North Korean-Manchurian border would be attacked and destroyed if more Red troops were sent against the United Nations forces in Korea."

And the next morning, November 6, General Douglas MacArthur finally let loose with his celebrated special communiqué accusing the Communists of committing "one of the most offensive acts of international lawlessness of historic record" by intervening in Korea from their "privileged sanctuary" across the border. The fat was in the fire.

CHAPTER 23

★

Mr. Truman Keeps Cool

THE reactions of the American government were curiously cool. In Kansas City the President said "there was nothing to be gained by commenting at this time on the enlarging role of Communist Chinese forces in the Korean War." In Washington the only reaction to the MacArthur statement at the State and Defense Departments was "no comment." At Lake Success a spokesman for the American delegation "expressed doubts that a complaint to the United Nations against the Peiping Government would be made simply on the basis of the information contained in General MacArthur's communication." This reserved attitude made it appear likely that the earlier report from Lake Success of a possible American complaint to the Security Council and the report from Washington of a threat to bomb the power dams were trial balloons sent up by officials who shared the views of General MacArthur, rather than actions seriously contemplated by the Truman Administration.

The MacArthur communiqué of November 6 spoke of the intervention by "alien Communist forces across the Yalu River," when the war in Korea itself seemed almost over, as "a possible trap . . . surreptitiously laid, calculated to encompass the destruction of the United Nations forces . . ." Perhaps one reason Washington was so unexcited by MacArthur's alarms was that he had violated its directives in sending American and British as well as South Korean troops into the border area, despite the knowledge that both the Chinese and the Russians were concerned about the dams and power facilities along the Yalu. Perhaps Washington, knowing MacArthur's views, felt that he had been deliberately looking for trouble. If a trap had been laid by the Chinese Communists, the way to avoid it was easy enough. It was to send only South Koreans into the border area, in accordance with the original order, and to keep even the South Koreans away from the power facilities where Chinese troops were stationed. To disparage the possibility of Chinese intervention after military intelligence already knew of the border crossing, to order United States and British troops to attack areas in which Chinese troops were already known to be deployed—as General Almond did on November 4—*was not to fall into a trap, but to arrange one.*

In case anyone failed to get the point of MacArthur's heavy reference to "the privileged sanctuary" from which this "new and fresh army . . . faces us," backed by reserves and supplies "within easy reach to the enemy but beyond the limits of our present sphere of military action," MacArthur Headquarters helpfully spelled it out for the correspondents at the briefing that day. By this "he indicated," cabled the *New York Times* correspondent in Tokyo, that this massing of reserves "in presumably neutral territory . . . might not forever command immunity." MacArthur was ready to extend the war into China.

The United Nations would be expected to do its share in this wider conflict. MacArthur Headquarters that day, while "calm and confident," was talking in terms of 300,000 Chinese Communist troops immediately available in Manchuria and another 300,000 "either in Manchuria or North China." The Associated Press reporting after the briefing said the Chinese Reds "thus have the potentiality of vastly outnumbering the present United Nations forces in Korea—if they intend to commit the entire force."

What followed in the dispatch accurately foreshadowed what was soon to happen in the war. "Militarily," the Associated Press continued, "the situation could become a greatly expanded version of the first days of the Korean War. That is, there would be a slow fighting United Nations' retreat back down the peninsula, brought about mainly by flanking and encirclement made possible by numerically superior Communist forces." Clearly MacArthur Headquarters already assumed the commitment of overwhelming force and a steady retreat; we shall see that the retreat kept rolling on even when the numerically overwhelming forces, if ever in the field, had long since disappeared. "Such action," the dispatch continued, "on the part of the Chinese Reds could touch off a big war." This is what Chiang Kai-shek had been hoping for; it would also suit the temporarily silenced advocates of a preventive war.

The possibility of a general war, the Associated Press said, was what MacArthur apparently meant by the sentence, "Whether and to what extent these reserves will be moved forward to reinforce units now committed remains to be seen and is a matter of the gravest international significance." The Associated Press added cryptically, "The key word is 'international.' " More plainly stated: if the situation produced a war, the war—in American slang—would be the UN's "baby."

Perhaps one reason that MacArthur hesitated so long to make an issue of Chinese intervention is that the Chinese still had not committed any sizable body of troops to North Korea. This would explain why MacArthur Headquarters on November 6 was talking of the number of Chinese available in Manchuria and of what would happen if they were committed to battle in North Korea. This would also explain the dispatch from Lake Success published the same day discounting an American complaint to the United Nations: "The United States, it has been reported, is considering the possibility of filing such charges if they are borne out by military information received. Thus far, however, it is felt that insufficient data have been available."

The data, when supplied later the same day by MacArthur, made big headlines: "U.S. BIDS U.N. ACT ON CHINESE IN KOREA AFTER MACARTHUR IDENTIFIES RED UNITS. . . ." The actual data, however, were not impressive. This may be the reason why MacArthur on November 6 issued two special communiqués instead of one. The first, issued in time for the American morning papers of the same day, contained the dramatic news of how "alien Communists" operating from their "privileged sanctuary" had committed "one of the most offensive acts of international lawlessness of historic record." The second communiqué, issued later that day in Tokyo and published in the next day's morning papers in America, gave the evidence. Had the two been combined in one, as would have been natural, the character of the evidence would have considerably deflated the sensationalism of the general charges. The general charges created the atmosphere. The evidence next day provided second-day supporting headlines. Few had time to examine the character of MacArthur's information.

The text may be found in the *New York Times* of November 7, in the international edition as well as the New York edition, and the reader will want to look at the report for himself. It presents "in summary form, . . . confirmed intelligence reports . . . that forces other than Korean are resisting our efforts to carry out the resolutions of the United Nations" and that United Nations forces "are presently in hostile contact with Chinese Communist military units deployed for action" against them.

Twelve specific supporting incidents are cited, lettered *A* to *L* inclusive. Five of these deal with occasions when there was antiaircraft fire from the Manchurian side of the Yalu against American bombers operating on the Korean side of the river. Two of these incidents dated back to August, weeks before MacArthur's forces had crossed the 38th Parallel, much less approached the frontiers. MacArthur cited fifty bursts of antiaircraft fire on August 22 against an RB-29 Radar Bomber flying "over Korea in the vicinity of Suiho (Supung) reservoir." On August 24, MacArthur cited forty bursts of antiaircraft fire against an RB-29 flying "over Korea in the vicinity of Sinuiju." The first bomber was flying at 7000 feet, the second at 10,000 feet. Neither was damaged.

These two incidents, which occurred at the time the United Nations forces were still fighting inside the Pusan beachhead, are so irrelevant to the charge of Chinese military intervention in late October and November as to make one suspect that

MacArthur must have been hard put indeed for proof. One wonders whether there were not many other instances of such antiaircraft bursts along the border in August, perhaps as legitimate warning to MacArthur's bombers to keep away. If one checks back over that period one will find that on August 28 the Chinese government sent the United States government a formal note protesting five different violations of the Manchurian frontier by American bombers on August 27, including two reconnaissance flights by B-29s and three strafing attacks by F-51s. This note was rejected by the State Department as United Nations, rather than United States, business. The attack was denied by the Air Force Headquarters in Tokyo, but later admitted by Washington in a note to the United Nations on October 3. One may legitimately wonder whether those two bombers on August 22 and August 24 were on the Korean side of the border. One may also see that gunners manning the antiaircraft on the frontier were not acting too unnaturally if they let loose some bursts at approaching aircraft.

The third incident cited by MacArthur occurred on October 15, when antiaircraft from the Manchurian side was alleged to have been aimed at "four F-51s flying near Sinuiju Airfield on the Korean side." One was shot down. There is no mention in the Air Force communiqués of that day of any such flight on the Korean side of the border. If Chinese antiaircraft shot down an F-51 on the Korean side, why was no protest made? Why was the incident kept a secret until it turned up in an entirely different context in the report of November 6? The answer may be supplied by the fact that less than two weeks before, as the aftermath of the October 3 note admitting the August 27 raid, "United States bombers were under orders not to get within thirty miles of Manchuria." The incident, which occurred the day MacArthur was meeting with Truman on Wake Island, would have been most embarrassing to the Supreme Commander if it had become known at the time. Ditto for the fourth antiaircraft incident cited by MacArthur: fifteen bursts of heavy antiaircraft fire on October 17 against an RB-29 flying at 10,000 feet over Sinuiju. This time no damage was done.

The fifth case of antiaircraft fire was on November 1 against thirteen F-80s in the vicinity of Sinuiju. One plane was shot down. Again, there is no mention either of the flight or of the lost plane in the communiqué issued on that day's military activity. If the plane was on the Korean side, why was no protest made? Could it be that plane raids in that area were still interdicted and that the raid was a violation of orders? It is interesting to notice that of the five cases of antiaircraft fire cited, all but the first occurred over Sinuiju, and the last three occurred there *after* the order early in October to keep thirty miles south of the frontier. Sinuiju lies on the Yalu directly across from Antung where the strafings of August 27 took place. (The first antiaircraft incident occurred, be it noted, against a plane over one of the Yalu River area power reservoirs.)

We have now covered five of the twelve instances cited by MacArthur to "prove" Chinese intervention. A sixth also dealt with an aviation incident—an alleged attack on a flight of F-51s early in the afternoon of November 1 by "six to nine jet aircraft which flew across the Yalu River into Manchuria." No damage was done. "A red star was observed" on the wing of one aircraft. Of the six aircraft incidents, this is the only one which supports the charge of Chinese or Russian intervention. Considering the number of border violations alleged by the Chinese and Russians and the fact that several were admitted by Washington, it could be argued reasonably that the jets were going into action to make it clear that aerial incursions on the border would be resisted. In this context, it may show intervention but it does not prove the intent was aggressive.

The six incidents remaining of the twelve all deal with intervention by land forces. The first was the crossing of the Yalu on October 16 to place some 2500 troops in the vicinity of the Changjin and Pujon dams; the second was the crossing on October 20 to place some 5000 troops south of the Suiho dam. These we have examined earlier. They indicate a determination to protect the dams. Had they been brought to public attention earlier, they would have emphasized the importance of keeping away from the dams. As it is, publicized only after the sensational charges of November 6, they were presented in a context which made them appear to the unwary and the hasty as proof of aggressive intent.

The other four incidents cited by MacArthur are these: On October 30 the interrogation of nineteen Chinese prisoners identified two additional regiments "in the vicinity of Chang-jin," where the troops who crossed on October 16 were stationed. On November 2, "Interrogation of prisoners of war indicates the Fifty-fourth C.C.F. [Chinese Communist Force] unit in Korea" made up of contingents from the 112th, 113th, and 114th Divisions of the Thirty-eighth C.C.F. Army. On November 3, "Further interrogation of Chinese prisoners of war indicates Fifty-sixth C.C.F. unit organized from elements of 118th, 119th and 120th C.C.F. Divisions of the Fortieth C.C.F. Army." The final item of proof, Paragraph *L*, says, "4 November: As of this date, a total of thirty-five C.C.F. prisoners had been taken in Korea." There could not have been so very much fighting if only thirty-five prisoners had been taken.

This ragout of intelligence information, some relevant, some not, was hardly enough to support MacArthur's reference to "one of the most offensive acts of international lawlessness of historic record." It is noteworthy that neither communiqué of November 6 cites or alleges one single instance of attack by Chinese troops in Korea. The communiqué giving the proof speaks of the United Nations forces "meeting a new foe" and being "presently in hostile contact with Chinese Communist military units deployed for action against the forces of the Unified Command." It does not say these Chinese forces attacked but that they were "deployed for action" and that United Nations forces were "presently in hostile contact" with them.

Judging from the attack launched by the Tenth Corps, the "hostile contact" originated from the United Nations side. MacArthur alleges nothing to the contrary. His conclusion is worth reading closely: "The continued employment of Chinese Communist forces in Korea and *the hostile attitude* assumed by such forces, *either inside or outside Korea,* are matters which it is incumbent upon me to bring at once to the attention of the United Nations." (Italics added.) Was a "hostile attitude . . . inside or outside Korea" the best that MacArthur was able to adduce when he got down to specific cases in his effort to show large-scale intervention with aggressive intent? Where was the proof of "a possible trap . . . surreptitiously laid, calculated to encompass the destruction of the United Nations forces"?

Hanson Baldwin, cabling the same day from Tokyo, summarized the facts less sensationally but more precisely: "The Chinese Communist intervention in Korea, so long anticipated and feared, is an established fact. . . . What is not clear as yet is the extent of that intervention and its precise purposes. . . . The minimum objective of the Chinese Communists is certainly protection of the Yalu River and the Changjin-Pujon reservoir power complex."

CHAPTER 24

★

The China Lobby Responds

THE military situation, as so often with MacArthur, was obscure. The political situation was clear. In Washington one of Chiang Kai-shek's staunchest champions, Senator William F. Knowland, Republican, of California, telegraphed to Secretary of State Acheson to demand that Chiang's July offer of Kuomintang troops for Korea now be accepted. The reason for rejecting the offer then, Senator Knowland said, was the fear of furnishing "the excuse for the invasion of Korea by Chinese Communists," but "since this has now happened anyway, General MacArthur should forthwith be authorized to accept with thanks." Four other Republican Senators issued a joint supporting blast against that "small willful group in the State Department intent upon appeasing the Chinese Communist revolution." From Taipei, Chiang's capital, came the news: "Now that Chinese Communist troops have struck in North Korea, Formosa is bubbling with excitement. Military men here are canvassing the situation, wondering if this new development may not mean they soon will see action," either because MacArthur "under strong pressure in North Korea . . . may reach for the only considerable pool of reinforcements he now enjoys in the Far East," that is, Chiang's troops, or because the United Nations and the Allied leaders "might decide the time was ripe for a Nationalist reinvasion of the mainland."

At Peking the radio was calling for "volunteers" and predicting that the Chinese would "destroy and dislodge the American imperialistic aggressors" in Korea, but more sober counsels seemed to be having their effect. The American delegation at Lake Success showed by two statements that it was really alarmed over what MacArthur might do. Ernest A. Gross of the American delegation told a press conference "that General MacArthur could not take any measures outside Korean borders without specific United Nations authority," as if using this method to put some curb on the dangerous possibilities at Tokyo. Even more indicative of a crisis atmosphere was Gross' statement at the same press conference that the United States "was willing to talk the situation over with the Soviet delegation if the latter wished to do so." Wh n the Security Council met at 3 P.M. on November 6, Austin read the MacArthur "special report" on Chinese aggression and asked that discussion be deferred two days. The United States was in no hurry for a war with China.

Neither was the United Nations. On November 7 the United Nations Interim Committee on Korea issued a statement intended, as its chairman, General Carlos P. Romulo of the Philippines, explained, "to reassure the Chinese Communists regarding their interests on the Korean-Manchurian border." There was talk at Lake Success of postponing Security Council discussion of the MacArthur charges until the representatives of Peking arrived. Caution was urged and, "as the spokesman of one great power delegation put it, the Chinese so far were only in the war on a small scale."

There also seemed to be a restraining influence in Peking. On November 7 came the news from Tokyo that "Chinese and North Korean troops in a surprise maneuver broke contact with United Nations forces on the defense line north of Anju this morning. . . ." MacArthur Headquarters did not seem to welcome this sudden stoppage of hostilities, for it was added that " 'vigorous' patrols by United States and South Korean elements this morning failed to find the enemy. . . ." As the lull continued, the UN forces on November 8 "expanded their bridgehead north and west of the Chongchon" where the enemy had broken off contact—in other words, the UN forces continued to move north and west in search of the enemy.

The sudden breaking off of hostilities was difficult to explain with certainty. In Tokyo a military spokesman "warned, however, that the enemy withdrawal seemed to be a pause to reorganize and regroup large concentrations of North Korean and Chinese Communist troops for a new onslaught rather than a retreat." How the military spokesman could be so sure this withdrawal merely portended new aggressive designs was not explained. The withdrawal might also reflect the peace talk at Lake Success. Peking's delegates were to arrive on November 15 to state their case on Formosa: they could hardly expect a favorable hearing if they were waging war against the United Nations in Korea. They had everything to gain, if not by peace, then at least by postponing hostilities.

MacArthur was taking no chances. At this moment there occurred an incident which demonstrates perhaps better than any other in the course of the war how desperately determined Tokyo Headquarters was to prevent peace from breaking out. The Security Council was to meet on November 8. The Communists had withdrawn their forces in Korea. Suddenly on November 7 a spokesman for the Air Force in Washington announced that "an earlier ban against flights within three miles of Manchuria" had been lifted and "United States pilots in Korea are operating right up to the Chinese border along the Yalu River." The phrasing was not "may operate" but "are operating." The reason for putting it this way was soon evident.

For that day seventy-nine B-29 Superfortresses and three hundred fighter planes attacked Sinuiju, the Korean city across the river from Antung, the danger spot where MacArthur had cited antiaircraft air bursts on four different occasions. They dropped 630 tons of bombs and were "said to have destroyed ninety percent of the city" and to have used "rockets, demolition bombs, and 85,000 incendiaries."

"The attack came almost simultaneously," Lindesay Parrott reported from Tokyo to the *New York Times*, "with an announcement by an Air Force spokesman in Washington that

United States fliers had received permission to bomb right up to the Manchurian border instead of remaining three miles south in an attempt to avoid possible frontier violations."

From the phrase used in the dispatch from Washington, "are operating," one would conclude that the "almost simultaneously" from Tokyo meant that the attack began before the announcement. Whether just before or just after is not really crucial. What is crucial is the fact that, just when there was a lull in the fighting and it looked as if peace were possible, MacArthur staged a gigantic and murderous raid directly across from the Chinese frontier, destroying most of a city in an area where bombings had been forbidden to prevent border violations. He had gotten the Air Force to lift the bombing restriction—how, when, or why nobody knows. Perhaps he did it by starting the raid first and asking permission afterwards. He likes the *fait accompli*. This is what he is reported to have done the very first week of the war, in forcing the President to "allow" him to bomb north of the 38th Parallel. ("There were reports," the *New York Times* said October 15, the day of the Wake Island meeting, "that General MacArthur had ordered the first bombings of North Korean cities without authorization from Washington.")

The pretext for the raid was "to eliminate Sinuiju as a future stronghold for supplies and communications." This was stated in the announcement later issued by Lieutenant General George E. Stratemeyer, commander of the Far East Air Forces. The description based on the briefing in Tokyo is not pleasant reading. The attack began in the morning "when fighter planes swept the area with machine guns, rockets, and jellied gasoline bombs." They were followed by "ten of the superforts" which "dropped 1000-pound high-explosive bombs on railroad and highway bridges across the Yalu River and on the bridge approaches." (If dropped on the bridges as well as the approaches, the bombers were obviously operating right up to the boundary line on the river itself.) After this, "the remaining planes used incendiaries exclusively on a two and one-half mile built-up area along the southeast bank of the Yalu." General Stratemeyer maintained that all targets were of a military nature and bomb runs "had kept away from the city's hospital areas." At the same time the Air Force claimed ninety percent of the city had been destroyed. How these statements can be reconciled I do not know. There is an indifference to human suffering to be read between those lines which makes me as an American deeply ashamed of what was done that day at Sinuiju.

Tokyo Headquarters, with or without connivance by Washington, ravaged a city when a truce was in prospect. It deliberately took action which might have provoked a third world war—when the Chinese, of whose intervention it complained, were withdrawing. That the military knew what they were doing is indicated by a short Associated Press dispatch from Seoul which was printed the same day as the news of the mass raid on Sinuiju. A United States Eighth Army spokesman said that "Chinese Communist troops might be avoiding a fight in North Korea pending high level diplomatic moves that would affect the course of the Korean War." This spokesman stated that the withdrawal of the Chinese in the northwest "has been gradual over a four-day period" while in the northeast "a Tenth Corps spokesman said the Chinese 184th Division was 'in retreat' from the giant Changjin hydroelectric complex." If the Chinese were even abandoning their dams, they must have wanted peace badly. Was the mass raid intended to goad them to war?

The mass bombing raid on Sinuiju November 8 was the beginning of a race between peace and provocation. A terrible retribution threatened the peoples of the Western world who so feebly permitted such acts to be done in their name. For it was by such means that the pyromaniacs hoped to set the world afire.

CHAPTER 25

★

Peking Suspects

THE Peking radio on November 8 said it was "foolish" to believe that the United States "has not and never had any intention of crossing the Yalu River" into Manchuria. With MacArthur in Tokyo it was hazardous to take Washington's assurances seriously, even if one granted their sincerity. At Lake Success that day the British representative, Sir Gladwyn Jebb, introduced a resolution inviting a representative of Peking "to be present during discussion by the Council of the special report of the United Nations Command in Korea." The American representative, Warren Austin, though complaining that Peking should have been "summoned" rather than "invited," voted for the resolution, which only Nationalist China and Cuba opposed. Peking had now won two invitations to participate in United Nations discussions, one on Formosa, the other on Korea.

Tokyo Headquarters seemed to be galvanized into action. Just as MacArthur's Headquarters belittled reports of Chinese intervention during the period in which this intervention actually began, so now it began to exaggerate the extent of the intervention as it ebbed away. The day after the Security Council voted to invite Red China to be present during the discussion of the MacArthur charges, the gap between the front-line reports and Headquarters' briefing was again ludicrously wide, but widening in the opposite direction. Again "on the ground there was . . . only minor contact with the

180

enemy on either the east or west coasts." The United Nations forces were having difficulty in locating the retreating enemy, but what made headlines was "60,000 CHINESE REDS IN WAR, MORE READY, MACARTHUR SAYS."

It was on November 9 that MacArthur Headquarters "officially stated . . . for the first time that strong forces of the Chinese Communist Army, estimated at 60,000 men, had entered the Korean War, with an equal number of reinforcements believed to be on the way. . . . In addition, headquarters believed that Mao Tse-tung . . . might have as many as 500,000 men . . . capable of reinforcing the Communist forces in Korea . . . over the short communications lines south of the Korean border . . . immune from attack on the Manchurian side." This emphasis on Manchuria's "immunity" to attack was to become a constant theme of MacArthur Headquarters.

"Yesterday's assessment of the extent of Chinese intervention in Korea," the *New York Times* correspondent in Tokyo noted on November 10, "was the most detailed yet made public here and was in sharp contrast with earlier declarations at General MacArthur's headquarters that the Chinese soldiers were 'volunteers' and that there was no cause for alarm."

It also contrasted not only with the news from the front lines, where the enemy had disappeared, but with the rather meager evidence brought forward by the Headquarters spokesman at the same briefing. He said that thus far only a hundred Chinese prisoners had been taken—a very small number if 60,000 Chinese Communists were already in Korea. Either the number in Korea was much exaggerated or they had done little fighting.

If patrols sent out by the forces in the field were having trouble locating the enemy, and if MacArthur's command had only a hundred prisoners, how could they be so sure—and be so sure so suddenly—that there were 60,000 Chinese in Korea? Actually when the spokesman got down to "brass tacks" it was hard to see where that 60,000 figure came from. The spokesman explained that interrogation of the Chinese prisoners "indicated that elements of three Chinese armies were facing the United States Eighth Army in the west, with the fourth opposing the United States Tenth Corps."

But the dispatch about the briefing did not say that four entire armies were in the field. It said, "The prisoners had knowledge of 'eighteen or nineteen units' presumably of regimental strength, in combat in Korea to date from all four armies." Eighteen or nineteen units "presumably of regimental strength"—could they add up to 60,000 men?

Whatever the number, the UN forces were still unable to get close enough to count them. November 11 was "relatively quiet" for the fifth successive day, being marked only "by patrol actions and light skirmishes." United States Marines from the First Division, advancing unopposed, had even been able to seize "the last of four huge hydroelectric plants" south of Pusong reservoir near Changjin. Vital parts stripped from the plants "were found nearby, heavily camouflaged." If the Chinese had 60,000 troops in Manchuria ready to fight, it is doubtful that they would abandon these power plants to possible destruction.

MacArthur Headquarters did its best nevertheless to picture this continued swift withdrawal as somehow infused with aggressive intent. The *New York Times* report on the Headquarters briefing of the 11th said that, while the front was "relatively quiet" behind the lines, "Chinese reinforcements continued to cross from Manchuria into North Korea, threatening a new drive against the UN forces as soon as the hostile buildup had been completed." A tortuous paragraph tried to explain how this conclusion was reached.

"With the enemy making no major effort," the dispatch reported, "the headquarters spokesman reiterated that no conclusion could be reached yet regarding the Communist intentions either for attack to the south or a defensive stand in the wide bridgehead based on the Yalu River. Intelligence sources said, however, that 'everything' pointed to the reinforcements still flowing across the frontier and there was no indication that the enemy on the front was digging important positions for defense."

This *non sequitur* was enough to drive a logician wild. The enemy had been withdrawing so rapidly for five days that it was difficult to maintain contact. A retreating force does not stop to dig "important positions for defense." To say that everything "pointed to" reinforcements flowing in, when "everything" seemed to show that the enemy troops were moving out, and then couple this with the absence of defensive preparations as signs of a coming attack was something of a feat.

In the air the "unified command" was still looking for trouble. On November 9 dive bombers from Navy carriers off shore attacked the long railroad bridge between ruined Sinuiju on the Korean side and Antung on the Manchurian side, and a vehicular bridge further upstream near the big Suiho hydro-electric plant was also hit. On Friday, November 10, "in the fourth incendiary raid since Sunday, B-29 Superforts . . . plastered the town of Uiju on the Yalu's south bank ten miles upstream from the burned-out city of Sinuiju, site of the principal bridge to Manchuria."

There was increased resistance in the air, and on November 10 at Lake Success Warren Austin interrupted a speech before the Security Council to say that "he had just received word that two United Nations B-29 bombers had been shot up by Russian-type planes seen coming across the border over the Korean city of Sinuiju across the Yalu River from Antung. He added that this state of affairs gravely prejudiced the successful completion of the UN mission in Korea." It might reasonably have been asked whether by this Austin meant the continued American mass bombings and burnings on a sensitive border in a hitherto interdicted area without permission from the United Nations or whether he meant the occasional retaliation from the other side.

The whole affair in retrospect seems fantastic. While the Western Powers introduced a resolution at Lake Success asking the Chinese to withdraw, the Chinese *were* actually drawing their forces back to the border. Tokyo Headquarters, waging skillful war in the headlines, managed to hide this hopeful development from view. Alongside the headline "WEST BIDS U.N. ASK PEIPING TO WITHDRAW MEN IN KOREA," in the *New York*

Times international edition of November 11, was the headline "CHINESE CONTINUE MARCH INTO KOREA DESPITE AIR BLOWS," over the day's dispatch from Tokyo. But the dispatch itself gave no supporting evidence other than the fact that unnamed "intelligence sources" said " 'everything' pointed to the reinforcements still flowing across the frontier." If "everything" pointed to this, one wondered why one or two sample "things" might not have been cited—especially since the terrific bombardment of the Yalu River bridges made one wonder just how those reinforcements were getting across. Not only the average newspaper reader, but even those of us who read the papers carefully as part of our business, missed the full implications in those hectic days. The picture that was being built up in the public mind of the West was that the Chinese were the aggressors—though there had been enough border violations and attacks on vital Chinese interests in the Yalu dams to provide justification for their entry into the war.

Let Americans think for a moment how they would react if the armies of another great power from across the seas were crushing a Mexican government friendly to the U.S.A., strafing Texas border towns, and operating under a general who threatened war against the U.S.A. itself.

CHAPTER 26

★

Home-By-Christmas

THE *New Yorker* published a profile of General Omar Bradley in March, 1951. The profile shed some new light on the Korean War. For one thing, it disclosed that the "home-by-Christmas" offensive of General MacArthur was originally scheduled for November 15 but later postponed to November 24. The dates are instructive. Originally the representatives of Communist China were scheduled to arrive at Lake Success on November 15. Their arrival, too, was postponed to the 24th.

The MacArthur offensive of the 24th put war headlines in the papers the day the Red Chinese delegation arrived. Some people hoped—others feared—that the appearance of spokesmen for Peking at the United Nations would be the beginning of peace talks. To open an offensive the day they arrived was to create a less than auspicious atmosphere. With an offensive under way, it was difficult for the Chinese to talk peace without losing face.

How did the offensive happen to be postponed until the 24th? A. J. Liebling, the author of the *New Yorker* profile, was told that the "jump off in North Korea" was delayed until the 24th because of "bad weather." It is a pity there was not a fuller explanation. The Air Force communiqués show unusually heavy air activity and no sign of bad weather for the ten days up to and including November 15. It was somewhat overcast on the 16th but not enough to prevent the Air Force from flying 516 sorties that day and carrier-based Navy planes "more than 140" sorties.

The synchronization of the offensive with the arrival of the Chinese delegation might be another of those coincidences so frequent in the history of the Korean War. On the other hand, if Tokyo Headquarters planned it that way, it had ample advance notice. Peking announced on October 24 that it would send representatives to attend the November 15 hearing on Formosa before the Security Council. Tokyo Headquarters knew and the Pentagon knew that the opening of the offensive would coincide with the arrival of the Peking delegation.

It would be useful if one could examine the communications between Tokyo and the Pentagon and see just when it was decided that the weather had turned too unfavorable. That the Chinese delegation would be unable to reach Lake Success on November 15 became known on November 11. On that day Trygve Lie received a cable from Chou En-lai, the Chinese Premier, saying that a nine-man delegation was leaving Peking for Prague where it hoped to pick up United States visas and arrive at Lake Success "about" November 18. It would also be enlightening to know when November 24 was picked as the next date for the offensive. It was on November 16 that United Nations transportation officials learned that the Chinese delegation had booked passage on BOAC Flight 509 arriving in New York Friday morning, November 24.

The choice first of November 15 and then of November 24 for the offensive might have been coincidence, though sheer coincidence twice repeated begins to put a strain on the law of probabilities. No one knows why these dates were chosen or exactly why the postponement from the 15th to the 24th occurred. But two things can be stated with assurance. MacArthur in Tokyo and the American military in Washington knew three weeks ahead of time the first date for the scheduled arrival of the Chinese Red delegation and eight days ahead of time the date to which the arrival had been postponed.

It cannot be proved that the American military picked the date for the offensive each time to coincide with the arrival. That might have been accidental both times. What one can prove is that they *did* know the arrival dates. And they can be condemned for going ahead with plans for opening an offensive which *would* coincide. American generals are not innocents when it comes to public relations. Both MacArthur in Tokyo and Bradley in Washington could hardly have been unaware of the political effects of what they were planning.

The problem of "face" was not confined to the Oriental participants. If the UN offensive were victorious, the Chinese would be made to seem suppliants in defeat. If the American forces were hurled back, it would become politically risky for the Truman Administration to make concessions for peace while suffering military reversals at the hands of the Reds. Either way something would be gained by those who wanted the war widened.

There is another aspect to this matter of the November offensive. In this, too, MacArthur's hand was quicker than the public's eye. Let us begin by looking at how the White House and the Pentagon reacted when the November 24 offensive provoked counterattacks and started a UN retreat. "Some members of the President's civilian entourage," Liebling relates in his profile of General Bradley, "angrily denounced MacArthur as the author of their sorrows. They told anybody who would listen that the Wisconsin Mikado had assured the President that the Chinese Communists would not come in." General Bradley himself said, "*Everybody* at the Wake Island conference was confident the Chinese would stay out," emphasizing the "*everybody*." (The italics are Liebling's.)

In any case, it is clear that the decisions at Wake Island, when MacArthur's forces were beginning to head north from the 38th Parallel, were predicated on a general agreement that the forward advance could safely continue because the Chinese would not intervene. This assumption proved incorrect. *The point about the November offensive is that it was launched after this assumption had been proved incorrect.* Chinese intervention, as we have already seen, began the day after the Wake Island conference, at least to protect the Yalu River dam and power installations in the Korean border area. That the calculation was wrong was finally admitted by MacArthur in his

November 6 statements, which not only acknowledged but imperiously denounced Chinese intervention. To go ahead with an offensive after that was not to make a miscalculation but deliberately to take a known risk, a risk which might set off World War III. This analysis applies as much to General Bradley as to General MacArthur.

The rationalizations of the Pentagon are reflected by Liebling. MacArthur, he writes, "had an authorization from the United Nations and a directive from the U.S. Joint Chiefs of Staff to restore order in all Korea, so that free elections could be held. . . . According to a view propounded by some British and American critics, MacArthur, having hit a lamppost—in this case, a Chinese lantern—on November 1st, should have called off his later attack. It seemed to him, however, that this second offensive would succeed, and his was the right to decide."

General MacArthur's directive was to "restore order" in Korea but to do it without involving the United States and United Nations in war with China. It was not necessary to occupy the border area with UN troops, especially with American and British troops, in order to "restore order" and allow free elections to be held. The North Korean regime had been overthrown, its capital occupied, and its troops smashed when the November offensive was decided upon. "Aggression" had already been repelled; the "police action" victoriously accomplished; world "law and order" upheld. There was no need to take the additional risk—unless one was determined to humiliate, alarm, and provoke Red China.

Were Bradley as candid, and Liebling as inquisitive, as they might have been? There was a directive to restore order in all Korea, yes. But what had been decided at Wake Island about the troops to be used in restoring order in the border zone? Truman, as we have seen, declared flatly that it was his understanding that South Korean troops were to be used for this purpose. A First Army Corps spokesman in Korea had stated that the Americans and the British and the other UN forces were not to go beyond a line forty miles from the border. Did MacArthur disobey orders? Or did he find a way to get around them? Events had shown how dangerous it was to allow United States and British troops to invade the border region. Was it not unwise to allow an offensive to be launched within it? Having hit the "Chinese lantern" once, why was MacArthur allowed to hit it again? This was not a case of trying a mere military maneuver a second time. It was risking war again, and risking it unnecessarily.

MacArthur was acting in the name of the United Nations. He owed a duty to it. Sometime in October the British "had circulated a paper proposing that the United Nations troops halt well before the Manchurian frontier and leave a buffer zone between the United Nations and Red China armies." According to the diplomatic correspondent of the *New York Times,* writing after the November offensive broke down, Mac-Arthur "took the view that these suggestions were jeopardizing the victories he had won. Moreover, he indicated that he could not be responsible for the security of his troops—a phrase used on several occasions—if any such policy of cautious waiting were adopted."

Obviously these objections from Tokyo had been decisive. They deserve closer examination. If we glance back we see that on November 6 MacArthur denounced Chinese intervention in Korea. We also see that on November 7 the Chinese Communist troops, in a surprise maneuver, suddenly broke contact and began a withdrawal. That withdrawal continued until after the new MacArthur offensive began.

This Chinese withdrawal could be interpreted in either of two ways. If it was what it seemed to be, a withdrawal from Korea, then to allow it peacefully to proceed would neither jeopardize MacArthur's victories nor endanger his troops. If it was a feint, to draw his troops into a trap, then the best way to avoid the trap was to keep away from it.

What makes the November offensive so shocking is that if one looks back over the newspapers before it was launched one sees that MacArthur Headquarters pictured the withdrawal, not as genuine, but as a screen to cover preparations for an aggressive push by overwhelming forces.

On November 10 it was "60,000 CHINESE REDS IN WAR, MORE

READY M'ARTHUR SAYS." On November 11, "CHINESE CONTINUE MARCH INTO KOREA DESPITE AIR BLOWS: REINFORCEMENTS POUR OVER RIVER." On November 13, "ENEMY CONTINUES TO MOVE MEN AND SUPPLIES FROM MANCHURIA." On November 15 "reports implied that about two-thirds of three Chinese Communist armies—estimated at 75,000 men—now had reached Korea from Manchurian bases." On November 18 Tokyo Headquarters estimated that the Chinese had not only concentrated 100,000 men in front of the UN forces but had also reorganized 40,000 guerrillas in their rear. On November 19 from Tokyo Headquarters "the big threat" reported "was the concentration of perhaps 250,000 Chinese Communist soldiers in Manchuria and what might happen if Mao Tse-tung decided to throw the force into Korea."

MacArthur Headquarters not only seemed sure a trap was being prepared but began to advertise how it might best be sprung. On November 20 the daily *New York Times* dispatch based on the military briefing contained a paragraph which—in the light of what was soon to happen—seems perilously clairvoyant. The dispatch said an estimated 40,000 Red guerrillas in the rear of the UN forces had orders, "according to various accounts," to "break out to the north in Central Korea, where there was only tenuous contact between the United States Eighth Army and the Tenth Corps on the east coast." Thus Tokyo Headquarters pointed out the famous "gap" through which "Red hordes" were soon to pour. Rarely has one army been so helpful to its enemy.

On only one day did Tokyo Headquarters paint a different picture from this one of peril fore and aft. The one deviation came on November 21, when " a headquarters spokesman gave some clue to the rather mysterious movements of the Chinese Communist soldiers who had forced United Nations troops to make withdrawals of up to fifty miles in their counteroffensive last month, then had broken off the attack and had largely avoided contact with United Nations forces."

From the questioning of about 150 Chinese prisoners the spokesman "indicated it was learned that the Chinese had quickly become demoralized by the fire power of a modern army and the total UN control of the air." But on the 22nd the Tokyo Headquarters briefing was back on the old line, estimating that 50,000 more Chinese Reds "might have entered Korea during the last three weeks since the Communists broke off their attack on the Western front"—which would indicate, it was explained, that there were now about 110,000 Red troops in Korea. This was about the number of United Nations troops in Korea, and on the 24th, with the news of the launching of the "home-by-Christmas offensive," Tokyo Headquarters explained that the opposing forces were "approximately equal as the UN assault was launched."

Thus, according to MacArthur's own Headquarters, he launched that assault (1) against an equal number of troops but (2) with 40,000 guerrillas in his rear ready to strike (if they read the reports of the briefings at Tokyo Headquarters) at the gap between the Eighth Army in the west and the Tenth Corps in the east and (3) with some 500,000 Red troops ready to move across the border from Manchuria. "Militarily," a dispatch out of Tokyo Headquarters had said prophetically as early as November 6, "the situation could become a greatly expanded version of the first days of the Korean war," forcing the UN troops into a "retreat back down the peninsula."

Never did a general so fully floodlight the trap into which he insisted on marching his troops, nor so clearly advise the enemy to get the trap ready because he was coming. "There are reports in the American press," said a November 22 dispatch from Washington published in the London *Times* of November 24, "that seven United Nations divisions—three of them American and four South Korean—as well as the British Commonwealth brigade, are ready for what is called the final push to clear the lower reaches of the Yalu River from the west coast to the point where South Korean troops have already reached it." The Washington correspondent of the *Times* thought this advance publicity announcing an offensive was "certainly a curious way to fight a war."

CHAPTER 27

★

Danger on the Thames

THIS offensive may have seemed military idiocy. It was political genius. It began a stampede in Washington and it began a stampede in Lake Success. In less than a week Truman was threatening to use the atom bomb. And in less than a month he had declared a state of national emergency and begun the full-scale mobilization of America for war.

The immediate danger the offensive of the 24th succeeded in scotching arose not on the Yalu but on the Thames. Britain was threatening to declare its independence of America, and the offensive in Korea was politically necessary to create a *fait accompli*. On November 17, twenty-two Laborite MPs, including two members of the Labor Party executive, Ian Mikardo and Tom Driberg, had filed two motions, aimed to end two wars, the big cold war and the little one. One motion asked the government to advance proposals for talks with Russia, the other urged an "immediate agreement" to limit the advance of the United Nations forces in Korea "with a view to bringing the fighting to an end as quickly as possible."

This was played in the American press as a left-wing revolt —but MacArthur, not Marx, lay behind the uprising. A series of "leaders" on MacArthur in the influential London *New Statesman and Nation* had helped to crystallize a widespread feeling of dissatisfaction with the reckless course of the war. But the signal for the revolt in Parliament had come not from the Left but from the Right. It was the address made on November 15 by the Conservative leader in the House of Lords, Lord Salisbury, which first broke the ice of Britain's own "bipartisanship" in foreign policy and gave Laborites courage —and ultrarespectable cover—for a challenge to their own governmental leaders. One of the twenty-two rebels, Richard H. S. Crossman, wrote of Lord Salisbury's address a few days later in the London *Sunday Pictorial*: "If any Socialist had talked like this at the Labor Party conference, he would probably have been bashed by Ernest Bevin as a crypto-Communist and steam-rollered by the block vote." Lord Salisbury, the London correspondent of the *Manchester Guardian* noted, not only "voiced what many Labor members had been thinking but dared not say lest they should be identified with Communists and their sympathizers" but at the same time raised a horrid question in the minds of Labor Party leaders: "What if it were to appear that the Conservatives were the only party genuinely seeking peace?"

The Conservative peer who opened a breach in an Anglo-American partnership in which one partner made the decisions and left the other to face the consequences was no Tory maverick. Before the war, as Viscount Cranborne, he occupied the No. 3 position in making foreign policy for the British government from 1935 to 1938. He was Parliamentary Under Secretary of State for Foreign Affairs during those years and resigned with Anthony Eden, then Foreign Secretary, in protest against the further appeasement of Fascist Italy in Spain and Ethiopia at the expense of British interest and collective security. Lord Cranborne went back into the government with Churchill in 1940 and served in various War Cabinet posts until 1945.

The occasion for Lord Salisbury's address was the Russian note of November 3 to the United States, Britain, and France asking for a conference on Germany, and the immediate reaction of Secretary of State Dean Acheson on November 8 that he saw no hope for the success of such a meeting because Russia had yet to show "genuine desire" for peace. Lord Salisbury warned against "a blank negative" and said the alternative to such talks "was a steady drift to war."

Ever so tactfully but unmistakably Lord Salisbury also pointed a warning finger toward MacArthur. "The danger in our present position," he said, "was that we had, if anything, advanced too far. We had reached a point where the enemy's lines of communication were not in Korea at all and could not therefore be attacked without grave diplomatic consequences. Surely it was far better in the long run to avoid such complications, even if it meant leaving a small area of North Korea unoccupied by the United Nations forces." A Socialist peer, Lord Chorley, went further. Declaring that he suspected that MacArthur had played "a dominant part in the decision to cross the 38th Parallel," Lord Chorley said this "played into the hands of those who had promulgated the view that the United States, supported by the English-speaking world, had imperialist and aggressive designs in the Far East."

The revolt had a certain amount of support even from those who favored the cold war. The fear was that MacArthur might precipitate action which would force the concentration of American military effort and aid on the Far East rather than on Europe. The day after Lord Salisbury spoke, Churchill rose in Commons to ask whether the government would "also bear in mind the great importance of our not becoming and of our allies not becoming too much pinned down in China, or in the approaches to China, at a time when the danger in Europe is undoubtedly occupying our minds?"

A few minutes later that irrepressible little Laborite battler, Sydney Silverman, rose to ask the 64-dollar question. A few days earlier, in a leader called "MacArthur Rides Again," the *New Statesman* of November 11 had made a sensational disclosure. Asserting that MacArthur "seems intent on turning the Korean War into a world war," the *New Statesman* said it understood that at the time the 38th Parallel was crossed "confidential instructions, suggested by the British and fully approved by the State Department, were sent to Tokyo." These instructions, according to the *New Statesman*, "urged MacArthur, if it were militarily possible, to halt his advance at the isthmus and so avoid contact with the Chinese forces which would be bound to cross the Yalu River in order to screen the Manchurian border and protect the valuable hydro-electric works." The *New Statesman* accused MacArthur of having "once again, as in the case of Formosa . . . deliberately disregarded the clearly expressed purposes of his superiors."

Silverman asked the Minister of Defense, who had just finished giving a report on the course of the war in Korea, a question which gave the government an opportunity to confirm or deny this report. "In view of the statement that instructions were given from time to time to the Commander-in-Chief about the line at which hostilities were to cease," Silverman asked the Minister of Defense, "would the Minister say when such instructions were given and whether they were always fully complied with?"

At this point the Commons was treated to the unusual spectacle of intervention by the leader of the Opposition to save the spokesman for the government from an embarrassing question put by one of the Labor Party's own back-benchers. Churchill suggested that it might be better to reserve "those questions which affect foreign policy to the debate on that matter." Neither then nor in the later debate on foreign policy was the question ever answered.

The answer would have required a humiliating admission on the part of the British government. The admission would have been that the United Nations, under the resolution establishing the "unified command," had no authority over the Commander to whom its troops were entrusted. The answer to Silverman's question was furnished two weeks later by MacArthur himself. In a telegram on November 30 to Arthur Krock, the chief Washington correspondent of the *New York Times*, the General asserted that he had received "no suggestion from any authoritative source that in the execution of its mission the Command should stop at the 38th Parallel or Pyongyang, or at any other line short of the international boundary."

The key to this answer lies in the phrase "any authoritative source" and in the next sentence of the MacArthur telegram: "To have done so would have required revision of the resolutions of the United Nations and the directives received in implementation thereof." The only "authoritative sources" which could have "suggested a stop-point," the *New York Times* explained in a note printed with the telegram, "are the United Nations Security Council, the General Assembly, and President Truman." The British government could, as the *New Statesman* suggested, withdraw or threaten to withdraw its troops, if it did not like MacArthur's conduct of the "unified command." But it could not recall or revise the blank check it gave him through the United Nations. It could urge, it could suggest, it could protest, it could deplore, but it could not instruct.

This tragic impotence was not clear to British public opinion at the time—it is doubtful whether it is clear to this day—but the British government was not entirely helpless. Neither MacArthur Headquarters nor Washington could be sure how far the growing protest in Britain might force the government to go. It was necessary to some extent to allay British fears and appease British wishes lest the government itself take drastic action. The British government might boldly suggest revision of the Korean resolutions at the United Nations. It could withdraw or threaten to withdraw British troops, as the *New Statesman* had just suggested in its issue of November 25. These had been furnished only on "recommendation" of the Security Council under Articles 39 and 42 of the Charter, and not in pursuance of its power under Articles 43 and 44 to require member states to participate in military sanctions.

Behind the scenes the British government seemed to be seeking desperately for some way to avoid a clash with China. The Washington correspondent of the London *Sunday Times* reported in its issue of November 19 that Sir Oliver Franks, the British Ambassador to the United States, had suggested a demilitarized "no man's land" zone along the frontier. And on November 21, at Lake Success, Britain angered John Foster Dulles by opposing the Chinese Nationalist motion for a United Nations commission to investigate Chiang's charges that the Soviet Union was threatening peace in the Far East by backing and dominating the Chinese Communist regime.

Dulles said it would be "a very black day indeed . . . if we bury this proposition." For Chiang it undoubtedly would. Such a commission would set the United Nations at logger-heads with both Red China and Soviet Russia.

On November 22 Secretary of State Acheson denied that any agreement had been reached on a demilitarized buffer zone. But the correspondent of the *New York Herald Tribune* added that "Well-informed sources, however, indicated agree-ment on the plan [on a buffer zone], to be presented to the Communist Chinese delegation at the United Nations, is near and is awaiting primarily approval of its military details by General Douglas MacArthur."

On November 23 Foreign Secretary Bevin sent Peking a conciliatory note in an effort to promote a political settlement of the Korean conflict. It was reported significantly that "the decision to approach the Chinese was made unilaterally by the British government." The adverb in this context seemed to mean without first clearing the move with Washington, though British sources still "maintained" that the move "fits in with" current Anglo-American-French talks on a Korean settlement.

Peace talk and peace rumors were everywhere on the eve of the November 24 offensive. The Chinese had released a hundred United States and South Korean prisoners with a message that China did not want war with America, and they were reported to have offered to release one thousand more. In Tokyo General MacArthur's spokesman acknowledged that there was a "special reason" why United Nations forces were not following up the Chinese Communists, but would not say whether it had anything to do with peace feelers.

At the same time there was an apprehension which was to prove only too well founded. Thursday the 23rd, the eve of the offensive, the Washington correspondent of the London *Telegraph* reported that British officials in the American capital feared "some irresponsible step" which would make "a peace settlement impossible." The Labor government faced a full-dress debate on Korea the coming week, in which there would be a showdown with its critics and a demand for a break away from American leadership on both Far Eastern and German policy.

Something had to be done quickly. MacArthur did it. "The offensive," said the London *Dail Mail's* correspondent at Tokyo Headquarters in a cable on November 24, "has cut through the web of rumors that negotiations were in progress for a diplomatic settlement. . . . General MacArthur's action makes it clear that he does not intend to keep his troops in a condition of stalemate in the bitter Korean winter while politicians try to hammer out a compromise."

The headline said, "MACARTHUR LAUNCHES 'END THE WAR' ASSAULT." The assault did not end the war. It did cut short the peace talk.

CHAPTER 28

★

Anti-Peace Offensive

PRESIDENT Truman was asked at his press conference on November 30 whether MacArthur had exceeded his authority in Korea. Truman answered sharply that the General had done nothing of the kind. MacArthur was asked at the time in a formal question-and-answer interview by the editors of *U.S. News and World Report* whether he had kept Washington advised of what he was doing. "Major operations," he replied, "are all reported and approved prior to being launched."

The American government often gives the appearance of a house divided against itself. It does not seem to have been in this case. Washington itself a few days earlier had launched a diplomatic offensive no less dangerous to the hopes of peace. At Lake Success on November 21 John Foster Dulles threw the support of the United States behind Chiang Kai-shek's proposal for a United Nations commission to investigate his charge that the Soviet Union was threatening peace in the Far East by backing and dominating the Chinese Communist regime. Such a commission, opposed by Britain, would have been as effective as the military offensive itself in undercutting the hopes of a peaceful solution, and in embittering relations between the United Nations and the two big Communist states.

To Peking, striving to assess the real purposes of the American government, this could not have seemed other than a hostile act, taken in open alliance with Chiang Kai-shek. Perhaps it did not prove an intent to make war, but it certainly showed no readiness to make peace. The day the military offensive began, the State Department revealed the details of another dangerous diplomatic push. The Department published the proposals for a peace treaty with Japan on which Mr. Dulles had been busily engaged. These seemed better calculated to lay the groundwork for war than for peace in the Far East. For they proposed to undo the Cairo declaration, which had promised Formosa and the Pescadores to China, and the Yalta agreement, which had given South Sakhalin and the Kuriles to Russia.

The proposals were so neatly framed as to be downright cute. The disposal of these four former Japanese possessions was to be left to joint decision by the United States, the Soviet Union, Britain, and China. If an agreement was not reached within a year, the question would be submitted to the General Assembly. Since the United States, Britain, and Russia disagreed even on the preliminary question of who should represent China, the question was bound to fall into the lap of the General Assembly, where the United States was sure of a majority. The United Nations could thus be committed to defend Formosa against Peking and to the task of dislodging the Russian occupation of South Sakhalin and the Kuriles. This was hardly the way to create an atmosphere conducive to successful negotiations for ending the Korean War. Peace was not brought nearer by having Dulles dangle the tempting carrot of these former colonies before a Japan being coaxed into American military harness.

Truman showed no eagerness to reassure the Chinese, except in reluctant words and general phrases, as in his statement of November 16, which said the United States "never at any time entertained any intention to carry hostilities into China . . . [and] will take every honorable step to prevent the extension of hostilities in the Far East." James Reston, the diplomatic correspondent of the *New York Times,* noted next day that other members of the United Nations had been urging such a statement for weeks and were criticizing this as too late and too vague. "Some well-informed persons here," he reported from Washington, "believe that such a statement, if made when the United Nations troops took the North Korean capital, might have prevented the Chinese intervention, particularly if the United States had also offered to allow a United Nations peace commission to take over a buffer zone on the Korean side of the Chinese frontier."

It was not known at the time that a new offensive had originally been scheduled, as we have seen, for the 15th but postponed at the last minute to the 24th. Had the original schedule been followed, Truman's vague assurances of the 16th would have been made to look all the less convincing by the launching of a new drive toward the Soviet and Chinese frontiers. The Chinese, to echo a favorite Washington phrase of the time, were also entitled to ask for "deeds, not words"— if not for deeds, at least for some specific words about their interests in the Yalu dam and power network. More disquieting than Truman's failure even to mention the dams on the 16th was Acheson's brusque denial on the 22d of any agreement for a buffer zone to protect them. This threatened to upset the negotiations the British were carrying on at Peking.

Reston, who has excellent British sources in Washington, lifted the curtain a little more in a brilliant dispatch of November 29. He said that the President, in making his statement "reassuring" the Chinese, had overruled MacArthur, and that he had also "denied a request by General MacArthur to chase Communist planes over Manchuria." Reston added, however, that "in the undercover dispute between the cautious policy proposed by the British and French and the bold policy sponsored by General MacArthur, the President backed the Supreme Commander nearly every time."

Caution in September might have brought peace. Truman preferred to push ahead across the Parallel. Caution in November might have brought peace. Truman preferred to push ahead into the Yalu border regions. Whenever peace came within talking range a common bond seemed to appear between Truman and Acheson on the one hand and MacArthur and Dulles on the other. While only the latter seemed bent on widening the war, none of them seemed eager for peace.

It is in such common points of agreement, usually unspoken, often invisible beneath the surface of real differences, half-hidden in the political subconscious, that the essence of a nation's policies is to be found. Sometimes this eludes the observer. Sometimes he may find it more politic to look the other way. In Britain and France, both dependent on American aid, trying fitfully to be independent partners but sinking repeatedly into the submissive role of loyal retainers, it was more comfortable to put the blame for America's Far Eastern policy on MacArthur and the Republicans.

In witty despair, the *Manchester Guardian* wrote early in December that while "Europe" was quite willing to "stand shoulder-to-shoulder with the Republicans—and the Democrats"—on Far Eastern policy, it would help if "Europe" could find out "where their shoulders are." The fact was, of course, that America's Republicans and Democrats were as much shoulder-to-shoulder on China policy as were Britain's Tories and Laborites. The differences in both countries were differences of degree.

Just as Britain's two big parties agreed on recognition and trade with Communist China, so both America's two big parties agreed on non-recognition and a refusal to trade. The difference which divided the British parties was how far a wise policy on China was to be allowed to interfere with Anglo-American relations and the cold war elsewhere. The difference which divided the American parties was twofold. The minor one was how far hostility to China was to be allowed to strain Anglo-American understanding. The major one was whether hostility was to become open conflict or try to halt at measures short-of-war. In both countries both parties were split internally by these differences, but in both a common national policy was also evident for those who wished to see it, or could afford to do so.

It was easier for the British and the French to pretend, in the hope of being able to persuade, and in the knowledge that too clear a view might strain a friendship on which so much depended. The *Manchester Guardian* editorial reflected the dominant tactic in that period when military operations were smothering peace negotiations. It blamed the Republicans for a tendency to see international policy "in terms of black and white, or rather red and white." In reality, the Democrats showed the same tendency. At the agonized Anglo-American conferences soon to be held in the wake of the MacArthur offensive and the counterattacks it had evoked, the *Manchester Guardian* lamented that Acheson "sounded to the British team like one of his more belligerent critics" and "would not consider inclusion of Formosa in any negotiations with the Chinese Communists." It blamed this on "Republican sniping" and was sure that Acheson's "was probably a stronger line than he really thought necessary."

Republican sniping and the emotional impact of renewed fighting must have had their effect, but the conclusion was doubtful. Acheson was an old and devoted friend, and the British always showed a weakness for him. He was their picture of what a foreign secretary should be: cultivated, personable, and superbly tailored. He was, as he demonstrated at such cost in the Alger Hiss case, what the Victorians called—in the best sense of both terms—a Christian and a gentleman. The British found it hard to believe that a man who so resembled their own idealized images of themselves could be quite sincere when he disagreed with them—as Acheson did on China.

What a public man "really" thinks is difficult to discover and rarely of much relevance when found. It is what the pressure of circumstance upon his own personality leads him to do and say that counts. What Acheson had long said and done committed him to a policy hostile to Communist China. Nothing could be more dangerous to a public figure in America than the mere suspicion of an urbane and compassionate view of history and humanity, a less than solemnly respectful attitude toward those feverish ideologies which turn up like maddened battle-cries in the wars as frequent among men as storms are on the sea. Safer almost to have a Communist Party membership card turn up in one's pocket than to let such detachment reflect itself in some unwary phrase.

Acheson could not let himself be objective about the Communist revolution in China—and remain Secretary of State. Whether he allowed himself to think differently in private, whether he had the iron resolution necessary for steadfast hypocrisy, was most unlikely. He was too much the man of honor to indulge in inner honesty at the price of living with the consciousness of public duplicity. If a hypocrite to start with, he could only become happy, like the man in Max Beerbohm's tale, when the mask had become the face. That he was a hypocrite was most improbable; only in the heat-distorted vision of cold-war America could Acheson be seen other than as he was: an "enlightened conservative"—to use a barbarous and patronizing phrase; a lawyer by profession, with a large corporate practice. Who remembered in these days of McCarthyism that Acheson, on making his Washington debut at the Treasury before the war, had been denounced by New Dealers as a "Morgan man," a Wall Street Trojan Horse, a borer-from-within on behalf of the big bankers?

That Acheson's opposite numbers in England, despite a similar background, took a different view of Red China was a puzzle the key to which lay in Hong Kong. America had no such economic stake to make objectivity respectable. Much that Acheson did as Secretary of State during the tortuous course of the Korean War becomes explicable if one turns back to the views he expressed in the famous American White Paper on China in August, 1949, and the speeches he made on China policy in the following spring, before the Korean War began. The point of view there recorded made it most difficult for him ever to sit down in peaceful negotiation with the Chinese Reds. A new foreign secretary is required when reversals of policy so extensive must be made.

Acheson's "Letter of Transmittal" provided the preface to the White Paper and prefigured the policy the United States was henceforth to take on China. The core of the White Paper, the famous long-suppressed report by Lieutenant General Albert Wedemeyer, darling of the China lobby and the hope of Chiang Kai-shek, did indeed propose expanded United States aid to China—but on conditions hardly flattering to the

Kuomintang regime. American business men, the Wedemeyer report stated, "felt that it would prejudice achievement of necessary reforms in China, if financial assistance were to be provided in any large amount with control of its use to be left in Chinese hands." General Wedemeyer felt that military aid should be conditional on "concurrent drastic political and economic reforms," with American military "advice and supervision" extended "to include field forces, training centers and particularly logistical agencies." Logistical agencies handle supplies; supplies in Nationalist China had a way of disappearing.

This proposal in September 1947 for a virtual protectorate over Kuomintang China was rejected by the Truman Administration, but while it did not wish to support Chiang it also did not wish to recognize his opponents. It persisted in the politically comfortable delusion that the Communist revolution was some kind of foreign plot, and committed itself to support of counterrevolution. This was the policy implied by the conclusion of Acheson's Letter of Transmittal. He expressed the belief that "ultimately the profound civilization and the democratic individualism of China will reassert themselves and she will throw off the foreign yoke." He said that the "implementation of our historic policy of friendship for China"—presumably American aid and trade—"will necessarily be influenced by the degree to which the Chinese people come to recognize that the Communist regime serves not their interests but those of Soviet Russia and the manner in which . . . they react to this foreign domination." The United States thus proposed to take over where Chiang had failed. From the standpoint of the Right, this policy made no sense: why let Chiang go down the drain, if one intended to encourage the overthrow of the Chinese Communists? It also made no sense from the standpoint of the Left: why drop Chiang and then fail to get the benefit of good relations with the new regime? The only sense the policy made was that it avoided the expense of underwriting Chiang, a hopeless task, without incurring the public odium of dealing with the Reds.

In pursuance of this policy, mythology gradually began to

triumph over observed fact, and Acheson began to live in an imaginary world—while General Wedemeyer had operated in a context of ruthless realism. General Wedemeyer's basic premise was that war threatened with the Soviet Union and that Chiang was a necessary instrument of American military policy. General Wedemeyer did not deceive himself about the nature of the Kuomintang regime. He spoke of "the reactionary character of Kuomintang leadership, the repressive nature of its rule and the widespread corruption among government officials and military officers." He warned that "adoption by the United States of a policy motivated solely toward stopping the expansion of Communism without regard to the continued existence of an unpopular repressive government would render any aid ineffective."

It is ironic that Truman and Acheson, after rejecting General Wedemeyer's proposals, should have been drawn by the Korean War into trying to do exactly what he warned would prove ineffective. The drift to the worst of policies in the absence of the vision and courage necessary for the best was marked by a series of speeches in which Acheson began to set forth a new image of the Chinese revolution, hardly recognizable to a reader of the White Paper. This new view subordinated the harsh realities which led to the revolution and substituted a bucolic fantasy; it was as if Marx had been rewritten by Theocritus.

This idyllic view, already beginning to be visible in the Letter of Transmittal, made its first full appearance in Acheson's famous talk to the Advertising Council at the White House in February, 1950, launching the "total diplomacy" campaign. "The Communists took over in China," Acheson explained, "at a ridiculously small cost"—an assertion some Chinese Communist survivors of the terrible years after the Shanghai massacre might be inclined to dispute. "What they did," Acheson narrated, "was to invite some Chinese leaders who were dissatisfied with the way things were going in their country to Moscow." There these leaders were "thoroughly indoctrinated . . . so that they returned to China prepared to resort to any means whatsoever to establish Communist control." They were, Acheson went on, "completely subservient to the Moscow regime." These "agents then mingled with the people and sold them on the personal material advantages of Communism. . . . They promised to turn over the land to them." This exposition of the possibility of "selling" Communism—as one might sell soap—must have fascinated the Advertising Council. These agents, Acheson went on to relate, did not "talk only in terms of economic interest." They invoked not only Marx and Engels but Terpsichore. "We have all seen pictures from China," Acheson recalled, "of native dances out in the fields which were put on by the local Communist organizations. In many cases they provided the only fun that these peasants had . . ."

Acheson's advice to the Chinese people was, as we have seen, to do less dancing and more plotting against the new regime. American attitudes would depend, as he said in the Letter of Transmittal, on how they reacted to "this foreign domination." Acheson expounded the view that the new regime was simply a Russian tool. It might fool the Chinese for a while, but America must refuse to recognize it while encouraging the people to rise against it. In the meantime America would help them along by restricting trade with China. As Acheson said in another of the "total diplomacy" speeches in March of 1950, "Trade requires certain standards of conduct." When the Chinese were prepared to conform, America would trade with them again. The sentence could have been punctuated with a pinch of snuff; it might have been Lord North's rebuke to the Boston Tea Party. This unconscious effort to meet twentieth-century problems with eighteenth-century hauteur would be wholly funny if it were not for the consequences.

The simplistic premises and hostile fixation of Truman-Acheson policy made it difficult for them to discuss peace with Peking. Truman either had to risk the ending of the cold war or its possible transformation into the real thing. He gave MacArthur the signal to go ahead.

PART V

PHANTOM WARFARE

CHAPTER 29

★

The Enemy Was Horrid

A PETULANT note appears in a communique issued by Tokyo Headquarters two days after the offensive began. "In the Chongju-Pakchon area," said Release No. 676 on November 26, "the enemy refused to make an appearance." This was horrid of him. The complaint would have been ground for disqualification in any medieval tournament. It seemed out of place coming from a Headquarters which had just launched an "end-the-war" offensive. The annoyance becomes less incomprehensible, however, if examined in the light of the political planning in Tokyo.

As early as November 11, the Tokyo correspondent of the London *Sunday Times* cabled that "diplomatic quarters" there had said that "Britain and the United States will call for a United Nations vote to permit them to bomb Manchurian bases if the Chinese continue to oppose the forces in Korea." The Chinese, however, after breaking off their attack in "a surprise maneuver" on November 7, were nowhere to be found. What if the November 24 offensive still failed to provoke an appearance?

Much depended politically on the November 24 offensive. As the Lake Success correspondent of the London *Observer* noted the day after it began, "the almost ceremonial trumpeting of the final offensive" had "brought the United Nations back to realities." The "realities" presumably were the realities of "Chinese aggression." But what if the Chinese did not "aggress"? "Diplomats here," said the same dispatch, "have stopped speculating on prospective deals, and are now waiting in nervous anticipation for news over which they know they have no control." What if the expected news failed to materialize? What if peace settled down on the battlefield again, as after November 7? MacArthur's Headquarters, for its own reasons, may have been as nervous as Lake Success.

The November 24 offensive precipitated some bloody fighting. In the east, the Marines fought their way out of entrapment around Chingjin reservoir, and the Tenth Corps was dramatically evacuated by sea from Hungnam under a curtain of naval and aviation firepower by December 24. In the west, where the principal action took place, the Eighth Army Corps was pushed back from the Manchurian borders, and retreated steadily down the peninsula, evacuating first the Northern capital at Pyongyang and then the Southern capital at Seoul. The headlines painted the picture of a headlong flight.

The flight was real enough, but after December 1 there was reason to question its necessity. MacArthur had said he hoped to get the boys home by Christmas. To look back carefully over the battle reports is to wonder whether the offhand promise might not have been kept. And to look back over the negotiations which Tokyo Headquarters was carrying on in October, when it seemed as if the war was won, also leads one to ask how seriously MacArthur could have meant that "home-by-Christmas" remark. For on October 29 General MacArthur was reported to be pressing Washington strongly to retain four or five of the eight divisions under his command. Richard Hughes, the Tokyo correspondent of the London *Sunday Times*, cabled that the officers who "customarily reflect his views are insisting that in no circumstances should the end of the Korean War be allowed to dissolve the tough fighting force . . . under the United Nations flag, and under General MacArthur's command, in Korea."

A good place to begin for a fresh perspective on those hectic weeks in December is with a dispatch that Lindesay Parrott sent the *New York Times* from Tokyo on December 21. Parrott noted that the only "contact" with the enemy the day before had been an encounter between a United States patrol and "a small group of North Koreans." He then added an observation which was in startling contrast to the general impression created by the headlines: "As for the last three weeks, there again was no contact with the Chinese Communists . . . in central Korea with a wide no man's land between them and the United Nations forces."

That was on December 21. Three weeks took one back to December 1. The MacArthur offensive had begun on November 24. It would appear from this that in the west, where the main fighting occurred, contact between the UN forces and the Chinese invaders was broken off six days after the offensive was launched.

This mercurial lack of persistence may explain the petulance visible in that communiqué we quoted. The first Chinese counterattacks began on October 31, and MacArthur had barely branded them as aggressors on November 6 before they broke contact on the 7th and began a swift withdrawal. It was difficult to keep up steam in a campaign to have the United Nations condemn the Chinese aggression when one's patrols moving northward could find no trace of the aggressor.

MacArthur acted more rapidly—and in reverse—the next time. On November 26 his troops on both the east and west were rolling northward "without encountering the enemy in any strength." On November 27 his Headquarters declared that "strong enemy counterattacks" had "stalled" the offensive. On November 28 Tokyo Headquarters said the UN line had "sagged back" under heavy attacks against the right and center of the UN positions, and later that same day the United States at Lake Success accused Communist China of "open and notorious aggression." This time MacArthur did not take any chances on a Chinese withdrawal. He began rapidly to withdraw himself.

At Tokyo on the 29th an Eighth Army spokesman disclosed that UN withdrawals had begun. "At some points" the withdrawals were made "under heavy pressure," but "in others contact with the enemy had been broken as United States and South Korean forces took up better positions for defense." The UN forces kept on withdrawing to "better positions for defense." If a lull in the fighting had become visible after December 1, as both sides stabilized their lines, or if the Chinese had again withdrawn, it would have been difficult to get them condemned as aggressors. MacArthur, by beating them to the retreat, let loose a cascade of headlines which pictured a hard-pressed United Nations force under disastrous attack by overwhelming hordes pouring across the border.

The Eighth Army not only ran but seemed determined to show the enemy just where to chase it, so that it would be forced to continue its strategic withdrawals. We have already seen that on November 20 the military briefing at Tokyo had generously pointed out the famous "gap" between the Eighth Army in the west and the Tenth Corps in the east, and had expressed the opinion that 40,000 Red guerrillas in the rear might have orders to break through at this point in the center where there was "only tenuous contact between the United States Eighth Army and the Tenth Corps."

Though the offensive did not begin until four days later, nothing seems to have been done to close this publicly advertised weak spot. On the contrary, on November 26, when the Eighth Army was pushing up the west coast and the Tenth Corps up the east coast without meeting resistance, Tokyo Headquarters again called attention to the vulnerable point between the two armies. To read the *New York Times* account of the briefing on the 26th is to see Achilles pointing frantically at his heel.

The dispatch said that while all was going well on both flanks, the enemy had counterattacked in the middle "and there were indications that a large-scale battle—if there is to be one before the end of the war—might shape up in that snowy mountain sector." The resistance in the center "while not in mass force was the strongest encountered," and it was added, almost seductively, that "the absence of major opposition raised the question of what the foe was doing in the wedge-shaped area fifty miles deep" between the two United Nations armies. A Victorian maiden could not have fluttered her eyes more unmistakably behind her fan as she moved shyly into the garden.

MacArthur Headquarters seemed to regard the possibility of a serious attack on its most vulnerable sector with noble equanimity. "The growing resistance in the middle of the sector," the dispatch continued, "may or may not provide the answer to that question soon. A spokesman at General MacArthur's headquarters said, 'We can only anticipate that we will run into stiff resistance. We haven't done so yet.' " One usually anticipates resistance at a weak point by stronger defensive measures, not by discussing one's weakness for publication round the world.

When resistance began, Tokyo Headquarters was ready to assume the worst and begin retreating. It was as if MacArthur were about to resume the plans to withdraw that he had ready on November 6, just before the Chinese Communists suddenly broke contact.

At that time, as the reader will recall, the Associated Press reported from Tokyo that "General MacArthur's Headquarters was calm today and confident." What it seemed confident of was just the kind of retreat which began on December 1. This calm and confidence were curious in view of the Headquarters estimate that day that Mao Tse-tung had 600,000 troops available in Manchuria and North China.

"The Chinese Reds thus have the potentiality of vastly outnumbering the present United Nations forces in Korea—if they intend to commit the entire force. Militarily," the dispatch from Headquarters continued, "the situation could become a greatly expanded version of the first days of the Korean war. That is, there would be a slow fighting United Nations' retreat back down the peninsula, brought about mainly by flanking and encirclement made possible by numerically superior Communist forces. Such action," the dispatch added thoughtfully, "on the part of the Chinese Reds could touch off a big war."

This is substantially what happened after December 1—except that MacArthur Headquarters did not wait to see whether such huge forces had in fact been committed by Mao Tse-tung. Another difference was that the retreat of the Eighth

Army was neither "slow" nor "fighting." A third was that the Chinese did not seem at all inclined to touch off that "big war" by pressing MacArthur too hard. But the steady retreat "brought about mainly by flanking and encirclement" went exactly according to that prophetic forecast of November 6.

When resistance began, MacArthur Headquarters was ready to assume the worst and to go on assuming it. Under cover of what seemed to be a "rout," there was a panicky stampede in Washington, London, and Lake Success. The military ignominy in Korea was more than compensated by the political successes elsewhere. Truman at last threatened to use the atom bomb against China, a threat which made peace talks virtually impossible. Attlee came rushing to Washington. On the home front the President issued a declaration of national emergency and set up the economic mobilization machinery which has twice been the prelude to American entry into a world war. France in the excitement swallowed the bitter pill of German rearmament, and Britain found itself being impelled toward quasi-mobilization by the Anglo-American equivalent of the old school tie. Few stopped to consider what was really happening in Korea. The fact is that the Chinese Communists had again failed to "aggress" on the scale that some feared and others hoped for.

At the very start of the "rout," the editors of the conservative British weekly, the *Spectator*, had the temerity to suggest in its issue of December 1 that "it is at least conceivable that China, having, by an astonishingly efficient stroke of strategy, thrust the United Nations back to what she considers a safe distance from her frontier, may be content to break off the battle and enter into some kind of negotiation." Without pausing over the implications, others had begun to notice that there was something odd about the retreat, or as MacArthur—quite rightly—insisted it should be called, the "planned withdrawal."

The MacArthur forces seemed in a great hurry to withdraw while the Communist forces seemed in no hurry to attack. This is not the usual procedure when an aggressor with overwhelming force at his command has the initiative against a weaker foe. There were sour souls who complained, as did Peter

Fleming, the military commentator of the *Spectator*, on December 8 that the Eighth Army's "successful disengagement" had left the Chinese Reds with no "more exacting role than that of sheep dogs." He noted dryly that "front-line reports suggest that an atmosphere has once more been generated in which, if the enemy sends a patrol round behind you, he is said to have 'cut' your 'escape route,' whereas—quite possibly—all he has done is to put part of his forces in a precarious position without benefit of their supporting arms." Fleming was unseemly enough to challenge the validity of Tokyo Headquarters' favorite nightmare, the Chinese "horde." "I can see no military considerations," he went on, "which would enable even the largest force of infantry to throw a modern army, supported by a large air force and an unchallenged fleet, into the sea."

Friendlier critics were just as embarrassing. The military correspondent of the London Sunday *Observer* on December 10 obviously thought he was being helpful. He pointed out that the Eighth Army after drawing back about a hundred miles in a week had been given "a good chance to re-form and reorganize" by the "leisurely pace of the Chinese advance." He suggested that the Eighth "seems to have put itself in a position to give battle, if the Chinese decide to carry the war on." Tokyo Headquarters had other plans. The Tokyo correspondent of the London *Sunday Times* that same day cabled that while the Chinese were "apparently in no hurry to resume battle" it was expected at headquarters that UN forces "will go south of the Parallel to see what the Chinese will do." In the meantime, in the headlines, the "rout" could go on.

Into the popular British press began to seep the grumblings of men of the British 29th Brigade who had been covering the withdrawal. "In spite of their covering mission," the London *Daily Mail* correspondent reported from Tokyo on December 13, "the regiments concerned in the rearguard action have yet to fire a shot in anger. None of them has yet seen a Chinese Communist. Some of the men are asking, 'What's all the hurry?' " The military correspondent of the London *Times* noted on December 18 that the Chinese had "made not the slightest attempt" to close with the rearguards of the Eighth

Army, that they did not "press its flank," and that there was "no clear evidence that they strove to bar its road." The fact is, as we shall see, that there was no clear evidence that the Chinese Communists were following it at all.

"It seems manifest," the *Times* military correspondent wrote of the Chinese, "that their one object was to shepherd it south of the 38th Parallel without further fighting, and, if that was so, they succeeded. It is not to be denied that the Eighth Army stood in great danger; but it will be of great interest to discover, when better information becomes available, whether this army, infinitely better armed than that which followed rather than pursued it to the Parallel, was unable to strike a blow, or was rightly ordered not to."

On December 21, in a special communiqué, MacArthur Headquarters made a bizarre admission. In the course of some characteristically tortuous double talk, it said, "The withdrawal after the battle of Sinanju was not dictated by battle losses or the acceptance of defeat but by the obvious discrepancy between the Chinese Communists and the United Nations potential." The "battle of Sinanju" ended the night of November 30. For three weeks the MacArthur forces had been executing a planned withdrawal, not under direct pressure from the enemy but on the calculation that his forces were too big to venture battle. Whether the enemy had in fact been pursuing the UN forces, whether the enemy's numbers were in fact overwhelming, were not at all clear—though MacArthur Headquarters in the same communiqué implied that one-fifth of China's total military manpower was in Korea "with fifteen to twenty-five additional divisions" massed behind the Yalu.

The UN forces, wrote Hanson Baldwin in his column of December 24, had violated "one of the first rules of war—never to lose contact with the enemy." He said that "we did so for days on end, and high commanders had to insist last week upon large-scale aggressive patrolling along the Eighth Army front to try to determine where the enemy was and how strong he was." As after November 6, those dratted Chinese seemed to have up and disappeared again.

CHAPTER 30

★

...*Like a Poorly Made Fire*

THE war was again in danger of dying out like a poorly made fire. MacArthur Headquarters was looking for (1) Chinese, or (2) a sizable force of North Koreans, and (3) an enemy offensive. The Chinese seemed hardest to find. On December 2, when the "rout" was well under way, with the Northern capital of Pyongyang about to be evacuated, MacArthur had accused the Chinese of waging "undeclared war" against the United Nations. He then had "nearly 145,000 prisoners of war," but when asked by correspondents that day how many were Chinese he replied, "Less than 300 of them are Chinese." On December 28 the *New York Times* reported that there were more than 120,000 North Korean prisoners of war and 616 Chinese in South Korean detention camps. The number of Chinese seemed remarkably few considering Tokyo Headquarters' estimate of the Chinese "hordes" mobilized against it.

There seemed to be even fewer Chinese along the battle-less battlefront. The news from Tokyo Headquarters on the 19th of December was discouraging. "South Korean sources said there were no reports of Chinese troops south of the 38th Parallel," and the "same indication came from nine United States, British, and South Korean war prisoners" who had just been released by the Reds. They reported no sign of Chinese while in enemy hands. A communiqué of December 21 put the Chinese back into the headlines but the evidence of their presence on the battlefield was not overwhelming. The communiqué spoke of an attack on the central front below the 38th Parallel and said that "the fact that horses and camels were reported to have been seen in the immediate area suggests that the attackers were Chinese Communist forces," but it admitted that "no positive identifications were obtained." A communiqué of December 23 said "four additional Chinese Communist armies (corps) believed to be operating under the Fourth Field Army are reported to have entered North Korea recently"—but that was still a long way from the 38th Parallel.

In the absence of Chinese, Tokyo Headquarters began to reassess the size of the North Korean forces. On November 6 MacArthur had declared the North Korean army totally destroyed. On December 19 he estimated that it had six divisions *more* than at the peak of its power. This military miracle deserves to be appreciated in its full proportions. In his famous communiqué of November 6 announcing to the United Nations that "a new foe" was in the field, MacArthur said the North Korean army had been liquidated as a fighting force. The General's arithmetic worked it out that with "the number of prisoners of war in our hands . . . well over 135,000, which, with other losses amounting to over 200,000, brought casualties to 335,000, representing a fair estimate of North Korean total military strength," the war had been "brought to a practical end" when the Chinese intervened.

Now six weeks later, with little evidence of Chinese in the fighting—or, better, the withdrawing—zone, MacArthur raised the North Korean army, like Lazarus, from the tomb. "The total organized strength" of the North Korean forces, this communiqué pleaded, "must approximate 150,000 men at this time," though why was not clear. In addition there were reports that North Koreans were being trained in Manchuria "and it is probable that another 50,000 conscripts and recruits are available, even though they are not actually in North Korea at the moment." This information was amplified at Headquarters.

"Discussing the reconstruction of the North Korean army," said the *New York Times* dispatch from Headquarters next day, "General MacArthur's intelligence section indicated that the Communists had been able to restore virtually all divisions that had made the attack on the Pusan perimeter last summer and had added half a dozen new ones." The "revised" intelligence reports now put the number of North Korean divisions at eighteen, and the number of men at 150,000, without counting the 50,000 more who were probably available in Manchuria. To reorganize an army of 150,000 men and eighteen divisions in six weeks was, if true, a military feat.

As early as December 15, some prisoners when interrogated were reported to have said *that the Chinese did not intend to fight below the 38th Parallel.* If the Chinese didn't, maybe the North Koreans would. With the North Korean army brilliantly reconstituted, at least in the estimates of Tokyo intelligence, the communiqués began to report that an offensive was imminent. "Continued strong probing attacks in various frontal areas," said a communiqué of December 22, "indicate the enemy's determination to seek out the details of the United Nations main line of resistance. This is normally the initial phase of an impending attack." The communiqué speculated on "the enemy intention to repeat his late November offensive."

There were portents. "Tokyo Headquarters privately expressed the opinion," said the *New York Times* weekly Sunday summary on December 24, "that the Chinese assault would come soon. Some officials guessed it might come tonight—on Christmas Eve. Their guess was based on the calendar. The moon is full tonight. Twice before the Chinese have struck on the full of the moon." It might have been a scene from ancient Rome, with the augurs peering into the fresh livers of the sacrifice to gather intelligence of an advancing army.

Why an army under constant bombardment and strafing from the air, with virtually no planes of its own for cover, should wait for a full moon to attack was not explained. But Tokyo Headquarters seemed so sure of that "guess based on the calendar" that it threw a powerful Chinese army south across the 38th Parallel and into the Christmas morning headlines without waiting to synchronize the effort with enemy action. "CHINESE SWEEP SOUTH OVER 38TH PARALLEL—FIRST WAVE HEADS FOR SEOUL; 100,000 TROOPS MASSED IN SUPPORT. GOVERNMENT FLEES FROM SOUTHERN CAPITAL," said the headlines Christmas morning in the Paris edition of the London *Daily Mail*. "CHINESE REDS CROSS PARALLEL FOR DRIVE," said the international edition of the *New York Times* for the same day. Unfortunately the international edition is not printed in Paris until the next day, and by then it was clear that nothing had happened. The Chinese were being uncooperative again.

The offensive had been expected for Christmas Eve. At Tokyo Headquarters everything was moving on schedule. "The first wave of a powerful Communist army," said the *Daily Mail's* dispatch out of Tokyo Headquarters, "has swept across the 38th Parallel into South Korea, heading for Seoul. Ten thousand Chinese and North Koreans are already reported over the border and another 100,000 are moving up behind them. The South Korean government is fleeing from Seoul . . . on the advice of the American military authorities. The full weight of the Chinese and North Korean onslaught is expected tomorrow." In the Paris edition of the *New York Herald Tribune* Christmas morning, headlines based on a similar Associated Press dispatch read: "CHINESE ARE REPORTED ACROSS 38TH PARALLEL IN 'CONSIDERABLE STRENGTH.' RED DRIVE ON SEOUL EXPECTED SOON." The *New York Times'* Lindesay Parrott also reported from Tokyo Headquarters early Christmas morning that Chinese Communist troops "in considerable strength" were reported to have crossed the Parallel for that expected drive on Seoul.

"REDS MASS ABOVE SEOUL," said the separate headline over this dispatch in the *New York Times*. The evidence for this seemed to be that "Korean Republican Troops patrolling on the left flank of the United Nations line north of Seoul killed two Chinese and captured two others in the Imjin River area a few hundred yards south of the border." The prisoners, according to Tokyo Headquarters, said the Chinese were "in strength" in the neighborhood of Korangpo, east of Kaesong, which was described as "the first important settlement south of the boundary along the main highway . . . toward the Republican capital" of Seoul. What the prisoners meant by "in strength" was not explained, but in Tokyo "Korean accounts" were said to have "indicated the Chinese numbered 7000 to 10,000—the equivalent of approximately one Communist division." It was this minor brush on patrol which seemed to have started that headline offensive Christmas Day on Seoul.

Tokyo Headquarters learned to its sorrow that four Chinese do not an offensive make. "REDS DELAY THEIR BIG ATTACK," was the news in the *Daily Mail* the day after Christmas. "The big Communist push into South Korea—regarded as a certainty for Christmas Day—has failed to materialize," its correspondent cabled from Tokyo. The UN troops, dug in below the border, had "maintained and improved their positions during the day" but there were "no new reports of Communist drives south of the Parallel, and statements yesterday that the Reds had crossed the Parallel are now denied officially." Despite the two Chinese reported killed and two captured and interrogated near the Imjin River just south of the border "an Eighth Army spokesman declared that no Chinese armies had yet been identified south of the border." There was still hope, however. "But there is no doubt," the dispatch went on, "that strong Communist forces are poised in the neighborhood of the Parallel. They are probing the Allied front within thirty miles of Seoul, which is being hurriedly evacuated by all noncombatants."

The evacuation of Seoul, however, was proving to be something of a problem. The South Koreans seemed less frightened than Tokyo Headquarters by those Communists supposedly "poised" on the border, as if ready to spring at Seoul. The Northern capital Pyongyang had been set afire and evacuated without a battle. There was some fear that the same fate might meet Seoul in the course of MacArthur's "planned withdrawals." On December 11 a *New York Times* correspondent in Seoul reported that the Eighth Army Headquarters there "has asserted that no decision has been taken on whether or not Seoul would be defended." He added, "Koreans are worried that it will not be."

The same day Syngman Rhee complained in an interview: "The Army wants to fight. Korean soldiers are not taught to back down. . . . They do not know the tactics of retreat. But they were ordered to come down and down." He said six of the colonels in his army had committed suicide the previous summer "in protest against the ordered retreat to the Taegu defense perimeter." The South Korean President announced that he was calling a mass meeting to explain the latest retreat and to tell the people "it would be unwise to flee Seoul this time." Apparently Rhee was then at least in favor of defending Seoul.

There is reason to believe that the United Nations military command had decided on the evacuation of Seoul even before the Christmas Eve offensive which failed to materialize. For a dispatch from Seoul, published in the Paris edition of the *New York Herald Tribune* on December 26, disclosed an arresting fact. In reporting that the South Korean National Assembly had voted to leave the capital for some spot "farther south . . . probably Pusan," the *Herald Tribune*'s correspondent, Ansel E. Talbert, added, "Previously, on December 22, the Assembly voted to defy President Rhee's request and remain in Seoul."

Apparently Rhee himself was under pressure from the American military. For the *New York Times* account quoted him as saying that the vote to evacuate the capital "had been taken 'with reluctance' at the advice of the United Nations military command." Rhee still "expressed confidence that the capital would be held, and appealed to Korean troops to fight to the end." In fact the United Press out of Seoul quoted him next day as saying that the South Korean government "has no intention of leaving its capital," complaining that a false impression had been created in Tokyo and declaring that he had instructed his minister there to make representations to MacArthur Headquarters.

So strong was the resistance to evacuation in Seoul, as the Christmas Day "offensive" evaporated, that on the 26th the *New York Times* correspondent in the South Korean capital reported "growing sentiment in some high government quarters in favor of a plan to ask the United Nations command to release the South Korean military forces so that the Koreans might fight for Seoul as long as possible if other United Nations forces were withdrawn from this area." It was not a defeat but a withdrawal that was feared. South Korean officials said, according to this same dispatch, "they had not been able to learn if the defense of Seoul was planned or if the city would be given up without a fight." South Korea did not seem to have much confidence in its defenders from overseas. This lack of confidence, as we shall see, was not without foundation. Seoul was soon to be gutted and given up by its United Nations defenders in a phantom battle with a phantom foe.

CHAPTER 31

★

Phantom Battle

THE Christmas offensive had barely ebbed out of the headlines when Tokyo Headquarters' intelligence was building up the threat of a new one. On December 28 it made public some alarming new estimates. An "intelligence service breakdown of the enemy strength" showed that MacArthur now faced 1,350,406 enemy forces, divided as follows:

Facing the Eighth Army: 171,117 men of the Chinese Communist Fourth Army.

Massed in the Hungnam area: 106,056 men of the Chinese Communist Third Army.

North Korean troops, including guerrillas: 167,233.

Combined enemy strength in Korea	444,406
In North China "or reported on the way"	906,000
Grand enemy total	1,350,406

The Census Bureau could not have done better. The figures, according to the Headquarters spokesman, were "partly based on the interrogation of several hundred prisoners." The phrase "partly based" was intriguing but Headquarters was discreetly silent about the other method or methods used—perhaps some wartime intelligence device secretly clicking off the enemy as they went by, like a New York subway turnstile.

Lindesay Parrott, the *New York Times* man in Tokyo, after reporting these figures added that their release "coincided with reports from Washington that no reliable intelligence assessment thus far had been received . . . to substantiate General MacArthur's estimate of the overwhelming Communist strength arrayed against his forces in Korea." Publication of the exact count may have been MacArthur's way of silencing the skeptics.

The most extraordinary news of all concerned the North Korean army. It was still growing by what might conservatively be described as leaps and bounds. This army, as the reader will recall, was reported by MacArthur totally destroyed on November 6, and then six weeks later on December 19 as miraculously reorganized with "half a dozen" more divisions than at its wartime peak. Now, eight days later, on December 27, a communiqué from MacArthur reported that "eleven reconstituted North Korean divisions have reappeared in the last twelve days, thus bringing the total identified North Korean units to twenty-six." This was an increase of eight divisions in eight days. Kim Il Sung was made to seem a modern Cadmus.

On December 19 Headquarters had thought it "probable" that there were 50,000 more North Koreans training in Manchuria. The number estimated had almost tripled by December 27. "There have been reports," the communiqué said, "that as many as 130,000 North Korean troops were undergoing training in Manchuria in late November," and it was "reasonable to assume that the enemy has the capability of placing several additional North Korean divisions in the field in the very near future." At this rate, even if Mao Tse-tung withdrew altogether, MacArthur and Kim Il Sung would be able to carry on alone.

With these vast enemy estimates deployed, MacArthur Headquarters made a new prediction. Its spokesman said on December 29 that the Communists, with twenty-two divisions ready to strike, would "be in a position to launch a coordinated attack against the United States Eighth Army in Korea by January 1." "The timing and strength of their expected offensive," it was explained, "can be deduced from time-distance factors and last-known Chinese positions." While the day's battlefront news, "as for the last fortnight," showed "only patrol actions," the Headquarters spokesman "asserted that 'limited attacks could be launched at any time' in strength of at least one Chinese corps." The breathless expectation of overwhelming attack, magnified many times in the headlines—an instrument on which Tokyo Headquarters played with mastery—hid the essential news: "For the last fortnight" there had been "only patrol actions."

This was not all. Tucked away unnoticed in a wordy communiqué of December 28 was a quietly sensational revelation. This Headquarters Release No. 768, the full text of which may be found in the following day's *New York Times*, said that the "last positive contact and identification as of December 12 placed the Chinese Communist forces generally . . . in the vicinity of Pyongyang." The last positive identification and contact thus had taken place sixteen days before. And it had taken place in the vicinity of the Northern capital, which was about seventy miles above the 38th Parallel. Pyongyang had been abandoned without a fight by MacArthur's forces on December 4; the first sign of any advancing enemy was on December 5, when observation planes reported that Communist troops had taken over an airfield on the northeastern outskirts of the city. For all MacArthur Headquarters knew to the contrary on December 28, the Chinese Communists were still around Pyongyang about a hundred miles north of Seoul.

On December 30, there was still no sign of that offensive, and "speculation . . . backed by intelligence estimates at General MacArthur's Headquarters, was that the mass offensive now was scheduled for sometime after New Year's Day." The Eighth Army's new commander, Lieutenant General Matthew Ridgway, after a three-day tour announced "complete confidence in the magnificent team" under his command, and in Seoul a spokesman for the South Korean government said it would not leave the capital "despite earlier plans for evacuation" because it now thought "the defense line north of the city would be held."

Not much happened on December 31, though Headquarters noted "the continued thickening of hostile dispositions." The

Associated Press reported from Tokyo that the enemy was wheeling into position "for an expected all-out smash at Seoul in the first days of the new year." A front-line dispatch said that the troops were confident they could hold, unless the Communists again placed too much "pressure against the left flank of the United Nations line, forcing it to fall back. There is fear among the United Nations line troops," the front-line correspondent reported to the *New York Times*, "that this may happen again." Headquarters seemed to be reconciled to this prospect. Three days earlier, in the communiqué discussing supposed enemy preparations, it said, "It is likely that the enemy will use his usual maneuver of attacking on the flank of the United Nations ensemble." Headquarters' spokesman amplified this by explaining that "it was considered probable that the enemy was preparing to repeat the maneuver of the 'end run' that forced the United Nations withdrawal last month from the Chongchon River line north of the Communist capital at Pyongyang." Then, too, as the reader will remember, Headquarters had obligingly pointed out its own weak spots. It was almost as if Tokyo Headquarters were trying to build up for another strategic withdrawal, this time at the expense of Seoul.

MacArthur was preparing the ground for evacuation even before it could be sure there would be an attack. These preparations were apparent in a dispatch which Richard J. H. Johnston filed with the dateline *"With United States Troops in Korea"* on December 30 but which was held up somewhere en route, for it was not published until January 1. (Because of the fourteen-hour time difference, Korean war dispatches often appeared in the New York morning papers the same day they were written.) This reported not only the expectation that Seoul would probably be abandoned "within a short time after the enemy's attack" but went on to say, "Whether United Nations forces would make a major stand south and west of Seoul on the opposite bank of the broad Han River in order to maintain Seoul's port of Inchon was not indicated as late as yesterday."

The Eighth Army officers with whom Johnston spoke seem

to have been considering seriously not only the abandonment of Seoul and Inchon but of all Korea. "A problem causing much concern here," Johnston cabled, was what to do with 130,000 prisoners "if the evacuation of United Nations forces is decided upon." A "closely related" problem was what to do with the South Korean army "in case of total evacuation." It was suggested "in some Korean quarters"—obviously rather extensive discussions were going on—that these troops, "numbering more than 100,000, be shifted to Cheju Island, sixty miles off the South Korean coast." It was also suggested that this rocky barren fishing island might become Syngman Rhee's "Formosa." It was "unofficially" suggested that Rhee might set up a government in exile on Cheju "similar to the Nationalist Chinese Government in Formosa."

The morale of the South Koreans "against this background," Johnston wrote, "probably is lower now than at any moment since the North Korean Communist attack of last June" but there was "an undercurrent of confidence" that the United Nations "ultimately" would "eject the enemy and unify the country." Johnston added at this point, "With the danger of a world war fully appreciated by the Koreans, however, the possibility that this victory will be long delayed is widely recognized."

A new world war was certainly possible. It had been possible since the beginning of the Korean War. If a new world war came, the position of the MacArthur forces in Korea would be untenable, for they would be caught in a vise between the Chinese in Manchuria and the Russians in Siberia. The Rhee forces would be lucky if they could hold out in Cheju. But why was all this being discussed so elaborately at this time, when there had been no real fighting on the main front since December 1, no positive contact with Chinese Communist troops since December 12, no real sign that they had ever moved past Pyongyang one hundred miles away?

"KOREA EXIT IS SEEN IF NEW WAR COMES," said the headline on the Johnston dispatch. Why the planning on world war when there was so little real warfare, even in Korea? There was no doubt now, and there had been no doubt from the beginning, that if the Chinese intervened wholeheartedly in Korea, alone or together with the Russians, they had the manpower and the material to push the United Nations forces into the sea. They had not done so. Russian submarines had not challenged the American Navy in the sea. There had only been rare, intermittent, and meager challenge by the Russians and the Chinese in the air. The forces in North Korea had little heavy equipment. The signs at the end of December, as from the beginning, were that the Russians and the Chinese had no desire to take up the American challenge in Korea. Why, then, all this talk and planning of a total evacuation and world war?

It is possible that there were some people in Tokyo and perhaps also in Washington for whom this question held no mystery. There was another set of conditions under which world war and evacuation of Korea *would* be necessary. If MacArthur were to bomb Manchuria, especially if he were to be allowed to use the atom bomb, there would be war with China and almost certainly also with Russia. In that event the troops in Korea would be caught in a trap. If Manchuria was to be bombed, it would be better to get the troops out of Korea first.

Some key to the mystery may be found if one turns back to the statements given to the press in Tokyo on December 6 by the Republican leader Harold E. Stassen after seeing General MacArthur. Stassen said that MacArthur was operating under "impossible" United Nations directives in the face of the Chinese attacks. In view of this, Stassen suggested an unconditional cease-fire ultimatum to the Chinese, to take effect in forty-eight hours. If the Chinese agreed, there would be mediation. If the Chinese did not agree, the Supreme Commander should be allowed to retaliate "by striking in any manner any objects of military significance either in Korea or China." When asked whether he included use of the atom bomb, Stassen replied, "I say any manner and any objects of military significance; that includes everything." He added that air bombardment and blockade should be supplemented "by orders to General Douglas MacArthur to withdraw land forces from Korea in as orderly a manner as possible in favor of long-range attacks."

Was MacArthur, under cover of alarmist statistics and predictions of offensives which failed to occur, withdrawing so rapidly because he hoped for permission soon to bomb that "privileged sanctuary" and turn the war into war with China? Were these repeated alarms an attempt to force, by military maneuver, decisions which had gone against him in the political councils? The same day that Stassen, fresh from his talks with MacArthur, suggested withdrawal from Korea and the bombing of China, a different decision seems to have been reached in Washington. For the news that day out of the Attlee-Truman conversations was that there would be no evacuation of Korea unless the United Nations' troops were actually pushed into the sea. This implied that MacArthur would not receive permission to bomb Manchuria, for the time being at any rate. In this perspective, the decision not to evacuate seems to have been the one concrete accomplishment of Attlee's otherwise inconclusive visit to Washington, where on the atom bomb itself Truman would give no more than a vague assurance of "consultation."

To look back at the news reports of early December from the vantage point of the end of the month is to see that Truman's threat to use the bomb was made under the impact of predictions of disaster which proved ridiculously untrue. On December 6 the diplomatic correspondent of the *New York Times*, reporting the Attlee-Truman decision not to evacuate, wrote from Washington as if a triple Dunkirk were ahead in Korea. "The United States and Britain," he reported, "will fight side by side in Korea until the very last moment. The Hamhung beachhead in the northeast may be in danger, but the Inchon-Seoul beachhead can probably be held for several weeks with the aid of naval gunfire, and three South Korean divisions in the south have a good chance of holding out for a while in the Pusan beachhead. Therefore no general evacuation should be ordered for the time being."

The Hamhung beachhead proved in no danger. Between December 12, when its evacuation began, and December 25, when it was completed, ships and planes removed 105,000 troops, 100,000 refugees, 17,500 vehicles, and 350,000 tons of equipment from the Hamhung beachhead. The three admirals in charge told a press conference at Tokyo afterwards that the beachhead "could have been held indefinitely"—meaning, as long as the Russians and Chinese refrained from putting submarines and aircraft, much less heavy guns, into an attack upon it. As for the references to a Seoul-Inchon beachhead and a new stand in the Pusan beachhead, events had proved such forecasts fantastic.

The forecasts had their political logic for MacArthur Headquarters. The London *Daily Mail's* correspondent in Washington cabled on December 6 that one reason for Truman's unwillingness to give Attlee "categoric assurances" against the use of the atom bomb was that the President "may be under pressure to keep his and General MacArthur's hands free to use all weapons to redeem what some people here believe to be approaching military disaster." The real disaster, narrowly averted with the aid of Attlee's dramatic flight to Washington, would have been to plunge into war with China and almost certainly thereafter with China's ally, the Soviet Union, on the dubious inference that the Chinese intervention set off by MacArthur's offensive of November 28 was intended to sweep the UN troops out of Korea.

As the year ended, it was beginning to become clear that the Chinese were not interested in taking over all Korea. On the west coast the last place the Eighth Army had fought, according to MacArthur, was at the "battle of Sinanju." On the east coast, no major military effort had been made to prevent the UN evacuation of Hamhung. A line from Sinanju to Hamhung is roughly the line of the Korean "waist," the narrows of the peninsula before it broadens out into the border zone. There was little evidence of Chinese interest in the rest of North Korea, much less the territory below the Parallel. Were this to seep beyond the scare headlines into the consciousness of ordinary folk, especially in America, it might be difficult to keep peace from breaking out. There had been in all but name a cease-fire on the main front since early in December. How could MacArthur win permission to bomb China if the Chinese did not fight? How bomb China if there was still a considerable body of UN troops in Korea, where they would be trapped by a world war? Tokyo Headquarters was steadily thinking in terms of total evacuation, despite the Anglo-American decision at Washington. A new Communist offensive might provide the military pretext. On New Year's Day Mac-Arthur Headquarters got what it needed, an enemy offensive— or at least so it seemed.

CHAPTER 32

★

Seoul Abandoned Again

ON JANUARY 1 Tokyo Headquarters announced that the long-expected offensive had begun. Early on the morning of January 4, Seoul was abandoned. The next day MacArthur's forces also pulled out of Inchon, the key South Korean seaport adjoining the capital.

The briefings at Tokyo Headquarters pictured a terrible battle against overwhelming odds. On January 1: "The Communists, who have an estimated 1,250,000 men at their disposal, were rushing division after division to the break-through points." On January 2: "Unofficial reports said three Chinese corps, plus nine reconstituted North Korean divisions, were advancing abreast in a total force estimated at more than 100,000 men." On January 3: "Red hordes, supported by tanks, swarmed southward under a deadly hail of rockets and machine-gun bullets fired by low-flying United Nations planes." On January 4: "The Red attack has been a series of hammer blows that have overwhelmed the UN troops by sheer weight of numbers." "The pathos of this retreat," said General Ridgway, the commander of the Eighth Army, shortly after the last Han River bridges were blown up to cover the retreat from Seoul, "ought to wake up the people at home like nothing else." It was revealing how many of MacArthur's generals seemed to have time—at their busiest moments—to keep a sharp eye on public opinion, almost as if they were engaged less in military actions than in gigantic advertising campaigns.

The heat was on again in Washington. Demands were made in Congress for a "second front" in China, to be opened by Chiang from Formosa, and for a complete withdrawal from Korea. Truman at his press conference on January 4 stood his ground, insisting that the United States did not intend to bomb China and that any such decision would depend on a Congressional declaration of war and could only be taken after consultation with the United Nations. His Secretary of Defense, General Marshall, said the United Nations forces were up against "odds . . . almost incredible in some respects"— which seemed to be true in more ways than was perhaps intended. Otherwise the Secretary seemed unsurprised. "The situation in Korea," General Marshall told the press, "is developing almost exactly as we anticipated and deployment of our forces is being carried out to meet this anticipation."

What may or may not have been anticipated was that this offensive, like its predecessors, would die down so soon. In the headlines the war raged on, but for those few who read beyond the headlines the situation on the ground was puzzling. On January 13 the Eighth Army issued a communiqué, No. 124, which finally confessed "eight days of nothing more than patrol action in the west." Eight from thirteen leaves five. Eight days takes one back to January 5. Seoul was abandoned on the 4th. A second communiqué the same day, No. 125, said: "From end to end on the Eighth Army front this morning the enemy was either out of contact or contained. At certain points Eighth Army troops were ranging farther north than at any time since soon after Seoul was evacuated." MacArthur was looking for the enemy again. The "strategic withdrawals" were again becoming too obvious. There was something almost wistful in the phrasing of Communiqué No. 124: "Despite eight days of nothing more than patrol action in the west, possibility of a major Communist attack there is not discounted." At the beginning of April, 1951, three months later, that "major attack" in the west was still being awaited. And MacArthur had crossed the Parallel again in search of the enemy.

Rarely, even in the Korean War as waged by MacArthur,

has defeat been accepted with such speed as in the second abandonment of Seoul. Despite the vivid reports (from Tokyo) of the usual "hordes" pouring down from the Parallel on the doomed capital, as early as January 2—one day after the offensive was supposed to have begun, two days before Seoul was evacuated—the Air Force seemed to have difficulty in finding many of the enemy. Christopher Rand, the *New York Herald Tribune's* correspondent in Tokyo, reported an Air Force spokesman as saying that "the lack of sufficient targets in the battle zone might have been due to the fact that withdrawing UN forces have lost contact with the Reds, or because the Communists have reduced the pressure against UN lines temporarily."

Rand added, perhaps with tongue in cheek, that "it seems fair to say that the UN is practicing a new type of warfare in Korea now—retiring with mechanized speed before Communist mass onslaughts." But Seoul is only thirty miles below the Parallel and MacArthur's forces were then still above the capital. No matter how fast they were retreating, the Air Force should have had no trouble finding plenty of targets between Seoul and the Parallel if Communist hordes were pouring over it to join the attack. The communiqués themselves, as distinct from the briefings, seemed hesitant. The communiqués are written, the briefings are oral. The former go into the official records, the latter supply material the correspondents use on their own responsibility. Every official knows the difference between a document he may have to defend and an informal talk with the press that he can always disavow. To go from the headlines to the briefings and from the briefings to the communiqués was a pilgrimage in anticlimax. MacArthur Headquarters took a long time before committing itself in writing to the fact that an offensive was under way against Seoul.

It is instructive to look at these communiqués. At 5:15 P.M. Tokyo time on January 1, Headquarters would go no further than to say that enemy forces opposite the Eighth Army "continue in the advance stages of preparations for an all-out offensive, predicted to be launched on January 1." It was not until 4 P.M. January 3 Tokyo time that Headquarters issued a communiqué saying that the offensive was under way. "On New Year's Eve," said Release No. 783 from MacArthur Headquarters that day, "the enemy launched his expected offensive in very great strength with three to four Chinese Communist armies (corps) abreast." If three to four Chinese Communist armies had been moving forward "abreast" since New Year's Eve, it seems queer that Headquarters should not have taken official notice of them sooner and that the Air Force should feel restive about lack of targets in the battle area.

Where were these armies going? "It is safe to assume," said the communiqué on the afternoon of January 3, "that the city of Seoul, the capital of South Korea, is a major, if not the major, objective." With "three or four armies" moving abreast to the attack since New Year's Eve, Headquarters three days later still had to make cautious "assumptions" about where it was going. The attacking horde must have been quite a way from Seoul on January 3 if the best that Headquarters could offer that afternoon about its intentions was this "safe to assume."

At the time this communiqué was being issued in Tokyo, MacArthur's troops were methodically burning and destroying Seoul in pursuance of "the United Nations Command's 'scorched earth' policy" which "has been to leave no facility standing which the enemy might use." The text of the communiqué appeared in the *New York Times* the same day with an eyewitness account from Seoul. This said the evacuation had been completed on the morning of January 4 "with such precision as to indicate that elaborate planning had preceded its abandonment."

This eyewitness account said that little was known about "the weight of the fighting" which had preceded the fall of Seoul, "although previous official accounts had said the Chinese were making their major assault regardless of casualties." Correspondents who had left the city by air the night before (January 3) "said there was some volume of rifle and machine-gun fire in the outskirts—apparently a rearguard engagement." The final attack had been expected early on the morning of the 4th, but by 8:30 A.M. "all United Nations troops had been withdrawn and were safely across the Han River."

The actual fighting that day to the north of Seoul indicated no irresistible mass onslaught. For several days Tokyo Headquarters had focused attention on the village of Uijongbu, twelve miles north of Seoul, as a key communications center through which an attack on the capital might be expected. Uijongbu was set on fire and abandoned by MacArthur's forces on the night of January 2. During the day of January 3 a puzzling incident occurred. Uijongbu was recaptured, as if by mistake, and then ordered abandoned again.

The story appeared not in the dispatches based on the briefings at Tokyo—these did not mention the incident—but in a front-line story filed from *"Outside Seoul"* early on the morning of the 4th by Michael James of the *New York Times*. James said that the order to evacuate Seoul came on the afternoon of January 3 and "was not as surprising to units in the rear as it was to front-line units." To explain why the order was a surprise to front-line units, he told the story of two successful counterattacks that day north of Seoul, one of them the recapture of Uijongbu.

James reported that the United States 24th Division sent out a unit of twenty Pershing tanks and 300 Australian infantrymen which made its way twelve miles northward out of the city and retook Uijongbu within two hours but "was then told to come back." If it was possible on January 3 for a striking force of that size to move twelve miles northward that quickly and retake so important a road center it would seem that the attacking forces were neither so large nor so invincible as reported. In a smaller action that day a company of Australian infantry with four British medium tanks took two small villages two miles inside the enemy lines.

"Both counterattacks," James wrote, "had a magic effect on the United Nations troops. Fighting men of all the United Nations have generally hoped that some sort of line would be formed around the capital. While it is true that two South Korean divisions took a severe battering on the defense line, the remainder of the troops were virtually undamaged. For the last week reports that the city would be defended did much to keep up morale. Today's counterattacks made it shoot sky-high. The order to retreat or 'withdraw' sent it down."

It is informative to notice how briefly the day's Headquarters communiqué dismissed these two counterattacks. Release No. 786 put out at 3:50 P.M. Tokyo time on January 4 spoke of "orderly withdrawals . . . in the Seoul area" and of continued enemy "pressure" to the northwest of the city, and then mentioned casually that "a vigorous counterattack by friendly forces regained two villages." This seems almost churlish, but Headquarters must have known what it was doing. How keep up the pretense of irresistible hordes if 300 infantrymen with twenty tanks and a company of infantrymen with four tanks could make that much progress that quickly north of Seoul the very day it was being burned and abandoned?

The discrepancy between these successful counterattacks by small groups of men and the overwhelming hordes supposedly attacking Seoul became embarrassing. So were certain aerial observations which were not mentioned in the briefings or the communiqués. An observation plane over Inchon on January 5 reported "no sign of enemy troops." An Associated Press correspondent, William C. Barnard, who was in that plane, also reported: "We flew over Seoul and found a dead city. Although we cruised over it for five minutes, there was not a single sign of life—not a person, not a single one, just empty streets and cold silent buildings." Tokyo Headquarters had created the impression that these cities had been abandoned "in the nick of time" to avoid inescapable defeat before impossible odds. Where was the enemy?

Tokyo Headquarters was forced to change its tune, at least for the more sophisticated. "A spokesman in Tokyo," the military correspondent of *The Times* of London noted on January 5, had stated "that the abandonment of Seoul was not due to the weight of the Chinese convergent advance on Seoul; at the only point where the main defensive position was breached on this front it was restored by a local counterattack"—a reference possibly to the retaking of Uijongbu. "The retreat was ordered," the *Times* correspondent went on to report, "in consequence of a strong thrust by the enemy which threatened to outflank, or even envelop, the defensive arc around Seoul." This thrust was in the direction of Wonju, fifty-seven miles southeast of Seoul, and "if it had reached Wonju before the retreat from Seoul had taken place, it might have turned west and caught the bulk of the Eighth Army in a trap." Since this appeared in *The Times* of January 5, it means that as early as January 4 Tokyo Headquarters was already explaining to those shrewd enough to look beyond the headlines that the abandonment of Seoul was not due to "the weight" of the attack against it but to a calculation that *if* other forces more than fifty-five miles away were to take Wonju and if they then were to turn west, they *might* outflank Seoul. The *Times* correspondent concluded that if "the policy of immediate retreat when a flank is turned" were continued, "the prospect of maintaining a hold on the Korean peninsula is virtually nil."

Seoul was another of those defeats-by-conjecture. The tenuous nature of this particular conjecture could be seen in the communiqués issued by Tokyo Headquarters. At 4 P.M. Tokyo time on January 3, Release No. 783 speculated that the four Chinese Communist armies and two North Korean corps previously estimated to be in the area of Hungnam "and now moving west and south, possibly have as their objective the important communications center of Wonju, fifty-five miles east and southeast of Seoul." It was then on the strength of this "possibility" that the UN troops were already setting fire to Seoul that afternoon. A communiqué the next afternoon, hours after Seoul had been destroyed and abandoned, was still speculating on this possible attack toward Wonju. It said again that the objective of the forces released in the east by the evacuation of Hungnam was "believed to be" Wonju. It conjectured that the force which thus might be moving toward Wonju contained "at least four and possibly seven Chinese Communist armies (corps), with a total strength of 120,000 men," and said that in addition two reconstituted North Korean corps "also are believed to be taking part in this movement." And if this force took Wonju, it might envelop the UN forces to the north and west and "exploit" the route south to Pusan.

Headquarters was telling correspondents on January 4 that the "head" of this force had reached the neighborhood of Hongchon, twenty-one miles south of the 38th Parallel and some twenty-five miles north of Wonju. But this also seemed to be conjecture, for the communiqué itself merely said cryptically, "Two enemy groups in the vicinity of Hongchon were engaged by friendly troops." It did not say how large the "groups" were nor what was the result of the engagement; in fact it looked very much like a brush on patrol and very unlike the spearhead of a force as enormous as the 120,000 men together with two North Korean corps supposedly advancing on Wonju. The *Times* military correspondent commented sensibly on January 6 that "no such force could exist or move simultaneously in these bleak foothills, through which run only a couple of poor roads and some still more indifferent tracks. Transport can be used on them only to a very small extent, and without transport there is little sustenance." His opinion was that "several divisions . . . strung out" were engaged on the central front "and it may be taken for granted that they are North Korean. There might be some small Chinese element in the force, though even that seems improbable."

The picture painted by MacArthur of overwhelming Chinese hordes pouring down on his men was also difficult to reconcile with a communiqué of January 9, Release No. 799, which said that villages on both sides of the Parallel "continue to be raided by armed bands in search of manpower." It described these bands as impressing all males between the ages of seventeen and forty-five and paying no attention to the political beliefs of the conscripts. Why impress politically unreliable and militarily untrained elements if huge Chinese armies, not to speak of those two reconstituted North Korean divisions, were already on the scene? In an effort to answer, Headquarters set a new mark in fatuity. It said this widespread impressment policy was "obviously designed to make maximum use of the huge manpower potential of Korea."

There was an outburst of criticism in the British press about the character of the "information" emanating from MacArthur's Headquarters. The *Daily Mirror* spoke of "FAIRY TALES FROM KOREA." The *Sunday Pictorial* asked in big red type, "IS THIS A PRIVATE WAR?" The Beaverbrook *Sunday Express* wanted to know how MacArthur's intelligence chief, Lieutenant General Charles Willoughby, could have counted the enemy troops to the last man as he did in the fantastic communiqué of December 26. On January 9 Tokyo Headquarters replied by suddenly imposing censorship regulations far more severe than any known in World War II. Selkirk Panton, Tokyo correspondent of the London *Daily Express*, reported that even speculation about the possible reasons for such severe censorship had been forbidden. "But," he added, as if in one last desperate effort to get the real story over, "this much can be said. . . . There has been no sign of any Chinese Communist 'hordes' in the front-line fighting."

On the central front around Wonju, the one sector where the UN troops did not withdraw but stood and fought, no Chinese hordes appeared. According to a Tokyo communiqué of January 4, Wonju was believed to be threatened by "four and possibly seven Chinese Communist armies (corps)" which were in turn believed to be "all or a major portion of the Chinese Communist forces subordinate to the Third Communist Chinese Field Army." Three days later in the *New York Times*, Hanson Baldwin wrote that the troops fighting around Wonju "said they knew nothing of the four Chinese Communist armies, but had been attacked by four reconstituted North Korean divisions." Baldwin added that "in any case the bulk of the Chinese Communist Third Field Army is not yet in Korea and probably not yet in Manchuria. . . . Some of its units were reported near Canton last week."

The explanation handed out for the abandonment of Seoul —after the hordes threatening it began to evaporate—was the danger that the Wonju salient some fifty miles to the east might give way and allow the Eighth Army to be outflanked. But the Wonju salient held. Its commander was then rewarded by being removed from his command. Commanders are usually removed in defeat, not in victory. The treatment given Major General R. B. McClure, commander of the United States Second Division, which held Wonju and prevented the flanking maneuver Tokyo Headquarters affected to fear, is another of the unexplained incidents in this strange war.

General McClure was one of the United States Army's top experts on China. He had been deputy chief of staff to Chiang Kai-shek. He was named commander of the Second Division on December 11. He took over a badly battered force. The Second Division, as a rearguard along the Chong River, covered the retreat of the Eighth Army from the Korean "waist" when it was pushed out of the border regions by the Chinese. The Division lost one-third of its men in killed, wounded, or missing in that operation. Under General McClure, it became a first-rate fighting force again. The London *Times* said that in the Wonju salient the Second Division "had blocked the enemy's attempt to advance southwards for sixteen days and caused him thousands of casualties." The London *Daily Mail* said of McClure's troops that "their five-day stand at Wonju has been one of the most dramatic actions of the campaign."

These tributes are from the British press. General McClure seemed without honor in his own country. In a war so replete with inglorious retreat, one would have thought that a Headquarters as publicity-conscious as MacArthur's would have built up the story of McClure's stand at Wonju. Instead, on January 15 came the cryptic news that General McClure "whose Second Division infantrymen conducted a brilliant defensive stand against eight Communist assaults at Wonju, has been relieved of his command, it was announced today. No reason for the action was given in a dispatch cleared by Eighth Army censorship, but the dispatch said he was highly regarded by division officers and correspondents at Second Division headquarters." It was announced that

General McClure would be replaced by Major General C. L. Ruffner and that pending his arrival the division would be led by the deputy commander. This swift and summary removal without explanation was painful punishment for a commander.

An odd incident occurred when the news of General McClure's removal reached his divisional officers. A field dispatch said "they promptly cut off the beards they had allowed to grow since the Chinese and North Koreans crossed the 38th Parallel a fortnight ago. Why they did so was not explained." Perhaps censorship did not permit it to be explained.

The new commander seemed a bit embarrassed about the beards. Next day an Associated Press dispatch said one of General Ruffner's first orders to his new command was to shave them off. This was not consistent with the field dispatch of the day before which said the beards were shaved as soon as McClure's removal was announced. At that time no explanation was given. Now a spokesman for the new commander had two explanations. One was that the beards were grown for identification purposes at night—the Asians have sparser whiskers than Occidentals. "I rather think it was a morale gesture, too," the spokesman said, "giving the men something to talk about." The men had begun to grow the beards when the enemy crossed the Parallel. Could it be that they had made one of those familiar battlefront vows not to shave again until the enemy were driven back?

Another of the new commander's first orders was to withdraw. The same day with the story about the order to shave, the *New York Times* published this short dispatch from Eighth Army Headquarters: "Allied troops have moved south from the Wonju salient that jutted deep into Communist territory in central Korea, the Eighth Army announced today. The withdrawal was carried out to the defensive line established after the pullback from Seoul, an Eighth Army communiqué said." This reference to the "defensive line established after the pullback from Seoul" is tantalizing. It suggests that McClure's troops were further north than they were supposed to be, that they had not withdrawn as planned.

But if the pullback from Seoul occurred for fear that Wonju would not hold, why had a new defensive line based on a withdrawal from Wonju been established "after the pullback from Seoul"? Was this an elaborate game of military leapfrog, in which there was a withdrawal in the west in fear of an outflanking maneuver on the east, and then a withdrawal in the east to meet the threat of an outflanking maneuver from the west? Was this the game McClure had disrupted by holding at Wonju? And is this why he was relieved?

The withdrawal, when it came, seemed so pointless as almost to appear vindictive. There had been no enemy attack. "There have been no contacts with the enemy in the area for twenty hours," said the communiqué announcing the withdrawal. No formidable threat was being built up by the enemy at Wonju. Three days later the London *Times* reported, "In Central Korea a patrol went into Wonju, and meeting no resistance, spent the night there, withdrawing safely on Thursday afternoon and picking up eighteen prisoners in villages nearby." Wonju was reoccupied next day by what was described as a "reinforced patrol."

Elsewhere in Korea, at the very time General McClure was removed and the Second Division ordered to retreat, the withdrawal had suddenly been ended and patrols sent northward again in search of the enemy. Why, at such a moment and under such circumstances, were an able commander and a valiant division humiliated? There have been wars in which commanders who successfully held strategic salients were promoted, while those who unnecessarily abandoned and destroyed a great city were removed or court-martialed.

General McClure and the Second Division had saved MacArthur from being outflanked by the North Koreans, but at the expense of allowing the Supreme Commander to be outflanked by the British. The evidence suggests that despite the agreement reached in the Attlee-Truman conversations, to stay in Korea, MacArthur was determined to evacuate the peninsula and clear the way for bombardment of Manchuria. While McClure's troops were successfully fighting on the

Wonju front, Tokyo Headquarters was preparing the public mind for the evacuation they were delaying.

Through every channel of communication it could reach, MacArthur Headquarters was spreading the idea that a general withdrawal was inevitable. And Hanson Baldwin, with the best of sources in both Tokyo and Washington, wrote flatly in the *New York Times* of January 7 that "the big retreat" would go on until the Pusan beachhead was reached again. Christopher Rand, the *New York Herald Tribune's* sharp-eyed correspondent at Tokyo, had the audacity to cable on January 8 that censorship was passing speculative stories based on hints thrown out by "high United Nations army officers . . . that our eventual retirement from Korea may be inevitable." Rand noted one difference between the atmosphere surrounding this "retirement" and the withdrawal to Pusan the preceding summer. "Last summer," Rand cabled, "we expected to drive back north again. Now we do not."

Something happened to change the picture. The British government intervened. "The rapid retreats of recent days," the Washington correspondent of the London *Daily Mail* reported on January 11, "raised fears in British official minds that the agreement reached by Mr. Attlee and President Truman in conference here last month, that every effort should be made to continue the fight, had been revised. These fears were aggravated by the stringent new censorship rules imposed by General MacArthur, which, in the words of the influential *Washington Post* today, 'Only serve to arouse suspicion that something fishy is going on.' "

The British government may have feared that evacuation would be followed by bombardment of Manchuria and war with China. Its ambassador, Sir Oliver Franks, was instructed to raise the question. On January 11 Sir Oliver was assured that American troops and United Nations forces would fight on and "make every effort to establish a defense position on the peninsula." The representations made by the British government must have been unusually forceful, because three days later Washington announced that General J. Lawton Collins, the United States Army Chief of Staff, and General

Hoyt Vandenberg, the Air Force Chief of Staff, had arrived in Tokyo for a conference with MacArthur. Present were Lieutenant General Walter Bedell Smith, head of Central Intelligence Agency, and Major General Alexander R. Bolling, Chief of Staff, Intelligence Section, Department of the Army. The conference was closely guarded and no announcement of its purpose or conclusions was made. But two things happened after it was over.

One was that General Collins, in a press conference at Eighth Army Headquarters on January 15, declared that the UN forces will "certainly stay in Korea and fight." From that time on, the general retreat was at an end. The other event which followed the conference was never connected up with it at all. On the night of January 15 Major General Emmett ("Rosy") O'Donnell, commander of the Far East Air Force's Bomber Command, was relieved of his post and left the bomber base in Japan for another assignment with the Fifteenth Air Force in California.

A *New York Times* correspondent cabled that "General O'Donnell, one of the most outspoken proponents of strategic bombing, is leaving a command fraught with frustrations." The nature of these frustrations was indicated by the General in an interview he gave the correspondent at the air base before leaving. "We have never been permitted," General O'Donnell said, "to bomb what are the real strategic targets, the enemy's real sources of supply." The General made his views even clearer—in fact, blatant—at a press conference when he took over his new post in California three days later. He said the strategic bombing command had been "designed to deliver the atomic offensive to the heart of the enemy" and indicated very clearly that he thought the bomb should have been used against the Chinese. When General O'Donnell's superior, General Vandenberg, now back in Washington, was asked about O'Donnell's statement, he replied sharply, "Obviously he doesn't speak for the Air Force."

One wonders whether General O'Donnell's removal in the wake of the Tokyo conference was purely coincidental or whether there were officials in both Washington and London who feared to leave a man with these views in command of the bombers which might at any time precipitate war with China. It may not be irrelevant to observe that five days earlier on January 10 Secretary of the Air Force Thomas K. Finletter appeared before a Congressional committee to testify in favor of a bill to reorganize the Air Force so that the Air Force Chief of Staff in Washington would be able to "command" rather than merely "supervise" tactical units in the field. "Without actually saying so," the Associated Press reported from Washington, "he left no doubt that one aim of the proposed reorganization is to have an authority in Washington that could stop an atom-bomb strike even after the planes had left a distant base if late information available only in Washington made the blow appear unnecessary." Was this the expression of fears of another *fait accompli* on a scale greater than ever?

The changes in the Far East seem to have been bitter pills for some of the American military to swallow. The night General O'Donnell left Japan "the Air Force said that the shift did not mean any let-up in the heavy bombardment of Korea" and announced that his deputy, Brigadier General James E. Briggs, "also is a disciple of the Air Force's strategic bombing doctrine." General Collins himself seemed none too happy on his return to Washington. He brusquely "cut short the interview" when reporters at the airport asked him whether the UN forces would be able to stay in Korea.

"General Collins' reluctance to discuss the military position in Korea," said the *New York Times* account, "could be interpreted as reflecting the considerable feeling in the Pentagon that a drawn-out defense of Korea, because of the numerical superiority of the forces facing the United Nations troops, is strategically unwise in the light of pressures elsewhere in the world."

The Pentagon, like MacArthur, though not necessarily for the same reasons, wanted to get out of Korea. The great retreat, once the Korean "waist" was passed, resembled a hoax more than a disaster. The UN troops, on orders delivered by General Collins, turned to face the foe—and confronted a mystery. "Where are the Chinese in Korea?" the London *Daily Mail's* correspondent asked in his dispatch from Tokyo the very day the about-face began. "UN forces today pushed forward to answer the question—and found nothing. They reentered Osan without a fight, another Allied column reached Kumyangjang, and a third is advancing west of the Seoul-Osan road." The hordes had vanished, like the figments of a nightmare.

PART VI
WAR AS POLITICS

C H A P T E R 3 3

★

Hiding the Lull

CLAUSEWITZ'S observation that war is only politics carried on by other means was never better illustrated than in Korea. Were MacArthur allowed to evacuate his troops, the humiliation of defeat would make peace almost impossible to negotiate. Were MacArthur to stay in the peninsula, however, and permit a lull in the fighting, it would become almost impossible to keep peace from breaking out. How could negotiations be prevented if public opinion at home began to realize that very little fighting was going on anyway? And how prevail upon the United Nations to condemn the Chinese as aggressors if it began to appear that they had ceased "aggressing"?

From the moment MacArthur was ordered to stop the withdrawal, his object was to find the enemy and resume the fighting. As long as there was fighting, the "security" of his fighting forces could be cited as paramount considerations, overriding any civilian political directives. Under cover of the plea of military necessity, the commander in the field could make the decisions. But unless battle, or the appearance of battle, were maintained, the initiative would slip from his hands. This is the key to events from the about-face in January, 1951, to the second crossing of the Parallel in force early in April of that year.

One of the five principles put forward by the UN's cease-fire negotiating committee on January 11 said, "When a cease-fire occurs . . . either as a result of a formal arrangement *or . . . as a result of a lull in hostilities* . . . advantage should be taken of it to pursue consideration of further steps to be taken for the restoration of peace." (Italics added.) The lull for which the United Nations hoped was the lull its military commander feared. MacArthur waged slow-motion war, stretching out a minimum of combat for a maximum of effect, hinting darkly every few days of enemy traps which were never sprung and enemy offensives which were never launched. "No one," he declared flamboyantly on January 20, when further retreat had been inescapably countermanded, "is going to drive us into the sea." There didn't seem to be anybody around.

This farce no doubt turned stomachs at the White House, the State Department, and even the Pentagon. Some twenty years earlier, Prussian military aristocrats and sophisticated Rhineland millionaires felt a similar distaste for the perhaps more vulgar but equally shrewd antics of Adolf Hitler. They swallowed rapidly and went along with Hitler. And in this case the White House, the State Department, and the Pentagon went along with MacArthur. During the latter half of January, the United States was threatening to withdraw from the United Nations unless the General Assembly obediently condemned Peking as an aggressor, and MacArthur was trying unsuccessfully to find some substantial body of enemy troops which might oblige with a little aggression. Though something close to a *de facto* cease-fire existed in Korea, MacArthur kept on valiantly shooting at an enemy who wasn't there, at least in any sizable quantity. Without that continual rumble in the press dispatches, the reluctant diplomats at Lake Success might not have been stampeded.

The lull was difficult to hide, but MacArthur managed, if not to hide it, then at least to confuse the public mind as to its duration and significance. On January 12, when the British Commonwealth parley urged direct talks with Stalin and Mao Tse-tung, a State Department spokesman said coldly, "We will not participate in these talks until the Chinese Communists have stopped fighting." They had. On the central front MacArthur's troops, as we have seen, were fighting North Koreans,

not Chinese. And the day after the State Department spokesman rebuffed the idea of direct talks, an Eighth Army communiqué disclosed that there had been nothing but patrol
action for eight days in the west. But these admissions were
always phrased so as to create rather than allay apprehension.
The wording was characteristic. "Despite eight days of nothing
more than patrol action in the west, possibility of a major
Communist attack there is not discounted." The UN troops
seemed always about to be overwhelmed. Catastrophe with
MacArthur, like prosperity with his old chief Herbert Hoover
in the early thirties, was always just-around-the-corner.

On January 20, when MacArthur said no one was going to
drive him into the sea, the communiqués still showed "little or
no enemy contact." Fifth Air Force fighters and bombers complained of "a paucity of enemy troops as targets," having
flown 260 sorties in the battle area and killed only forty of
the enemy, an average of less than one enemy casualty for
every six sorties—hardly a profitable operation. But Mac-
Arthur warned that "the entire military might of Communist
China is available against this relatively small command" and
"only by maneuver" could the allies "avoid the hazards con-
fronting inferior forces in face of the masses of a determined
enemy." It always seemed quite a miracle that MacArthur's
little band survived at all, though these masses never seemed
to move out of the headlines.

Alarums were audible in the briefings and the headlines,
even when the communiqués showed that little actually was
going on. Attention was focused on a "lull" only when it was
—almost triumphantly—announced that it had at last been
broken. The break in the lull always of course confirmed the
most recent prediction of an enemy offensive, but the battle
reports when read closely usually showed little sign of enemy
masses. "U.N. TROOPS YIELD ICHON AS LULL ENDS ON KOREAN
FRONTS," the *New York Times* proclaimed on January 22.
"ICHON, WONJU ARE GIVEN UP BY U.N. FORCES," said the Paris
edition of the *New York Herald Tribune* the same day;
"CHINESE ATTACK 12 HOURS AT ICHON IN THEIR FIRST BIG ACTION
SINCE SEOUL." The first "big" action since Seoul—almost three

weeks—was an attack "by an estimated three enemy platoons." The affair at Wonju was an American drive into the town against an "estimated" enemy regiment which seized Wonju the day before "but failed to follow up," said the United Press from Tokyo, "with an anticipated drive." The enemy had a habit of disappointing these anticipations; the UN column entered the town, held the Wonju air strip for three hours, exchanged fire with the enemy, and left at dusk. The three platoons at Ichon were termed Chinese, but it was again admitted that on the central front the fighting had been "carried out principally by North Korean units."

Rarely has an aggressor shown himself so perversely unwilling to advance. Never has an aggressor so stubbornly resisted victory by holding back his overwhelming hordes from the eager victim. While the United States Senate was unanimously passing a resolution on January 23 demanding that the United Nations brand China an aggressor, the UN forces were probing deep into a no man's land, reoccupying one ghost town after another without finding the aggressor. On the 25th an Allied column had penetrated past Wonju into Hoengsong only thirty-three miles below the Parallel without being able to report more than "two sharp fights with an enemy force estimated at more than one company." The lull was becoming noticeable at Lake Success. Sir Benegal N. Rau, fighting desperately for peace, said the lull "may not be without significance." There was desperation reflected in next day's headlines from the curiously unembattled battlefront: "U.N. SHIPS BOMBARD INCHON," said the *New York Times*, "AS PATROLS SEARCH FOR ENEMY." MacArthur's search for the enemy was disrupting the UN's search for peace. If someone at Lake Success had dared challenge the Supreme Commander's activity, even the constant plea of military necessity could hardly have covered this frantic effort to move his troops within shooting range of that elusive enemy.

While the United States put the pressure on at Lake Success to brand the Chinese as aggressors, Tokyo Headquarters was hard put to maintain the semblance of major combat. On January 28, with UN patrols only fourteen miles from Seoul, enemy opposition was said to be "hardening," and a "major clash" was said to be "in sight." On the 29th "approximately 1000 of the enemy" actually turned up in a night attack and "MASSING OF FOE" was "REPORTED." On January 30 the United Nations forces were "seemingly coming into contact with advance posts of the Chinese and North Korean defense." Next day the Political and Security Committee of the United Nations voted 44-7 to brand China an aggressor and initiate a study of sanctions. On February 1, the day the Assembly had to vote, fighting reached a new "intensity." Along the front generally "enemy resistance" was described as "long and sporadic," while at one point an attack by "an estimated two enemy regiments" was reported, the largest concentration of enemy troops actually encountered in many days. The Air Force listed among its own exploits against aggression that day "a strike on two enemy-held villages east of Seoul" which "destroyed or damaged 1200 bags of rice and hit several buildings." It was in the face of such mounting evidence that the Assembly formally ratified the finding of aggression. International law and order were vindicated.

CHAPTER 34

★

Lost and Found

"FOR three weeks," said the *New York Times* war summary on February 4, "UN patrols have been probing for the main body of the Chinese army. Last week—after a fifteen-mile advance through no man's land—the UN forces finally found it. The Chinese were dug in along a forty-mile line, stretching from just south of Seoul on the west, along the southern bank of the Han River, up to the central mountain spine." Tokyo Headquarters was proved wrong again. Advancing patrols found that no man's land extended to the very gates of Seoul. "YONGDUNGPO QUIET DISTURBS CAPTORS" said the *New York Times* headline on the battlefront dispatch describing the taking of Seoul's industrial suburb six days later. The troops marched unopposed "through silent empty streets, . . . past bomb-wrecked factories and shrapnel-pocked houses." When Seoul itself was entered "no enemy contact" was reported. Headquarters hinted that the enemy had probably pulled back to mass on the central front; those Chinese always seemed to be massing—in Headquarters estimates—where the fighting wasn't.

Though the enemy was difficult to find, he was being slaughtered in astronomical numbers. "Enemy troops in almost full division strength fell before the UN onslaught each day this week," said a report from Eighth Army Headquarters on February 10. "An enemy division is generally estimated to contain 6000 troops." How were they able to kill so many when there was so little contact? The paradox was not made any clearer by an examination of the daily communiqués during this period. The day with the biggest number of announced ground casualties was February 4, when 8635 casualties were said to have been inflicted. But the communiqué which gave this figure spoke of limited advances against "moderate resistance" at one point and "light" resistance at another. It spoke of six enemy attacks along the front, two by unspecified numbers, two by an estimated two enemy companies each, one by an estimated enemy company, and one by "two enemy platoons." In no case did the communiqué claim to have annihilated these enemy forces; it only reported that they were repulsed or contained. How, then, did MacArthur's forces manage to inflict such huge casualties?

Eighth Army Headquarters claimed to have killed or wounded 69,500 of the enemy from January 25 to midnight February 9, an average of about 4600—or, as Headquarters put it, "almost" a "full division" a day. Comparisons with the peak battles of World Wars I and II will indicate what a feat this was, if true. Divisions vary a good deal in size, but it is worth noting that in the great Battle of Verdun in 1916, one of the most terrible battles of attrition in history, the Germans lost forty-three and a half divisions from February 21 to July 1, an average of ten divisions a month. The rate claimed in those ten days before reaching Seoul would be the equivalent of thirty divisions a month.

If the figures given out that day at Lieutenant General Matthew Ridgway's Headquarters were correct, then that push through the no man's land south of Seoul must rank with the Battle of Stalingrad, the climax of World War II, the point at which the German armies began the long retreat back to defeat. The high point at Stalingrad was the twenty-day period from January 10 to January 30, when Marshal von Paulus was taken prisoner and his famous Sixth Army destroyed. The Red Army claimed in those twenty days to have killed 100,000 German officers and men. That is an average of 5000 a day. The average of the estimates given in the communiqués for the first ten days of February before Seoul adds up just a shade better than that—to 5510 casualties a day! Were MacArthur's generals military marvels or military Münchhausens?

These figures did not seem so strange to a newspaper-reading public in America which had been led to picture Chinese hordes "marching abreast" and "in human waves" against American guns, in supposed "Oriental" disregard of their own lives. Belief in fairy tales is not limited to childhood. The experts paused to wonder, but expert analysis does not make headlines.

MacArthur Headquarters had claimed to have killed or captured 134,616 Chinese since mid-October, about 36,000 a month—not a bad total for an army which had spent most of its time in full retreat and out of contact with the enemy. Hanson Baldwin in the *New York Times* of February 11 wrote that the "only exact" part of this estimate was the number of prisoners: "We knew we had exactly 616 Chinese Communist prisoners." He did not think that number in four months was "encouraging," comparing as it did with 8531 Americans listed as "missing." Baldwin assumed that most of these "missing are probably prisoners." Were Americans more easily captured than Chinese? Or were there errors in the count of the casualties? Could it be that so few Chinese Communists had been taken prisoner because so few had been fighting in Korea?

Figures like these—and the obscene advertising slogan "Operation Killer" which grew out of them—were part of military operations which might have seemed almost comic, were it not for the effect on the Korean people. If there was any reality in "Operation Killer" it lay in what was happening to the Koreans and their country as MacArthur's troops maneuvered up and down the South and finally crossed the Parallel in force again in April, without once meeting that major enemy offensive which continued to be predicted. "Reports of Chinese concentrations continue to come in," the military correspondent of the London *Times* reported as late as April 2. "Opinion in Washington expects a strong hostile offensive to be launched in the near future. This belief naturally damps hopes of any successful negotiation, at all events for some time to come." It must also have damped the hopes of Koreans North and South for some end to the frightful process of their liberation.

The Mongols, to whom Truman compared the Chinese Communists in calling for a "moral mobilization" against them, could not have hoped to match the depredations of Korea's liberators. Not only the industrial potential of the cities but the poorest possessions of the countryside were ravaged. "Allied troops in the Wonju sector," the London *Times* reported on January 15, "pursuing a scorched-earth policy, have burned twenty-two villages and set fire to three hundred haystacks." A policy which is truly heroic when practiced by a bravely resisting people on their own homes becomes as truly atrocious when practiced by a powerful "ally" on a helpless partner.

An article published by the London *Times* on November 16, 1950, showed that the North Korean command rejected a scorched-earth program and left the countryside over which they retreated little touched by war. The contrast recalls the legend about Solomon and the two mothers who each claimed the same child; he found the true one by suggesting that the child be cut in half and divided between them. Korean opinion, to which so little attention was paid by either side, was no doubt heartily sick of both. A *New York Times* correspondent from Taegu described it as "dislike and distrust of the Communists, with no great love for the South Korea regime." But the same correspondent noted that "when the Koreans saw that the Communists had left their homes and schools standing in retreat while the United Nations troops, fighting with much more destructive tools, left only blackened spots where towns once stood, the Communists even in retreat chalked up moral victories."

Ground troops in retreat left ghost towns in their wake, while terror rained down upon the land from the skies. As early as September, 1950, Far East Air Forces Headquarters announced that the first stage of its bombing program, aimed at industrial installations, was complete, and that there was now a "paucity" of industrial targets for bombers. One of the problems which began to trouble the Air Force in Korea, judging by the communiqués, was that there was nothing left to destroy. These communiqués must be read by anyone who wants a complete history of the Korean War. They are literally horrifying.

"Crews on B-26 light bombers of the 452nd Bomb Wing," said the Fifth Air Force operational summary at 5 P.M. Tokyo time, January 31, "reported a scarcity of targets at Hamhung today." According to Staff Sergeant Clark V. Watson of Hutchinson, Kansas, "It's hard to find good targets, for we have burned out almost everything."

Other Air Force units were still managing. "The Eighth Fighter Bomber Wing F-80 jets," said the same communiqué, "reported large fires in villages in the western sector following attacks with rockets, napalm, and machine guns. A village was hard hit south of Chorwon." *Why* was not explained. Whether the village represented some military objective was not stated. Sometimes a possible military objective seemed to have been hit by accident. In the same communiqué it was announced that the navigator of one of the light bombers that attacked Pongung near Hamhung reported: "One of our napalms must have hit a gas or oil dump. It landed and there was a big belch of orange flame and black smoke." Peasants do not detonate so colorfully.

Sometimes the reason offered for bombing a defenseless village was that it was "enemy-occupied." The same communiqué said, "One flight dive-bombed the enemy-occupied village of Takchong and then rocketed and strafed the area, reporting several buildings destroyed and large fires started." Were all villages in enemy territory regarded as enemy-occupied? The ratio of civilian to soldier dead in these raids must have been very large. This same communiqué said the "largest claim of troops casualties inflicted" in the day's raids were 100 enemy troops killed or wounded by one group of planes. Even in a small village more civilians than that could be killed in one raid.

A complete indifference to noncombatants was reflected in the way villages were given "saturation treatment" with napalm to dislodge a few soldiers. George Barrett, a front-line correspondent of the *New York Times*, drew an unforgettable picture of such a village in a dispatch early in February. He was with an armored column which "took" a village north of Anyang and found what he described as "a macabre tribute to the totality of modern war":

> A napalm raid hit the village three or four days ago when the Chinese were holding up the advance, and nowhere in the village have they buried the dead because there is nobody left to do so. This correspondent came across one old woman, the only one who seemed to be left alive, dazedly hanging up some clothes in a blackened courtyard filled with the bodies of four members of her family.
>
> The inhabitants throughout the village and in the fields were caught and killed and kept the exact postures they had held when the napalm struck—a man about to get on his bicycle, fifty boys and girls playing in an orphanage, a housewife strangely unmarked, holding in her hand a page torn from a Sears-Roebuck catalogue crayoned at Mail Order No. 3,811,294 for a $2.98 "bewitching bed jacket— coral." There must be almost two hundred dead in the tiny hamlet.

Such were the realities behind efficient notations like the following, in Fifth Air Force operational summary February 4: "Other F-80s from the Eighth reported excellent results in attacks on villages near Chorwon, Kumchon, Chunchon, and Chunchon-ni. The villages were hit with bombs as well as rockets and napalm." The results were . . . "excellent." Not all the reports were so brisk. There were some passages about these raids on villages which reflected, not the pity which human feeling called for, but a kind of gay moral imbecility, utterly devoid of imagination—as if the fliers were playing in a bowling alley, with villages for pins.

An example was Fifth Air Force operational summary 5 P.M. Tokyo time Friday, February 2. This told how the two-man crew of a downed Mosquito patrol plane was rescued by helicopter "from the midst of an enemy troop concentration near Hongchon." Some fifty enemy troops had been sighted and between 300 and 400 foxholes reported so it was decided to give the whole area "saturation" treatment.

A mass flight of twenty-four F-51 mustangs poured 5000 gallons of napalm over the area. The flight leader, Lieutenant Colonel James Kirkendall, of Duluth, Minnesota—the Air Force communiqués gave names, as if to foster individual pride in such handiwork—reported that "his flight hit every village and building in the area." Perhaps it was some uneasy qualm which led him to add, "There was plenty of evidence of troops living in the houses there." The evidence itself was not disclosed. It might have been hard to find, for Colonel Kirkendall added that "smoke blanketed the area, rising to over 4000 feet when they left."

His subordinates were cheerful. Captain Everett L. Hundley of Kansas City, Kansas, who led one group of four planes, was quoted by the communiqué as saying, "You can kiss that group of villages good-bye." Captain Hugh Boniford of Montgomery, Alabama, said he saw "tracks and other evidence of enemy activity in the area." He added, "That place can really be called devastated now."

Captain Boniford's remark applies to all Korea.

CHAPTER 35

★

The Deadly Parallel Again

THE MacArthur story belongs in Buddhist annals. The Korean War was an exercise in eternal recurrence. The same half-truths, the same hesitations, and the same tactics all reappeared when MacArthur's forces approached and finally crossed the Parallel again in the spring of 1951. Again we were told that it was only an imaginary line; so are most boundaries. Again it was said that no hard-and-fast directives could be given a commander when a war was on; perhaps—in a real sense—every subordinate must be given some margin of discretion. The answer is not the absolutely rigid directive—though that, too, is sometimes necessary. The answer is the removal of the subordinate who abuses his discretion. In this the United Nations showed itself not merely a flabby executive, but again became through timidity the tool of its own commander.

For the United Nations, the basic question at the time was not the Parallel at all. It was whether MacArthur was to be permitted to go on drumming up alarums of combat when the enemy obviously was prepared for a *de facto* cease-fire during which public opinion could cool off and peace might be negotiated. Despite the threats of the Peking radio and congratulatory messages from Stalin, nothing had been done to reestablish the North Korean regime. If Russia and China had sought to convert all Korea into a satellite state, the abandonment of Seoul in January could have provided a political symbol of the first magnitude. The establishment of a Communist regime in Korea's ancient capital, with a claim to rule the whole peninsula, would have committed Russia and China to a political settlement which would have barred the door to peace. No such move was made. Even when Pyongyang was retaken, there was no pointedly dramatic reinstallation of the Communist regime. It should have been clear, it would have been clear but for the synthetic offstage clamor of battle, that neither Moscow nor Peking wished to commit themselves.

What should have been obvious on the political plane was even more obvious on the military plane. The North Koreans and the Chinese "volunteers" in that period not only lacked air and naval support, they lacked even small arms. A dispatch from Tokyo on February 20 said advancing UN troops "picked up quantities of abandoned Communist equipment, including twenty bamboo spears six feet long and tipped with eight-inch steel blades. It was estimated," the dispatch continued, "that about twenty percent of the Chinese Reds were armed with spears and no other weapon." General Ridgway at a press conference the day before had shown these spears to correspondents and commented, "In the year of Our Lord 1951, they attack our troops with these crude spears that were in style five thousand years ago." In the year of His Lord 1951 this was how a Christian general leading a crusade against "godless" Communists and Oriental heathen sneered at the inferiority of their weapons of destruction.

The political significance of this was completely ignored. The Russians with a huge armament industry, even the Chinese with some five million men under arms, could certainly have supplied the troops fighting in North Korea with better weapons than improvised spears had they so chosen. That they did not choose at that time to do so gave testimony, like their failure to engage again in a major battle after the first days of December, to their desire for peace. Yet the United Nations lacked the resolution to recognize that here was the *de facto* cease-fire it wanted. It feared even to impose firm restrictions on MacArthur, though it became obvious to anyone who studied the battle reports closely that his troops could sweep across the Parallel again any time he chose. With full command of the skies, his reconnaissance reports must have shown that the failure of that long-predicted mass offensive to turn up was no real cause for surprise.

The State Department, a house divided, much of it more sympathetic to MacArthur than loyal to Acheson, did what it could to discourage any effort to curb the Supreme Commander. As early as February 2—in the wake of rumors that a new buffer zone was being discussed—it issued a statement saying that the restoration of peace in Korea "would not be helped by 'speculation' about whether United Nations forces would or would not" cross the Parallel again. This was the obverse of the truth. The first essential for the restoration of peace was to focus public attention on the problem. That the time to act was growing short became clear ten days after the Department's chilly little statement, when Eighth Army Communiqué No. 183 at 10:15 A.M. Tokyo time February 12 announced that South Korean forces on the east coast "reported light scattered enemy resistance as they advanced to Yangyang five miles north of the 38th Parallel." The news startled both Paris and London. In Paris the foreign office spokesman said feebly that the issues involved in any new crossing of the Parallel were "matters to be discussed and decided by the United Nations." In London the Prime Minister made a statement on the subject in the House of Commons that afternoon, which disclosed a similar weakness.

For Attlee's statement merely revealed that the British government was still at the mercy of MacArthur. The best Attlee could say was that the British government had discussed the matter with the American government while the UN forces "were advancing northward" and had found "the fullest comprehension of the political implications" involved in crossing the 38th Parallel. This was not the same as a commitment to consult beforehand, much less a promise not to cross again. The fact that a banker shows "the fullest comprehension" of a borrower's inability to meet a payment on a mortgage is no assurance that he will not foreclose. Somebody had held Sir Oliver Franks' hand, but there was no evidence of more than sympathy, sincere or simulated. In fact Attlee foreshadowed his own failure when he expressed the fuzzy view that there should be no crossing "in depth" before consultation. MacArthur had already shown that he was fully capable of reaching the Yalu if the right to make one so-called "tactical" step across the Parallel was left within his discretion.

The London *Times* said gently what the Prime Minister should have said firmly and loudly to all the world. It said that a halt on the Parallel was important because "there are even now some signs that the Chinese government might be ready for some kind of cease-fire, perhaps even a tacit or unacknowledged arrangement about the 38th Parallel; and the latest Chinese statement in reply to the United Nations 'condemnatory' resolution did not rule out the possibility of talks among directly interested Powers. There is, in fact, a period of uneasy watching and waiting in Korea." This was the lull, which might break out into peace—if only MacArthur would permit it.

February 12 was a Monday. That was a week of almost contemptuous comedy, as if played out deliberately by a master of buffoonery. The crossing was announced and then denied, though not too firmly. Eric Downton, the London *Daily Telegraph* correspondent at Tokyo, was allowed to cable past censorship next morning this comment on the denial. He said that while "it may well be that there are now no South Koreans officially across the Parallel . . . one cannot help suspecting that the international political reaction to the earlier announcement had some influence on the subsequent 'correction.' " Downton put the quotation marks around the word *correction*.

There was a barrage of statements from Washington and Tokyo intended to show that everything was going to be all right. Acheson "indicated" at his press conference on the 14th that a new crossing of the Parallel was for the United Nations to decide. General Collins told the National Press Club in Washington that there would be no new crossing of the Parallel until current political discussions were completed. General MacArthur himself said in his fruity prose, which often reminded one of W. C. Fields as a traveling patent medicine salesman, that "talk of crossing the 38th Parallel at the present stage of the campaign, except by scattered patrol action incidental to the tactical situation, is purely academic."

Under cover of these reassuring falsehoods, moves of quite a different character were going on. From Washington, the day after MacArthur spoke, came a Reuters' dispatch saying that MacArthur had just asked again and been refused permission (1) to bomb Manchurian bases and (2) to use Chiang Kai-shek's troops. From Tokyo came the news that South Korean Marines protected by Allied naval units had established a beachhead at Wonsan ninety miles north of the Parallel. Ninety miles north of the Parallel was quite a long way for a "scattered patrol action incidental to the tactical situation." If the British protested, they got a cold rebuff. At his press conference on Thursday, February 15, Truman said that a crossing of the Parallel was for MacArthur to decide, a matter with which the President did not intend to interfere. Apparently the British government had found something less than "the fullest comprehension" Attlee claimed in Commons.

What happened to the South Korean Marines who landed at Wonsan ninety miles above the Parallel? No one knows. The strictest censorship curtain of the war was dropped over Wonsan. It did not lift until some six weeks later. On March 29 Rear Admiral Allen E. Smith told a press conference in Tokyo that a UN naval task force had been bombarding Wonsan for forty-one "straight days and nights . . . the longest sustained naval or air bombardment of a city in history . . . with United States, British, Australian, and South Korean warships participating." He said the bombardment was still going on, and he described life under bombardment in this city of 35,000 people. "In Wonsan," he told the press, "you cannot walk in the streets. You cannot sleep anywhere in the twenty-four hours, unless it is the sleep of death." The Admiral said his guns had reduced the population to "suicide groups" and that two other ports in the same area, Songjin and Chongjin, were being given the same kind of continuous bombardment.

Why had this massacre been cloaked by censorship? To keep

the news from the enemy? The people of Wonsan, with death raining down upon them for forty-one days and nights, did not have to depend on the news dispatches from Tokyo to know what was happening to them. The only conceivable purpose of the censorship was to hide from public opinion at home the fact that, while a crossing of the Parallel seemed to have been delayed, naval forces were subjecting three ports far to the north to a savage bombardment without precedent in naval history, imposing untold suffering on the population and embittering the enemy—at a time when there were renewed hopes of peace talks. There were British warships participating. Why did the British government keep silent while this was going on? Was it any less a crossing of the Parallel in force than if it had been purely an infantry operation? Did their silence not show MacArthur that he was dealing with officials who, after protest, would swallow whatever bitter pill he chose to ram down their throats?

The Wonsan bombardment showed the enemy he had to deal with MacArthur, not Attlee or even Truman. And it showed once again that MacArthur wanted war, not peace. While this was being demonstrated under cover of censorship above the Parallel, a small-scale Communist attack on the central front was puffed up by Tokyo Headquarters into a mass offensive, as if to distract attention from the Parallel controversy and to blanket talk of a *de facto* cease-fire. Some patrols advancing northward from Wonju ran into opposition late Sunday night February 11. By Tuesday morning the 13th, the day MacArthur dismissed the question of crossing the Parallel as "academic," Tokyo Headquarters had built this up into a monster offensive. Estimates of the number of enemy troops engaged ran from a niggardly 30,000 to a possible 150,000. Some graphic, if mixed, metaphors were emerging from Tokyo's descriptions of the battle. The London *Times* said enemy reinforcements were "reported to be 'swarming like mountain goats' over the ridges," and the London *Daily Herald* correspondent said the enemy "swarmed out of the hills like fleas." Nobody seemed to notice the discrepancy between these "human waves" and the Air Force figures for the day. The Air Force flew almost 600 "close-support missions" against these attacking hordes and "estimated more than 650 Communists were killed in bombing, strafing and napalm attacks." That makes an average of only a fraction over one enemy casualty per sortie. If the planes were really strafing an enemy in such numbers that they seemed to be swarming like goats or fleas, it seems incomprehensible that each sortie—even by the Air Force's own sometimes generous estimates—could not average more than one and a fraction men killed.

By Thursday February 15 the dispatches quoted exuberant field commanders who were calling the affair "the Wonju Shoot," and it was said the slaughter had been so great that the defenders dubbed the area "Death Valley." (Tokyo Headquarters had a gift for making the war sound as if it were being run by men temporarily on leave from the more juicy advertising agencies.) That same day Major General Edward M. Almond, commanding general of the Tenth Corps on that front, was promoted to Lieutenant General. He told reporters at the front that the UN offensive in the west had shown "where the enemy mass wasn't" while on the central front the UN's "multiple columns stabbing northward" had located "what we think is an enemy mass." On the third day of the great battle against "human waves" the commanding general still wasn't sure. The fighting petered out next day. Whatever its military magnitude, it had served its purpose. In the face of such headlines and battle dispatches, who dared continue to suggest that it was better to stop at the Parallel because the time was ripe for a cease-fire?

CHAPTER 36

★

MacArthur Upsets the Applecart

AFTER the "Wonju Shoot" MacArthur seemed content to maneuver up and down in South Korea, as long as he felt there was a chance the United Nations might vote sanctions against China and permit him to bombard Manchurian bases. On March 7 he issued a statement saying the war would become a "stalemate" unless political decisions "on the highest international levels" resolved the "unsolved problems raised by Red China's undeclared war in Korea" and, he implied, lifted what he called the "abnormal military inhibitions" under which he had to operate. He also took advantage of the occasion to predict once again that major enemy offensive: "Even now there are indications that the enemy is attempting to build up from China a new and massive offensive for the spring." A month later—with his troops crossing the Parallel in force again, unopposed—MacArthur was still predicting that same offensive. These predictions were calculated to have a political effect. As the military correspondent of the London *Times* wrote on April 2, "this belief" that a major offensive was impending "naturally damps hopes of any successful negotiation, at all events for some time to come."

MacArthur did not begin a new sprint toward and across the Parallel until it began to look as if the United Nations were moving toward new negotiations. On March 13, the day before his troops retook Seoul a second time—again without

267

a shot—the news from Lake Success was disturbing. "U.N. DROPPING IDEA OF UNIFYING KOREA BY MILITARY FORCE," said a headline in the *New York Times* next morning, "DIPLOMATS SAY U. S. IS TAKING POSITION ARMS TASK WILL END AROUND 38TH LINE." MacArthur's "stalemate" prediction was being used against him. The diplomats seemed to feel, if an indefinite stalemate were in view, why not negotiate an end of the conflict? The Supreme Commander declared in alarm on March 15 that it would be almost impossible to hold a "static" defense line near the Parallel. And the same day, vacationing in Key West, Truman again said that the decision to cross the Parallel was a tactical matter, within the authority of MacArthur.

MacArthur did not wait for reinforcements, to take advantage of the green light given him by Truman. "ENEMY RESISTANCE DECLINES," said the *New York Times* main battlefront headline on March 17, "AS ALLIES DRIVE ON PARALLEL." On the 18th, "ALLIES CHASE FOE TOWARD PARALLEL; CONTACT IS SLIGHT." On the 19th, advancing troops found what was supposed to have been a big enemy base at Chunchon only eight miles south of the Parallel "apparently . . . abandoned." On the 20th, five separate groups of UN troops were within seventeen miles of the Parallel. That night, correspondents in Tokyo were handed a memorandum forbidding them to mention the Parallel in any of their dispatches, and were warned that "no synonym in any form for the 38th Parallel" would be cleared by the censor. The order was rescinded next morning, but it indicated Tokyo Headquarters' frame of mind as the old line came in sight again, and new protests began from London and Ottawa.

The race between peace and provocation once more was becoming intense. On the 22nd, Israel's astute chief delegate at the United Nations, Abba Eban, was circulating a new peace plan, shrewdly calculated to bridge the gap between the Chinese Communist desire for a general conference and the American insistence on an unconditional cease-fire. Stockholm had begun sounding out Peking on peace. The sixteen nations whose troops were fighting under MacArthur's command were drafting a statement of aims, designed to persuade Mao Tse-tung to agree to a cease-fire. The British government was hoping "that Mao might be led to accept a tacit, unnegotiated truce along the Parallel."

A tacit truce might easily lead to a formal armistice. A formal armistice would reopen the door to solution of those major political problems which could be settled only at the expense of America's hold on Formosa and the final liquidation of the Chiang Kai-shek regime. The same danger was taking more formidable shape behind the scenes in negotiations being held by London and Paris with Washington for a formal declaration of United Nations aims in Korea. This declaration, the Washington correspondent of the *Sunday Times* of London cabled his paper at the time, was expected not only to lead to peace in Korea, "but would open the door to negotiations for a general settlement of Far Eastern problems." This was the general settlement MacArthur had been trying all along to avoid. If there was a truce, he wanted that truce divorced if possible from consideration of the broader problems involved in a general political stabilization in the Far East.

It did not become known till later that Truman himself had been trying to resist the pressure for such a statement of United Nations aims. But the pressure grew so strong that there were prolonged negotiations between the State Department and the Joint Chiefs of Staff on the content and phrasing of the statement. A draft was prepared with the concurrence of both on March 19. That same day MacArthur was told that a statement of this kind was being prepared. MacArthur decided on countermeasures of his own.

On March 24 MacArthur issued, without authorization, an announcement declaring he was ready at any time to meet the commander in chief of the enemy forces to discuss a truce, saying that this should not be hard to achieve "if the issues are resolved on their own merits without being burdened by extraneous issues . . . such as Formosa and China's seat in the United Nations." He ended with a scarcely veiled threat of war on China. This was designed to take the initiative from the diplomats, to forestall any effort to couple Korea with Formosa, and to make it as hard as possible for

Mao to talk without losing face. One paragraph was deftly brewed poison for the new China's national pride. "The enemy therefore must by now be painfully aware," Mac-Arthur wrote, "that a decision of the United Nations to depart from its tolerant effort to contain the war to the area of Korea through expansion of our military operations to his coastal areas and interior bases would doom Red China to the risk of imminent military collapse." This is how one leads up to a demand for unconditional surrender, not to new peace negotiations.

Nehru, lonely in his search for peace, under the constant threat that his independence might cost him the food that famine-stricken India needed, treated this statement as it deserved. "Certainly no field commander," Nehru said, "is going to lay down the policies of the government of India. Political policies are laid down by governments." But the fundamental Anglo-Saxon and traditionally American notion that the military ought always to be subordinate to the civil power did not fare so well in its homelands.

In this case a military subordinate had done his civilian superior a favor by insubordination. MacArthur's disruptive truce offer of March 24 came as a relief to the Truman Administration. It succeeded in upsetting the international negotiations for the statement of United Nations aims in Korea which Truman was reluctant to make. This accounts for Washington's reaction to MacArthur's insubordination. Acheson, after consultation with Truman, stated mildly that MacArthur had touched on political issues "beyond his responsibility as a field commander." Acheson's ambiguity and the State Department's failure clearly to disavow MacArthur's offer were sharply pointed out at the time by James Reston in the *New York Times*.

If the Administration had really resented MacArthur's interference on that occasion, there was one clear way to rebuke him. The Administration could have reassured the Chinese and our own allies by cooperating in completing and releasing to the world that statement of principles for which the United Nations was pressing. Weeks later the text of the proposed Presidential message along these lines went into the record of the MacArthur inquiry but the text was kept secret, with bipartisan approval. This was, as Senator Connally said on that occasion, "a communication they were going to submit to the United Nations, but the MacArthur action stopped it." Just why this "stopped it" was never explained, and none of the Senators seemed interested enough to ask. Neither then nor later was there any effort from Washington to revive the project of a joint statement of United Nations aims in Korea. An official declaration of United Nations aims in Korea would have limited American freedom of action.

With peace negotiations stymied for the time being, MacArthur in Tokyo moved to end the lull in hostilities. Several hours after his challenging truce offer, he issued a formal order to the United States Eighth Army in Korea authorizing it to cross the Parallel "if and when security makes it tactically advisable." "Security" at once made this "tactically advisable" on an ever wider scale. On the 26th it was announced that South Korean patrols had crossed several times against little resistance. On the 27th they captured a village three miles above the Parallel. As the movement northward continued, the British government on March 30 was reported formally to have notified the American government that United Nations forces should halt at the Parallel, with the usual exception for "tactical necessity." Next day the first United States armored column pushed across. The new British Foreign Secretary, Herbert Morrison, declared on April 2 that the "psychological moment" had come for peace talks. MacArthur had decided it was the psychological moment for a new offensive.

By April 6, troops of six countries—Americans, British, South Koreans, Australians, Greeks, and Siamese—had been led across the line. By April 7, elements of nine separate divisions, six American, were advancing beyond the Parallel. A new full-scale offensive was in the making, paced as usual by huge estimates of enemy strength and foreboding forecasts of enemy intentions. MacArthur worked it out on April

3 that the enemy had sixty-three divisions, totaling more than 440,000 troops, "massed" in Korea. While the demands in England and America for MacArthur's removal reached a new intensity, the Supreme Commander's predictions of a big offensive just around the corner had their usual inhibiting effect. As the London *Daily Mail's* Washington correspondent said on April 9, "With a major Communist offensive apparently imminent, the difficulty of the problem is obvious."

Liberal opinion in the United States looked to General George C. Marshall as the one man in American public life who might bring MacArthur under control. But, as the *Washington Post* said, there was fear in Washington that "he seems to think it is none of his business." Certainly the Marshall press conference of March 27—his first conference in the six months since he had been Secretary of Defense—was an almost tongue-in-cheek performance. All Marshall really said was that, in crossing the Parallel, MacArthur would be guided by "the demands of security"—which is just what MacArthur said. When a reporter asked whether this meant MacArthur might go as far as the Yalu if he chose, the Secretary replied that "such a move might prove to be a little extreme." It had certainly proved so once before.

Secretary Marshall seemed more concerned about the danger of a letdown in the emotional mobilization than he did about the danger of a widened conflict in China. It was to warn against the dangers of a letdown, not to hold back MacArthur, that he called his first formal press conference. "GENERAL ASTONISHED," said the *New York Times* headline, "AT PUBLIC AND CONGRESSIONAL APATHY TO PREPAREDNESS EFFORT; FEARS LOSS IN MOMENTUM." Marshall warned that the world danger was greater than ever, but "would not clarify his remark about how the world crisis had worsened."

How could generals working overtime to maintain enough tension to put universal military training through Congress be expected to put any controls on the only man who really knew how to keep the heat on? An Administration whose whole program depended on an ever greater injection of alarums feared the consequences of peace, the "letdown" which would follow. The American public didn't seem too interested in the Korean War anyway. Official Washington, Arthur Krock reported, was asking itself one crucial question: "Can anything but a plain threat of immediate war produce the official and public psychology that is required?" How could one expect the Administration to clamp down on Mac-Arthur when its own House leader, Speaker Sam Rayburn of Texas, struggling to get the universal military training bill through the House—and fresh from a White House conference—pulled a war scare of his own? "This complacency," he said to a House still unwilling to commit its eighteen-year-olds to battle, "this winning of a little battle in Korea, had better not lull the American people to sleep, because I think we stand in the face of terrible danger and maybe the beginning of World War III."

The words were literally true, but the source of the danger was not the apathy of the American people. The danger was in Tokyo and in Washington. Its embodiment was the Supreme Commander, General Douglas MacArthur. The danger was that the crisis would eventually be resolved Mac-Arthur's way, because Truman and his Administration still feared peace. Fortunately, at that critical moment, MacArthur made a serious mistake.

PART VII
STALEMATE AND TRUCE TALKS

CHAPTER 37

★

Why MacArthur Was Fired

MAC ARTHUR'S mistake was his letter to Joseph W. Martin, Jr., Republican leader of the House of Representatives. MacArthur had received a letter in Tokyo from Martin. The Republican leader enclosed the text of an address he had made suggesting that Chiang Kai-shek's forces on Formosa be used to open "a second Asiatic front to relieve the pressure on our forces in Korea." Martin asked for MacArthur's views "on this point, either on a confidential basis or otherwise." MacArthur replied that his own views were well known. "They follow the conventional pattern of meeting force with maximum counter-force as we have never failed to do in the past," MacArthur wrote. "Your view," he informed Martin, "with respect to the utilization of the Chinese forces on Formosa is in conflict with neither logic nor this tradition."

MacArthur's letter endorsed Martin's proposal and concluded with an appeal to those Republicans who opposed the Administration's policy of focusing major attention on Europe. "It seems strangely difficult," MacArthur wrote, "for some to realize that here in Asia is where the Communist conspirators have elected to make their play for global conquest . . . here we fight Europe's battle with arms while the diplomats there still fight it with words . . . if we lose the war to Communism in Asia the fall of Europe is inevitable." The letter embodied MacArthur's fundamental thesis and appealed to the Republicans to support it against the President.

274

It was one thing for MacArthur to communicate with the Chinese military commander without authorization from Truman and the United Nations. It was quite another to communicate, over Truman's head, with the Republican leader of the House of Representatives. The former move did Truman a favor anyway. The latter not only challenged the President's authority at home, but invaded that field of action in which Truman did not need to rely on diplomats or generals. MacArthur's letter to Joseph Martin was politics, and politics was something on which no one needed to coach Harry Truman. It was this letter which led to MacArthur's dismissal on April 11.

MacArthur pretended not to understand. Weeks later, two days after the Malik offer of peace terms, the deposed General complained to an audience in Boston: "I was relieved of my command by the same authorities who since have received so enthusiastically the identical proposal when made by the Soviet government." The Malik offer was, indeed, like MacArthur's offer to meet the Chinese commander in the field, based on the idea of limiting the talks to strictly military negotiations for a strictly military armistice. The advantage from the Truman Administration's point of view was that such talks avoided the troublesome questions sure to arise in any attempt at a real political settlement in the Far East. To this extent Truman and MacArthur agreed.

But MacArthur's complaint was unfounded, and disingenuous. His dismissal was not precipitated by his unauthorized message to the Chinese commander on March 24 but by the release to the press on April 5 of his letter to Martin. It was MacArthur's intervention in domestic, not world, politics which finally led Truman to remove him. MacArthur was not only directly challenging the President, his declared policies, and the constitutional principle of civilian supremacy, he was entering into open alliance with the Republican opposition. The day after Martin read MacArthur's letter to the House, Truman's press secretary announced that no change in China policy was contemplated. Five days later MacArthur was dismissed.

The use of Chiang's troops on the mainland would have extended the war, and committed the United States to reinstate Chiang in power by military intervention. To this Truman was still opposed, and it was on this issue that he and MacArthur parted. On the other question, the question of ending the war in Korea, Truman remained in close agreement with MacArthur. The President made a nationwide radio address, on the night of MacArthur's dismissal, outlining his terms for peace in Korea. They were, like MacArthur's terms to the enemy commander, an offer of military negotiations only. Truman stated that the United States was ready at any time to negotiate peace on a three-point basis: "(1) The fighting must stop, (2) Concrete steps must be taken to insure that the fighting will not break out again, (3) There must be an end of the aggression." All the President offered was that "a settlement founded upon these elements would open the way for the unification of Korea and the withdrawal of all foreign forces." Even within the peninsula itself Truman would make no political commitments; the reference to unification of Korea was vague enough to leave the door open for Syngman Rhee's program for joining the North to the South in special elections which would leave his own regime intact. All the wider political issues whose settlement was essential to stabilization of the situation in the Far East—the related questions of Formosa and the admission of Red China to the United Nations—were excluded by Truman's terms as they had been by MacArthur's.

Even on this basis, his own and MacArthur's, Truman was reluctant to negotiate. The story of the negotiations behind the scenes which followed MacArthur's removal is still hidden, but their upshot on June 23 was a dramatic victory for Truman. The Russians by the Malik offer on that date were put in the position of suing for peace and of committing themselves and their allies in advance to the terms laid down by Truman. The Malik offer omitted the three political conditions on which the Chinese and North Koreans had laid such stress: withdrawal of foreign troops from Korea, the return of Formosa to China, and the seating of the Peking government in the United Nations. Malik offered instead a pure and simple military armistice in the field. And these were Truman's terms.

The Malik offer, coming two days before the first anniversary of the war, could have been hailed in Washington as a Russian surrender and an American victory. The United States, if peace was what it wanted, could then have suggested an immediate cease-fire to take effect on the anniversary while the armistice details were negotiated. The principle of a cease-fire first and negotiations afterwards had been put forward in January by the United States and the United Nations, and had then been rejected by the Chinese Reds. This, too, could have been represented as a victory, and the United States by the cease-fire proposal would have gained a propaganda advantage in the battle over peace.

But any such response to the Malik offer would have led to a world-wide relaxation of tension, and the maintenance of tension was a prime objective of Truman's foreign policy. The Korean War was being drawn toward a truce by military realities: neither side could hope to win a limited war in the peninsula, neither side was willing to launch World War III over Korea. But while neither side could win the war, only one side —from Truman's point of view—could win the peace. Once peace broke out, it would become difficult to hold Formosa, to keep Peking out of the United Nations, and to force acceptance of a Japanese peace treaty permitting Japan to rearm and the American military to keep its bases in Japan. It would also become difficult to maintain the increasing tempo of rearmament at home and abroad.

Washington regarded peace, even on its own terms, as a kind of trap. Constantine Brown, the well-informed diplomatic correspondent of the *Washington Star*, a favored confidant at the Pentagon, indicated what the trouble was. Official quarters, he reported, feared that if peace came it would be hard to keep Communist China out of the United Nations even though the subject were excluded from the truce negotiations. Washington therefore preferred to "let the other members of the UN take the lead in whatever negotiations may result. . . . From the standpoint of domestic politics, this is a 'must.'"

Unfortunately, the domestic political situation in the United States was such as to leave little leeway for those "other members" of the United Nations. The sixteen nations which had contributed troops to the war in Korea had no direct liaison with the "unified command" in Tokyo. Their channel of communication was indirect; the "unified command" reported to the United States Chiefs of Staff which in turn reported to the State Department. The State Department assigned an Assistant Secretary of State to meet once a week with a committee representing the sixteen nations, to give them their briefing. But this official, Dean Rusk, was himself the darling of the China lobby and even declared in a speech at the Waldorf-Astoria on May 18 that the United States recognized Chiang Kai-shek because he "more authentically represents the views of the great body of the people of China" and would help them if they tried to throw off Communist "tyranny."

The repercussions of the Rusk speech showed how difficult it would be for the other members of the United Nations to "lead" the negotiations in the direction of a settlement with Communist China. Senator Taft declared triumphantly that the State Department had adopted MacArthur's policies. That the speech succeeded in limiting the Department's freedom of action was indicated by Secretary Acheson's weak effort to disavow this interpretation of it at the press conference which followed. One reporter asked whether Rusk's "statement to the effect that the Peking regime does not represent the people of China" meant that the United States would refuse to negotiate a settlement with that regime in Korea. To this Acheson replied that, well, as he had pointed out, if you are going to stop fighting with people that are fighting with you, you would have to deal with the people who are fighting with you. He thought MacArthur stated that, that everybody had stated it.[1]

The reporter then pressed the real question. "Mr. Secretary,

[1] The wording is that of the official transcript of the May 23, 1951, press conference at the State Department. Direct quotation of the Secretary's words is forbidden by the Department's rules, but this and similar quotations are given as exactly as possible in indirect discourse. This particular conference was discussed in my column, New York *Daily Compass*, May 28, 1951.

if a cease-fire were arranged, would we be willing to negotiate with the Red China regime a permanent settlement?" Acheson replied that he thought he had said enough on the subject, and did not intend to say any more.

But could peace be achieved in the Far East if this, the crucial question, were evaded? The inescapable point had been made the day before by Walter Lippmann when he said that if the Rusk speech were to be adopted as policy "then the Administration has worked itself into a fantastic predicament. It has made the issue with Red China not the repulse of its aggression in Korea but that of its survival. Regimes do not negotiate about their survival . . . These issues are not negotiable. They can be settled only by total victory."

CHAPTER 38

★

"Every Time Stalin Smiles"

WITH America's allies increasingly eager to end the Korean War, with the Soviet Union ready to end it on Truman's terms, talks could not be avoided. Yet before these talks had even begun, top American officials set out to make public opinion distrustful and to stress the dangers of peace. The first reactions in Washington to the Malik offer were chilly. The State Department said that if Malik's recommendation "is more than propaganda, adequate means for discussing an end to the conflict are available." Acheson did not seem to think that it warranted any change in his previously prepared statement marking the first anniversary of the war on June 24. "They," he said, "talk of peace and plan for war." Truman, in a speech prepared for delivery on June 25, inserted a few noncommittal sentences expressing wary interest. And Acheson next day instructed the House Foreign Affairs Committee that the Malik offer might only be "camouflage" to cover designs on Iran or Burma.

Some hours earlier the same day in Tokyo there occurred the first of those supposedly accidental leaks to the press which turned up several times during the truce talks and helped make public opinion suspicious of them. This leak supplied the very first item on American news tickers the morning of June 26 and seemed designed to throw a monkey wrench into the works before the truce talks could get under way. "The United States State Department," the United Press ticker reported from Tokyo, "suspects Russia's cease-fire proposal may be just an attempt to dupe the Allies . . ." And the Associated Press said that a State Department memorandum, made available to the press in Tokyo, "virtually branded" the Malik offer "a move . . . to place the enemy in a better position militarily." The memorandum was distributed "through the mimeographing department of General Ridgway's public information officer." It looked as if the General were moving in the footsteps of his illustrious predecessor.

There was a bipartisan barrage of warning, in which both the "internationalist" and "isolationist" wings of the Republican Party joined. The "internationalist" Dewey said, with that paranoia so characteristic of American politics in this period, "Every time the Soviets make a peace move, I get scared. . . . Every time Stalin smiles, beware." The "isolationist" Taft warned that it looked as if the talks were headed toward recognition of the "Chinese aggressors." Within the space of a week, beginning with Defense Secretary George C. Marshall's appearance on June 29 before the House Foreign Affairs Committee, all the top Administration military and civilian mobilization officials made speeches or statements warning against any letdown in the mobilization effort if there was peace in Korea. Economic Stabilizer Eric Johnston, Chief of Naval Operations Forrest P. Sherman, Joint Chiefs of Staff Chairman Omar N. Bradley, Defense Mobilizer Charles E. Wilson, W. Averell Harriman, and General Dwight D. Eisenhower—they all echoed Marshall's "I'm worried . . . whether we'll relax after the Korean action." Truman made a Fourth of July speech warning that even if the Korean War should end "we face a long period of world tension and great international danger." Once again he and MacArthur found themselves in agreement. The dismissed General told the New York *Daily News* on July 11 that if the United States cut down its armed forces after a Korean truce it would be "caught like a mouse in a trap."

The peace talks were regarded by these leaders as a kind of diabolic plot against rearmament. The often semi-authoritative *Washington Post* said, in a widely reprinted editorial called

"Peril of Communist Treachery," that "Moscow's desire for an armistice apparently springs from a belief that the extraordinary stimulus that the aggression in Korea gave to rearmament in the free world must be allowed to subside." This sternly suggested, as did so much official propaganda, that the Korean War was a benefit of which we should not permit ourselves easily to be deprived. *"What is likely to come out of the forthcoming negotiations in Korea,"* the editorial continued, *"is not real peace but a new kind of struggle that will be more difficult in every way,* except in the sacrifice of human life." All but the last phrase, added as if in hasty awareness of an oversight, was in italics. The emphasis was on the greater dangers of peace, not on the saving of lives. Truman himself a few weeks earlier had implied that the loss of life in Korea was of minor significance. He told the Highway Safety Conference in Washington on June 13 that "the sabotage press" was exaggerating Korean casualties. There had been "less than 80,000" casualties in Korea as compared with 1,035,000 people killed and injured on United States highways the previous year.

Most disturbing of all, at this early stage, even before the truce talks began, were indications that officials were thinking seriously of adopting MacArthur's ideas and bombing China if the talks failed. The *Washington Post,* though pro-Administration and anti-MacArthur, struck this note in the editorial just quoted—a note which was to be heard again and again in official quarters as the truce talks dragged on. "The Chinese," the *Washington Post* said, "should also understand that if they put forth no genuine effort to bring about a cessation of hostilities in the forthcoming negotiations the resumption of the war would not be on the limited scale that has characterized it to date. The world-wide desire for a cessation of hostilities cannot be trifled with."

On July 8, two days before the truce talks began, Arthur Krock reported from Washington in the *New York Times* that among the questions uppermost in the minds of those in all "three branches" of the government (presumably Krock felt the Supreme Court was also pondering the matter) was this:

"If the armistice negotiations fail, in circumstances which will justify the official accusation that they were undertaken as a cover for an offensive military buildup by the enemy in Korea, should the United States insist that the United Nations authorize the Allied commander to use every military instrument at his disposal to end the war, including air bombing of the enemy bases outside Korea?"

"Should this authority," Krock went on, "be extended to the use of atomic weapons in the commander's discretion? And if the United Nations refuses to give this latitude to the commander, even that which excludes atomic weapons, shall the United States 'go it alone,' and if so could it count on sufficient public support?"

Krock said it was the consensus of official opinion that if the parleys proved a cover for a military buildup, with a new enemy offensive to be accompanied by air attack, the United States would win its demand to "shoot the works" and would be supported by public opinion. It was the possibility of such grave decisions arising from the truce talks which "explains why there is no dancing in the streets of Washington this Saturday night by informed and responsible persons in the government." Surely, on the other hand, it was grounds for a hurried jig or two in MacArthur's private suite in the Waldorf-Astoria and among the MacArthurite generals in the Far East. To hint in advance that the generals could bomb China if the truce talks broke down was to encourage them in advance to break them down.

CHAPTER 39

★

Cease-Fire Switch

AT THE very start of the negotiations on July 10, as if to make sure that peace did not break out inadvertently, the American military insisted that hostilities were to continue until all the issues of the truce had been negotiated. This, as already noted, was in sharp contrast to the situation in January, when it was the United Nations which proposed and the Chinese Reds who objected to an immediate cease-fire and negotiations afterward. "The purpose of a cease-fire," Chou En-lai had declared on January 17, "is merely to obtain a breathing space for the United States troops." Six months later, it was the Americans who were arguing that a cease-fire before the negotiations had been successfully concluded would merely procure a breathing space for the Chinese and North Korean troops. "Hostilities," said Admiral Joy on July 10, in a formal statement which had been endorsed by General Ridgway, "will continue until such time as there is an agreement on the terms covering the armistice, and until such time as an approved armistice commission is prepared to function." This was to prove a long time, indeed.

The talks began on July 10. They were broken off on July 12. The charge was that the Reds had barred twenty UN newspapermen from the scene of the truce talks. Though the break came purportedly over the right of the American press to have access to Kaesong, the correspondents themselves seemed to take an acid view of this sudden solicitude on the part of generals and admirals who had never been unduly liberal in their own press relations and proved extraordinarily restrictive in the weeks that followed. Jim Becker, the Associated Press war correspondent, in a dispatch filed from Munsan under dateline of July 12, said "it was generally conceded by newsmen here that the issue was badly handled—both by the press and by the army." He quoted as the majority viewpoint among the correspondents that expressed by Hal Foust of the *Chicago Tribune,* one of those stopped by the Reds. "It is a hell of a note," Foust said, "to stop a peace conference over such petulant trivialities. We 'weren't going to attend the conference sessions anyway. Everyone acted hastily and short-tempered in this matter. Some more American kids are going to get killed because of it." Becker himself reported in his dispatch: "There was a good deal of criticism here over the harsh tone of Vice Admiral C. Turner Joy's reply to the rather conciliatory message of the Reds which preceded it. The Communist attitude was that they would like to have newsmen present, but only after the talks had made greater progress."

The talks were resumed on July 15, three days after they were broken off. The first topic was preparation of an agenda, and the first snag was Communist insistence on putting on the agenda the question of withdrawal of troops from Korea. The Reds dropped this demand after General Marshall on July 24 told a news conference in Washington that the Communists were bringing up the issue too soon, and "withdrawal of foreign troops from Korea will naturally follow a satisfactory peace settlement." Next day General Nam Il offered to accept the Marshall formula. The agenda was adopted next day, the 26th, and discussion began on Point Two: "Fixing a cease-fire line and demilitarized front-line zone."

It looked as if the talks were at last under way. Within twenty-four hours there occurred the next in that series of disruptive news "leaks" which did so much to confuse and poison the public mind in America against the talks. An Army officer held a briefing session at the Pentagon on Friday afternoon, July 27, accusing the Reds of bad faith in Korea and declaring that they were using the comparative lull on the battlefield to carry out a tremendous buildup for future attacks. The officer said the United States Eighth Army had the Reds "on the ropes," when it was forced to pause by the truce negotiations. The briefing set off alarmist headlines in the press. "RED TRICK TO DODGE DEFEAT SEEN," said the New York *Daily News*. "CHINESE 'SAVED' BY PARLEY," said the banner headline on the front page of the *New York Journal American*. The Pentagon briefing said the Chinese had just suffered "their most disastrous defeat" of the war when the Malik offer led the United Nations forces to halt "in the interest of peace, at the very moment when they were in a position to achieve an even greater success."

Judging by Ridgway's next fortnightly report to the United Nations, the picture given by the briefing officer was a false one. But it made scare headlines all over the country while the Ridgway report, released the next day, was virtually ignored by the press. Ridgway's report covered the period from June 15 to June 30 during which the Malik peace offer was made. The Malik offer was on June 23 and the preliminary talks began July 8. The Ridgway report mentions no "disastrous defeat" from which the Reds were saved nor does it support the picture of the Reds utilizing the truce period for a buildup. According to Ridgway, a buildup in the Red forces had been going on since March, and augmented strength had been noted "in supporting arms—particularly artillery and anti-tank units." The briefing officer had said the Reds were on the ropes when truce talks were opened. But Ridgway said: "In mid-June counterattacking UN ground forces were meeting increased resistance." An enemy showing increased capacity to resist attack is not an enemy on the ropes. The briefing was disavowed and an investigation was said to have been ordered by Secretary Marshall, but no more was heard of this investigation. And the very next day the President himself made a speech expressing distrust of the negotiations. "We do not yet know," he said at Detroit on July 28, "whether the Communists really desire peace in Korea or whether they are simply trying to gain by negotiations what they have not been able to get by conquest. We intend to find that out . . ."

The Reds may well have asked themselves whether the United States "really" wanted peace or was simply trying to see how much more it could gain by negotiations. It was in this period that the American negotiators raised their price for a cease-fire agreement. On June 26, three days after the Malik offer, Acheson had told the House Foreign Affairs Committee that the United States military objective in Korea would be satisfied if the Reds withdrew behind the 38th Parallel. Even earlier, on March 12, Ridgway had told correspondents in Korea that if the war ended on the 38th Parallel it would be "a tremendous victory" for the United Nations. But to accept the Parallel as the dividing line was to reestablish the situation prevailing before the war, to accept the existence of a North Korean regime again. There began to be talk of obtaining a more "defensible" line. And on August 1 Acheson, ignoring his commitment made five weeks before, handed out this statement: "The 38th Parallel is unacceptable as a line of demarcation for the buffer zone because it is militarily indefensible." Whether the 38th Parallel was any more or less defensible than any other line in that general area was not explained.

What the State Department says publicly is not always the same as the "not-for-attribution" background which it feeds out to trusted newspaper sources. John M. Hightower, Associated Press correspondent at the Department, reported in a Washington dispatch published July 30 by the *Nippon Times* that the Reds, by insisting on the 38th Parallel as the line of demarcation, "are trying to regain the political *status quo,* something they were unable to achieve by military means." The *New York Times* reflected the same point of view in an editorial on July 31: "Even if it is admitted that the Parallel can be properly discussed as a possible cease-fire line, the political objections to it are insurmountable." To restore the Parallel, the editorial went on, would be to restore the *status quo ante,* the old political division of the peninsula: "The *status quo* in this case was no good to start with, and there can be no good in merely going back to it."

These were political, not strategic, considerations, and were another example of the pervasive swing back toward MacArthurism. MacArthur had also objected to restoration of the Parallel. His argument against the Parallel in March undercut the arguments being used against it in July and August. When Ridgway on March 12 had said that a truce on the Parallel would be a satisfactory ending for the war, MacArthur cabled Hugh Baillie of the United Press three days later that there were "no natural defense features anywhere near" the 38th Parallel. MacArthur was implying that the war must go on until all Korea was conquered if victory was to be secure. But if there were, as MacArthur said, "no natural defense features anywhere near" the 38th Parallel, then it did not really matter very much whether the line was on the Parallel or in its general vicinity. It soon appeared that the military were merely trying to drive as hard a bargain as possible.

From July 27 to August 4, while the truce talks were deadlocked on the question of the cease-fire line, it was assumed that the UN negotiators were holding out for the existing battleline. On August 4 the *New York Times* carried a dispatch from its correspondent, Lindesay Parrott, datelined the same day, saying that "an Allied spokesman" had denied that Ridgway's headquarters "had demanded a demarcation line well north of the present combat area, as the Communist radio has been reporting." But the same day an Associated Press dispatch datelined "*UN Advance Headquarters in Korea*" said obscurely that the Reds were being reminded that since the Allied air and sea fronts "extend over most of North Korea" the United Nations forces were "entitled to some compensation for this in the fixing of a buffer zone." Just what this meant was made clearer by a curious revelation that same day in Tokyo. The United Press reported that day, and so did the Associated Press the next, that three days earlier the Civil Information and Education Section of Supreme Headquarters had issued, to the Japanese press, information still denied the American press. This information was labeled as "background material" to help the Japanese press understand the demands being made by the UN negotiators at Kaesong. It indicated that the UN negotiators were seeking a truce line not on the existing battlefront but somewhere between the battleline on the ground and the Manchurian border.

"In the air and on the sea," the Headquarters information bulletin said, "the United Nations Command forces have gained and continued to maintain control up to the line of the Yalu and Tumen Rivers . . . It is here in the zone between the present ground front and the air and sea fronts on and adjacent to the northern boundaries of Korea that the military situation is stabilized—that the military forces are in balance. The military demarcation line upon which we must reach agreement therefore lies somewhere between the air and sea front on the Yalu and the ground front."

The *Sunday Times* of London, in a dispatch from its Tokyo correspondent, Richard Hughes, on August 5 referred to two "handouts" from Ridgway Headquarters to the Japanese press and quoted a second one which seems to have been written in the style of Syngman Rhee. This pointed out that the UN air and sea front was on the Yalu River and said: "The Korean people do not wish the Communists to be poised on the 38th Parallel again. These are the facts. The sooner the Reds face them the sooner the Kaesong negotiations will come to a successful end."

The Associated Press, in calling attention on August 5 to the information bulletin explaining why the Allied negotiators were asking a line between the battlefront and the Yalu, said: "United Nations armistice envoys have not publicly announced their buffer zone demands made during the closed session at Kaesong. However, Army officers at the Allied advance headquarters near Munsan recently expressed the view that the Allies must have a defensible line."

The authenticity of the material given to the Japanese press was not denied, but on August 6 General Ridgway told the American press that the defensible line sought by the UN command was "in effect the line now generally held by the UN forces." The "in effect" and the "generally" were not explained. But eleven days later an International News Service story in the *Nippon Times* of August 17 described a new "background information" story from Ridgway's Public Information Office which "repeated Admiral C. Turner Joy's Kaesong arguments that UN air and sea superiority have a definite relation to the military armistice line under discussion but that they are not completely reflected in the ground battle line."

This was the same old tune all over again. Lindesay Parrott, chief correspondent of the *New York Times* in Tokyo—who had completely ignored the information bulletin disclosure of August 4—cabled his paper on August 20: "The United Nations representatives consistently have insisted that, when the air and naval attacks . . . were called off under an armistice, a corresponding advantage . . . on the ground must be conceded by the Communists." It is difficult to avoid the conclusion that Ridgway had been telling the truth to the Japanese press—and misleading our own.

The discrepancy was hidden from sight, however, in a more sensational disclosure. At 9:30 P.M. Saturday, August 4, Ridgway called a conference at his headquarters in Tokyo which lasted five hours and twenty minutes. It was announced that he had been in touch with the Pentagon during that time. Early on the morning of Sunday, August 5, Ridgway broadcast a message to the Communists breaking off the peace talks on the ground that an armed infantry company had been seen Saturday marching past within a hundred yards of the house in which the truce talks were going on. Ridgway called this a "flagrant violation" of the agreement for the talks and said these would be resumed only if the Reds furnished "a satisfactory explanation" of the incident and assurances that there would be no recurrence. The truce talks were off again.

CHAPTER 40

★

Ridgway Stands "Firm"

AMID the cheers for Ridgway's "firmness," there were some quieter voices. "General Ridgway's statement," the Washington correspondent of the London Sunday *Observer* reported August 5, "is not the ultimatum which has seemed to be in the air for the last two days, but it has more significance than a mere protest at Communist violation of the Kaesong 'neutrality' rules." This suggested that some kind of ultimatum had been expected, before the violation occurred. The dispatch indeed went on to say, "It was confidently expected here that the week-end would produce, either at Kaesong or from General Ridgway in Tokyo, some demonstration of counterpressure on the Communists which would show that the Allies knew just how far they were prepared to go and that they had no intention of going farther." In fact the *Observer* correspondent seemed to feel that the incident was the pretext rather than the occasion for the breaking off of the truce talks. For he went on to say, "As it happens, General Ridgway has been able to make a display of toughness, on a sound legalistic basis."

The Ridgway broadcast was made early on the morning of the 5th. On the 6th, the Reds replied that the troops had marched through the neutral zone "by mistake," and asked Ridgway to send his negotiators back to Kaesong and not to break off the talks because of such "minor matters." Ridgway responded that the incident was "neither minor nor trivial."

On the 9th, the Reds replied with assurances of their "strict adherence" to the truce zone agreement and said that any further interruption of the talks was "inconceivable . . . unless you should deliberately fabricate incidents." The new pledge was accepted and the talks resumed on August 10. General Nam Il had eaten a hearty slice of humble pie.

The truce talks resumed but the same deadlock recurred. "Plainly," the *New York Times* said on August 12, "the Communists do not want the talks to break down—three times they have given way to prevent that. Yet they apparently will not budge on the cease-fire line." General Nam Il insisted, "The 38th Parallel is the basic condition of any armistice." On August 13, he declared the talks "will not make any progress" until the UN negotiators "change the distorted demands they have made so far." But there was evidence that both sides were beginning to give. A UN communiqué late August 12 declared that "a mutually acceptable area in which further exploratory discussion might be held" seemed to have been uncovered. Ridgway on the 14th declared: "The present battle line . . . is approximately the line upon which the cease-fire must occur. It is militarily defensible." Next day (according to a Peking radio broadcast two days later) General Nam Il indicated that while the Reds still wanted the 38th Parallel as the dividing line, "it is possible to adjust this line on the basis of the terrain and mutual defense positions of the demilitarized zone if they are necessary and reasonable." Bargaining had begun. That same day Admiral Joy proposed that a two-man subcommittee —one from each side—handle the problem of the truce line. The Reds next day asked instead for a two-man team from each side. Joy agreed.

That was on Thursday, August 16. Next day, Friday, the Peking radio broadcast General Nam Il's readiness to adjust the truce line "on the basis of the terrain and mutual defense positions." Judging from a disclosure made ten days later by General William Nuckols, official spokesman of the UN delegation, General Nam Il had even "hinted that the Sino-Korean delegation was prepared to accept the present battlefront as a cease-fire line." On Saturday the Associated Press reported from Munsan that "for the second straight day Saturday the UN and Communist junior teams had met in a friendlier atmosphere than any shown when the full delegations wrestled with the impasse. . . . Muffled words and occasional laughter drifting from the Kaesong conference room indicated that the four-man armistice subcommittee met again in a spirit of friendly informality." Late Saturday, official sources in Washington said the two sides "were trying to figure out which line each army thinks it can defend in the general area of the 38th Parallel. The space between the two lines then would become the buffer zone." "REDS SEEN YIELDING," said the headline in the *Nippon Times* on August 18, and "ACCORD SEEN NEARER" on Sunday, August 19. A release prepared for the Sunday papers by Ridgway's press information office said that if the Reds were sincere "the actual armistice may be in sight."

It was at this moment, when peace at last seemed in sight, early on Sunday morning of August 19, that UN troops "behind one of the most devastating artillery bombardments of the Korean War" launched "the heaviest attack since the Kaesong armistice talks began." At the same time, about dawn on Sunday, a band of armed men invaded the Kaesong neutral zone, ambushed a Communist military police platoon, killed its commander, and wounded one of its men. Next day the United Press reported that "a third of the Korean battlefront was aflame."

The same day Eighth Army Headquarters reported, falsely, that the offensive was being made entirely by South Korean troops. The truth did not come out until later. On September 4, Eighth Army Headquarters officially released the fact that three United States divisions had been on a "limited offensive" since August 18. "Until last night," David McConnell cabled the *New York Herald Tribune* on September 5, "censorship forbade mentioning other than South Koreans being in battle. Three weeks ago in Seoul, correspondents were told that the military did not want to disturb the American public with news that United States troops were taking part in an offensive while the peace talks were in progress." It would have been more precise to say that the American military had launched the offensive just when it looked as if the truce talks might succeed, and had kept the attack secret.

The fact that American troops had opened an offensive did not become known until eighteen days after it began. In the meantime there was a series of incidents which led the Communists to break off the talks on August 23. They protested on August 19 that their military police had been ambushed; on August 20 that one of their truce team jeeps, on its way to the talks the day before, had been shot up by a United States Air Force plane; and on August 22 that a UN plane had bombed Kaesong. When the Reds broke off the talks on the 23rd, Ridgway in Tokyo denounced the Red "frame-up" and Truman in Washington spoke of the Kaesong talks as a Red "masquerade." The impression created was that the Reds had somehow manufactured these incidents as an excuse to upset the truce talks. Censorship still hid the fact that the incidents coincided with an American offensive. "Ridgway Warns of Red Trickery" was the featured exclusive interview published by *U.S. News* August 17 on the eve of the offensive. "NO SIGN OF PEACEFUL INTENT BY FOE," said a headline over the interview itself. It is not difficult to imagine the headlines in the American press if it had been Nam Il and not Ridgway who launched an offensive just at the moment when an armistice line agreement at last seemed possible. And what if it had been American MPs, not Chinese, who had been ambushed?

Were these incidents fabricated, as Ridgway and Truman implied by their statements of August 23? Let us take them one by one. The UN command's formal statement on the ambush as published in full text by the *New York Times* on August 21 denied neither the fact nor the manner of the attack. It merely made the point that no evidence had been uncovered to indicate that the attack had been made by uniformed personnel. "The possibility exists," the statement admitted, "that the shooting was the work of a politically guided civilian group operating under instructions to create an atmosphere of tension which would tend to support the breaking of the current military armistice conference."

The description fitted Syngman Rhee. He had long opposed a truce. When the talks broke down on August 23, a Rhee spokesman at once issued a statement welcoming the breakdown. Rhee had at his command armed troops, South Korean guerrillas, and quasi-Fascist civilian bands. But the UN press officer, General Nuckols, "hinted," according to the United Press on August 20, "that North Korean troops disguised as civilians might have carried out the plot," though under questioning by the press he also "admitted South Korean irregulars might have been to blame." Official propaganda amplified the ingenious Nuckols "hint" that the Reds somehow ambushed themselves, citing this as further evidence of Communist bad faith and desire to intimidate the UN. A *New York Times* correspondent, Murray Schumach, offered a less ingenious but more likely explanation: "It is quite possible that a soldier was killed by South Korean guerrillas, who occasionally operate in small bands without close supervision from the Eighth Army." The possibility was brushed aside.

The second incident, the strafing of a truce team jeep north of Kaesong, was not denied by the UN command. Admiral Joy's reply on August 22 was that the jeep had not borne agreed truce team markings. Joy warned, the Associated Press reported, that such vehicles "even though marked with white flags" would be subject to air attack "unless the UN is informed in advance of their time and route of movement." The North Korean and Chinese Communist negotiators may well have decided to take their chances on the open road rather than trust a sometimes trigger-happy Air Force to know in advance just when and by what route they would be traveling to Kaesong.

As for the bombing, a release from Tokyo headquarters on August 23 showed that all the UN command had was a report from its Colonel A. J. Kinney, "based on investigation on the spot, but in darkness." The report said that the holes shown to Colonel Kinney "might actually be the result of a Communist plane dropping small cans of napalm and small explosive charges such as grenades." Could it not also perhaps have been an anti-Communist plane? What made Colonel Kinney think that if there was a bombing the Communists must have been bombing themselves? The report also mentioned that the Fifth Air Force picked up an unidentified aircraft by radar west of Kaesong shortly before the alleged bombing occurred.

The little that is known suggests the need for impartial investigation and hardly supports a finding of Communist fabrication. Correspondents were not only operating under censorship but in at least one case were kept from the scene. "United Nations correspondents," Eric Downton, Korea correspondent of the London *Daily Telegraph*, reported in its issue of August 21, "were not allowed by American officers to go to the scene of the alleged shooting." Can anyone doubt that correspondents would have been rushed to the scene if Ridgway could have proved a frame-up? The tone taken by Ridgway was not that of a man reacting to a provocation he deplored or an unfortunate incident he was determined to investigate but of a man throwing up a smoke screen to cover himself and his agents.

Even if one could believe that the Reds ambushed, bombed, and strafed themselves, one would still have to explain the American offensive of the 18th and the censorship which hid its full import from the American public. The best evidence that the Reds were not seeking by manufactured incidents to break off the talks lies in the fact that the Peking radio the night of August 23 hastily explained that the Communists meant only to break off the meeting that day, not the entire armistice conference. The Red commanders next day sent Ridgway a message denouncing the UN for a plot to murder their delegates but expressing hope that truce talks would be resumed and "proceed smoothly" to a "just and reasonable agreement." By then it was too late. There was every sign that the United States military had the break they wanted, and that civilian Washington wanted, too.

A quick succession of headlines showed the way the wind was blowing. The *Nippon Times* on August 24 already had a story from Washington, "TRUCE TALK BREAKDOWN HELD DICTATED BY U.S.S.R." Two days later, it was "TROOPS IN FIGHTING TRIM—GENERAL VAN FLEET ASSERTS U.N. FORCES READY IF TALKS

FAIL." On August 25, Rashin, uncomfortably close to the
Russian border and long interdicted as a target to MacArthur,
was bombed. In Washington the American press was told that
the bombing was ordered because reconnaissance showed a
buildup in that area. But the UP story from Washington
in the *Nippon Times* on August 27 said, "Air Force Superforts
carried the war to within seventeen miles of Russia's border
Saturday—with Washington's permission—in an attack that
implied a warning to the Reds that the UN was prepared to go
'all out' if the Communists end the Kaesong peace talks."

The day after the offensive of August 18 began in Korea,
eight of the Republican Senators on the MacArthur inquiry
filed a minority report declaring that "any peace short of
the liberation and unification of Korea is a delusion." The
statement, though filed jointly, was termed "a statement of
individual views" rather than a minority report, perhaps to
put a better face on the pro-Administration majority's failure
to file any report at all. The minority was allowed to state
without challenge that one of the thirty points on which the
Committee showed "a remarkable unanimity of agreement"
was the need for stronger American support of Chiang Kai-
shek and the proposition that "a temporary lull in Korea,
which later develops into a Far Eastern Munich-type appeasement of the Chinese and Korean Communist aggressors, is
no guarantee of peace or security for the free world."

"Had the majority made a report," I commented at the time
in my column, "it would have been forced to argue the case
against a wider war in order to defend Truman's removal of
MacArthur. But one may well begin to wonder whether Truman wants to be 'defended' in that way. It is hard to avoid
the conclusion that the upshot of the inquiry fits a different
pattern. The Administration seems more interested in preparing public opinion at home and abroad for the breakdown of
the peace talks than in building up support for a cease-fire."

All the emphasis seemed to be on the failure of the talks
even before the incidents and the offensive which accompanied
their breakdown on the 23rd. The chairman of the Mac-
Arthur inquiry, Senator Russell of Georgia, told the United

Press on August 17, two days before the minority report was released for publication, that the MacArthur hearings "might prove especially valuable if the Korean truce talks 'should fail.' " The Senator said the hearings would lead to "a better understanding" with our allies "and result in the war being waged much more vigorously in Korea by the United Nations." Senators Smith and Taft may have helped to spell out what Senator Russell meant by waging the war "more vigorously" when they declared on August 18 that, if the cease-fire talks broke down, the United States would be forced to widen the war and bomb Manchurian bases. Even before the talks broke down, on the eve of the offensive and the incidents, the stage seemed to be set for a reversion to MacArthurism.

Six days after the truce talk breakdown, the *Wall Street Journal's* Washington bureau reported, "Military men and diplomats are discussing General Douglas MacArthur's old proposals for winning the Korean war in a hurry—if the truce attempt is really washed up." The mood was hardly one of earnest searchers for peace.

CHAPTER 41

★

Postponing Peace Again

THERE was an immediate diplomatic and political reason why a successful outcome of the truce talks in August would have been embarrassing. Senator Russell, in announcing that there would be no formal majority report from the MacArthur hearings, explained that "to renew a bitter discussion of the methods for waging war as advocated by General MacArthur would not help the successful conclusion of a cease-fire or the signing of a Japanese peace treaty at San Francisco."

The treaty conference was to open in San Francisco on September 4. The Russians at the last moment had decided to attend the conference, though they had been ignored in drafting the treaty. The announcement on August 13 that the Russians were coming threw the State Department into something of a panic.

"The State Department," the *Wall Street Journal* reported on August 17, "sizes up the Russian peace strategy along these lines: Russians want to mess up the San Francisco parley on a Jap peace treaty starting September 4. One move will be to demand that Red China take part. A cease-fire in Korea on the eve of the conference would make the Chinese Communists look nicer, maybe win them some votes at San Francisco. The United States reaction is to demand more in Korean talks than we expect the Communists ever to concede. Barring a complete cave-in by the Reds, the State Department would prefer no cease-fire deal until after the San Francisco conference ends."

The day this was published was the day that the Peking radio broadcast General Nam Il's readiness to compromise on the question of the cease-fire line. It looked like that "cave-in by the Reds" the Department seemed to fear. The offensive, the ambush, and the other incidents followed. The break-down in the truce talks on August 23 suited the political needs of the State Department as well as the dominant mood of the American military. Three days after the break the *New York Times* noted cheerfully in its "News of the Week in Review": "One thing seems clear—the time lost on the neutral zone fracas makes it unlikely, though not impossible, that there can be a truce agreement by September 4 when the San Francisco conference on the Japanese peace treaty begins. Many United States officials had believed the Russians wanted a Korean truce concluded before the conference. The Russians, the theory runs, want to use the armistice to document their claim to peace-maker and win allies in their fight against the treaty from among those Asian nations who are already op-posed to some of its provisions."

This understated the relationship between the Korean War and the Japanese treaty. Only the war made the treaty possible. There were many objections to it: the treaty had been drafted without consulting Japan's most important neighbor, China; both the Nationalists and the Communists were bitter about this. It was opposed by Japan's other big neighbor, Russia. It was unsatisfactory to India. A treaty of peace with Japan which was unacceptable to the three biggest Far Eastern powers was hardly a stabilizing factor. All the Asian and Pacific countries plundered by the Japanese were angered by its virtual abandonment of their claim to reparations. All were alarmed by the provisions allowing Japan to rearm. The British agreed with many of these objections. They feared the impact on their own markets of Japanese economic revival and of any moves which tended to shut Japan off from her natural markets in China and force her exports into Britain's African and Southeast Asian markets. Were the Korean War ended and peace established in the Far East, it would become more difficult to exclude Communist China from the settlement with Japan and it would become more difficult to make our own allies accept Japanese rearmament.

These anxieties were felt in Washington on the very eve of the peace talks in Korea. Three days before they began, Arthur Krock in his July 7 dispatch from Washington to the *New York Times* indicated that the pending treaty with Japan was bulking as large as Formosa itself in the apprehensions aroused by the prospect of peace talks. Krock said one of the questions bothering official Washington was, "Suppose one of the Communist conditions for subscribing to an armistice which will be satisfactory to our side is the inclusion of Moscow and Peiping in the Japanese peace treaty negotiations or the suspension of those negotiations until the other questions have been reviewed?" Suppose that were "the judgment of our treaty-making associates?" Should the United States agree to that condition "or refuse its assent?" And "in which position could the government count on the support of American public opinion?"

American policy makers were as much worried by "the judgment of our treaty-making associates" as they were by the views of the Russians and the Chinese Reds. This explains the rather hoggish way this peace treaty was framed. It was drafted by the United States on the basis of principles which were developed with General MacArthur and had the full approval of both parties. (This explanation was given by John Foster Dulles, widely proclaimed as the "architect" of the treaty.) These principles included Japanese rearmament and the lifting of all restrictions on Japanese industry. The draft was shown to the other interested nations (except China, Communist or Nationalist), virtually on a take-it-or-leave-it basis.

The United States was willing to listen and even to make minor changes. "However, in the last analysis," as Dulles had warned unctuously on March 31, "the United States cannot, in justice to our own people, or indeed to others, become co-sponsor of a peace settlement which, in our judgment, made

. . . without arrogance and in humbleness of spirit, would throw unnecessary and intolerable burdens of a military or economic character upon the United States . . ." This meant that the United States reserved the right to dictate the terms irrespective of the wishes of other nations.

The reason offered for rearming Japan was to lessen the military burden on the United States. Likewise, the reason for lifting restrictions on her industries and absolving her from reparations was to lessen the economic burden on the United States. The price, for Japan, was the acceptance of a collateral agreement giving bases in Japan to the American military. So long as the Korean War went on, and China was involved in it, the United States could always argue that a real peace conference among the interested powers was impossible. So long as the Korean War went on, the American military could always insist that they had to have bases in Japan to carry on the war and to protect Japan itself from invasion. The United States could not afford to have a cease-fire before the San Francisco conference. It could not even afford a cease-fire until after the treaty—and the military agreement which went with it—had been safely ratified in both Washington and Tokyo. The Korean War made Japan a prisoner of American policy. Peace in Korea threatened to loosen the bonds.

Dulles called his handiwork "a peace of reconciliation." It was so in the sense that it forced the victims of Japanese aggression to reconcile themselves to the rebirth of Japanese militarism. It was not so much a treaty binding up the wounds of World War II as a forced military alliance laying the basis for World War III. The Yalta settlement, which had recognized Soviet sovereignty over the Kuriles and South Sakhalin, was disregarded in the treaty. Japan renounced its claims to these territories, no mention was made of their ultimate ownership. In the hearings on Senate ratification, Dulles pointed out this reversal of the Yalta commitment. Here were the seeds of future conflict with the USSR. At the same time American policy strove to force Japanese recognition of Chiang Kai-shek, a step which would put Japan into hostile relations with Communist China. Dulles had so far succeeded in this as to elicit a personal letter from the Japanese premier, Shigeru Yoshida, pledging that Japan would not establish either economic or political ties with Communist China. The treaty was thus laying firm foundations for irreconcilable hostility between Japan and its nearest and largest neighbors. A Korean cease-fire in this perspective could only be a temporary and perhaps inconvenient lull in the preparations for a much larger and wider conflict. The sudden burst of "incidents" in Kaesong at the end of August served to prevent "incidents" at San Francisco in September. Under circumstances as diplomatic as a steam-roller, the treaty was signed, sealed, and delivered at San Francisco in four days.

CHAPTER 42

★

"The Dreaded Softening Process"

THE PEACE talks were broken off on August 23. They did not resume until October 25, after a sixty-three day lapse. The period opened with an incident which hardly showed good faith on Ridgway's part in dealing either with the other side or with the American public. On August 28 the Reds demanded that liaison teams "reinvestigate" the alleged bombing of the neutral zone on August 22, and asked for publication of all documents exchanged between the two sides during the truce talks "in order to enable people throughout the world to understand the full and true picture of the incident." Publication of all documents would have provided not only a picture of the exchanges over the incident but a full picture of the issues in dispute at the time—especially as to the exact location of the armistice line. Ridgway was silent on the demand for publication of the documents, and these were withheld. Lindesay Parrott explained in his cable to the *New York Times* from Tokyo Headquarters that the proposed publication of the documents was "a maneuver some observers believed was an attempt to force the United Nations to go on record publicly with definite proposals for an armistice line." But if definite proposals were made to the Reds during the negotiations, why should Ridgway keep hidden from American and United Nations public opinion what was already known to the enemy? Perhaps because the demands he was making would not have been supported? This was the same period in which censorship was also hiding from American public opinion the fact that American troops were engaged in an offensive begun just when the truce talks had taken a turn for the better. The withholding of the documents was another example of the highhandedness with which the military treated the press and the bluntness with which it decided what the American people should and should not be allowed to know about the war.

In the case of the alleged bombing, as in that of the withheld documents, Tokyo Headquarters had nothing to lose by disclosure—unless it had something to hide. If the bombing was a "frame-up," as Ridgway charged the day it happened, why not investigate and prove it? His own Headquarters release had disclosed, "The Fifth Air Force reports an unidentified aircraft picked up by radar west of Kaesong at 2130 (9:30 P.M.)." That was one hour and fifty minutes before the bombing allegedly took place. The purpose of radar is to enable the air force to spot enemy planes and go after them before they can do any damage. Was an effort made to find out what this unidentified aircraft was doing so close to United Nations lines? Were any UN planes sent up to find and intercept it? None of these questions was ever answered. Except for one old-fashioned box crate which had made a sensational appearance on the enemy's side some weeks before, enemy air action had been largely confined to air battles over the Yalu, on the Manchurian frontier.

The appearance of an unidentified plane on the radar screens that night might have been expected to create a minor scurry. Why was it passed over so quickly in the formal release? These were questions which called for investigation. And the refusal to investigate, like the circumstances, leads one to wonder whether the "unidentified" plane created so little excitement because its mission was known. The UN investigating officers admitted the holes they examined in the ground at Kaesong might have been caused by "a Communist plane dropping small cans of napalm and small explosive charges such as grenades." Why did they say "Communist" plane? Might it not have been an "anti-Communist" plane operated by South Koreans? If the unidentified plane spotted on the radar screen was a Communist plane, then one would have expected Tokyo Headquarters to institute a drastic investigation of another kind. There was something dangerously wrong with the reporting and interception system if a Communist plane could operate so near UN lines without being intercepted and shot down after it was spotted. Of all the fishy incidents in the Korean War, this was one of the fishiest.

The dubious character of the whole affair was underscored when the Communists charged that a B-26 had penetrated and strafed the neutral zone early on the morning of September 10. UN investigators again pooh-poohed the charges. The *New York Times* headline next day on its report of the inquiry said, "KAESONG EVIDENCE HELD INCONCLUSIVE" and the headline over the *Herald Tribune* cable said, "U.N. LIAISON OFFICERS VISIT KAESONG TO INVESTIGATE, SAY CHARGE LOOKS FALSE." The Associated Press quoted one of the investigators, Colonel Don Darrow, as asking, "How do we know the plane was one of ours? Why not one of yours?" Yet late that night Tokyo Headquarters disclosed that the strafing was in fact done by a B-26 which was spotted on the radar screen at 1:41 A.M. on September 10. This meant that all the time Joy's investigators were finding the evidence at Kaesong "inconclusive" and wondering whether the strafing might not have been done by a Communist plane, Far East Air Forces knew that the neutral zone had been violated and strafed by one of our B-26s.

Questions began to be asked by the press in Tokyo. The Headquarters release of Tuesday night the 11th showed "the bomber was picked up by radar and in response to a challenge executed a directed identification turn." This led to "speculation that the radar operator knew, and the pilot must eventually have realized, that the plane was in the restricted area." Was the pilot warned away? If he was warned that he was over Kaesong "or realized a navigational error had been made before the strafing, why was his post-flight briefing report not immediately forwarded to top Fifth Air Force officers for action?"

Two American correspondents, David McConnell of the

New York Herald Tribune and George Herman of Columbia Broadcasting System, wanted to know what precautions were being taken to prevent a repetition and what mechanisms were being set up "to give the United Nations armistice team quicker notice in the event a similar incident should occur." They went to "a major, then a lieutenant colonel, a colonel, and Brigadier General William P. Nuckols, Far East Air Force information officer" without getting anywhere. "One Army officer," McConnell reported, "at first advised correspondents that their questions were 'none of your business' but later recanted." When they got to Brigadier General Frank A. Allen, chief Army public relations director, "he challenged the correspondents with the assertion that as a reader he would not be interested" in the answer to the questions they put. From him they finally learned "officially . . . that other than to reiterate to pilots to stay away from Kaesong, no other precautions have been taken." General Allen's first reaction to the queries as reported by McConnell had been a warning to the correspondents, "Don't forget which side you're on." The remark provided a vivid glimpse of the atmosphere at press headquarters in Tokyo. It also hinted that in trying to get at the truth about the bombing, they were hurting their own side. This implied in turn that full disclosure would reflect badly on the UN forces. General Allen's unrehearsed remark was a small-scale confession.

The military indicated that its interest was not in resuming the truce talks but in another round. "My hope for peace," General Van Fleet, commander of the Eighth Army, told correspondents on September 12, "is with United Nations' military might. And right now the enemy is hurt badly. We will hurt him much more before the winter is over and then he will want peace. He will need peace and badly, whether he attacks or just tries to sit out the winter." It was the UN not the Reds who were on the offensive. "In clashes during the past month," Murray Schumach reported to the *New York Times* from Eighth Army headquarters on September 15, "it has been the United Nations forces who attacked. Almost every time when the Communists attacked it has been as a countermeasure in an attempt to regain ground we had taken."

These weeks of so-called "limited offensive" were costly, and began to arouse criticism. Between the start of truce talks on July 10 and the end of September, official casualty totals for Americans alone were already close to 10,000 killed, wounded, and missing. General Van Fleet in a statement issued at the end of the month felt impelled to make an answer, as the *New York Times* correspondent in Tokyo explained on October 1, "to some critics who think less aggressive and less costly operations should be conducted as long as cease-fire negotiations give even faint indications that peace may still come to Korea." Van Fleet's own statement was as interesting for its omissions as for what it said. Nowhere did it say that casualties were due to Communist attacks which had to be repulsed. On the contrary, it was designed to show why the command felt it had to go on attacking.

"We suffered many of these casualties," General Van Fleet argued, "in taking hills which on the surface appeared minor in significance." But, Van Fleet elaborated, it was "militarily essential to take those hills to deny the enemy commanding terrain in close proximity." Just what this military gobbledygook meant was not clear. Hanson Baldwin, himself just back from Korea, thought the Van Fleet statement "smacked too much of propaganda and too little of fact." "Korea, like Italy," Balwin objected, "is simply one hill mass and 'dominating terrain feature' after another; the process of winning hills could be an unending one."

Perhaps because General Van Fleet himself thought this talk of "commanding terrain in close proximity" might sound less than "militarily essential" to informed opinion, he added a second "imperative" explanation. The General said it was "imperative that the Eighth Army remain active to forestall the dreaded softening process of stagnation . . . I could not allow my forces to become soft and dormant." Thus the fighting, despite its unfortunate tendency to kill people, did provide military exercise. "While these attacks," he went on, "served further to cripple the Communist aggressor, United

Nations forces were working at their trade . . . absorbing new lessons and gradually learning the profession of fighting." The Eighth Army, he himself said, "was utilized more and more as a combat school." So was Korea. The General seemed unwilling to call off operations in which, as he said, "replacements are steadily assuming the poise that attends combat experience."

Back home we had been told that American lives had to be spilled in Korea to repel aggression. Now the generals were beginning to explain brightly that Korea represented an opportunity to improve the fighting caliber of "their" armed forces. We were told that the repulse of the aggressors, forcing them back across the 38th Parallel, would reestablish law and order. Now the generals were speaking as if a real truce would regrettably bring a useful training operation to an end. This was no longer "liberating" Korea. It was using the unhappy country as a ground for live field maneuvers. Van Fleet compared those who died in those operations to "the storied boy hero of Holland" who put his finger in the dike. The comparison was less than happy. If the Dutch boy had operated like General Van Fleet, he would have gone around punching holes in the dikes to make sure that the flood control squads were spared "the dreaded softening process of stagnation."

CHAPTER 43

★

Talks on Whether to Talk

TALKS on whether to resume the talks lasted two months. The night of August 23 the Red radio explained, as we have seen, that its negotiators only meant to break off for the day. The Reds wanted a reinvestigation of the Kaesong bombing. This was refused by Ridgway. On September 6 he suggested a new site instead, but in a message which declared the Red charges that the UN had violated Kaesong's neutrality "baseless and intentionally false." This was deliberate insult. The admission of the September 10 strafing by Ridgway gave the Reds a face-saving out, however, and on September 20 they asked resumption of the truce talks. Rhee the same day opposed resuming the talks unless the Chinese withdrew from Korea. Ridgway replied three days later offering not resumption of the truce talks but resumption of talks between the liaison committees to prepare for the truce talks. Four days later he proposed to remove the talks to Songhwan eight miles east of Kaesong. The Reds insisted there was nothing wrong with Kaesong, that the trouble lay with the UN command's failure to curb its fliers and South Korean irregulars. On October 4 they rejected the proposal to move the talks from Kaesong, but in negotiations on October 8 and 9 both sides finally agreed on Panmunjom. On October 11 the UN truce talks team dismantled its old "peace camp" at Munsan and prepared to set up a new one a mile from Panmunjom.

It looked as if the truce talks were at last to begin again. "After suspending the truce negotiations for seven weeks on trumped up grounds," the *New York Times* said in an editorial on October 11, "the Communists have now agreed to resume the talks at a new site and under new neutrality controls." The reference to "trumped up grounds" proved unfortunate. The very next day "there was another boggle." The phrasing was that used by the *Times* in recounting the incident in its next "News of the Week in Review" section. What was this new "boggle"? The boggle was a Communist charge that on October 12 a UN plane had strafed the neutral zone around the Red truce talks camp at Kaesong, killing one child and wounding another. UN liaison officers, the *New York Times* related, "after a preliminary investigation in which they viewed the body of a twelve-year-old boy, were not certain whether the Communists' charges were true." Dourly the *Times* added, "It is expected the Communists will use the new incident—true or not," in asking stricter guarantees of the neutral zone.

The *New York Times* seemed ready to believe that the Communists had strafed their own portion of the neutral zone and killed a small boy to "trump up" another incident. But on October 15 Ridgway admitted that at 5:30 P.M. on October 12 three American-piloted jet fighters returning to base after a rail-cutting mission had made two strafing attacks "in violation of standing instructions" to avoid the neutral zone. The second strafing run "riddled with machine-gun fire a road near Panmunjom" killing one boy and wounding his two-year-old brother. The Peking radio said thirty .50-caliber machine-gun slugs were dug out of the road at that point. The picture of United States planes stopping on their way home after a day's "work" to strafe a deserted road with their machine guns and potshot two small boys was not one to fill thoughtful Americans with pride. Ridgway in officially expressing "heartfelt grief to the bereaved Korean family for their tragic loss" said he was especially pained because "It has heretofore been, and will continue to be, the prime objective of the UN command to avoid loss of life and destruction of property of the noncombatant population." I append a foot-note to enable the reader to judge for himself the worth of these condolences.[1]

[1] On June 25, 1951, Major General Emmett O'Donnell, Jr., commander of the Far Eastern Air Force Bomber Command during the first six months of the Korean War, testifying before the MacArthur inquiry, ex-plained his hopes at the beginning of the conflict:

"GENERAL O'DONNELL. It was my intention and hope, not having any in-structions, that we would be able to get out there and to cash in on our psychological advantage in having gotten into the theater and into the war so fast, by putting a very severe blow on the North Koreans, with advance warning, perhaps, telling them that they had gone too far in what we all recognized as being a case of aggression, and General Mac-Arthur would go top side to make a statement, and we now have at our command a weapon that can really dish out some severe destruction, and let us go to work on burning five major cities in North Korea to the ground, and to destroy completely every one of about 18 major strategic targets.

"CHAIRMAN RUSSELL. . . . As I understood you intended to give them notice you had better get out of the war or we will burn your cities?

"GENERAL O'DONNELL. I thought that would take care of the humane aspects of the problem. We thought we could do it. Tell them to either stop the aggression and get back over the 38th parallel or they better have their wives and children and bedrolls to go down with them because there is not going to be anything left up in North Korea to return to.

"CHAIRMAN RUSSELL. What decision was made at that suggestion of yours?

"GENERAL O'DONNELL. We were not at that time permitted to do it. . . .

"SENATOR STENNIS. Well, early in your testimony this morning you said that the O'Donnell plan had 18 major strategic targets, I believe, in Korea?

"GENERAL O'DONNELL. Roughly; yes, sir.

"SENATOR STENNIS. And then you had five primary spots of some kind. Did you not mention that figure?

"GENERAL O'DONNELL. The main cities were Pyongyang, first, the capital, Seishin, Rashin, Wonsan, and Chinnampo . . . We thought that the impact of taking those quickly, and getting—we could have gotten the 5 cities—I could have done that in 10 days flat, and we think that maybe that terrific impact would so shock them that it might have pressed them into getting out.

"SENATOR STENNIS. . . . Now, as a matter of fact, Northern Korea has been virtually destroyed, hasn't it? Those cities have been virtually destroyed.

"GENERAL O'DONNELL. Oh, yes; we did it all later anyhow. . . . I would say that the entire, almost the entire Korean Peninsula is just a terrible mess. Everything is destroyed. There is nothing standing worthy of the name. . . . Just before the Chinese came in we were grounded. There were no more targets in Korea.

"CHAIRMAN RUSSELL. . . . I think you have demonstrated soldierly qual-ities that endeared you to the American people."

So much for the attitude toward North Korea. What of the attitude toward South Korea? The authoritative British military publication,

General Ridgway promised "prompt and appropriate disciplinary action" for the road strafing. There were some who did not think this enough. "Disciplinary action was promised," the Washington *Evening Star* pointed out in an editorial, "after a similarly erroneous allied strafing of Kaesong on September 11 but this did not prevent the more serious incident last Friday." The *Star* urged more positive safeguards. "What is urgently needed now is some preventive action that will make the truce-negotiations site reasonably secure from further mistakes that could prolong or imperil the critical discussions at Panmunjom." The strafings had occurred in daylight and "no explanation of how the mistake occurred was offered." The five-mile neutral radius established around the neutral zone was clearly not enough. "A five-mile margin is a very thin line of demarcation for a jet plane. The nearest active combat zone on the western front is about thirty miles away—and even this is too close for comfort." And the editorial ended with the suggestion that, since the western front had been "relatively quiet of late," it might be wise to concentrate UN air units "farther east and northward." The incidents should be stopped, it was argued, "even if it should mean the temporary grounding of our air units operating in the vicinity of the neutral zone."

Brassey's Annual: The Armed Forces Yearbook, has this to say in its 1951 edition:

"The war was fought without regard for the South Koreans, and their unfortunate country was regarded as an arena rather than a country to be liberated. As a consequence, fighting was quite ruthless, and it is no exaggeration to state that South Korea no longer exists as a country. Its towns have been destroyed, much of its means of livelihood eradicated, and its people reduced to a sullen mass dependent upon charity . . . Few attempts were made to explain to the American soldier why he was fighting . . . The national hatred and fear of Communism was sufficient in most cases to inflame him with a rather indiscriminate belligerence . . . It failed, however, to bring about any kind of sympathy for South Koreans, except, of course, in the thousand and one little kindnesses troops offer to children and lost dogs . . . The South Korean, unfortunately, was regarded as a 'gook,' like his cousins north of the 38th parallel."

It is against this background that one must read Ridgway's assurance that it had always been "the prime objective of the United Nations command to avoid loss of life and destruction of property of the noncombatant population."

This criticism was not offered by Radio Peking. Even the Reds never went so far as to suggest the UN planes be moved farther east and northward or even grounded to avoid further accidents. The criticism was offered on October 16 by the conservative, ultra-respectable Washington *Evening Star*. It is quoted here at such length because it was Ridgway's unwillingness to take preventive action, and indeed his insistence on making the neutral zone even smaller than it was before, which played so large a part in delaying resumption of the truce talks at this stage. When one got out of the atmosphere of propaganda and got down to brass tacks on the practical questions of how to prevent further incidents, a conservative American newspaper not only found itself in (of course inadvertent) agreement with the Reds but went even further than they did.

When the Reds, bowing to Ridgway's demand for a new site and for no further discussion of previous incidents, picked Panmunjom as the place in which to resume the talks, they asked that the neutral zone be widened. They also took Ridgway up on his demand for joint policing of the neutral zone but went further. They suggested that a joint committee on enforcement be appointed which "should discuss concrete stringent regulations regarding the neutral zone and assume responsibility to enforce the regulations." Ridgway's negotiators insisted on a neutral zone of 1000 yards around the tent at Panmunjom for the truce talks, neutral zones around the UN camp at Munsan and the Red camp at Kaesong, and a system of safe-conducts for truce teams traveling between their respective camps and Panmunjom. Nothing was said about neutrality regulations or enforcement machinery, and the Reds were finally forced to accept these terms.

The Reds also urged that planes be forbidden to fly over the neutral zone. "The UN command maintains," one dispatch explained during the negotiations, that this would give the Reds an "unearned and unwarranted military advantage." The Panmunjom accord, made public in Tokyo on October 22, said nothing about the question of "overflights," but two days later the UN command announced at Munsan that five "understandings" had been reached during the talks which had the same force as the agreement though not forming part of it. One of them was that military planes of neither side should fly over the neutral zone except under "weather or technical conditions beyond control."

Ridgway's negotiators were also reluctant to restrain action by so-called "irregular" elements. This was important in the light of the incidents which had occurred toward the end of August. Whether the attack on the Chinese Communist military police near Panmunjom late in August was the work of "irregulars" or of South Korean troops was never investigated. That South Korean troops held the line near the Kaesong neutral zone was not disclosed in the dispatches at the time. But on October 8 Lindesay Parrott, reporting to the *New York Times* from Tokyo, said that the wider neutral zone asked by the Reds in the negotiations "presumably would mean shifting some South Korean troops out of positions they now hold near the extreme west of the allied line." Parrott added, perhaps *sotto voce* under censorship: "whether it [the extension of the zone and the shift in the South Korean troops] also might curb the guerrilla activities that Vice Admiral Charles Turner Joy, senior United Nations truce delegate, held were responsible for some of the incidents within the Kaesong zone was an unsolved question." If the incidents were committed by irregulars, why should shifting regular South Korean troops have any bearing on the matter?

CHAPTER 44

★

Ridgway's Own Iron Curtain

THERE was a good deal of dissatisfaction at the time among Allied correspondents. The military command, which had dramatically broken off the talks in July on the issue of freedom of access by the press, had been giving the correspondents as little news as possible. Its delegates were living behind a little iron curtain of their own, and Allied correspondents were beginning to depend on what they could glean from the two English-speaking correspondents on the other side, Alan Winnington of the London *Daily Worker* and Wilfred Burchett, an Australian reporting for the leftist *Ce Soir* of Paris. As usual in such situations it was left to a "visiting fireman" to expose what was going on. The regularly accredited correspondents are subject to reprisals, ranging from denying them some bit of news given a competitor to withdrawing their accreditation. A visiting correspondent can more easily afford to tell the truth. There had been some hints of what was going on, but it was a cable by Marguerite Higgins from Panmunjom to the *New York Herald Tribune* which finally broke the truth about Allied press relations. The dispatch, logically enough, was held up two days in transmission. It described the scene vividly: "At the noon recess in the truce negotiations Allied officials—whom Allied newspapermen are not permitted to approach—stalk off to their helicopters, which fly them back to the base camp. This in turn is surrounded by barbed wire and military policemen, and no newspaperman is permitted to enter without being officially invited or under officer escort." Miss Higgins said the "UN liaison officers attending the truce talks are forbidden to speak to the press."

The UN delegation, Miss Higgins reported, gave only one briefing a day, "by a general officer not present at the liaison talks." This briefing came at the end of the day, so that during the noon recess "the Allied correspondents have been dependent on information volunteered by their Red colleagues." Miss Higgins added, "The Communist briefings have been quite accurate and, until the last couple of days, more informative than the Allied evening briefings." She described a talk she had with Wilfred Burchett, whom she had formerly known as the London *Daily Express* correspondent in Berlin. Shortly before noon, when the truce meeting broke up, "Mr. Burchett excused himself to go and talk to the Communist liaison officers. 'I'll go find out what's happened so I can give you chaps (referring to the news agencies) a fill-in,' Mr. Burchett said. He produced the fill-in as promised, and it was through him that we learned the essence of the morning discussions."

Complaints seem to have penetrated to publicity-conscious Tokyo Headquarters. On October 16 Ridgway held what the *New York Times* correspondent described as "one of his rare press conferences." In this he acknowledged that "full and timely information" had not been supplied Allied correspondents. He promised "some steps would be taken to correct the situation." The promise was made somewhat watery by the General's contention that it would be "bad faith" to give out certain kinds of information and his statement that material would continue to be presented in a manner "best serving our interests." This very manner had been sharply characterized a few weeks earlier by Hanson Baldwin in the *New York Times*. Baldwin said that in "the pattern of most of the announcements from Korea since the start of the war— embellished adjectives had replaced facts." He recalled that "the military communiqué used to be simply worded, often terse," but Korea had set a new fashion in which the communiqué had "become a grab-bag of service claims, so-called 'action' verbs and descriptive phrases, instead of a terse recital of fact." And Baldwin warned that "the result is all the more dangerous since censorship in Korea has been severe and often captious."

It is one thing, however, to issue canned releases on a take-it-or-leave-it basis. It is quite another to stand up to questioning at a press conference—which is perhaps why Ridgway, like MacArthur before him, held so few. In holding the October 16 press conference Ridgway did have to answer questions, and in answering them he made two rather handsome giveaways. These showed exactly what was meant by his promise of "prompt and appropriate disciplinary action" against pilots who bombed or strafed the neutral zone. They also showed how lacking in forthrightness was the attitude of Tokyo Headquarters toward incidents caused by so-called "irregulars."

Apparently the press corps had been trying for a month to find out what punishment if any had been visited on the airmen guilty of the first admitted strafing of the neutral zone, that of September 10. For at this press conference of October 16 Ridgway "revealed for the first time that his promise of 'prompt and appropriate disciplinary action'" against those fliers "had been carried out." The punishment was a "reprimand." And "he was unable to state whether the reprimanded bomber crew was still flying over Korea." He also "made it plain that the identities of the culprits would be withheld." Ridgway "excused the incident" as due to "faulty navigation." No mention was made of any punishment for those responsible for the second strafing of October 12, when one boy was killed and another wounded. It is hard to believe that no questions were asked about this, but if they were the censor elided both the questions and the answers. The General said of this latest incident, somewhat in the manner of an indulgent parent, "Problems which confront young pilots can well exceed human capacity at any given time." Just what military "problem" would lead these pilots returning home from a bombing mission to stop and strafe a lonely roadside along which two small boys were playing was not explained. It is easy to imagine the

American public's reaction if this were a Chinese Communist general condoning the action of his "young" pilots who killed an American boy in a neutral zone.

The questioning at this conference also led Ridgway for the first time to admit responsibility for South Korean guerrillas. In the attack on the Chinese military police patrol in the neutral zone in late August, the UN command had claimed that these shootings were due to guerrillas over which neither side had control. Now Ridgway admitted responsibility for guerrilla bands operating in his territory but said "this could not apply to South Korean irregulars in the zone policed by the enemy." At the same time "he declined to say whether or not Allied forces armed South Koreans to operate behind the Communist lines."

Ridgway's negotiators at Panmunjom were proposing at the time "that guerrilla actions should not constitute violations of neutrality." This would have encouraged South Korean forces to upset the truce talks again with further incidents whenever they wanted to, with or without a nod from the Allied command. One of the "understandings" Ridgway was finally forced to accept before the truce talks resumed on October 25 was that the term "armed forces" as used in the Panmunjom accord was to include "armed units or individuals who are controlled by or prompted overtly or covertly by one side or the other."

There was one more revelation—of a kind—in that Ridgway press conference. This had to do with the results achieved by the offensives he had launched so flamboyantly from time to time during the gap in the truce talks. Communiqués and briefings had been unusually noncommittal on the outcome of attacks in which so many lives were being lost, as in the long and terrible fight for "Heartbreak Ridge." When the first offensive of August 18 ended on September 4, Van Fleet's special communiqué "on the outcome of the severe fighting that began seventeen days ago" was discreetly vague on the question of what ground, if any, had been won. The Red radio claimed that the attacks had been successfully repulsed. Lindesay Parrott from Tokyo on September 5 replied, "By no stretch of the imagination could the Allied attacks begun August 18 be judged as anything other than successful," but he too failed to specify just what had been won. On October 6 a dispatch to the *New York Times* from Tokyo recounting how far north of the Parallel two patrols had penetrated (twenty-two and forty miles respectively) said, "Censorship hitherto had prevented mention of how far into Communist territory the UN forces had pushed."

The hope of winning some sensational victory on the ground during the truce talks never materialized, and the gains made never seemed to match the advance billings given these offensives. When General Bradley with his aides made a flying visit to Korea at the end of September, he "found confidence bordering on cockiness at army, corps, and division levels during their visit to Korea, and left with the impression that the Eighth Army would welcome a Communist offensive as an opportunity to deal the North Korean and Communist armies another crippling blow." The same day a new offensive was opened by the Allied command. "U.N. UNITS ADVANCE ON A 40-MILE FRONT; TRUCE SHIFT UPSET—U.S., BRITISH, GREEK, FILIPINO, SOUTH KOREAN, TURKISH UNITS FOLLOW UP HEAVY BARRAGE," said the *New York Times* headline on October 4. Back in Washington that day Bradley declared that "there is a chance of winning a military decision in Korea." But next day the news was that the big offensive had bogged down, making "little headway" against strong counterattacks. Fighting continued but with little change and at his October 16 press conference Ridgway acknowledged "the situation from some standpoints 'could readily be construed as a military stalemate. It all depends on how you look at it,' he said."

CHAPTER 45

★

Atrocities to the Rescue

THERE always seemed to be a reason for fearing that the Korean cease-fire talks might be successful. In August it was the forthcoming Japanese peace conference. In October it was the forthcoming session of the United Nations General Assembly. As early as October 4, speaking to a luncheon of the United Nations Correspondents Association in New York, Ernest A. Gross, deputy United States representative on the Security Council, warned that a cease-fire in Korea would enable the Soviet Union to launch a "phony" peace offensive when the Assembly met in Paris. Gross said the Soviet objective would be to weaken "the sense of urgency that has developed in the free world as a result of Soviet actions." This was the old bugaboo—"relaxation of tension"—which loomed whenever a settlement came into view. Gross revealed that the United States was thinking not of ending but of expanding the Korean War. He told the correspondents that "if the Korean talks fail and full-scale war is resumed . . . the Assembly would have to consider additional measures to employ against the foe there."

Tokyo Headquarters was cheerfully pessimistic. "Even if . . . full-dress sessions again began," said a Sunday *New York Times* "dope story" out of Tokyo on October 20, "few believed that an armistice would come much nearer." Three days later there were additional reassurances from Hanson Baldwin. Unless the UN was "willing to pull back to the 38th Parallel all along the front . . . there is not likely to be a cease-fire." The truce talks resumed on the 25th, but the negotiators did not get down to business until the 26th. And on that day there was disturbing news: "KOREAN FOE DROPS DEMAND FOR TRUCE ON 38TH PARALLEL." The talks had reopened in October at the point where incidents and an offensive had helped to break them off in August. Now the Reds were ready to yield on the 38th Parallel. It looked as if it would be difficult to keep peace from breaking out. By November 4 the Communists had "finally yielded to UN insistence that the armistice line should be generally based on the line of battle contact," had agreed on a neutral buffer strip one and a quarter miles wide, and were "largely in agreement" on the location of the line itself.

The situation looked desperate, but a stumbling block happily turned up. Though the UN negotiators had insisted all along that the armistice line generally follow the battle line, and the Reds had agreed to this, the former now insisted that the UN territory must include Kaesong, which the Reds held. It was over Kaesong that the talks bogged down again. "In Washington—especially in diplomatic quarters," the *New York Times* reported on November 11, "there was some mystification why Kaesong had taken on such importance when both sides had agreed on the principle that the battlefront should be the basis for the armistice line." The place had no strategic value. "It was pointed out," the *Times* account continued, "that the battered town lay in a plain dominated by hills and hence had little military value."

When the deadlock over Kaesong continued in the following week, "there was an outcropping of criticism of the way the UN truce team was conducting the negotiations—not only by our Allies in Korea but also within the United States government." At the weekly meeting of Allied representatives with the State Department "there was a growing uneasiness" reported behind the "outward show of unanimity." There was "a belief that after the Communists had made the big concession on the line the United Nations officers might be sticking at straws." There was criticism in the British press and "a fear," the *New York Times* reported on November 18, "that the UN was giving the Communists a propaganda opportunity to claim that the Allies did not really want a truce."

This restiveness spread to the troops in the field. On the heels of the Communist concessions as the truce talks resumed, "in many places along the Korean front the muttering guns fell silent. Ground fighting was almost at a standstill though air battles went on. The foxhole to foxhole grapevine on the UN lines was active with rumors. The GIs had hopes that an end to this fighting might not be far off—hopes which had been raised before and dashed before." Radio Peking on November 11 broadcast the statement that "if the Americans give up their demand for Kaesong a settlement can be reached in a matter of hours." "A matter of hours" referred to a new proposal the Allied negotiators apparently found even more troubling. The Reds proposed that once the truce line was agreed on there be an immediate cease-fire while the remaining issues were negotiated. Van Fleet in an Armistice Day message to the troops called for "business as usual" until "the Communist aggressors terminate their violation of human liberty"—a formulation broad enough in American terms to keep the war going for many years. On November 14 the United Press reported from Tokyo Headquarters that in suggesting an immediate cease-fire once the truce line was agreed on, "The Reds openly repudiated their long-standing agreement that hostilities would go on until a full armistice was signed." The blackguards were trying to bring the war to an end.

The GIs in the foxholes seem to have had other feelings about this than the brass in Tokyo. On November 12 the *New York Times* published an Armistice Day dispatch from George Barrett on the central front in Korea saying that everywhere along the front the same question came up, "Why don't we have a cease-fire now?" Barrett cabled that, so far as "the troops who have to fight the war" are concerned, "the unadorned way that an apparently increasing number of them see the situation right now is that the Communists have made important concessions, while the United Nations Command, as they view it, continues to make more and more demands." In most of the gatherings Barrett had observed along the front lines, "the

United Nations truce team has created the impression that it
switches its stand whenever the Communists indicate they
might go along with it." Recent developments "have convinced
some troops," he said, "that their own commanders, for reasons
unknown to the troops, are throwing up blocks against an
agreement."

Something had to be done and done quickly. Something
was. "This was the state of affairs," as the *New York Times*
summarized it, "when the issue of Communist atrocities was
suddenly interjected into the situation." On November 14 in
Pusan, Colonel James M. Hanley, Judge Advocate General of
the Eighth Army, called in the local Korean "stringers" who
covered that out-of-the-way place for the big news agencies and
gave out one of the biggest sensations of the war. "U.S. REVEALS
REDS KILLED 5500 G.I. CAPTIVES IN KOREA," said the headlines
next day. And on November 16, when the estimate was raised
to 6270, the Associated Press sent out a gory compilation,
"REDS BUTCHERED MORE AMERICANS THAN FELL IN '76."

The purpose was indicated by the explanations which followed. The Associated Press reported that in an interview at
Pusan on November 16 Colonel Hanley said he "divulged the
Reds' 'wanton murder' of American prisoners because he
thought American soldiers at the front ought to know what
they are up against." Beginning the next afternoon, the Armed
Forces Radio "broadcast the atrocity story . . . and repeated it
at intervals." Troop dissatisfaction over the delay in the truce
talks was to be countered with an injection of hate. The
alleged atrocities also were used to explain the delay in arrang-
ing a cease-fire. "A highly placed Allied officer," the Associated
Press reported from Tokyo on November 16, "said today the
announcement that the Communists in Korea have murdered
thousands of American prisoners has stripped the mystery from
what has been holding up Korean armistice talks." He hinted
darkly, "The Communists don't want to have to answer questions about what happened to their prisoners."

General Ridgway himself saw the hand of Providence in the
whole affair. "It may perhaps be well to note with deep rev-
erence," Ridgway said in a formal statement on November 17,

"that in his inscrutable way God chose to bring home to our people and to the conscience of the world the moral principles of the leaders of the forces against which we fight in Korea ... It may well be that in no other way could all lingering doubts be dispelled from the minds of our people as to the methods which the leaders of communism are willing to use, and actually do use, in their efforts to destroy free peoples and the principles for which they stand." The General devoutly added that "the publication of the information" in Colonel Hanley's statement "had, of course, no connection whatever with the current armistice negotiations."

Some were impious enough to doubt this. There were British to whom the Hanley release "seemed evidence of bungling propaganda or a deliberate effort to sabotage the negotiations," and the *New York Times* correspondent in London added that "a suspicion exists that the United States, for some inexplicable reason, wants to prolong the fighting." The astute James Reston reported to the *New York Times* from Washington that the circumstances did look peculiar. "Several days ago," he wrote on November 15, "it appeared that a compromise finally had been arranged on the cease-fire line, at which time Secretary of State Dean Acheson, speaking in the United Nations meetings in Paris, attacked the Chinese Communists for conduct below the level of 'barbarians.' When this attack was followed during the critical moment of the armistice negotiations by the publication of Colonel Hanley's atrocities report, even officials here conceded that it might look to the world as if the United States was purposely trying to avoid a cease-fire in Korea."

And so the fighting continued.

CHAPTER 46

★

Weird Statistics

THE figures alone show that Hanley and Ridgway did not handle this matter like responsible men dealing with a grave subject. It does not help prisoners in the hands of the enemy to make charges of mistreatment if these charges are false, nor does it help their families. Let us begin with the bare record. The first story given out by Colonel Hanley on November 14 was that the Reds had killed 5500 American and 290 other Allied prisoners of war. Two days later the Colonel gave out revised figures: 6270 Americans, 7000 South Koreans, and 130 other Allied prisoners—a total of 13,400. Ridgway's formal statement of November 17 confirmed Hanley's "information" but gave no figures. On November 20 Ridgway issued a second statement. This time he said it was "possible" that 6000 American soldiers listed as missing in action might have been killed as prisoners but that there was proof of only 365 such murders; he made no reference to other Allied prisoners. Two days after this statement, a fourth estimate turned up, also by Ridgway. The daily batch of documents arriving by air courier from Paris at UN New York headquarters contained the text of Ridgway's fortnightly report as "unified commander" in Korea, dated November 12 and covering the two weeks from August 16 to August 31. This report, which had been released—but ignored—in Paris on November 13, the day before Hanley's first statement, alleged that 8000 Americans had been killed as prisoners of war. So there were now five sets of figures on the number of American POWs murdered:

Ridgway (November 13)	8000
Hanley (November 14)	5500
Hanley (November 16)	6270
Ridgway (November 20) "possibly"	6000
"definitely known"	365

And on November 29 Ridgway issued yet another statement in an effort to explain these discrepancies. This time he said that figures on the killing of prisoners of war were subject to "constant re-evaluation," that the 8000 figure was an earlier estimate, that the 6000 figure "was the most up-to-date and included 'all United Nations forces'" except for South Koreans. On November 20 Ridgway had said that it was "possible" that 6000 Americans had been killed as prisoners of war. Nine days later he said this figure included other UN forces as well. This, as the wire services reported, "actually had the effect of further reducing the number of actual known atrocities suffered by American forces in Korea."

Perhaps the most amazing wrinkle of all is why Ridgway on November 20 did not cover up his own 8000 figure of November 13 by saying that it was "possible" that 8000 not 6000 had been slain. One figure was surely as "possible" as the other. Had Ridgway forgotten? To excuse oneself later by saying that atrocity reports were subject to "constant re-evaluation" and that the 6000 was the more "up-to-date" figure was to admit that these reports and estimates were so unreliable that in one week this process of "constant re-evaluation" cut Ridgway's estimates by 25 percent, while Hanley's figures rose by 14 percent. This is sheer statistical slapstick, understandable enough if the purpose was merely to stir up hate and upset peace talks, utterly inexcusable if intended as a serious accounting on the murder of American men by the enemy.

There was one revealing figure in the various totals given out by Ridgway. MacArthur, in his own fortnightly reports to the United Nations as "unified commander," had cited a number of atrocities against American prisoners of war. Just one year earlier, in his report dated November 6, 1950, covering the war to the period ending October 31, MacArthur gave an estimate as to the number of American POWs killed by the enemy. The figure MacArthur gave was "approximately 400." And a year later we find Ridgway saying that only 365 such cases were "definitely known" although thousands more were "possible." Ridgway's 365 "definitely known" and MacArthur's "approximately 400" sounded much like the same figure. The suspicion that Ridgway was in other respects talking through his hat was strengthened by the lofty vagueness with which he put forward that estimate of 6000 "possible" murders. His actual words were: "Of the 10,836 persons still carried as missing in action, there is no conclusive proof as to the number of dead, though there is considerable evidence to justify a presumption of death by atrocity of a large number which may approximate 6000. Neither the fact nor the manner of death in individual cases has yet been established."

MacArthur flew into Newark airport the night of November 16 when the Hanley statements were spread in banner headlines over the American press. He refused to comment then or since on these "revelations." The refusal to comment becomes less surprising if one examines MacArthur's own references to atrocities in the fortnightly reports he made to the United Nations during the period of his command. The full text of these may be found reprinted at pages 3384-3462 of Part 5 of the Senate MacArthur inquiry hearings. There were sixteen reports, beginning July 25, 1950, and ending March 26, 1951. Eight of these deal with the period before Chinese intervention and eight with the period after. In the first eight reports there are six specific atrocity incidents involving Americans, from which one can obtain a total of 98 killed. In the eighth report MacArthur gives two estimates, one the number of Americans killed in atrocities and the other the number of atrocities inflicted on South Koreans. MacArthur placed the former at 400, the latter at 26,000. Colonel Hanley twelve months later gave virtually the same figures for atrocities inflicted on South Koreans—he put them at 25,575. But Hanley now gave a figure eight times as large for non-Korean prisoners of war.

He told the press on November 16 that the North Koreans before Chinese intervention killed "about 3000 non-Korean prisoners of war."

If MacArthur had so grossly underestimated North Korean atrocities against American soldiers in that period of the war, it was incumbent on Hanley to give names, dates, and places; to show how new cases had come to light; to give some indication of the kind of evidence he had. A statement of this kind would have carried weight with Allied countries and with world opinion. Hanley was chief of the Judge Advocate section of the Eighth Army, which had the responsibility for compiling and investigating all atrocities and other war crimes; he had at his disposal all the specific information there was on such incidents. But his formal written statement, unlike his two oral statements, contains no figure at all on the number of atrocities committed by the North Koreans before the Chinese entered the war. Instead all we have about this period in the Hanley report is that "incidents involving the killing of from one to 1250 UN war prisoners at a time are recorded in the United Nations Command files. The killing of 1250 involved Americans killed near the Yalu River in North Korea by North Koreans between the 16th and 18th of September, 1950." This is the only specific case cited by Hanley of Americans killed by North Koreans before the Chinese entered the war. It is one of the few specific incidents in his formal statement which cannot be found in MacArthur's reports. The report leaves unclear whether all of the 1250 were Americans or whether the slaying "involved" some Americans. Hanley said the 1250 were transported from a prison camp near Pyongyang "and shot in groups after being fed rice and wine, according to the report of the incident." The source of "*the* report" was not given. How did Colonel Hanley hear of this? Why did the Reds transport the prisoners all the way from Pyongyang to the Yalu if they were going to kill them? Why were they first fed "rice and wine"? One suspects that this was a wartime rumor picked up from the local population which MacArthur himself did not think reliable enough to include in any of his reports.

The discrepancy between Hanley's "information" and the MacArthur reports is even more striking when one comes to the period after November 1, when Chinese intervention in force began. For where Hanley alleges (in his formal statement) more than 2500 prisoners slain, MacArthur alleges none at all. On the contrary, with the Chinese in the field, a new note is struck in MacArthur's reporting. His tenth report, dated December 27, said "no reports of any atrocities have been received from the areas recently taken by United Nations troops." MacArthur went on to say, "Reports from the very small number of wounded UN troops recently released by the Chinese Communists of humane treatment is in marked contrast with all other reports in this regard received since the beginning of hostilities." This was a roundabout way of saying that the Chinese seemed to be treating prisoners much better than the North Koreans had. What followed was pure MacArthur: he was eager to take credit for the change and reluctant to admit it had taken place. "Too few have been released," MacArthur informed the United Nations, "to draw any valid conclusions as to whether the actions taken and publicly announced by the UN command to insure the punishment of war criminals have convinced the enemy of the necessity that all prisoners of war and all noncombatants receive the humane treatment required under international law and demanded by modern civilization."

The enemy seemed nevertheless to have been "convinced." For in none of the succeeding MacArthur reports were any atrocities alleged. Even unofficially there was no report of any Chinese Communist atrocity against prisoners of war until June 16, 1951, when a United Press dispatch from the Korean central front said retreating Communists had "shot and bludgeoned" seven United States prisoners and wounded an eighth near Hwachon. The dispatch added: "The mass murder was the first such atrocity reported since the beginning of the year. Many prisoners were brutally slain during the headlong retreat of the Korean Communists last fall."

Hanley's own formal statement said that, since Chinese intervention in the war, 147 American prisoners of war had been killed by North Koreans, and 2513 by Chinese Communists. In addition he says 130 other prisoners of other or unknown nationality were killed during this period. That makes 2790. But he gives only three specific incidents: the alleged murder of 200 United States Marines near Sinhung on December 10, 1950; of seventeen Turkish prisoners of war on May 15, 1951, near Yanggu; and of twelve more Turks on April 10 near Yonchon. None of these appeared in MacArthur's reports. Yet the alleged murder of 200 United States Marines occurred when MacArthur was still in command in Tokyo. How and when did it come to light? Why was it never mentioned before? I tried to find answers to these questions in Washington. At Marine Headquarters I was told, both by the Marine Corps liaison officer at the Pentagon press room and by the officer in charge at Marine Corps Headquarters itself in the Naval Annex, that the Marines had no record of any such incident.

Ridgway's own fortnightly reports contain no mention of this incident—a very serious one, if true. Only three of Ridgway's reports before the time of the Hanley statement made any mention of atrocities. His report dated April 26, 1951, alleged a case in which six UN prisoners—nationality not specified—had been shot by North Koreans in September of the year before. His report dated May 18 alleged three atrocities against soldiers: one American killed by North Koreans; one American killed by Chinese; ten Americans and one South Korean slain by guerrillas. Thus Ridgway added nineteen new cases to the "approximately 400" alleged by MacArthur. Then, suddenly, in Ridgway's report dated November 13, 1951, there appeared the sensational estimate of 8000 Americans killed.

This was the largest estimate yet or since. Yet Ridgway himself devoted only one paragraph to it in a report of ten mimeographed pages, where it was buried on page 9. Tokyo Headquarters did not call it to the attention of the press, nor did the Pentagon or the State Department, both of which clear these fortnightly reports before they go to the United Nations. This is how the paragraph was worded:

Documentation and investigation of reported war crimes incidents are continuing. As of July 20, 1951, approximately 8000 United States military personnel have been reported killed as war crimes victims. Of this number, approximately 7000 were reported killed by North Koreans and the remainder by Chinese Communists.

This was in absolute contradiction to the Hanley statement released next day in Pusan. For this began, "The Chinese forces in Korea have committed most of the Communist atrocity killings of UN prisoners of war since the entry of Red China into the conflict late last year." Hanley's statement said the Chinese Communists had killed 2513 American prisoners of war. Ridgway's report to the United Nations, released the day before, attributed most of the killings to the North Koreans and gave the number killed by the Chinese as approximately 1000. There is one explanation which would account for the conflicting stories from the General and the Colonel. We may be dealing here, simply and plainly, with a couple of clumsy liars.

With unrest growing among the troops at the front because of the bogdown in truce negotiations, Hanley and Ridgway were determined to drum up hate against the Chinese. This appears clearly from the wording of the Hanley formal statement, which begins with the charge that the Chinese committed most of the atrocities and declares this "in sharp conflict with the Chinese claim of compliance with the Geneva Convention for the Treatment of War Prisoners." Hanley said, "Last winter the Chinese released a small number of American prisoners on various occasions in an obvious propaganda attempt to create a favorable atmosphere for future captures." And went on: "That the attempt was futile and so recognized by the Chinese is evident from the record of the number of atrocities and their failure since early last spring to release additional prisoners." The purpose obviously was to persuade the troops that the reports of good treatment by the Chinese Communists were untrue.

The Communist radio at Peking called the Hanley atrocity story a "fabrication" and "a new excuse manufactured in order to delay the Korean armistice talks." Radio Peking "alleged that UN military authorities for several months have kept Allied correspondents from interviewing prisoners the Chinese have returned to the UN lines for fear that the UN public might learn that the captives were well treated by the Communists." Lindesay Parrott reported to the *New York Times* from Tokyo: "The charge is partly true. Newsmen often are not permitted to speak with returned prisoners. A good many such interviews have crept through the censorship regulations, however."

The most widely circulated of the interviews which did get through censorship was embodied in an article published by the *Saturday Evening Post* in its issue of August 25, 1951. The article was called "They Tried to Make Our Marines Love Stalin." It was written by Harold H. Martin and it carried the subtitle: "A Post editor in Korea got this eyewitness account from nineteen American fighting men who were prisoners of the Reds for six months. They weren't beaten or starved—but the propaganda torments they went through would curl your hair." Eighteen of these men were Marines, and they said that "so far as they knew" from six months of captivity the Chinese "never struck, beat, or in any way physically maltreated a prisoner." Some North Korean civilians tried to strike and kick them while they were being marched to their prisoner of war camp, but their Chinese guards "would drive their tormentors back with gun butts." At camp they were told to regard themselves as "newly liberated friends." The worst that happened to them, as the *Saturday Evening Post* subtitle indicated, was the obligation to sit through interminable Communist speeches during indoctrination sessions.

The atrocity story faded out of the headlines and the dispatches within two weeks. Soon afterwards a long wrangle over prisoners of war began in the truce negotiations. But the question of the treatment of American prisoners was apparently never even raised. The Hanley-Ridgway sensation evaporated like a stink bomb, but while it lasted the American press as a whole took it at face value. President Truman, vacationing at Key West, said the Hanley account was the most uncivilized thing which had happened in this century, but was smart enough to add "if true." On the other hand, in sophisticated New York, supposedly astute editors seemingly took the story at face value. The *New York Herald Tribune* had an editorial headed "The Communist Brutes." The *New York Times* editorial spoke of how the Communists had "butchered prisoners in cold blood." The *New York Post*, while criticizing Hanley, added quickly: "Let no one minimize the gravity of Hanley's charges. The Communists are ruthless enemies whose disregard for human life is notorious."

Tokyo Headquarters' disregard for facts should also by this time have been notorious. Only in Washington, where editors had readier access to the Pentagon, was the press skeptical. The mildly liberal *Washington Post* and the conservative *Evening Star* both expressed doubt of the figures. The Washington *Times-Herald*, the *Chicago Tribune's* affiliate in the capital, a paper also owned by Colonel Robert R. McCormick, went even farther. It inserted an editor's note right in the middle of a Tokyo dispatch on the front page November 17, citing a "top Pentagon authority" as having "said flatly Army headquarters has no conclusive evidence of atrocities or other barbaric acts committed by Chinese Reds in the Korean War. He said the only atrocities which are known have been traced to North Koreans early in the fighting."

CHAPTER 47

★

Six Months of Futile Slaughter

AS THE year 1951 ended and the year 1952 began, there was stalemate on the ground and stalemate in the air. After all the highly publicized offensives which had marked—and interrupted—six months of prolonged truce talks, the best that Hanson Baldwin could say in striking a military balance sheet on January 6, 1952, was that "the UN advances made since the truce negotiations started approximate as much as fifteen miles on the eastern front." This meant the gains were even less on the west and center. For six months there had been very little change in the battleline across Korea; it was still roughly in the neighborhood of the 38th Parallel.

Unfortunately it was impossible to report as little change in the casualty lists. When the truce talks began, battle casualties for the United States forces alone were slightly more than 75,000; six months later they were a little more than 103,000. An average of 4666 American casualties was the price paid for every month's delay in the truce negotiations—the price paid for American insistence on carrying on the fighting while the talks proceeded. True, Tokyo Headquarters claimed that during the same period enemy casualties had soared from 1,191,-000 to 1,518,000, an average of 54,500 a month. But by that time the public had grown so sour on Tokyo's inflated claims of enemy casualties that even the Hearst *New York Journal American* protested, "American military authorities have adopted the policy of reporting their estimates of enemy casualties . . . in such a manner that our own losses are made to seem small by contrast." In an editorial called "Doubtful Facts," the *Journal American* wanted to know how the military arrived at these estimates, asked whether the military thought "the American people are going to be more complacent about their own casualties because the enemy's losses are heavier," and ended with the disturbing thought: "For that matter, how do we know we are being told the truth about American casualties, when there is so much room for doubt about the supposed facts given us in connection with enemy losses?"

The enemy seemed to make more sober estimates of UN casualties. The Peking radio October 1 on the second anniversary of the establishment of the Chinese Communist government claimed that the Korean War had cost the UN more than 317,000 casualties. An Associated Press dispatch from Paris January 16, 1952, put total United Nations casualties, including South Korean troops, since the beginning of the war at 414,945. This was what began as a simple "police action."

At the beginning the American troops had been outnumbered. After the Chinese intervention there was so much talk of Chinese "hordes" that this became a joke among the correspondents. "Always there were hordes," *Brassey's Annual* observed ironically of this period, "until war correspondents who observed some of the actions asked how many hordes there were to a platoon." *Brassey's* estimated that in February, 1951, enemy forces must have totaled less than 350,000 men while the UN command had about 275,000 combat troops. Peter Kihss, one of the ablest reporters covering United Nations Headquarters in New York, estimated that by the end of 1951 the UN had total forces of 805,000 men in Korea. This was based on a shrewd series of arithmetical deductions from a speech made by Congressman George H. Bender which gave percentages derived from official figures cleared by American security officials. This may explain General Bradley's remark on leaving Tokyo for Washington October 3 after a trip to the Korean front: "We certainly have enough men over here to keep anyone from running over us." It was not for want of numbers that there was a stalemate on the ground.

More serious than the stalemate on the ground was the stalemate in the air, if it could be called that. Airpower had steadily been deflated as a decisive weapon in Korea. "There have been many puzzling aspects of the campaign in Korea," wrote British Air Vice-Marshal W. M. Yool, "of which not the least has been the apparent failure of airpower to exercise any great influence upon the course of events." This deflation proceeded in several stages. The first occurred within a few days of the outbreak of the war, when wildly inflated hopes of victory-by-airpower were in the air. "The word which reached Tokyo on the night of June 27 announcing that General MacArthur had been authorized to commit United States Air Force units in defense of South Korea," said a survey in the British *National Air Review* quoted by Air Vice-Marshal Yool, "was immediately followed by predictions of a 72-hour pushover. Reporters, rushing to get to the front, had already decided it would be all over before they even had time to dig old war correspondents' uniforms out of stateside attics." Within three days this expectation was exploded and President Truman, on MacArthur's request, was forced to commit ground troops.

In the next stage of the war, control of the air again failed to be decisive. As Air Vice-Marshal Yool summarized it, "We have had a situation in which the United Nations forces enjoyed practically complete air supremacy both before and after the intervention of the Chinese, and yet their forces were almost thrown into the sea at the outset of the campaign, and subsequently, after their triumphant advance to the Yalu River, were driven back headlong south of the 38th Parallel." The third stage in the deflation of airpower occurred in the fall of 1951 when it failed even in the lesser and humbler task of interdicting enemy supply, though the UN had complete air supremacy at the time. In August, at this stage of "Opertation Strangle"—the avidly sadistic phrase backfired on its makers—General Ridgway had set out to cut off enemy supply and push the enemy back for a more favorable truce line.

Air Chief of Staff General Hoyt S. Vandenberg gave a graphic description of Operation Strangle in a speech to the California Chamber of Commerce in Los Angeles at the end of November, 1951: "Day after day our F-84s have ranged over the enemy's vital supply route, blowing up tracks, destroying bridges, and preventing movement by daylight. For 100 miles behind the enemy's most forward positions no through rail traffic has moved for weeks. His army has become dependent for supply upon trucks, moving entirely at night. As this night road traffic developed, our B-26 light bombers, operating with a precision and regularity hitherto unknown in darkness, have ranged over the roads, disorganizing the convoys and destroying great numbers of trucks."

But even at the time General Vandenberg spoke it was already clear that this glamorously organized night-and-day interdiction program had failed to interdict. "Operation Strangle," Hanson Baldwin wrote on November 28, "has not strangled, and the ground battlefront is virtually stabilized." In a succeeding article he drew certain conclusions from the Korean experience which ought to have saddened the planners and publicists who had pictured easy victory through such tactics in a new world war. "There is no such thing," Baldwin wrote, "as real isolation or interdiction of any continental battlefield by airpower. The enemy's supply lines can be cut finally and irretrievably only when ground forces are firmly astride them." Inflated hopes had collapsed again. There was worse to come. On October 23, 1951, the United States Air Force lost a major battle in the air and became sharply aware of three dramatic developments, with important implications for world peace.

The Air Force suddenly faced the prospect of losing control of the air over Korea. It found that the long-distance strategic subsonic bomber, on which the Americans had relied for delivery of the atom bomb, was obsolete. It woke up to discover that the despised and technologically backward Soviet Union was producing better jet planes than the United States.

These discoveries came on October 23 when eight B-29

Superforts escorted by about 100 fighters staged a raid on Namsi air strip, a jet fighter air base under construction in North Korea. They were intercepted by about 150 MIGs. The Air Force acknowledged that three B-29s were shot down, but the dispatches added significantly the next day that "details were not available on other bomber losses."

General Vandenberg admitted at a press conference a month later that in the Namsi battle we "suffered our heaviest loss of any single action of the Korean war . . . three bombers were shot down, while the remaining five sustained some damage." The nature of the damage may be indicated in Hanson Baldwin's article on "The Challenge of the MIG" in the *New York Times* Sunday magazine December 9. Baldwin wrote: "In one famous raid, eight of eight was the score—three B-29s lost, the rest cracked up in landing or ditched or badly damaged."

Just the day before the Battle of Namsi, Vandenberg had held a cockily confident press conference in Washington. "Our boys," he said, "are knocking their socks off." A month later, after a hurried trip to the battlefront, he told the press at the Pentagon, on November 21, "as regards the air situation in Korea, a significant and, by some standards, even sinister change has occurred . . . Almost overnight China has become one of the major air powers of the world . . . the air supremacy upon which we have relied in the past is now faced with a serious challenge."

"Serious challenge" was an understatement. To examine the situation carefully was to see that the Battle of Namsi and its aftermath represented a military, technological, and strategic setback of the first magnitude.

According to Vandenberg's statement at the November 21 press conference, United States intelligence discovered in September, 1951, that three "particularly large airfields about ninety miles below the Manchurian border in northwestern Korea were being expanded and improved with amazing speed." Each of these fields, according to the Far East Air Forces communiqué on the Battle of Namsi, had runways of 6400 feet or more. "It was obvious from their dimensions," Vandenberg said, "that they were intended for jet use." Strong antiaircraft defenses were being established around them. "While none of the fields has been put into operation," the communiqué on Namsi explained, "their use by enemy aircraft would give Communist air power an effective operational range which could pose a menace to United Nations air and ground operations in the battle zone, operations which have been virtually unopposed by enemy air since the early days of the war." Once these fields were ready for use by jets, the enemy could begin to operate in the air over the battlelines for the first time since the tiny North Korean air force was destroyed early in the war.

On October 18 the United States Air Force began a series of heavy attacks on these three fields. The field at Saamcham was attacked by Superforts on October 18, without enemy air interference. The second field at Taechon was hit October 22, with some enemy air action, and "one Superfort was lost to enemy air action in this raid." The surprise, Vandenberg told the press, came next day at Namsi, and this initiated a week of "violent air battles—for seven straight days our formations in North Korea encountered flights of 100 MIGs or more." The decision was then taken to shift to night bombing. This was an admission that enemy air had effective control of the sky during the day.

Explaining what had happened, Vandenberg said that "the air space between the Yalu (the Manchurian border) and Pyongyang (the North Korean capital about a hundred miles south of the nearest Manchurian point), in which we had previously been able to operate unhindered, is now 'a no man's air' and has become the area of decision in the Korean War . . . Unmistakably the enemy is intensifying the efforts in the air despite his forced acceptance of a stalemate on the ground. And we must expect that if he wins in the air the stalemate on the ground is not likely to continue." To end the stalemate on the ground under these circumstances meant that the enemy might succeed with a new offensive in pushing the UN troops back below the Parallel again.

If the truce talks broke down, the stage was thus being set for something new in the Korean War, as Vandenberg indicated in his address on November 29 to the California State Chamber of Commerce. "It will be remembered," Vandenberg said, "that while we have scrupulously avoided attacking targets inside Manchuria or China proper, the enemy air force has also refrained from air attacks on our troops and air bases in Korea . . . While we have pressed a continuous air offensive clear to the Yalu, the enemy has never taken the offensive in the air." In that situation, Vandenberg said, the enemy must either agree to a truce "or again step up his investment by throwing in new forces." He continued that "one kind of a force that could offer a solution to his problem would be an offensive air force." The offensive air force, according to Vandenberg, was available. "Almost overnight," Vandenberg told his Pentagon press conference, "China has become one of the major air powers of the world."

The Air Force Chief of Staff admitted at that conference that "Soviet technicians have mastered the design and production problems of extremely high-speed aircraft to a degree which equals and in some respects excels all that we are able to demonstrate in warfare at the present time." There followed a sentence of historic import. "Fortunately for us," General Vandenberg said, "there is more to war than mere technical achievements." The Air Chief of the most advanced industrial power on earth was admitting that the United States had been outstripped technologically. Vandenberg said American pilots and crews, however, made up the deficiency by training and morale: "Their aggressive fighting spirit and their unfailing skill in performance have outweighed the numerical odds against them." The "hordes" were now in the air. The comfortable notion that the Russians were a backward enslaved people allied with even more backward colored Asiatics, and that technological proficiency in air warfare was not to be expected from either of them was one of the casualties of the Korean War as 1952 dawned. The truth had yet to penetrate a general feeling of cocky complacency and American superiority. But the realization that we could not look forward to a swift and easy Buck-Rogers-style victory over helpless masses of "gooks," "Chinks," and "Russkies" was already sobering military circles.

In the American and British aviation industries there was growing awareness that the planes encountered in the skies over Korea were not mere models copied or stolen from the West by designers sweating it out in fear of the secret police. "Russian airframe and engine designers," said a report in the summer of 1951, "are very unusual people. Gifted, original, individualistic, and intensely practical, the lives they live are for the most part the exact antithesis to what most Americans would expect in a Communist state." The quotation was not from some transmission belt for Red propaganda, but from a special issue on Russian aviation published by *Aviation Age*. Such information, of course, was limited to trade journals published for a comparative handful in the aircraft industry. Many newspaper readers knew that the Russian MIG-15s in Korea were powered by copies of a British Rolls-Royce engine. But few knew that the Russians had done things with this engine that surprised its British designers. The December 3, 1951, issue of *Aviation Week*, a McGraw-Hill publication, carried a dispatch from its London correspondent on the "wave of concern" in British air circles. The British were curious to know how the Russians got so much more power out of this engine than the British did. "How have the Russians," the question was put, "obtained such high performance from a centrifugal flow engine?" The *Manchester Guardian's* aviation correspondent was quoted as asking how the Russians had managed to "fly at the speed of sound" with such an engine. *Aviation Age* had warned, in its special Russian survey number, that "the industrial-technical gap between the U.S.A. and the USSR is not as great as some Americans think."

The anti-aircraft gunnery on the ground and the flying skill in the air which the enemy began to show in the fall of 1951 was indeed the source of speculation as to the possible presence of "Caucasians" on the Red side. If complicated guns were so well manned and complicated planes so well flown, surely there must be white men at the controls? There was even speculation that maybe Americans were flying planes for the Reds. A McGraw-Hill correspondent with the Fifth

Air Force in Korea reported in the December 17 issue of *Aviation Week*: "Who flies the MIG is still unprovable. 'For all we know,' one F-86 Sabre jet pilot of the 4th Fighter Interceptor Group says, 'there may be some ex-American World War II fighter jockeys up there.'" The men flying the Red jets could not have asked for a more naive and sincere compliment. The McGraw-Hill correspondent speculated that the fliers probably included "Chinese, North Koreans, Poles, Germans, Mongols, Russians, and perhaps others." But no "Caucasians" had yet been reported found in downed planes. There was no doubt that most of the fliers were of Asian colored races—and doing a competent job.

A glimpse of the highly involved technical problems in a jet plane attack was provided by the McGraw-Hill correspondent: "The MIGs take off, . . . climb into the sun to high altitudes. There they are picked up by other radar-tracking equipment and vectored into attacking positions. They then press the attack home against our B-29 medium bombers in a high-speed downhill pass that is virtually impossible to stop . . . MIGs coming downhill can't be headed off even if the Sabre pilots see them at maximum visibility. By the time the Sabres turn 90 degrees to meet the attack the MIGs pass and are on the bombers."

Thus in the fall of 1951, while truce talks dragged on, Red fliers wrested supremacy of the air from the United States in northwest Korea from the Yalu ninety miles south to the Chongchon. The United States was forced to shift over to night bombing. The demonstration was momentous. For it showed that the subsonic bombers on which the American military had depended for delivery of the atom bomb in a future war against Russia were indefensible against jet interceptors flying at or above the speed of sound.

In Korea this meant that, if the truce negotiations broke down and the war resumed on a limited scale, it would be difficult if not impossible to prevent the enemy from establishing jet air bases in northwest Korea to be used in attacks against UN troops on the battlefield. It meant that if the war were extended to Manchuria, with its much more highly developed radar and other defenses, the B-29s would be slowly moving shooting-gallery ducks for the much faster interceptor jets. Western Europe had seen that while American airpower could destroy any country we set out to liberate, airpower by itself could not win a decisive victory. Now it saw that America's famous atomic strategy had become obsolete. The defense had outstripped the offensive. Hanson Baldwin wrote in the *New York Times* in December, 1951, that the MIG had "forced some of our most ardent advocates of strategic bombing to take another good hard look at our prospects. Any very deep long-range penetration of Russia by planes like the B-29, the more modern and faster B-50, or even by the huge but still relatively slow B-36, could not possibly be accompanied by any fighters we now have . . . the supply difficulties of sending swarms of fighters deep into Russia would be terrific." But the difficulty was not merely one of supply. Korean experience had shown that jet fighters, even when available, were little defense against each other; their fantastic speeds explained the slight losses in battles between them. It was very difficult for jets to prevent other jets from getting at the big, slow, relatively unwieldy bombers they escorted.

The subsonic bomber proved obsolete over Korea and with it the foreign policy based upon the subsonic bomber. The atom bomb was still a "deterrent to aggression"—from either side. It was no longer a threat with which either side could hope to dictate terms. The Truman-Acheson dream of "building up strength," to the point where Moscow—and half the world with it—would be forced into unconditional surrender, had disintegrated in the skies over Korea. Whichever side attacked the other must expect a stalemate in the air as on the ground; whichever side fought away from its own borders would be at a crucial disadvantage. Neither the Soviet bloc nor the Western hemisphere could be brought to its knees by strategic bomber and atom bomb. True, they could ruin all the lands that lay between them as they had ruined Korea, a small country which demonstrated the wider fate to be expected by a world divided, as Korea was, in two. Western Europe's possible fate was written out in advance in Korea's blood.

CHAPTER 48

★

Van Fleet Sums Up

A WORLD in which neither side could impose terms on the other was a world in which peaceful settlement— at least settlement without war—was dictated by military realities. As this book went to press there seemed to be a growing awareness of this in every capital but Washington. Who started the war and how was still a mystery, as it is still a mystery just how we got into the Spanish-American War. In fact, George F. Kennan, the newly appointed American Ambassador to Moscow, spoke of the Spanish-American War— in his astute and sophisticated lectures on American foreign policy at the University of Chicago early in 1951—in terms which may some day be used of the Korean War. "We can only say," Kennan declared, discussing the war and its extension to the Philippines by Dewey's attack on the Spanish fleet in Manila, "that it looks very much as though, in this case, the action of the United States government had been determined primarily on the basis of a very able and very quiet intrigue by a few strategically placed persons in Washington, an intrigue which received absolution, forgiveness, and a sort of public blessing by virtue of war hysteria." No one really seemed to know just how the United States had been drawn into the Korean War, but as it continued there was less and less doubt as to who wanted to stop it and who wanted to continue it. Chiang Kai-shek and Syngman Rhee, its principal political beneficiaries in Asia, still wanted it to continue. John Foster Dulles and Governor Dewey were campaigning for broader American involvement in the Far East, along the lines of the Pacific Pact that Chiang had long been urging. Truman and Acheson were their prisoners, sometimes eagerly, sometimes hesitantly, as in a sense the whole American economy had become the prisoner of war fever and war addiction.

An almost hysterical fear of peace made itself felt when the shooting stopped on November 28, 1951, the day after agreement on a cease-fire line, the day when Red troops played volleyball within range of UN trenches. There was an almost frantic reaction from Key West, where the President was vacationing. Truman showed himself more insistent even than General Van Fleet that the fighting in Korea must continue until every last item in the interminable negotiations had finally been thrashed out. Again there were new political obstacles. The day the negotiators finally agreed on a cease-fire line, Eisenhower in Rome was pleading with the North Atlantic Council for a speed-up in Europe's rearmament. The *Wall Street Journal*, which had been carrying on an admirable fight for a saner foreign policy, dryly underscored the difficulty in an editorial on Korea and Rome: "It is understandable that peace in Korea, or even talk of peace, should make people—in the United States as well as Europe—less eager to sacrifice civilian standards for arms . . . if there is peace in Korea the position of the United States as the prime mover of European defense will be more difficult—and much more costly."

One could almost feel the relief in Washington as the truce talks bogged down again in an endless wrangle over air bases and the exchange of prisoners. A month earlier Tokyo Headquarters had been worrying noisily in public about the alleged mistreatment of American prisoners by the Reds. Now it was worrying, not about speeding up the exchange and releasing our prisoners from the enemy, but about "saving" Red prisoners who did not wish to be repatriated. Their safety seemingly took precedence over the now forgotten danger to Americans in the hands of "Communist brutes." Tokyo Headquarters was still dragging out an obscene farce while Truman in his conversations with Churchill paved the way for extension of the war to China. "The United States," the *Wall Street Journal* reported from Washington January 17, "has wrung an informal okay from reluctant Britain, for American bombing and naval blockade of Red China if Korean talks fail." The dispatch showed that American military men were still scheming toward a "limited" war with China which would somehow involve neither American ground troops nor war with Russia.

This was MacArthur's dream. "The MacArthur plan for dealing with Chinese Communists is being dusted off again by United States military planners," *U. S. News and World Report* said in its issue of February 1, 1952, "just about one year after the General was fired for suggesting it." But it was now MacArthur who lagged behind Truman. *U. S. News* added, "General MacArthur himself feels that the delay of one year, permitting Communists to build up, makes the plan he suggested out of date." Unfortunately the same political and economic factors that pressed for the Korean War now pressed for its extension. Chiang Kai-shek and Rhee still feared that peace would be the end of them. Dulles feared that peace would fatally interfere with the plan to rebuild the old Axis powers for a new anti-Soviet crusade. Truman and Acheson feared that peace would confront them anew in an election year with the need to face up to the Far Eastern problem and recognize the government of Communist China. America's allies were growing restive. Britain and France with the rest of Western Europe and practically the whole of the Middle East abstained or voted "No" when Chiang with American support put through the United Nations General Assembly in Paris a resolution condemning the Soviet Union in effect for Chiang's own richly deserved fall from power. It looked as if extension of the war, a new provocation, was necessary if the cold-war front was to be held together.

While the arms race and the attendant inflation were ruining America's allies, American leadership was still gripped by dread of the consequences of peace upon the economy. This dread was dictating the actions of the politicians and business leaders. An economy accustomed to ever larger injections of inflationary narcotic trembled at the thought that its deadly stimulant might be shut off. The road to war was more than ever the path of least resistance in 1952. If peace came in Korea, there might be new Koreas in the making in Indo-China and Burma. If not there, then with American troops in Korea some new "incident" might start up the war again. The dominant trend in American political, economic, and military thinking was fear of peace. General Van Fleet summed it all up in speaking to a visiting Filipino delegation in January, 1952: "Korea has been a blessing. There had to be a Korea either here or some place in the world." In this simple-minded confession lies the key to the hidden history of the Korean War.

APPENDIX

★

New Light on the Korean Mystery:
Was the War No Surprise to Chiang Kai-shek?

This article is reprinted from the first issue of I. F. Stone's Weekly, *January 17, 1953. Since it contains information not available to Stone at the time he was writing the book, we append it for the reader's information.*

The Senate report on Joseph McCarthy makes it possible to throw new light on one of the most tantalizing episodes in the Korean War. This concerns the burst of speculation in soybeans on the eve of the war. In touching on McCarthy's own successful flier in soybeans later that same year, the report asks whether he had confidential information "with respect to the trend of the soybean futures market" and adds an intriguing parenthesis. It says: "Just prior to the transaction in question, the Commodity Exchange Authority of the Department of Agriculture conducted an investigation of alleged soybean market manipulation involving, among others, a number of Chinese traders."

The report on McCarthy is not too intrepid a document. It was not surprising, on inquiry at the Department of Agriculture, to discover that the Senate Subcommittee on Privileges and Elections had omitted from the report its own biggest news "scoop" in the soybean story. Inquiry at the Department turned up 1) the full text of a report on its investigation into soybean speculation and 2) a list of the Chinese who took part in this trading. The original report, issued on August 10, 1950, passed almost unnoticed at the time outside grain publications. It withheld the names of the Chinese speculators. But in the file of the Agriculture Department's later press releases on the subject there turned up a statement of last

349

November 26 saying that the Senate Subcommittee on Privileges and Elections had asked for the names and addresses of the Chinese traders "referred to, but not identified" in the original report. Attached was a list of names, with their holdings in soybean futures when the Korean War began.

The Department declined to identify the names further, but one of the largest speculators on the list turned out to be T. V. Soong's younger brother, T. L. Soong. "T. V." is, of course, Chiang Kai-shek's brother-in-law. One of the smaller speculators was Nationalist China's executive director on the board of the International Bank for Reconstruction and Development. These directors are appointees of the governments they represent. Though such names confirm what had hitherto only been suspected—that "insiders" close to Chiang and his government played a prominent part in the speculation—the Senate committee did not even mention its discovery.

If the Korean War was a surprise attack, how is it that Chinese close to Chiang began to speculate in soybeans in the weeks before the fighting broke out? The question was first raised by the *Monthly Review* in its issue of October 1951. A "Footnote to Korea" by the editors, Leo Huberman and Paul Sweezy, called attention to the unsuccessful effort of the late Senator McMahon during the MacArthur hearings to elicit information from Secretary of State Acheson on reports that certain Chinese had cornered the American soybean market at the time the Korean War began. The "Footnote" put that obscure colloquy into new and startling light by coupling it with an item published two months later, on August 16, 1951, on the financial page of the *New York Herald Tribune*. This item said some fifty Chinese living in the United States and abroad had cleaned up $30,000,000 in speculative operations in soybeans "just before" the war.

Just how extensive these operations were was not clear until now. The original Department of Agriculture study to which the McCarthy report calls attention shows that Secretary Acheson was perhaps less than candid in his answers to Senator McMahon. The Senator wanted to know whether Acheson had ever discussed with Secretary of Agriculture Brannan "a corner that's supposed to have existed in the soybean market a year ago last June in the hands of certain Chinese in this country." A "year ago last June" was when the Korean War began. The casual listener would assume from the Acheson replies that the matter was of little importance and that little was known about it (p. 2187, vol. 3, MacArthur hearings) :

SECRETARY ACHESON: Yes, I have discussed it with him.

SENATOR McMAHON: Is there anything you can say at this time concerning the personalities who were engaged in that operation . . . ?

SECRETARY ACHESON: I don't know that I ever knew who the personalities involved were.

In the light of the information now turned up, this "I don't know that I ever knew" seems superbly evasive. If the Secretary of State discussed the matter with Secretary of Agriculture Brannan, they must have considered it of more than routine importance. Brannan could hardly have failed to tell Acheson that a full investigation had been made by the Agriculture Department's Commodity Exchange Authority and that the names of all the participants were known, as the report of August 10, 1950, shows.

This neglected report begins to indicate the full dimensions of the skeleton the Secretary of State wished to keep securely closeted. The story the Department of Agriculture report unfolds begins several months before the Korean War. The war broke out on June 25, 1950. Four months earlier, the Commodity Exchange Authority of the U. S. Department of Agriculture began to receive "a large number of complaints" from processors of soybeans in this country that the soybean futures market had fallen "so completely under the control of speculators" that it could no longer serve for legitimate hedging operations. One complainant pointed out that more soybeans were being traded on the Chicago market than all the other principal grain futures combined; another, that the sudden sharp rise in soybean prices "is helping only the speculators as a large majority of the farmers have already disposed of their farm holdings." The Commodity Exchange Authority began to investigate and found "very sizable trading by persons with Chinese names, and in some instances with Hong Kong addresses." Speculation in futures by Chinese is not unusual but "no previous instance had been found," it said, "in which Chinese held as large a proportion of the total open contracts in any commodity."

The Commodity Exchange Authority wondered why the Chicago Board of Trade reduced speculative margins on soybeans on March 13 "from the already low level of 8.3 percent to 6.1 percent . . . in the face of an active market." In the four weeks which followed, the daily average volume of trading rose to fifteen million bushels a day, as compared with ten million daily in the preceding four weeks. Since few suspected that war was coming in the Far East, it was thought that Chinese Nationalist interests were trying to corner the market. On August 7, 1950, the Chicago *Journal of Commerce* carried a front page item stating that the President of the Chicago Board of Trade had refuted previously published reports that a virtual corner of soybeans by "Chinese Nationalist" interests had been instrumental in causing prices to soar from $2.20 to $3.45 a bushel. The refutation was made to look somewhat sickly when three days later the Commodity Exchange Authority issued its report on "Speculation in Soybeans," the report from which the quotations here were taken. This showed that by June 30, 1950, fifty-six Chinese accounts held almost half of all open contracts for July futures on the long side of the market, i.e., of those playing for a rise in price.

The inference is irresistible though not necessarily correct that inner Chinese Nationalist circles knew war was coming and cashed in on their knowledge. If this ugly inference is false, the Nationalists should be anxious for a Congressional investigation which would clear them of suspicion that a group of them made themselves a nice little profit of $30,000,000 on a war which has cost the American people and its allies heavily in lives and money. It may be, of course, that they had informers in Red China who tipped them off to a coming attack from North Korea. It may also be, as I indicated in my book, *The Hidden History of the Korean War*, that Chiang and Syngman Rhee provoked the attack from the North. It should not be forgotten that in this, as in any other unsolved crime, it is useful to begin by determining who benefited. The biggest beneficiary of the Korean War was Chiang Kai-shek. The war diverted the Chinese Reds from their plans to attack Formosa. It gave him a virtual American protectorate over Formosa, and an increased flow of American aid. The $30,000,000 in that perspective is small change, but an investigation into that small change might throw a flood of new light on the origin of the conflict which threatens to engulf the globe in World War III.

References

NOTE. These references cite the page and line in the text where the direct quotation or source material first appears. The reference is not repeated if subsequent quotation is clearly from the same source. References have not been given for newspapers or periodical articles when the text specifies both the date and the name of the publication. Dispatches quoted from the *New York Times* will be found in both the domestic and the international editions; dispatches from the Paris editions of the *New York Herald Tribune* and the London *Daily Mail* have been so identified.

CHAPTER 1

Page 1, line 3. *United States Policy in the Korean Crisis*, Department of State Publication 3922, Far Eastern Series 34, July 20, 1950, p. iii. (Hereafter referred to as the State Department White Paper on Korea.)
Page 1, line 5. Report to United Nations Security Council, June 27, 1950. (Quoted from the State Department White Paper on Korea, p. 3.)
Page 1, line 8. John Gunther, *The Riddle of MacArthur* (New York: Harper and Brothers, 1951), p. 166.
Page 2, lines 1, 15, 24. *New York Times*, June 26, 1950.
Page 2, line 33. *New York Times*, June 27, 1950.
Page 3, line 11. *New York Times*, June 27, 1950.
Page 3, line 23. Gunther, *The Riddle of MacArthur*, p. 166.
Page 4, line 10. *New York Times*, June 27, 1950.
Page 4, line 30. *New York Times*, June 28, 1950.
Page 5, line 11. *New York Times*, June 26, 1950.
Page 5, line 19. *New York Times*, June 27, 1950.
Page 5, line 28. *New York Times*, August 19, 1950.

CHAPTER 2

Page 7, line 8. *Daily Telegraph* (London), June 27, 1950. (Dispatch from Washington.)
Page 7, line 11. *United Nations Commission on Korea Report, New York Times*, September 15, 1950.
Page 7, line 16. Robert T. Oliver, "Why War Came in Korea," *Current History*, September, 1950, quoting from his article in *Periscope on Asia*, June 9, 1950.
Page 8, line 3. *New York Herald Tribune*, June 30, 1950. (Paris edition.)
Page 8, line 12. State Department White Paper on Korea, p. 3.
Page 8, line 22. *New York Times*, September 15, 1950, text.
Page 10, line 17. State Department White Paper on Korea, p. 22.
Page 11, line 13. State Department White Paper on Korea, p. 11.
Page 12, line 12. *U. S. News and World Report*, May 2, 1950.
Page 12, lines 24, 28. *Nippon Times*, May 5, 1950. (Reuters' dispatch from Washington.)
Page 13, line 1. Robert T. Oliver, *Why War Came to Korea* (New York: Fordham University Press, 1950), p. 14.

CHAPTER 3

Page 14, lines 9, 18, 24. Gunther, *The Riddle of MacArthur*, pp. 168, 169.
Page 15, line 30. *Facts on File*, 1950, p. 203 K.
Page 15, line 35. *United States State Department Bulletin*, June 26, 1950, p. 1061.
Page 16, line 16. George M. McCune, *Korea Today* (Cambridge: Harvard University Press, 1950), p. 234.
Page 16, line 26. *New York Times*, June 28, 1950.
Page 16, line 29. *New York Times*, June 27, 1950.
Page 18, lines 3, 6, 10. *Facts on File*, 1950, pp. 106 N, 114 M-N, 171 F.
Page 18, line 21. McCune, *Korea Today*, p. 255.
Page 18, line 26. *New York Times*, June 20, 1950.
Page 19, line 18. Speech at Herald Tribune Forum, *Facts on File*, October 24, 1949, p. 349 B.
Page 20, line 33. *Christian Science Monitor*, June 22, 1950. (Dispatch from Tokyo.)
Page 21, lines 3, 6. *New York Times*, June 23, 1950.
Page 22, line 5. *U. S. News and World Report*, May 2, 1950.

CHAPTER 4

Page 23, line 3. *New York Times*, June 15, 1950.
Page 23, line 6. *New York Times*, March 23, 1939.
Page 23, line 9. *New York Times*, October 29, 1939.
Page 24, line 5. *New York Times*, September 6, 1943.
Page 24, line 23. *New York Times*, August 17, 1944.
Page 25, line 14. *Facts on File*, 1946, p. 195 G.
Page 25, line 16. *Facts on File*, 1947, p. 135 K.
Page 25, lines 37, 38. *New York Times*, May 19, 1933.
Page 26, line 1. *New York Times*, May 19, 1933.
Page 26, line 14. *Facts on File*, 1947, p. 69 G.
Page 26, lines 34, 37. *Facts on File*, 1950, pp. 81 J, 153 K.
Page 27, line 3. *New York Times*, June 21, 1950.
Page 27, line 5. *New York Times*, June 22, 1950.
Page 27, line 21. *The Times* (London), June 23, 1950.

CHAPTER 5

Page 32, line 19. *Sunday Times* (London), June 25, 1950.
Page 33, line 9. *New York Herald Tribune*, June 15, 17, and 20, 1950. (Paris edition.)

CHAPTER 6

Page 35, line 13. *The Times* (London), June 8, 1950.
Page 36, line 10. *The Times* (London), June 8, 1950.
Page 36, line 10. *Facts on File*, 1950, p. 178 N.
Page 36, line 16. *The Times* (London), June 8, 1950.
Page 36, line 30. *The Times* (London), June 7, 1950.
Page 37, lines 6, 11. *The Times* (London), June 19, 1950.
Page 37, line 15. *Facts on File*, 1950, p. 205 N.
Page 37, lines 20, 22. *The Times* (London), June 19, 1950.
Page 38, line 18. *Observer* (London), June 18, 1950.
Page 39, line 11. *New York Times*, June 20, 1950.
Page 39, line 23. London *Daily Mail*, June 19, 1950. (Paris edition.)
Page 40, line 6. Richard Hughes, *Sunday Times* (London), June 18, 1950.
Page 41, line 12. Lindesay Parrott, *New York Times*, June 18, 1950.

CHAPTER 7

Page 42, line 22. Report by United Nations Commission on Korea, June 29, 1950. (Quoted from State Department White Paper on Korea, p. 22.)
Page 43, line 32. James Reston, *New York Times*, June 27, 1950.
Page 44, line 27. Gunther, *The Riddle of MacArthur*, p. 164.
Page 44, line 31. State Department White Paper on Korea, p. 11.
Page 44, line 34. Lindesay Parrott, *New York Times*, June 26, 1950.
Page 45, line 8. State Department White Paper on Korea, p. 1.
Page 45, line 12. Gunther, *The Riddle of MacArthur*, p. 165.
Page 46, line 3. "Enforcing the Peace in Korea," United Nations Bulletin, July, 1950.
Page 46, line 22. State Department White Paper on Korea, p. 11.
Page 48, line 4. *New York Times*, June 26, 1950.
Page 48, line 27. State Department White Paper on Korea, p. 12.
Page 48, lines 29, 36. *New York Times*, June 26, 1950.
Page 49, line 7. *New York Times*, June 26, 1950.
Page 49, line 24. *New York Herald Tribune*, June 26, 1950. (Paris edition.)
Page 49, line 30. *The Times* (London), June 27, 1950.
Page 49, line 37. *New York Times*, June 26, 1950.
Page 52, line 13. State Department White Paper on Korea, p. 21.

CHAPTER 8

Page 53, line 13. *Senate Appropriation Committee Hearings on State, Justice, Commerce, and the Judiciary Appropriation for 1952*, p. 1086. (Hereafter referred to as Senate Appropriations Hearings.)

CHAPTER 9

Page 58, line 1. *Military Situation in the Far East; Hearings Before the Committee on Armed Services and the Committee on Foreign Relations, U. S. Senate, 82nd Congress, First Session: To Conduct an Inquiry Into the Military Situation in the Far East and the Facts Surrounding the Relief of General of the Army Douglas MacArthur from his Assignments in that Area*, p. 37. (Hereafter referred to as MacArthur Hearings.)
Page 59, line 11. MacArthur Hearings, p. 1991.
Page 60, line 31. MacArthur Hearings, p. 3384.

CHAPTER 10

Page 61, line 25. MacArthur Hearings, p. 3320.
Page 62, line 4. Gunther, *The Riddle of MacArthur*, pp. 165, 166.
Page 62, line 11. MacArthur Hearings, p. 3320
Page 62, line 17. Gunther, *The Riddle of MacArthur*, p. 171.
Page 62, line 23. MacArthur Hearings, p. 3320.
Page 64, line 2. *New York Times*, October 8, 1949.
Page 64, line 6. *New York Herald Tribune*, November 1, 1949.
Page 64, line 19. MacArthur Hearings, p. 1992.
Page 65, line 37. Senate Appropriations Hearings, p. 1087.
Page 66, line 18. MacArthur Hearings, p. 375.
Page 66, line 25. Walter Sullivan, *New York Times*, July 31, 1950.

CHAPTER 11

Page 67, line 6. *Manchester Guardian*, June 26, 1950.
Page 68, line 11. Associated Press dispatch from Baltimore, *New York Herald Tribune*, June 26, 1950. (Paris edition.)
Page 68, lines 15, 20. *New York Herald Tribune*, June 26, 1950. (Paris edition.)
Page 68, line 26. *New York Times*, June 26, 1950.
Page 68, line 33. State Department White Paper on Korea, pp. 16, 17.
Page 69, lines 14, 20, 31, 37. *New York Times*, June 27, 1950.
Page 71, line 8. *New York Times*, June 28, 1950.
Page 72, line 31. Associated Press dispatch, *New York Herald Tribune*, June 24, 1950. (Paris edition.)
Page 73, line 2. *New York Times*, June 26, 1950. (Dispatch from Tokyo.)
Page 73, line 7. *New York Times*, June 27, 1950. (Dispatch from Tokyo.)
Page 73, lines 27, 36. Gunther, *The Riddle of MacArthur*, pp. 25, 170-171.

CHAPTER 12

Page 75, line 6. *United Nations Temporary Commission on Korea Report*, October 8, 1948, Vol. 1, p. 28.
Page 76, line 34. McCune, *Korea Today*, p. 227.
Page 77, line 5. McCune, *Korea Today*, p. 230.
Page 78, line 6. State Department White Paper on Korea, pp. 66, 67.
Page 78, line 22. *New York Times*, July 8, 1950. (Dispatch from Lake Success.)
Page 79, line 1. *New York Times*, July 8, 1950.
Page 79, line 9. *New York Times*, July 9, 1950.
Page 79, line 30. Gunther, *The Riddle of MacArthur*, p. 17.
Page 80, lines 5, 11. Gunther, *The Riddle of MacArthur*, pp. 20, 21.
Page 80, line 18. *New York Times*, July 9, 1950.

CHAPTER 13

Page 82, line 23. *New York Times*, July 26, 1950, text.
Page 83, line 16. *New York Times*, July 26, 1950.
Page 84, line 2. *New York Times*, July 27, 1950. (Dispatch from Tokyo.)
Page 84, line 17. Walter Sullivan, *New York Times*, July 27, 1950.
Page 84, line 28. *New York Times*, July 30, 1950.
Page 85, line 19. *New York Times*, July 19, 1950.
Page 85, line 32. *New York Times*, July 21, 1950.
Page 86, line 22. State Department White Paper on Korea, p. 63.
Page 87, line 5. State Department White Paper on Korea, p. 64.
Page 87, line 37. *New York Times*, July 20, 1950.
Page 88, line 5. *New York Times*, July 21, 1950.
Page 88, line 22. *New York Times*, July 28, 1950. (Dispatch from Lake Success.)
Page 89, line 4. *New York Times*, August 1, 1950.

CHAPTER 14

Page 92, line 28. *New York Times*, August 26, 1950.
Page 92, line 32. *New York Times*, August 27, 1950.
Page 92, line 34. *Facts on File*, 1950, p. 285 F.
Page 93, line 2. *New York Times*, September 1, 1950.
Page 93, line 14. *Facts on File*, 1950, p. 275 K.
Page 93, line 20. *New York Times*, September 2, 1950.
Page 94, lines 24, 29. *New York Times*, September 18, 1950.
Page 94, line 33. *New York Times*, September 19, 1950.
Page 96, line 1. *New York Times*, September 19, 1950, photograph.
Page 99, line 10. *New York Times*, September 17, 1950.

CHAPTER 15

Page 101, line 4. *New York Times*, September 22, 1950.
Page 102, line 2. *New York Times*, September 28, 1950.
Page 102, line 12. *New York Times*, September 22, 1950.
Page 102, line 27. *New York Times*, September 16, 1950.
Page 102, line 33. *New York Times*, September 17, 1950.
Page 103, line 26. *New York Times*, September 26, 1950.
Page 105, line 1. *New York Times*, September 29, 1950.

CHAPTER 16

Page 108, line 7. *New York Times*, September 29, 1950.
Page 108, line 11. *New York Herald Tribune*, September 22, 1950. (Paris edition.)
Page 108, line 19. *New York Times*, September 29, 1950.
Page 109, lines 6, 22. *New York Times*, September 29, 1950.
Page 109, line 28. *New York Times*, September 28, 1950.
Page 111, line 16. *New York Times*, October 1, 1950.
Page 111, line 34. *New York Times*, July 14, 1950.
Page 112, line 22. Associated Press dispatch, *New York Times*, October 1, 1950.
Page 113, line 10. *New York Times*, September 29, 1950.
Page 113, line 15. *New York Times*, September 30, 1950.
Page 113, line 34. United Press dispatch from Seoul, *New York Times*, October 1, 1950.
Page 114, lines 3, 24. *New York Times*, October 1, 1950.

CHAPTER 17

Page 116, line 16. *New York Times*, July 15, 1950.
Page 116, line 19. Thomas J. Hamilton dispatch from Lake Success, *New York Times*, July 14, 1950.
Page 117, line 14. Associated Press dispatch from Moscow, *New York Times*, July 14, 1950.
Page 117, line 31. Thomas J. Hamilton dispatch from Lake Success, *New York Times*, August 24, 1950.
Page 117, line 37. United Nations Document A/Ac 19/80, p. 117: cited by George M. McCune, *Korea Today*, p. 228.
Page 118, lines 6, 19, 24. *New York Times*, August 24, 1950.
Page 118, line 31. *New York Times*, August 21, 1950.
Page 119, line 9. *New York Times*, September 28, 1950.
Page 119, line 26. *New York Times*, September 29, 1950.
Page 120, line 2. *New York Times*, September 26, 1950.
Page 120, line 24. *New York Times*, September 28, 1950.
Page 121, line 2. *New York Times*, October 1, 1950, text.
Page 122, lines 22, 34. *New York Times*, October 4, 1950. (Dispatch from Tokyo.)

CHAPTER 18

Page 124, line 5. Hanson Baldwin, *New York Times*, September 1, 1950.
Page 124, line 7. *New York Times*, September 8, 1950.
Page 124, line 17. *New York Times*, September 22, 1950. (Dispatch from Belgrade.)
Page 124, line 23. James Reston, *New York Times*, September 24, 1950.
Page 125, line 10. *New York Times*, September 24, 1950. (Dispatch from Hong Kong.)
Page 126, lines 9, 12, 16. *New York Times*, October 2, 1950.
Page 127, line 23. MacArthur communiqué no. 94, *New York Times*, July 20, 1950.
Page 127, line 29. *New York Times*, October 7, 1950.
Page 127, line 37. *New York Times*, October 4, 1950.
Page 128, line 8. *New York Times*, October 4, 1950.
Page 128, lines 29, 31. *New York Times*, October 2, 1950.
Page 129, line 16. *New York Times*, October 3, 1950, text.
Page 129, line 37. *New York Times*, October 4, 1950.
Page 130, line 28. *New York Times*, October 3, 1950.
Page 130, line 34. *New York Times*, October 4, 1950.
Page 131, line 3. *New York Times*, October 6, 1950.
Page 131, line 16. *Facts on File*, 1950, p. 314 E.
Page 131, line 34. *New York Times*, October 1, 1950.
Page 132, line 17. *New York Times*, October 1, 1950.

CHAPTER 19

Page 133, line 6. *New York Times*, June 28, 1950, text.
Page 133, lines 9, 13. *New York Times*, September 29, 1950. (Dispatch from Lake Success.)

Page 134, line 9. *New York Times*, September 29, 1950.
Page 135, lines 13, 17, 25. *New York Times*, October 10, 1950.
Page 135, line 30. *New York Times*, October 11, 1950.
Page 136, lines 3, 8. *New York Times*, October 11, 1950.
Page 137, line 12. *New York Times*, October 14, 1950.
Page 137, line 32. *New York Times*, September 7, 1950, text of the Soviet note.
Page 138, line 2. United Press dispatch from Moscow, *New York Times*, September 7, 1950.
Page 138, line 8. *New York Times*, September 6, 1950.
Page 138, line 10. *New York Times*, September 7, 1950.

CHAPTER 20

Page 139, line 15. *New York Times*, October 11, 1950.
Page 140, lines 11, 29. *New York Times*, October 20, 1950.
Page 141, line 22. *New York Times*, October 11, 1950.
Page 141, line 35. *New York Times*, October 12, 1950.
Page 142, lines 10, 26. *New York Times*, October 11, 1950.
Page 142, line 33. *New York Times*, October 12, 1950.
Page 143, line 30. State Department White Paper on Korea, p. 25.
Page 143, line 38. *New York Times*, October 11, 1950.
Page 144, lines 6, 15, 23. *New York Times*, October 12, 1950.

CHAPTER 21

Page 145, line 5. MacArthur Hearings, p. 1115.
Page 146, line 13. *New York Times*, October 15, 1950.
Page 146, line 24. Substance of *Statement Made at Wake Island Conference on October 15, 1950, Compiled by General of the Army Omar N. Bradley, Chairman of the Joint Chiefs of Staff . . . for the Use of the Committee on Armed Services and the Committee on Foreign Relations, U. S. Senate,* Washington, 1951, p. 8.
Page 147, line 24. *New York Times*, October 15, 1950.
Page 147, line 33. Gunther, *The Riddle of MacArthur,* p. 1.
Page 147, line 35. *New York Times*, October 14, 1950.
Page 149, lines 24, 29, 38. *New York Times*, October 16, 1950.

CHAPTER 22

Page 151, line 12. *New York Times*, October 19, 1950.
Page 152, line 16. *New York Times*, October 21, 1950. (Dispatch from Tokyo.)
Page 152, line 21. United Press dispatch, *New York Times*, October 21, 1950.
Page 153, line 3. United Press dispatch, *New York Times*, October 24, 1950.
Page 154, lines 5, 11. *New York Times*, October 25, 1950. (Dispatch from Tokyo.)
Page 155, lines 7, 13. *New York Times*, October 27, 1950.
Page 155, line 32. *New York Times*, October 28, 1950.
Page 156, lines 4, 7, 9. *New York Times*, October 28, 1950.
Page 158, line 5. *New York Times*, October 25, 1950.
Page 158, line 30. *New York Times*, October 28, 1950.
Page 159, line 2. *New York Times*, October 28, 1950.
Page 160, lines 2, 30, 38. *New York Times*, October 29, 1950.
Page 161, lines 16, 19. *New York Times*, October 30, 1950.
Page 161, line 35. *New York Times*, October 31, 1950.
Page 162, line 17. Associated Press dispatch from Washington, *New York Times*, October 31, 1950.
Page 162, line 31. *New York Times*, November 1, 1950.
Page 163, line 21. *New York Times*, November 1, 1950.
Page 163, lines 32, 39. *New York Times*, November 2, 1950.
Page 164, lines 7, 10. *New York Times*, November 2, 1950.
Page 164, line 19. *New York Times*, November 3, 1950. (Dispatch from Tokyo.)
Page 164, lines 22, 31. *New York Times*, November 3, 1950. (Dispatch from Hamhung.)
Page 165, line 25. United Press dispatch from Tokyo, *New York Times*, October 30, 1950.
Page 165, lines 29, 34. *New York Times*, November 4, 1950.
Page 166, lines 8, 19. *New York Times*, November 5, 1950.
Page 166, line 28. *New York Times*, November 6, 1950.

CHAPTER 23

Page 167, lines 2, 6, 8. *New York Times*, November 6, 1950.
Page 168, lines 22, 32. *New York Times*, November 6, 1950.
Page 169, line 28. *New York Times*, November 6, 1950.
Page 171, line 4. *New York Times*, August 28, 1950.
Page 171, line 31. *Facts on File*, 1950, p. 314 G.
Page 174, line 11. *New York Times*, November 7, 1950.

CHAPTER 24

Page 175, lines 8, 13, 15. *New York Times*, November 7, 1950.
Page 176, line 12. *New York Times*, November 7, 1950. (Dispatch from Lake Success.)
Page 176, line 25. *New York Times*, November 8, 1950.
Page 176, line 34. *New York Times*, November 7, 1950.
Page 176, line 36. *New York Times*, November 8, 1950.
Page 177, lines 4, 23. *New York Times*, November 8, 1950.
Page 177, line 33. *New York Times*, November 9, 1950.
Page 178, line 23. *New York Times*, November 9, 1950.
Page 179, line 16. *New York Times*, November 9, 1950.

CHAPTER 25

Page 180, lines 1, 8. *New York Times*, November 9, 1950.
Page 180, line 25. *New York Times*, November 10, 1950.
Page 181, lines 3, 5, 38. *New York Times*, November 10, 1950.
Page 182, lines 10, 14, 24. *New York Times*, November 11, 1950.
Page 183, line 10. *New York Times*, November 10, 1950.
Page 183, lines 14, 21. *New York Times*, November 11, 1950.

CHAPTER 26

Page 185, line 20. *New Yorker*, March 10, 1950.
Page 186, line 7. *Facts on File*, 1950, p. 340 C.
Page 186, line 16. *New York Times*, November 12, 1950.
Page 186, line 22. *New York Times*, November 17, 1950.
Page 187, line 19. *New Yorker*, March 10, 1950.
Page 189, lines 9, 15. James Reston, *New York Times*, November 30, 1950.
Page 189, line 38. *New York Times*, November 10, 1950.
Page 190, line 1. *New York Times*, November 11, 1950.
Page 190, line 3. *New York Times*, November 13, 1950.
Page 190, line 4. *New York Times*, November 15, 1950. (Dispatch from Tokyo.)
Page 190, line 7. *New York Times*, November 18, 1950. (Dispatch from Tokyo.)
Page 190, line 10. *New York Times*, November 19, 1950.
Page 190, line 30. *New York Times*, November 21, 1950. (Dispatch from Tokyo.)
Page 191, line 3. *New York Times*, November 22, 1950.
Page 191, line 10. *New York Times*, November 24, 1950.
Page 191, line 18. *New York Times*, November 6, 1950.

CHAPTER 27

Page 192, line 16. *New York Herald Tribune*, November 18, 1950. (Paris edition.)
Page 193, line 7. *Sunday Pictorial* (London), November 19, 1950.
Page 193, line 12. *Manchester Guardian*, November 23, 1950.
Page 193, line 31. *Facts on File*, 1950, p. 356 B.
Page 193, line 36. *The Times* (London), November 16, 1950.
Page 194, line 11. *The Times* (London), November 16, 1950.
Page 194, line 22. *The Times* (London), November 17, 1950.
Page 195, line 9. *The Times* (London), November 17, 1950.
Page 195, line 31. *New York Times*, December 1, 1950.
Page 196, line 6. *New Statesman and Nation*, November 25, 1950.
Page 196, line 33. *Manchester Guardian*, November 23, 1950.
Page 197, line 8. *New York Herald Tribune*, November 23, 1950. (Paris edition.)
Page 197, line 15. *New York Herald Tribune*, November 24, 1950. (Paris edition.)
Page 197, lines 23, 27. London *Daily Mail*, November 24, 1950. (Paris edition.)
Page 197, line 35. *Daily Telegraph* (London), November 24, 1950.
Page 198, line 3. London *Daily Mail*, November 25, 1950. (Paris edition.)

CHAPTER 28

Page 199, line 3. *New York Times*, December 1, 1950.
Page 199, line 7. *New York Times*, December 2, 1950.
Page 199, line 14. *New York Times*, November 22, 1950.
Page 200, line 9. *New York Times*, November 25, 1950.
Page 200, line 32. *New York Times*, November 17, 1950.
Page 201, line 19. *New York Herald Tribune*, November 23, 1950. (Paris edition.)
Page 201, line 24. *New York Times*, November 30, 1950.
Page 202, line 13. *Manchester Guardian*, December 16, 1950.

Page 205, line 1. "United States Relations with China," Department of State publication 3573, August, 1949, p. 798. (Hereafter referred to as State Department publication 3573.)
Page 205, line 6. State Department publication 3573, p. 810.
Page 205, line 17. State Department publication 3573, pp. xvi, xvii.
Page 206, lines 7, 10. State Department publication 3573, pp. 777, 768.
Page 206, line 30. *New York Times*, March 10, 1950.
Page 207, line 24. Speech at The Commonwealth Club, San Francisco, March 15, 1950.

CHAPTER 29

Page 208, line 3. *New York Times*, November 27, 1950.
Page 208, line 12. *Sunday Times* (London), November 12, 1950.
Page 208, line 22. *Observer* (London), November 26, 1950.
Page 209, line 31. *Sunday Times* (London), October 29, 1950.
Page 209, line 39. *New York Times*, December 21, 1950.
Page 210, line 24. *New York Times*, November 26, 1950.
Page 210, line 26. *New York Times*, November 27, 1950.
Page 210, line 27. *New York Times*, November 28, 1950.
Page 210, lines 29, 35. *New York Times*, November 29, 1950.
Page 211, line 16. *New York Times*, November 20, 1950.
Page 212, line 17. *New York Times*, November 6, 1950.
Page 214, line 26. *Sunday Times* (London), December 10, 1950.
Page 214, line 32. London *Daily Mail*, December 13, 1950. (Paris edition.)
Page 214, line 38. *The Times* (London), December 18, 1950.

CHAPTER 30

Page 216, line 7. *New York Herald Tribune*, December 4, 1950. (Paris edition.)
Page 216, line 12. *Facts on File*, 1950, p. 422 B.
Page 216, line 19. *New York Times*, December 19, 1950.
Page 216, line 24. Release No. 752, *New York Times*, December 23, 1950.
Page 217, line 7. Release No. 755, *New York Times*, December 24, 1950.
Page 217, line 20. *New York Times*, November 6, 1950.
Page 217, lines 28, 37. *New York Times*, December 20, 1950.
Page 218, line 10. *New York Times*, December 15, 1950.
Page 218, line 16. Release No. 752, *New York Times*, December 23, 1950.
Page 219, line 32. *New York Times*, December 25, 1950.
Page 220, line 36. *New York Times*, December 12, 1950.
Page 221, line 2. *New York Times*, December 12, 1950.
Page 221, line 24. *New York Times*, December 25, 1950.
Page 221, line 29. *New York Herald Tribune*, December 27, 1950. (Paris edition.)
Page 221, line 37. *New York Times*, December 27, 1950.

CHAPTER 31

Page 223, line 4. *New York Times*, December 28, 1950.
Page 224, line 15. Release No. 766, *New York Times*, December 28, 1950.
Page 224, line 34. *New York Times*, December 29, 1950.
Page 225, line 18. *New York Times*, December 5, 1950.
Page 225, lines 27, 31. *New York Times*, December 30, 1950.
Page 225, line 38. *New York Times*, December 31, 1950.
Page 226, lines 2, 4. *New York Times*, December 31, 1950.
Page 226, line 11. Release No. 768, *New York Times*, December 29, 1950.
Page 226, line 32. *New York Times*, January 1, 1951.
Page 228, line 24. *New York Herald Tribune*, December 7, 1950. (Paris edition.)
Page 228, line 30. *New York Times*, December 6, 1950.
Page 228, line 33. *New York Herald Tribune*, December 7, 1950. (Paris edition.)
Page 228, line 35. *New York Times*, December 6, 1950.
Page 229, lines 10, 27. *New York Times*, December 7, 1950.
Page 229, line 36. *New York Times*, December 25, 1950.
Page 230, line 3. *New York Times*, December 29, 1950.
Page 230, line 11. London *Daily Mail*, December 6, 1950. (Paris edition.)

CHAPTER 32

Page 232, line 7. *New York Times*, January 1, 1951.
Page 232, line 10. *New York Times*, January 2, 1951.
Page 232, line 13. *New York Times*, January 3, 1951.
Page 232, line 16. London *Daily Mail*, January 4, 1951. (Paris edition.)
Page 233, line 10. *New York Times*, January 5, 1951.
Page 233, lines 21, 25. *New York Times*, January 14, 1951.
Page 234, line 9. *New York Herald Tribune*, January 3, 1951. (Paris edition.)

Page 234, line 36. Release No. 777, *New York Times*, January 2, 1951.
Page 235, lines 1, 22. *New York Times*, January 4, 1951.
Page 235, line 27. Michael James, *New York Times*, January 4, 1951.
Page 235, line 35. Lindesay Parrott, *New York Times*, January 4, 1951.
Page 236, line 8. Lindesay Parrott, *New York Times*, January 3, 1951.
Page 236, line 25. *New York Times*, January 4, 1951.
Page 237, line 8. *New York Times*, January 5, 1951.
Page 237, line 25. *New York Herald Tribune*, January 6, 1951. (Paris edition.)
Page 238, line 26. *New York Times*, January 4, 1951.
Page 238, line 33. Release No. 786, *New York Times*, January 5, 1951.
Page 239, line 10. Release No. 786, *New York Times*, January 5, 1951.
Page 239, line 17. *The Times* (London), January 6, 1951.
Page 239, line 31. *New York Times*, January 10, 1951.
Page 240, line 9. *New York Times*, January 9, 1951. (Dispatch from London.)
Page 240, line 16. *Daily Express* (London), January 10, 1951.
Page 240, line 24. Release No. 786, *New York Times*, January 5, 1951.
Page 240, line 30. *New York Times*, January 7, 1951.
Page 241, line 17. *The Times* (London), January 15, 1951.
Page 241, line 21. *The Times* (London), January 17, 1951.
Page 241, line 23. London *Daily Mail*, January 15, 1951. (Paris edition.)
Page 241, line 32. United Press dispatch from Tokyo, *New York Times*, January 15, 1951.
Page 242, lines 1, 8. *The Times* (London), January 15, 1951.
Page 242, line 21. *New York Times*, January 16, 1951.
Page 243, line 13. Release No. 129, *New York Times*, January 16, 1951.
Page 243, line 17. *The Times* (London), January 19, 1951.
Page 243, line 21. *The Times* (London), January 20, 1951.
Page 244, line 19. London *Daily Mail*, January 12, 1951. (Paris edition.)
Page 244, line 34. *New York Times*, January 12, 1951.
Page 244, line 37. London *Daily Mail*, January 15, 1951. (Paris edition.)
Page 245, line 11. *New York Times*, January 15, 1951.
Page 245, lines 14, 19. Michael James dispatch from "An Airbase in Japan," *New York Times*, January 16, 1951.
Page 245, lines 30, 35. *New York Times*, January 19, 1951.
Page 246, line 9. *New York Herald Tribune*, January 12, 1951. (Paris edition.)
Page 246, line 19. *New York Times*, January 16, 1951.
Page 246, line 27. *New York Times*, January 19, 1951.
Page 247, line 1. London *Daily Mail*, January 16, 1951. (Paris edition.)

CHAPTER 33

Page 248, line 25. *New York Times*, January 12, 1951.
Page 249, line 9. *New York Times*, January 20, 1951.
Page 249, line 35. London *Daily Mail*, January 13, 1951. (Paris edition.)
Page 250, line 6. Release No. 124, *New York Times*, January 14, 1951.
Page 250, lines 13, 19. *New York Times*, January 21, 1951.
Page 251, line 1. *New York Times*, January 22, 1951. (Dispatch from Tokyo.)
Page 251, lines 4, 11. *New York Herald Tribune*, January 22, 1951. (Paris edition.)
Page 251, line 18. *New York Times*, January 23 and 24, 1951.
Page 251, lines 22, 25, 27. *New York Times*, January 26, 1951.
Page 252, line 1. *New York Times*, January 28, 1951.
Page 252, line 2. *New York Times*, January 29, 1951.
Page 252, line 5. *New York Times*, January 30, 1951.
Page 252, lines 11, 15. *New York Times*, February 2, 1951.

CHAPTER 34

Page 253, line 1. *New York Times*, "News Of The Week In Review," February 4, 1951.
Page 253, lines 13, 15. *New York Times*, February 11, 1951.
Page 253, line 21. *New York Times*, February 10, 1951.
Page 254, line 5. Release No. 170, *New York Times*, February 6, 1951.
Page 254, line 15. *New York Times*, February 10, 1951.
Page 256, line 5. *New York Times*, December 24, 1951.
Page 256, line 25. *New York Times*, February 21, 1951.
Page 256, line 36. *New York Times*, September 15, 1950.
Page 257, line 6. *New York Times*, February 1, 1951.
Page 258, line 7. *New York Times*, February 9, 1951.
Page 258, line 24. *New York Times*, February 5, 1951.
Page 258, line 34. *New York Times*, February 3, 1951.

CHAPTER 35

Page 261, lines 14, 21. *New York Herald Tribune*, February 20, 1951. (Paris edition.)
Page 262, line 10. *New York Times*, February 3, 1951.
Page 262, line 18. *New York Times*, February 12, 1951.
Page 262, line 23. London *Daily Mail*, February 13, 1951. (Paris edition.)
Page 262, line 31. *New York Times*, February 13, 1951.
Page 263, line 33. *New York Times*, February 15, 1951.
Page 263, line 35. London *Daily Mail*, February 16, 1951. (Paris edition.)
Page 264, line 2. *New York Times*, February 14, 1951.
Page 264, line 8. London *Daily Mail*, February 15, 1951. (Paris edition.)
Page 264, line 10. *The Times* (London), February 15, 1951.
Page 264, line 27. *New York Herald Tribune*, March 30, 1951. (Paris edition.)
Page 265, line 34. *The Times* (London), February 13, 1951.
Page 265, line 36. *Daily Herald* (London), February 13, 1951.
Page 266, line 1. *New York Times*, February 13, 1951. (Dispatch from Tokyo.)
Page 266, lines 11, 21. *New York Times*, February 15, 1951.

CHAPTER 36

Page 267, line 6. *New York Times*, March 8, 1951.
Page 268, lines 1, 6. *New York Times*, March 14, 1951.
Page 268, line 11. *New York Times*, March 16, 1951.
Page 268, line 20. *New York Times*, March 19, 1951.
Page 268, line 21. *New York Times*, March 20, 1951.
Page 268, lines 24, 26. *New York Times*, March 21, 1951.
Page 268, line 31. *New York Times*, March 23, 1951.
Page 269, line 2. *New York Times*, April 1, 1951.
Page 269, line 14. *Sunday Times* (London), March 25, 1951.
Page 269, line 25. MacArthur Hearings, p. 1608.
Page 269, line 32. *New York Times*, March 24, 1951.
Page 270, line 14. *New York Times*, March 29, 1951.
Page 270, line 28. *New York Times*, March 25, 1951.
Page 271, lines 1, 4. MacArthur Hearings, p. 1608.
Page 271, line 17. *Facts on File*, 1951, p. 97 E.
Page 271, line 19. *New York Times*, March 26, 1951.
Page 271, line 21. *New York Times*, March 27, 1951.
Page 271, lines 23, 26. *New York Times*, March 31, 1951.
Page 271, line 29. *New York Times*, April 3, 1951.
Page 271, line 32. *The Times* (London), April 7, 1951.
Page 271, line 34. *New York Times*, April 7, 1951.
Page 272, line 1. *New York Times*, April 3, 1951.
Page 272, line 12. *The Times* (London), April 5, 1951, quoting the *Washington Post*.
Page 272, lines 18, 27. *New York Times*, March 28, 1951.
Page 273, line 4. *New York Times*, March 28, 1951.
Page 273, line 10. *New York Times*, April 5, 1951.

CHAPTER 37

Page 274, line 6. MacArthur Hearings, pp. 3543, 3544.
Page 275, line 15. *New York Times*, July 26, 1951, text.
Page 277, line 32. Washington *Evening Star*, June 26, 1951.
Page 278, line 14. *New York Times*, May 19, 1951.
Page 279, line 8. *New York Herald Tribune*, May 22, 1951.

CHAPTER 38

Page 280, line 8. *New York Times*, June 24, 1951.
Page 280, line 15. *New York Times*, June 26, 1951.
Page 281, line 12. *New York Times*, July 4, 1951.
Page 281, lines 14, 16, 23, 33. *Facts on File*, 1951, pp. 209 F, 209 H, 210 C D F, 218 H.
Page 282, line 1. *New York Times*, July 6, 1951.
Page 282, line 16. *New York Times*, June 14, 1951.

CHAPTER 39

Page 284, lines 8, 14. *Facts on File*, 1951, pp. 14 D, 218 A.
Page 285, line 9. *Daily Compass*, July 13, 1951.
Page 285, line 26. *Facts on File*, 1951, p. 233 D.
Page 286, line 25. I. F. Stone, *Daily Compass*, July 31, 1951.
Page 286, line 33. *New York Times*, July 29, 1951.
Page 287, line 7. *New York Times*, June 27, 1951.
Page 287, line 11. *New York Times*, March 13, 1951.

Page 287, line 17. *New York Times*, August 2, 1951.
Page 288, line 8. *New York Times*, March 16, 1951.
Page 288, lines 27, 30. *New York Herald Tribune*, August 4, 1951.
Page 288, line 31. Associated Press dispatch, *New York Herald Tribune*, August 5, 1951.
Page 289, line 3. *New York Herald Tribune*, August 4, 1951.
Page 289, line 26. *New York Herald Tribune*, August 5, 1951.
Page 289, line 34. *New York Times*, August 6, 1951.
Page 290, line 18. See chronology in United Press dispatch, *Nippon Times*, August 6, 1951.

CHAPTER 40

Page 292, line 13. *Facts on File*, 1951, p. 257 D.
Page 292, line 17. United Press dispatch, *Nippon Times*, August 13, 1951.
Page 292, line 19. *Facts on File*, 1951, p. 257 D.
Page 292, line 24. *New York Herald Tribune*, August 17, 1951.
Page 292, line 36. *Nippon Times*, August 29, 1951.
Page 293, line 8. *New York Herald Tribune*, August 19, 1951.
Page 293, lines 15, 17, 19. United Press dispatch, *Nippon Times*, August 20, 1951.
Page 293, line 24. *Nippon Times*, August 21, 1951.
Page 295, line 3. *Facts on File*, 1951, p. 273 D.
Page 295, line 14. *New York Times*, August 26, 1951.
Page 295, line 22. *New York Times*, August 22, 1951.
Page 296, line 9. *Daily Telegraph* (London), August 21, 1951.
Page 296, line 26. *Nippon Times*, August 24, 1951.
Page 296, line 31. *Facts on File*, 1951, p. 265 K.
Page 297, line 26. *Daily Compass*, August 22, 1951.
Page 298, line 9. *New York Times*, August 19, 1951.
Page 298, line 15. *Wall Street Journal*, August 29, 1951.

CHAPTER 41

Page 300, line 12. *New York Times*, August 26, 1951.
Page 301, line 11. *New York Times*, July 8, 1951.
Page 301, line 26. *New York Times*, April 14, 1951.
Page 301, line 35. Speech at Whittier College, *New York Times*, April 1, 1950.
Page 302, lines 33, 38. *New York Herald Tribune*, January 22, 1952.

CHAPTER 42

Page 304, lines 9, 18. *New York Times*, August 28, 1951.
Page 305, lines 14, 35. *New York Times*, August 23, 1951.
Page 306, line 14. *New York Times*, September 11, 1951.
Page 306, lines 15, 18. *New York Herald Tribune*, September 11, 1951.
Page 306, line 28. David McConnell dispatch from Tokyo, *New York Herald Tribune*, September 13, 1951.
Page 307, line 4. David McConnell dispatch from Tokyo, *New York Herald Tribune*, September 16, 1951.
Page 307, lines 27, 36. *New York Times*, September 16, 1951.
Page 308, line 18. *New York Times*, October 1, 1951.
Page 308, line 24. *New York Times*, October 2, 1951.
Page 308, line 33. *New York Times*, October 1, 1951.

CHAPTER 43

Page 310, line 8, *Facts on File*, 1951, p. 282 H.
Page 311, lines 7, 14. *New York Times*, October 14, 1951.
Page 311, lines 23, 29. *New York Herald Tribune*, October 15, 1951.
Page 311, line 35. *New York Times*, October 15, 1951, text.
Page 312, footnote. MacArthur Hearings, pp. 3063-3114.
Page 313, footnote, line 3. *Brassey's Annual: The Armed Forces Yearbook*, London, 1951, pp. 110, 111.
Page 313, line 3. Washington *Evening Star*, October 16, 1951.
Page 314, line 22. *New York Times*, October 8, 1951.
Page 314, line 33. *New York Herald Tribune*, October 19, 1951.
Page 314, line 35. *New York Times*, October 22, 1951, text.
Page 315, line 4. *New York Times*, October 24, 1951, text.

CHAPTER 44

Page 316, line 16. See Lindesay Parrott's dispatch, *New York Times*, October 12, 1951.
Page 316, line 21. *New York Herald Tribune*, October 19, 1951.
Page 317, line 24. *New York Times*, October 16, 1951.
Page 317, line 34. *New York Times*, October 2, 1951.
Page 318, line 21. *New York Times*, October 16, 1951.
Page 319, line 16. *New York Times*, October 16, 1951.

Page 319, line 23. *New York Times*, October 24, 1951, text.
Page 319, line 33. Dispatch from Eighth Army Headquarters, *New York Times*, September 5, 1951.
Page 320, line 5. *New York Times*, October 6, 1951.
Page 320, line 12. *New York Herald Tribune*, October 4, 1951.
Page 320, line 22. Associated Press dispatch from Washington, *New York Herald Tribune*, October 5, 1951.
Page 320, line 24. *New York Times*, October 5, 1951.
Page 320, line 27. *New York Times*, October 16, 1951.

CHAPTER 45

Page 321, line 11. *New York Times*, October 5, 1951.
Page 321, line 20. *New York Times*, October 21, 1951.
Page 321, line 25. *New York Times*, October 23, 1951.
Page 322, line 4. *New York Times*, October 27, 1951.
Page 322, line 9. *New York Times*, November 4, 1951.
Page 322, lines 29, 33. *New York Times*, November 18, 1951.
Page 323, line 5. *New York Times*, November 4, 1951.
Page 323, line 11. *New York Herald Tribune*, November 11, 1951.
Page 323, line 18. *New York Times*, November 11, 1951.
Page 324, line 8. *New York Times*, November 18, 1951.
Page 324, line 14. *New York Herald Tribune*, November 15, 1951.
Page 324, line 18. *New York World Telegram and Sun*, November 16, 1951.
Page 324, line 21. *New York Herald Tribune*, November 16, 1951.
Page 324, lines 25, 29. *New York Herald Tribune*, November 17, 1951.
Page 324, line 37. *New York Times*, November 17, 1951, text.
Page 325, line 16. *New York Times*, November 17, 1951. (Dispatch from London.)
Page 325, line 19. *New York Times*, November 16, 1951.

CHAPTER 46

Page 326, line 7. Associated Press dispatch from Pusan, *New York Herald Tribune*, November 15, 1951.
Page 326, line 9. United Press dispatch from Tokyo, *New York Times*, November 17, 1951.
Page 326, line 14. *New York Times*, November 21, 1951.
Page 326, line 25. *New York Herald Tribune*, November 24, 1951.
Page 327, line 9. United Press dispatch from Tokyo, *New York Herald Tribune*, November 30, 1951.
Page 328, line 12. *New York Times*, November 21, 1951.
Page 329, line 18. *New York Times*, November 15, 1951, text.
Page 330, line 31. *New York Times*, June 17, 1951.
Page 332, line 1. *New York Herald Tribune*, November 24, 1951.
Page 332, line 8. *New York Herald Tribune*, November 15, 1951.
Page 332, line 25. *New York Times*, November 15, 1951.
Page 332, line 38. *New York Herald Tribune*, November 17, 1951.
Page 333, line 2. *New York Times*, November 17, 1951.
Page 334, line 6. *New York Herald Tribune*, November 17, 1951.
Page 334, line 8. *New York Times*, November 18, 1951.
Page 334, line 22. *Washington Times-Herald*, November 17, 1951.

CHAPTER 47

Page 335, line 6. *New York Times*, January 6, 1952.
Page 335, line 25. *New York Journal-American*, November 3, 1951.
Page 336, line 15. *New York Times*, October 1, 1951.
Page 336, line 24. *Brassey's Annual*, 1951, p. 108.
Page 336, line 31. *United Nations World*, February, 1952.
Page 336, line 38. *Facts on File*, 1951, p. 314 D.
Page 337, lines 5, 12, 25. *Brassey's Annual*, 1951, pp. 397, 398.
Page 338, line 4. *U. S. News and World Report*, December 14, 1951, text.
Page 338, line 16. *New York Times*, November 28, 1951.
Page 338, line 22. *New York Times*, November 29, 1951.
Page 339, line 8. *U. S. News and World Report*, November 30, 1951.
Page 339, line 17. *Facts on File*, 1951, p. 337 H.
Page 339, line 35. *New York Times*, October 25, 1951, text.
Page 341, line 2. *U. S. News and World Report*, December 14, 1951.
Page 342, line 7. *Aviation Age*, July, 1951.
Page 344, line 9. *New York Times*, December 9, 1951.

CHAPTER 48

Page 345, line 12. George F. Kennan, *American Diplomacy: 1900-1950* (Chicago: University of Chicago Press, 1951), p. 14.
Page 346, line 22. *Wall Street Journal*, November 27, 1951.
Page 348, line 11. United Press dispatch from Eighth Army Headquarters, *New York Journal-American*, January 19, 1952.

Index

Acheson, Dean, 12, 18, 20, 28, 35, 87, 109, 197, 201, 325, 344-347
  at MacArthur hearings, 59-65
  on China, 203-207
  on Formosa, 72, 203
  on 38th Parallel, 262, 263, 287
  on peace moves, 193, 270, 278-280
Air Force, 257-258, 337-344
Allen, Brig. Gen. Frank A., 307
Allied Council in Tokyo, 80
Almond, Maj. Gen. Edward M., 129, 163-164, 168, 266
Anderson, Maj. Gen. Orvil A., 93
Antung, 91
Associated Press, 109, 112, 125-126, 168-169, 212, 219, 237, 242, 246, 281, 285-295, 306, 324, 336
Atom bomb, 192, 213, 230, 245, 283, 344
Attlee, Clement, 213, 229, 230, 243, 244, 262-265
Austin, Warren, 78-79, 91, 96, 111, 117-122, 132, 138, 140, 150, 176, 180, 183
Aviation Age, 342
Aviation Week, 342-343

Baguio Conference, 29-30
Baillie, Hugh, 288
Baldwin, Hanson, 4, 16, 83-85, 92, 124-125, 152, 174, 215, 240, 244, 255, 308, 317-321, 335-339, 344
Barnard, William, 237
Barrett, George, 258, 323
Becker, Jim, 285
Bender, George H., 336
Bevin, Ernest, 29, 193, 197
Bolling, Maj. Gen. Alexander R., 245
Bombings of border, 90
Boniford, Capt. Hugh, 259
Bourdet, Claude, ix
Bradley, Gen. Omar, 27, 32, 38ff., 72, 101-103, 145-148, 185-188, 281, 320, 336
Brassey's Annual, 313 (footnote), 336
Bridges, Styles, 2, 4, 60, 66
Briggs, Brig. Gen. James E., 246
British attitude, 240, 244, 249, 271
Brown, Constantine, 277
Burchett, Wilfred, 316, 317

Casualty figures, 114, 254-255, 335-336
Censorship, 240
Ce Soir, 316
Chang, Dr. John M., 118, 120
Chiang Kai-shek, 10, 19-20, 28-29, 43, 88-90, 104, 151, 166, 175, 196, 199-200, 204-205, 233, 241, 264, 269, 274-278, 297, 302, 345· 347
Chicago Tribune, 285, 334
Chifley, Prime Minister of Australia, 28
China, *see* Communist China
Chou En-lai, 126, 153, 186, 284
Chorley, Lord, 194
Churchill, Winston, 24, 193-195, 347
Collins, Gen. J. Lawton, 244-246, 263
Commission to Study Bases of a Just and Durable Peace, 23
Communist China
  Admission to U.N., 30-31, 276-277
  aid to North Korea, 62, 97-98, 166
  air power, 338-344
  and truce talks, 291-292, 310, 322
  atrocities, 324-333
  delegation to U.N., 177, 185-186
  military maneuvers, 124-125, 153-157, 177, 179, 250-251
  protests on bombings, 171, 304
  treatment of prisoners, 197
Connally, Tom, 12, 13, 19, 21, 69, 271
Cosmopolitan, 58, 60
Craig, George N., 92
Crossman, Richard H. S., 193

Daily Compass, viii, ix, 278
London *Daily Mirror*, 240
Daily Worker, 70
Darrow, Col. Don, 306
Dewey, Thomas E., 24, 281, 346
Downton, Eric, 263, 295
Driberg, Tom, 192
Dulles, John Foster, 15, 16, 17, 19-21, 37, 42, 44, 57, 346, 347
  and Chiang, 196-202
  and MacArthur, 72-74
  "architect" of Japanese Treaty, 301-302
  background, 23-27

364

Eban, Abba, 268
Eden, Anthony, 193
Eisenhower, Gen. Dwight, 115, 281, 346
Emmerich, Lt. Col. Dick, 128
Evacuation of Korea, 227-229

Fair Deal, 105-106
Farley, James A., 26
Federal Council of Churches of Christ, 23, 25
Ferguson, Senator, 55, 56, 65, 66
Finletter, Thomas K., 101, 103, 246
Fleming, Peter, 214
Formosa, 6, 12, 19-21, 31-32, 43, 87-91, 146, 151, 200, 276-277
Foust, Hal, 285
France-Soir, 63
Franks, Sir Oliver, 196, 244, 262

Gross, Ernest A., 45, 49, 176, 321
Gunther, John, 1, 3, 7, 14-15, 44-45, 62, 73-74, 79-80

Hamilton, Thomas J., 69, 99
Handley, Capt. Everett L., 259
Hanley, Col. James M., 324-334
Harriman, W. Averell, 90, 148, 281
"Heartbreak Ridge" and other hills, 308-309, 319-320
Herman, George, 307
Hickenlooper, Senator, 60, 145-147
Hickerson, John D., 53-56, 65, 66
Higgins, Marguerite, 316, 317
Hightower, John M., 287
Hillenkoetter, Rear Admiral Roscoe H., 2-5, 9, 11, 16, 53-54
Hindustani Times, 30
Hiss, Alger, 203
Holt, Captain Vyvyan, 49
"Home-by-Christmas" offensive, 185, 209
Hoover, Herbert, 19, 250
Howley, Frank, 35
Hughes, Richard, 40, 41, 209, 289
Hull, Cordell, 24

Ickes, Harold, 26
International News Service, 289

James, Michael, 114, 236
Japan
    elections, 35, 36
    Korean policies, 122, 123
    repression in, 36, 37
Japanese Treaty, 32, 299-303, 384
Jebb, Sir Gladwyn, 78, 180

Jessup, Philip, 93, 148
Johnson, Louis, 27, 32, 37-42, 72, 93
Johnston, Eric, 281
Johnston, Richard J. H., 226, 227
Joy, Admiral C. Turner, 284, 290, 292, 295, 306, 315

Kaesong truce talks, 284-290, 292, 294, 295, 301-302
Kalinov, Col. Cyril Dimitrievitch, 62, 63
Kennan, George F., 345
Kim Il Sung, 224
Kim Tai Sun, 111
Kihss, Peter, 336
Kirk, Ambassador to Russia, 71
Kirkendall, Lt. Col. James, 259
Knowland, William F., 2, 4, 175
Koo, V. K. Wellington, 28
Korea Today, 77
Korean Aid Bill, 18
Krock, Arthur, 71, 72, 195, 273, 282-301
Kuriles, 200, 302

Lee Sun Keun, Col., 128
Lehman, Herbert, 19
"Letter of Transmittal," 204-205
Lie, Trygve, 30, 43, 46, 49, 111, 153
Liebling, A. J., 185, 187, 188
Lippmann, Walter, 33, 279
London *Daily Express,* 240, 317
London *Daily Herald,* 265
London *Daily Mail,* 198, 214, 219, 220, 230, 241, 244, 247, 272
London *Daily Telegraph,* 197, 263, 295
London *Daily Worker,* 316
London *Economist,* 127
London *Observer,* 38, 208, 214, 291
London *Sunday Pictorial,* 193, 240
London *Times,* 35-37, 40, 49, 191, 196, 208-209, 214-215, 237-239, 241, 243, 255, 256, 263, 265, 269, 289

MacArthur, Gen. Douglas, 1, 3, 6-8, 14, 17, 19-21, 27, 35-42, 44-45
    and Dulles, 72-74
    and Truman, 140-150, 199, 201-202
    at Seoul, 107, 113-115, 235
    at Wake Island, 140-150
    atrocities, reports on, 327-330
    border bombings, permission for, 90ff.

MacArthur, Gen. Douglas—*Cont.*
  crossing of 38th Parallel, 108, 129-132, 195-196, 260, 264, 271, 288
  extension of war demanded, 82, 229, 264, 267
  intervention of Chinese, reports on, 82-83, 94-98, 157-158, 162, 166ff., 181, 217ff.
  military situation, reports on, 57ff., 77ff., 186ff., 198, 210, 248
  press relations, 240ff.
  removal from office, 272-273, 274ff.
  surrender terms, 110, 111-112, 198, 269
McCarran, Senator, 53, 54, 55
McCarthy, Senator, Joseph, 20
McClure, Maj. Gen. R. B., 241, 242, 243
McConnell, David, 293, 306
McCormick, Col. Robert, 334
McCune, George, 77
McDermott, Michael J., 135, 162
Malik, Jacob, 65, 66, 88, 89, 103, 275-277, 280, 286-287
Manchester Guardian, 67, 202, 203, 342
Mao Tse-tung, 62, 181, 190, 212, 213, 224, 249, 268-269, 270
Marshall, Gen. George, 26, 66, 75, 76, 93, 102-103, 233, 272, 281, 285-286
Martin, Harold T., 333
Martin, Joseph W. Jr., 274
Maryland Committee for Peace, 103
Matthews, Francis P., 92
Melbourne military conferences, 38
MIGs, 339-344
Mikardo, Ian, 192
Millikin, Eugene D., 69
Monthly Review, x, xi
Morrison, Herbert, 271
Morse, Wayne, 58
Mowrer, Edgar Ansel, 26
Muccio, John J., 44-47, 147, 148

Nam Il, 285, 292, 294, 300
Namsi, 339-340
Napalm raid, 258
Nation, viii
National Air Review, 337
National Conference on Problem of Germany, 26
Nehru, 28-29, 87, 116-117, 133, 134, 270

Neutral zone violations, 304-307, 311, 318
New Statesman and Nation, 192, 194-196
New York Daily News, 281, 286
New York Herald Tribune, see References
New York Journal-American, 286, 335-336
New York Post, viii, 334
New York Times, see References
New Yorker, 185
Nippon Times, 12, 13, 287, 289, 293, 296
North Korean Army, 46, 84, 131, 210-215
  estimates of numbers, 165, 217-218, 223
  lack of weapons, 261
  pre-invasion activity, 4, 5, 7, 8, 9, 11, 66
  rejection of scorched earth policy, 256
Nuckols, Gen. William, 292, 295, 307

L'Observateur, ix
O'Donnell, Maj. Gen. Emmett, Jr., 245, 246, 312 (footnote)
Oliver, Robert T., 7, 12
"Operation Killer," 255
"Operation Strangle," 337-338

Pace, Frank, 148
Pacific Pact, 10, 28, 29
Panmunjom peace talks, 310, 319
Panton, Selkirk, 240
Parrott, Lindesay, 39, 41, 44, 45, 159, 177-178, 209-210, 219, 223, 288, 290, 304, 315, 319, 333
Peace negotiations, 116, 269, 271, 276, 282
Pescadores, 200
Philadelphia Record, viii
Pilot, 92
Presidential Air Policy Commission, 101
Pyongyang, 152, 216, 220, 225

Quirino, President of Philippines, 29

Radford, Admiral Arthur W., 148
Rand, Christopher, 234, 244
Rashin, 90
Rau, Sir Benegal, 251

Rayburn, Sam, 273
Rearmament of Japan and Germany, 102-103
Republican Postwar Advisory Council, 24
Reston, James, 80, 88, 120, 200, 201, 270, 325
Reuters', 111, 264
Ridgway, Gen. Matthew, 225, 232, 254, 261, 281, 284, 291ff.
atrocities, reports on, 324-326
neutral zone violations, reports on, 311-314, 318
press relations, 304ff., 307, 316-320
truce talks, 290, 310, 319
Roberts, Brig. Gen. William L., 8, 9
Romulo, Gen. Carlos P., 176
Roosevelt, Franklin D., 23, 24, 34, 105-106
Roosevelt, Mrs. Franklin D., 26
Ross, Charles, 139, 140
Ruffner, Maj. Gen. C. L., 242
Rusk, Dean, 148, 278, 279
Russell, Senator, 61, 297, 299, 312 (footnote)
Russia,
aid to North Korea, 62, 63, 96, 97
air attacks protested, 135, 137
in U. N., 65, 66, 76, 88, 193, 299
willingness to negotiate Korean peace, 22, 86, 87, 99, 117, 300
Ryokufukai, 35

Salisbury, Lord, 193, 194
Saturday Evening Post, 333
Schacht, Hjalmar, 26
Schumach, Murray, 295, 307
Schuman, Robert, 29
Senate Appropriations Committee, 2, 3, 4, 53ff.
Senate Foreign Relations Committee, 20
Seoul, 113-114, 219ff., 225, 232, 235, 237, 254
Sherman, Forrest P., 281
Sihn Sung Mo, Captain, 7
Silverman, Sydney, 194
Sinanju, 215, 230
Sinuiju, 177-178
Slim, Field Marshal Sir William, 38
Smith, Rear Admiral Allen E., 264
Smith, Senator, H. Alexander, 61, 62, 297
Smith, Lt. Gen. Walter Bedell, 245

South Korea
army organized for defense, 10
army poorly equipped, 7, 8
government recognized as "Republic of Korea," 77
need for reforms, 118
police repression, 111
South Sakhalin, 200, 302
Soviet Union, see Russia
"Soybean story," xi-xii
Spectator, 213
Spender, Percy C., 127
Stalin, 85, 87, 107, 137, 249, 260, 281
Stassen, Harold E., 228, 229
State Department, 1, 19, 71, 135, 140, 249, 262, 269, 280-281
Stennis, Senator, 311 (footnote)
Stratemeyer, Lt. Gen. George E., 178
Sullivan & Cromwell, 25
Sunday Express, 240
Surrender terms, 110-112
Syngman Rhee, 7, 10, 12-15, 18, 28-30, 43, 44, 64, 111, 113-115, 116, 120, 117-118, 151, 221, 276, 289, 295, 310, 345, 347
Szu-Tu, 10

Taft, Robert, 19, 278, 281, 297
Talbert, Ansel E., 221
Thirty-eighth Parallel, 80, 108-113, 118, 122, 126, 132-133, 260-266, 271, 287-288, 292, 322
Tito, Marshal, 124
Tokyo Asahi, 36, 37
Truman, Harry S.
atom bomb, possible use, 192, 213, 230
at Wake Island, 139-150
distrust of truce talks, 286, 294, 297
fear of peace, 104-107
pledge of aid to South Korea, 75ff.
surrender terms, 112-115, 142, 276
Thirty-eighth Parallel, 108-110, 264, 265, 268
views on MacArthur, 91ff., 199-202, 270, 275
war may be extended, 281, 344-347
Truman, Mary Jane, 139
"Trusteeship" for Formosa, 32
Tydings, Millard F., 142

Uijongbu, 236, 238

United Nations
  Korean question considered, 11, 48, 49, 75, 77, 169, 183-184
  Peking accused of aggression, 210, 249, 252
  Peking to send delegates, 180
  post-war planning for Korea, 117-118
  Thirty-eighth Parallel, resolutions on, 108-110, 133-134, 268
  truce team criticized, 322
  uninformed of MacArthur's moves, 131-132, 260-261
United Nations Commission on Korea, 1, 8, 9, 11, 42, 48, 50-52, 117-118
United Nations Forces, attack, 293
  depredations by, 256
  morale of, 236-237, 323
  retreat, 209, 210, 214-215, 245
United Press, 19, 20, 114, 280, 288, 295-296, 323, 330
United States Government, 37, 69, 139-140, 251
United States Military Advisory Group to South Korea, 8, 9
U. S. News and World Report, 12, 21, 199, 294, 347
Universal Military Training, 102, 273

Vandenberg, Gen. Hoyt, 245, 246, 338-341
Van Fleet, Gen., 296, 307-309, 319, 323, 345, 346, 348

Veterans of Foreign Wars, 91
Vishinsky, 25, 26, 137

Wake Island, 145
Walker, Lt. Gen. Walton, 160
Wall Street Journal, 298, 299, 346, 347
Washington *Evening Star,* 313, 314, 334
Washington Post, 244, 272, 281, 282, 334
Washington Times-Herald, 334
Watson, Clark V., 257
Wedemeyer, Lt. Gen., 204, 205, 206
Wheeler, Burton K., 23
White Paper on China, 204
White Paper on Korea, 1, 9, 45, 46, 50, 51
Whitney, Brig. Gen. Courtney, 45, 147-148
Willoughby, Lt. Gen. Charles, 57, 58, 79, 240
Wilson, Charles, 281
Winnington, Alan, 316
Wonju, 238-239, 240ff.
"Wonju shoot," 270
Wonsan, 152, 264, 265
World Council of Churches of Christ, 25

Yalu River, 91, 125ff., 152-154, 160, 161, 172, 174, 183, 201
Yool, Air Vice-Marshal W. M., 337
Yoshida, Shigeru, 35, 36, 303
Yugoslavia in U. N., 11, 47, 48, 75

Zakharov, Gen., 63

About the Author

Born in 1907, I. F. Stone has been a working newspaperman since the age of fourteen when, during his sophomore year at a small-town high school, he launched a monthly, *The Progress*, which supported — among other causes — the League of Nations and Gandhi's first efforts at freedom for India.

While at school and college, he worked for daily newspapers in Camden, New Jersey, Philadelphia, and New York.

Since 1940 he has served in succession as a Washington correspondent and commentator for *The Nation*, the newspaper *PM*, the *New York Post*, and the *Daily Compass*. In 1953 he launched *I. F. Stone's Weekly*, a legendary venture in independent, one-man journalism, which he edited and published for nineteen years. He has written extensively for the *New York Review of Books* and long served as a contributing editor. He writes a Washington column at irregular intervals for *The Nation* and for many daily papers at home and abroad, including the *Philadelphia Inquirer*, on which he worked while he was in college.

In semiretirement Mr. Stone returned to the philosophy and classical history he had studied in college. He taught himself ancient Greek and wrote *The Trial of Socrates*, a controversial probe of the most famous free-speech case of all time, widely acclaimed on publication in 1988.

Mr. Stone and his wife, Esther, live in Washington. They have three married children.